OTHO HOLLAND WILLIAMS
IN THE AMERICAN REVOLUTION

Otho Holland Williams
in
The American Revolution

By

JOHN H. BEAKES, JR.

The Nautical and Aviation Publishing Co. of America
Charleston, South Carolina

Copyright © 2015 by The Nautical and Aviation Publishing Company of America, Inc., 845A Lowcountry Blvd., Mount Pleasant, South Carolina 29464. All rights reserved. No part of this publication may be reprinted, stored in a retrieval system, or transmitted in any form by any electronic or mechanical copying system without the written permission of the publisher.

Library of Congress Catalog Card Number: 2015947161
ISBN: 978-1-877853-79-2

Printed in the United States of America

First Printing: 2015

Jacket Design by Katherine A. Simes, Carlisle, PA

The portraits in this book are reproduced courtesy of the National Park Service unless specifically noted otherwise.

CONTENTS

Dedication ix

Introduction 1

Chapter 1 – Eutaw Springs 8

Chapter 2 – Service in a Rifle Company 12

Chapter 3 – From Prisoner of War to Adjutant General 44

Chapter 4 – Transfer to the South; Southern Terrain 72

Chapter 5 – The Battle of Camden; Rebuilding the Army 102

Chapter 6 – Greene Takes Command of the Southern Army 149

Chapter 7 – The Battle of Guilford Courthouse 201

Chapter 8 – The Battle of Hobkirk's Hill 215

Chapter 9 – The Siege of Ninety-Six 239

Chapter 10 – The Battle of Eutaw Springs 258

Chapter 11 – Williams' Final Days with Greene's Army 271

Chapter 12 – Return to the North 287

Chapter 13 – After the War 304

Illustrations .... between pages 60 and 61

Bibliography 327

Index 340

DEDICATION

This book is dedicated to my wife of 49 years, Rosemary.

To my parents, John and Martha Beakes, who taught me to love history.

To my children and grandchildren, who I hope will live in a world that honors the founders and defenders of our great country.

INTRODUCTION

The Rotunda of the United States Capital and the Maryland State House both display large paintings of George Washington resigning his commission before Congress at the end of the Revolutionary War.[1] We are all familiar with some of the prominent men who are shown, for example Thomas Jefferson, James Madison, James Monroe, and Alexander Hamilton. But there is a virtually unknown individual near General Washington in both paintings who is identified as Brigadier General Otho Holland Williams. If General Williams was prominent enough to be witness to this important event, why do we know so little of him?

In this, our third book in a series about George Washington's best officers, our goal is to tell the full story of the military career of this exceptional soldier. Very few members of the Continental Army served in such a variety of roles, with such distinction, or for so long.

Williams' Revolutionary War record is compelling, and typical of the young men who left their farms, shops, and homesteads to fight for independence from Great Britain. They continued to learn and grow throughout the war, and they developed from being the greenest volunteers into soldiers in one of the finest armies in the world. They did it by sheer hard work and study – and without the benefit of military academies, officer candidate schools, or any formal institutions of military learning.

The three officers described in this series to date, John Eager Howard, Light Horse Harry Lee, and Otho Holland Williams, were all in their twenties when they joined the Continental Army. Williams was twenty-six years old when he received his first commission in 1775; Howard joined at twenty-three and Henry Lee, at twenty. Howard came from a close-knit, prosperous family northwest of Baltimore, and Lee was the son of one of the wealthiest and most prominent families in Virginia. Williams, on the other hand, was raised in less favorable circumstances in Western Maryland, having been orphaned at age 13, and therefore left largely to his own intelligence and persistence to find his way. The records of his youth are sparse, possibly reflecting his family's economic circumstances and his own apparent reluctance to write about those years.

What we do know is that Otho Holland Williams was born on March 1st, 1749 in Prince George's County, Maryland, the oldest son of parents of Welsh descent, Joseph Williams and Prudence Holland Williams. He had one older sister, Mercy, four younger sisters, and one younger brother, Elie. The family moved to Washington County, Maryland the year after Otho was born, and settled where the Conococheague Creek empties into the Potomac River.[2*] One writer who was familiar with Williams' wartime correspondence described the region where Otho spent his boyhood, and provided insight to his strong affection for home and family that would often appear in his wartime letters:

> *In that beautiful region of country, watered by the stream that lends its name to the valley, were spent the few short years of his boyhood. There he learned to love the aspect of fields and groves, the memory of which was his solace long after, in many dark and trying hours, for we find in the midst of the toils of the camp, that his spirit yearns for rural peace and solitude.*[3]

Otho's father Joseph Williams died when Otho was thirteen, and his sister Mercy's husband George Ross helped Otho obtain a position in the Clerk's Office of Frederick County, Maryland. He was eventually promoted to be in charge of that office, and then transferred to a similar position in Baltimore. Shortly before the war, Williams returned to Frederick and entered a commercial business.[4] There are no known records of Otho's schooling, although it is clear from his gifted pen that he mastered the art of narrative writing, and his occasional reference to names such as Pindar indicates that he had some exposure to the classics.

While he was young, Otho had demonstrated competence, responsibility, and administrative skill. He was described as being "… about six feet high, elegantly formed; his whole appearance and conduct much beyond his years; his manner such as made friends of all who knew him."[5] George Washington Greene, the grandson and biographer of Williams' great military partner during the war, General Nathanael Greene, described Williams in manhood:

> *In personal appearance Williams is said to have been graceful, with a military erectness of carriage, and an open, expressive countenance. In character he was warm-hearted and expansive; but upon moral questions firm to a degree which savored somewhat of sternness. As a soldier he was rigid in discipline, requiring from his subordinates the prompt obedience which he always paid to his superiors. Beginning his military career with*

---

*This is the site of current day Williamsport, Mayland, which is named for Otho Holland Williams.

Barnes & Noble Booksellers #2940
1 East Joppa Road Suite 100
Towson, MD 21286
410-296-7021

STR:2940 REG:002 TRN:7339 CSHR:Curt J

BARNES & NOBLE MEMBER   EXP: 05/26/2017

Otho Holland Williams in the American Re
9781877853791   T1
(1 @ 28.95) Member Card 10% (2.90)
(1 @ 26.05) Item Cpn 20% (5.21)
#VZ2GE8T2W3J11
    (1 @ 20.84)   20.84

Subtotal   20.84
Sales Tax T1 (6.000%)   1.25
TOTAL   22.09
ELECTRONIC GIFT CARD   15.00
  Card#: XXXXXXXXXXXXXXX4936
  Auth: 000000
  Entry Method: Swiped
  Card Balance: 0.00
CASH   10.00
CASH CHANGE   2.91-

MEMBER SAVINGS   2.90

Thanks for shopping at
Barnes & Noble

101.41A   07/29/2016 12:25PM

CUSTOMER COPY

Policy on receipt may appear in two sections.

Return Policy

With a sales receipt or Barnes & Noble.com packing slip, a full refund in the original form of payment will be issued from any Barnes & Noble Booksellers store for returns of undamaged NOOKs, new and unread books, and unopened and undamaged music CDs, DVDs, vinyl records, toys/games and audio books made within 14 days of purchase from a Barnes & Noble Booksellers store or Barnes & Noble.com with the below exceptions:

A store credit for the purchase price will be issued (i) for purchases made by check less than 7 days prior to the date of return, (ii) when a gift receipt is presented within 60 days of purchase, (iii) for textbooks, (iv) when the original tender is PayPal, or (v) for products purchased at Barnes & Noble College Booksellers that are listed for sale in the Barnes & Noble Booksellers inventory management system.

Opened music CDs, DVDs, vinyl records, audio books may not be returned, and can be exchanged only for the same title and only if defective. NOOKs purchased from other retailers or sellers are returnable only to the retailer or seller from which they are purchased, pursuant to such retailer's or seller's return policy. Magazines, newspapers, eBooks, digital downloads, and used books are not returnable or exchangeable. Defective NOOKs may be exchanged at the store in accordance with the applicable warranty.

Returns or exchanges will not be permitted (i) after 14 days or without receipt or (ii) for product not carried by Barnes & Noble or Barnes & Noble.com.

Policy on receipt may appear in two sections.

Return Policy

With a sales receipt or Barnes & Noble.com packing slip, a full refund in the original form of payment will be issued from any Barnes & Noble Booksellers store for returns of undamaged NOOKs, new and unread books, and unopened and undamaged music CDs, DVDs, vinyl records, toys/games and audio books made within 14 days of purchase from a Barnes & Noble Booksellers store or Barnes & Noble.com with the below exceptions:

Returns or exchanges will not be permitted (i) after 14 days or without receipt or (ii) for product not carried by Barnes & Noble or Barnes & Noble.com.

no advantages of military training, his rare intelligence led him directly to the true sources, and gave him a clear perception of the fundamental principles of the science. His counsel was always the counsel of a clear, deep, and perspicacious mind. His conduct in the field was ardor, tempered by judgment and self-possession.[6]

In early 1777, Congress took note of his strong military aptitude and promoted the twenty seven year old Williams to full Colonel. With many challenging assignments throughout his military service, he established a reputation for leadership and for ably handling the complex tasks of managing the men and materials of the entire army. Transferred to the southern theater with the Maryland troops in April, 1780, he served as a wise and experienced advisor to the army commanders, a tireless practitioner of army discipline and readiness, and a brave, decisive battlefield commander. He was awarded a sword by Congress for his performance at the Battle of Eutaw Springs in September, 1781, and his career reached its pinnacle when Congress granted him a commission as a Brigadier General in May, 1782.

From the time of his service as acting Adjutant General under Washington beginning in December 1779, he served in the dual roles of a line commander of troops and Adjutant General of the command in which he served. These dual responsibilities imposed a heavy workload, but they were also a clear indication of the high regard in which he was held.[7] Williams served loyally in the face of many difficulties. He had contracted a disease during his time as a prisoner-of-war (almost certainly tuberculosis from the symptoms recorded) and it would gradually weaken him and shorten his life. He was badly wounded in combat, and he had fought in a series of discouraging battlefield defeats. But Williams fought on in the face of many adversities. His is a story worth telling.

Since this first military biography of Otho Holland Williams is being written over two-hundred and twenty years after his death, the story must be assembled from sources that will never be sufficient to provide as complete a picture as can be developed for individuals such as Washington, Jefferson and Hamilton from whom we have large volumes of correspondence and official records. The archives of the Maryland Historical Society have the much less extensive Papers of Otho Holland Williams and a military journal that he kept for a short time after the Battle of Camden in 1780. Williams is occasionally mentioned in the Papers of George Washington, particularly during his short term as acting Adjutant General in the winter of 1779/1780.

The Papers of General Nathanael Greene contain many letters to and from his Commanding General and friend Nathanael Greene.

The Papers of Daniel Morgan in the New York Public Library provide additional helpful insights in the correspondence between these two completely different friends – the rough frontiersman Morgan and the more elegant, restrained Williams. The wonderful "Founders Online" series from the National Archives provides a few snippets of information, such as the exchanges between Williams and Alexander Hamilton. Early chroniclers of the Revolutionary War such as William Gordon, David Ramsay and William Moultrie described Williams' service in the southern campaign of 1780/81, and later writers such as William Johnson (1822) and George Washington Greene (1850-1880) developed that record.

Light Horse Harry Lee wrote favorably of his friend Williams in his memoirs, and Lee's son Henry Lee, IV expressed his respect in his book *The Campaign of 1781 in the Carolinas*. Modern historians of the Southern Campaigns all note the contributions of Williams when they are writing of the events in which he participated. Various references on prisoners-of-war, the Battle of Fort Washington, and other varied aspects of Williams' career help to fill in some of the blank spots.

Nevertheless, these sources leave us with an incomplete record, particularly of his youth and the early years of his service in the Revolutionary War. There are very few records of his family and personal life until he joined the army at age twenty-six, and the large collections of correspondence such as the Washington Papers rarely mention officers who were as junior as Williams in the early stages of the war. We have no journal or diary kept by Williams during those early days, and very few letters from that period have survived. The situation is the same for Williams as it was for our previous subjects, John Eager Howard and Henry Lee – it is necessary to infer what we can about these officers in the early parts of the war from the activities of their units and the action around them. For example, in Williams' case, we know a considerable amount about the rifle companies that were formed at the outset of the war, and about the riflemen and their leaders– Michael Cresap, Thomas Price, and Daniel Morgan. We have very little information about Otho Holland Williams himself during this time, but we do know that he was a junior officer in one of these units.

We can therefore reasonably assume that his leadership style developed under tough, experienced frontier leaders, and that he must have served competently with the rugged frontiersman that made up these units. He would not have been accepted as a leader of such men if he were not strong and healthy, capable of participating in the rifle companies' remarkable march at the start of the war from Western Maryland to Boston in just a few weeks. It also seems reasonable that he would not have been accepted by such a unit without some knowledge of the frontier rifle and backwoods battle tactics. With scant information on Williams himself during this time, we can only surmise the influences that he experienced and the activities that he encountered as we build the picture of his maturing character.

We also know that George Washington understood these riflemen from his long service on the frontier, that he was anxious for them to arrive in Boston, and that he intended to use them for gathering intelligence, capturing British prisoners, and generally creating havoc among the British troops. Washington wrote little about these activities, probably at least partially for fear of revealing his thoughts to his enemies, and Williams himself is therefore hidden from us beneath a cloud of secrecy during the siege of Boson in 1775/1776. Still, we can discern the outline of his likely activities by studying the scant information on the actions of the command in which he served. Other parts of the story, such as his rapid promotions to Captain and then Major, are evidence that he had an aptitude for soldiering and rapidly mastered its requirements. There are many times, especially early in the war, when we know generally where Williams was stationed, and have some sense of what he and his comrades were doing, but are unable to know the time and place of his thoughts or actions.

Williams' papers include well-written first-hand accounts of some Revolutionary War events, and we rely heavily on them in this book when we are describing scenes in which he participated. This includes his narrative of the 1780 Campaign, including the Battle of Camden, which is published as an Appendix B to William Johnson's 1822 *Life and Correspondence of Nathanael Greene, Volume I*; his letter to a friend describing the Battle of Guilford Courthouse written two days after the battle which is in the library at the Guilford Courthouse Battlefield Park; and his description of the Battle of Eutaw Springs, published in R.W. Gibbes' 1853 Volume of his *Documentary History of the American Revolution*, which covers the years 1780 and 1781.

Williams corresponded with early historians of the Revolutionary War, including David Ramsay and William Gordon, and he apparently intended to write his own history, but was unable to achieve that objective. However, he had an important impact on the early histories of the war. For example, William Gordon noted that "recourse has been had to the detail of facts written by the deputy adjutant general, Col. Otho H. Williams…"[8] Williams himself went a little further, writing to Henry Lee that Williams recognized that "whole pages" of his own narrative had been incorporated into Gordon's book. Williams had sent many of his papers to Gordon in Boston to be used in Gordon's history, but many were lost at sea when the documents were being returned to Williams.[9] Given the thoughtfulness, precision and care with which Williams prepared his historical documents, the loss of these papers has surely deprived us of valuable first-hand observations that would greatly enhance our understanding of the war and his place in it.

And, sadly, Williams did not live long enough to write what would have been, from all indications, a compelling history of the Revolutionary War, as he had experienced it.

Williams had some very human faults. He had a tendency to become testy when he was tired and under heavy pressure, which caused some other officers to complain to higher authority of his rigidity while he served as Washington's Adjutant General. He once snapped at his commander, Nathanael Greene, in a letter when he thought that his maneuvers were being questioned. All the sources we have seen describe him as very strict in the administration of discipline, as he was rigid in his obedience to his seniors. The army paperwork that survives, such as his muster lists for the army and lists of wounded after the various battles, reflect an unremitting demand for accuracy and precision, not bad traits in themselves, but sometimes annoyances to the officers who were required to assemble and submit the data when the war was keeping them busy with many other pressing responsibilities. The riflemen that he commanded at the skirmish at Weitzel's Mill in March, 1781 felt that he had needlessly exposed them to enemy attack to protect the Continental soldiers under his command. William Richardson Davie, a North Carolinian with solid military reputation, left a written criticism that Williams had permitted the enemy to steal a march on him in the same engagement. He was in overall command of the Maryland Line at both the battles of Guilford Courthouse and Hobkirk's Hill when various units of highly-respected Maryland troops broke and ran, although his personal actions were never officially challenged. In 1793, when President George Washington was evaluating experienced senior military officers to decide who would lead the American army, he noted that Williams was "…a sensible man, but not without vanity."[10]

Williams' imperfections are discussed in these pages to provide the most complete possible story. Although he was a fine officer, it would do him no honor to gloss over his faults. The glory of his service is that he rose above these weaknesses to make a vital contribution to our country's success in the Revolutionary War.

INTRODUCTION

Toward the end of the war, Nathanael Greene wrote Williams a letter that included a brief summary of their shared accomplishments during their year-plus of service together in the Southern Campaigns from December, 1780 through February, 1782:

> *I think that the public are not a little indebted for our exertions. The southern states were lost, they are now restored; the American arms were in disgrace, they are now in high reputation. The American soldiery were thought to want both patience and fortitude to contend with difficulties; they are now remarkable for both.*[11]

These words are a lasting tribute to the soldierly conduct of Otho Holland Williams and to his many contributions to victory during his long and arduous service in the War for Independence.

---

1 The painting of this event by John Trumbull hangs in the Rotunda of the United States Capital; the one by Edwin White is in the Maryland State Capitol. Ref: (1) Weir, John F. (Director of the Yale School of Fine Arts.) *John Trumbull, A Brief Sketch of his Life to Which is Added a Catalogue of His Works*. Charles Scribner's Sons. New York. 1901. Pp.69-70. (2) Maryland State Archives Web Site. msa.maryland.gov. ("what we have"/state art collection/ paintings/ "historical/ allegorical"/"Washington Resigning His Commission."

2 See Footnote.

3 Tiffany, Osmond. *A Sketch of the Life and Services of General Otho Holland Williams* (hereafter Tiffany, Sketch) Baltimore, 1851.Pp. 3-4.

4 Boyle, Esmeralda and Pinkney, Frederick. *Biographical Sketches of Distinguished Marylanders* (hereafter Boyle and Pinkney, Sketches.) Kelly, Piet and Company. Baltimore. 1877. Pp. 158-160.

5 IBID. P. 159.

6 Greene, George Washington. *The Life of Nathanael Greene, Major General of the Army of the Revolution in Three Volumes. Volume 3* (hereafter, Greene, *Life of Greene*.) Hurd and Houghton. Cambridge University Press. New York. 1871. Pp. 108-109.

7 Williams once confided in a relative that that he wished he could decline his additional duties to focus on his own regiment, for he considered its discipline and military achievements to be the soundest basis for his own reputation as a competent commander. Ref: Otho Holland Williams letter to John Stull. Written near Hillsborough, N.C. September 23rd, 1780. Calendar of the Otho Holland Williams Papers in the Manuscript Collections of the Maryland Historical Society (hereafter *Williams Papers*.) MS 908. Part 1/ 8.) (Item #53.)

8 Gordon, William. *The History of the Rise, Progress, And Establishment, of the Independence of the United States Of America: Including An Account Of The Late War and of the Thirteen Colonies, From Their Origin To That Period. In Four Volumes. Volume 3* (hereafter Gordon, *History*.) Printed for the Author; and sold By Charles Dilly, in the Poultry; and James Buckland, in Pater-Noster-Row. London. 1788. P. 450

9 Williams, Otho Holland. Letter to Governor Henry Lee of Virginia. Written at Baltimore, March 15th, 1792. *Williams Papers*. Part 4/8. (Item #688.)

10 Memorandum on General Officers, 9 March 1792," Founders Online, National Archives (http://founders.archives.gov/documents/Washington/05-10-02-0040, ver. 2014-05-09). Source: *The Papers of George Washington*, Presidential Series, vol. 10, *1 March 1792–15 August 1792*, ed. Robert F. Haggard and Mark A. Mastromarino. Charlottesville: University of Virginia Press, 2002, pp. 74–79.

11 Boyle and Pinkney, *Sketches*. P. 174.

CHAPTER 1

EUTAW SPRINGS

In sweltering heat at Eutaw Springs in South Carolina on September 8th, 1781, a small force of 250 Continental troops of the Maryland Line waited in formation to join the fight that was raging up ahead. They had set out at 4 a.m. and marched seven miles to reach their current position, encouraged along the way by a brief stop for a ration of rum intended to help prepare them for the coming ordeal. The soldiers heard the sounds of heavy combat up ahead, where militia units were fighting hard against a determined and well-led British force. They knew that they would soon be rushing into that inferno, which the commander of this southern army, Nathanael Greene, described as "by far the most obstinate and bloody I ever saw."[1]

In front of this little force was their thirty-two-year-old commander, Colonel Otho Williams, one of the most experienced and battle-tested senior officers in the Continental Army. Williams' battlefield experience had been built over the past six years since he joined the army as a junior officer in a rifle company at the very outset of the war. During these years of service, Williams demonstrated his combat prowess in the fighting during the siege of Boston in 1775/76; in the heroic but ultimately unsuccessful stand of the riflemen at the Battle of Fort Washington near New York in November, 1776; and in his solid, occasionally brilliant performance in the southern campaigns of 1781 and 1782, where he saw action in the Battle of Camden, the Race to the Dan, and the battles of Guilford Courthouse, and Hobkirk's Hill.

As he had done for previous battles, Williams helped General Greene plan the order of battle that morning so that the army would enter the field in the proper sequence to support Greene's objectives, a duty that stemmed from his position as Assistant Adjutant General. It would probably have been easy for Williams to avoid the danger of the front lines by pointing out that his proper place was with his commander. But it was not his way to serve behind the lines when a standup fight was imminent. He and his fellow Marylanders were particularly intent this day on erasing the memories of the poor performance of some Maryland units at the earlier Battle of Hobkirk's Hill.[2]

Williams' 250 men formed the left of the second American line. To their immediate right were Lieutenant Colonel Richard Campbell (Williams called him "the gallant Campbell[3]) and two battalions of Virginia Continentals totaling 350 men, who held the center of this line. To the right of Campbell and his Virginians on the far right of this second line were three battalions of North Carolina Continentals totaling 350 men under General Jethro

Sumner.⁴ All of the units in this second line were Continentals, Greene's most dependable troops.

Eventually, the British left faltered, and Greene sent Sumner and his North Carolinians forward into the fight, leaving Williams behind in command of the second line, now composed only of the Marylanders and Campbell's Virginians, to await further developments. Greene's instructions were not long in coming. When he saw the left of the British line move forward too aggressively and lose formation, he ordered:

*Let Williams advance and sweep the field with his bayonets.*⁵

Greene's official report of this action, written just two days after the fight, described what happened next:

> *...the Virginians under Lieut Colo Campbell, and the Maryland Troops under Colo Williams were led on to a brisk charge with trailed Arms⁶, through a heavy cannonade, and a shower of Musquet balls. Nothing could exceed the gallantry and firmness of both Officers and Soldiers upon this occasion. They preserved their order, and pressed on with such unshaken resolution that they bore down all before them. The Enemy were routed in all quarters.*⁷

Williams later reported that at this critical moment "shouts of victory resounded through the American line," yet the fight was not over. Richard Campbell, commander of the Virginia Continentals who fought next the Marylanders, was shot in the chest, and was supported in the saddle by his son, who had fought at his father's side. The wound would prove mortal. Still, an American victory seemed assured, as British commissaries destroyed their stores, and the road behind the British lines was flooded with panicked British soldiers, civilians, and American deserters retreating headlong for Charleston.⁸

In his account of this battle, Otho Williams wrote that the when victorious Americans reached the main British camp, they could not resist the allurements of the unaccustomed luxury around them. According to Williams, many "fastened upon the liquors and refreshments they afforded, and became totally unmanageable." The attack lost momentum, many of the troops lost formation, and those who retained enough discipline to pursue the British soon found that they were unsupported.⁹ ¹⁰ The chance for total victory was lost. In the meantime, elements of the British force had managed to put together a staunch defense centered on a nearby brick mansion, and Greene reluctantly decided to retire and leave the field to the enemy. It had been a closely-fought battle, and both sides claimed victory.

The British commander could claim possession of the battlefield at the end of the fighting, but he left the field and headed for the safety of Charleston the next evening, leaving sixty unburied dead and seventy severely wounded men behind to be cared for by Greene.[11] The British also smashed 1,000 muskets and threw them into the spring, while also destroying substantial amounts of stores.[12] These are hardly the acts of an army that has won an overwhelming victory. It happened that this was the last large engagement between British and American forces in the Carolinas for the remainder of the war, as afterwards the British mostly stayed close to their fortifications at Charleston.

A few days later, when Greene looked back over this battle as he was writing his report to Congress, the exploits of Otho Williams shone even more brightly. Greene was himself an experienced combat leader who had seen many battles since joining the army around Boston six-and-a-half years earlier, yet he felt that the charge that Williams led at Eutaw Springs stood out from any previous exploit he had witnessed on any previous field:

> *I cannot help acknowledging my obligations to Colonel Williams for his great activity on this and many other occasions in forming the army, and for his uncommon intrepidity in leading on the Maryland troops to the charge, which exceeded any thing I ever saw.*[13]

Congress responded to Greene's report by presenting Williams with a sword to commemorate his "…great military skill and uncommon exertions on this occasion."[14]

Otho Williams wore the uniform of his country from Congress' first call for troops on June 14th, 1775 until the major fighting had ended over seven years later. For every day he served in the face of danger on the field of battle, there were many more days of training, marching, administering, planning, and disciplining. He excelled in all of these areas, and he was continually relied upon by senior commander such as Washington and Greene to fulfill these essential military duties.

But the career of an exceptional soldier cannot be built on administrative skill alone, no matter how extensive. The core skill of soldiering is performance in battle.

At the Battle of Eutaw Springs the courage, military skill, clear-headedness, and decisiveness of Otho Williams stood out for all to see. He had exhibited these characteristics in many battles since the beginning of the war, but in roles where his individual performance was not as visible. At Eutaw Springs, we have our most insightful glimpse of Williams in battle.

---

1   Greene, Nathanael. Letter to William Smallwood. Written at the High Hills of the Santee, S.C. September 18th, 1781. Conrad, Dennis, M., Editor.; Parks, Roger N. Senior Associate Editor, and King, Martha J. Assistant Editor. *The Papers of General Nathanael Greene. Volume IX. 11 July 1781 - 2 December 1781.* The University of North Carolina Press. Chapel Hill and London. Published for the Rhode Island Historical Society. 1997. P. 369. (Volumes 7 through 11 of the *Papers of General Nathanael Greene* are referenced in this book. All will be cited as *Greene Papers*, with the Volume and page number indicated as follows: 9:369.)
2   Williams, Otho Holland, et. al. *Battle of Eutaw. Account Furnished by Col. Otho Williams, with additions by Cols. W. Hampton, Polk, Howard, and Watt.* From Gibbes, Robert W., M.D. *Documentary History of the American Revolution, Consisting of Letters and Papers Relating to the Contest for Liberty, Chiefly in South Carolina, in 1781 and 1782* (hereafter Williams, *Battle of Eutaw*, in Gibbes.) Published by Banner Steam-Power Press. Columbia, South Carolina. 1853. P. 150.
3   Ibid. Pp. 151.
4   Ibid. P. 146.
5   Ibid. P. 149.
6   According to *A New and Enlarged Military Dictionary* by Charles James, printed at the British military library, near Whitehall in 1802: "To Trail literally means to draw along the ground. In military matters it signifies, to carry the firelock in an oblique forward position, with the butt just above the ground. Hence Trail Arms, a word of command for that purpose." Essentially, these Maryland and North Carolina Continental troops were running with their heads bent forward and their muskets in their right hands, held near the muzzle, and tilted about 30 degrees from the vertical, with the bayonet fixed, as they charged into the musketry and cannon fire up ahead. Note: this is on a page headed "T R A" in the cited text, which does not have page numbers other than in the Introduction, but instead is organized alphabetically by military terminology.
7   Greene Nathanael. Letter to Thomas McKean, President of the Continental Congress. (Report of the Battle of Eutaw Springs.) Written at Martin's Tavern, near Ferguson's Swamp, South Carolina, September 11th, 1781. *Greene Papers.* 9:331.
8   Williams, *Battle of Eutaw*, in Gibbes. Pp. 151-154.
9   Some writers argue that, for various reasons, the story that the American soldiers were distracted by the allurements of the British camp cannot be true. However, our subject, Otho Holland Williams (who was present on the field) described the incident as it is recounted here. In addition, Williams wrote to Major Edward Giles on September 23rd, 1781, less than three weeks after the battle, that "…the eagerness of the pursuit had thrown most of the troops into disorder, which could not now be remedied. Some were taking prisoners and others plundering the enemy's camp…" Reference: Otho Holland Williams to Major Edward Giles, written at Camp, High Hills of the Santee; 23rd of September, 1781. In *Graham's American Monthly Magazine of Literature and Art, Volume XXVI.* George R. Graham, Editor and Proprietor. 98 Chestnut Street, Philadelphia. 1845. (The article on the Battle of Eutaw Springs is on pages 253-258.)
10 Williams, *Battle of Eutaw*, in Gibbes, Pp. 153-154.
11 Williams, Otho Holland. Unfinished raft of a letter to Major Edward Giles, written in the hand of Otho Holland Williams. Written at the High Hills of the Santee, South Carolina. September 23, 1781. *Williams Papers.* Part 1/8. (item # 116.)
12 Williams, *Battle of Eutaw*, in Gibbes P. 156.
13 Greene Nathanael. Letter to Thomas McKean, President of the Continental Congress. (Report of the Battle of Eutaw Springs.) Written at Martin's Tavern, South Carolina, September 11th, 1781. *Greene Papers.* 9:333.
14 Journals of the Continental Congress. Volume XXI. 1781. July 23--December 31. Monday, October 29th, 1781. P. 1085.

CHAPTER 2

SERVICE IN A RIFLE COMPANY

The frontier regions of western Virginia, Maryland, and Pennsylvania were stirring in June, 1775, as dozens of hardy frontiersmen packed their bedrolls, filled their shot pouches and powder horns, and marched off to join the American army. On June 14th, the Continental Congress had called for the formation of companies of "expert riflemen" who were to "...march and join the army near Boston, there to be employed as light infantry, under the command of the chief Officer in that Army."[1] Twenty-six year-old Otho Holland Williams was among the western Marylanders who answered this call.

Events were moving quickly in these early days of the conflict with Great Britain. The Battles of Lexington and Concord had been fought in Massachusetts on April 19th, less than two months earlier, and in the interim a large, loosely-knit assemblage of New England volunteers had formed around Boston. On June 15th, the day after the call for the rifle companies, Congress appointed George Washington to be Commander-In-Chief of all the American forces. Three days later, on June 17th, the fighting around Boston continued, as the British troops tried to dislodge the Americans from their entrenchments in what is called the Battle of Bunker Hill.[2] The British high command could claim a victory in that battle, but American muskets had killed and wounded a large number of redcoats, and the British officers who fought on that bloody hill would always remember how costly it had been to attack American troops entrenched behind fortified lines.

In accordance with a resolution passed by the full Congress, Maryland's Congressional delegation sent instructions to the Committee of Safety of Frederick County, Maryland to raise two companies of riflemen for the new Continental Army. The enlistment was to be for one year, ending on July 1st, 1776, and recruiters were to focus on men from the frontier regions for two specific reasons:

> ..we hope it will appear to you as to us, prudent to get the men as far back[3]* as may be, not only because there is a fair chance of their being as good as any others, but that those whose situations will permit, may be left at hand, to act in our own province, if unhappily there should be occasion.[4]

---

*The term "far back" meant that the Committee was to recruit men from as far into the frontier backcountry as possible.

In other words, Maryland's elected leaders opted to answer Congress's requisition by sending Westerners to Boston, and keeping troops from the more populous regions closer to home in case they were needed to defend population centers such as Baltimore and Annapolis.

The men who streamed in from the countryside were tough, lean, self-reliant sons of the frontier - inured to hardship, and masters of the skills needed to survive in a rugged, untamed wilderness. In short, these men were very well suited for soldiering, the forebears of today's Navy Seals, Recon Marines, and Special Forces operators. They were the first men to be considered troops of the Continental Army,[5] as the various units encircling Boston still served at the behest of their individual colonies. The United States Army dates its birth from June 14th, 1775, when these riflemen came down from the mountains to serve their country. Otho Holland Williams was one of these first soldiers to serve in the Continental army.

Each volunteer brought his own equipment, and wore typical frontiersman's clothing- a fringed hunting shirt and pants.[6] There were more volunteers than needed to fill the quotas established by Congress, so the "best of the best" were selected for the service, based primarily on marksmanship. Just about every man in the frontier regions could handle a rifle with considerable skill, but the selection process insured that only the finest sharpshooters would come into the Continental service.

The frontier rifle was a lethal weapon in the hands of such skilled marksmen. It could be deadly accurate at a range of two-hundred yards and beyond, while the smooth-bored musket carried by traditional infantrymen was notoriously inaccurate at any range, and especially so beyond one hundred yards. The rifle's superior range and accuracy came from the spin imposed on the bullet by grooves (called "rifling") on the inside of the barrel.

While the rifle was the perfect weapon for the "hit and run" tactics of frontier warfare, it had definite limitations in traditional eighteenth century infantry combat. The standard infantry battle of that era consisted of opposing lines of soldiers, standing shoulder-to-shoulder, and facing each other no more than 100 yards apart, which was the range of their muskets. After each of the lines fired a few massed volleys, they would often charge with fixed bayonets.

The rifle was virtually useless in close infantry combat because it was not built to hold a bayonet, and because reloading it was a slow and difficult process. While a competent infantryman could load and fire his musket up to four times a minute, the rifleman took two to three times as long to reload, because he had to force the bullet down the long, grooved barrel.[7]

Another disadvantage was that the narrow rifle barrel could become clogged with powder residue when it was hot from repeated firing.⁸

The riflemen were proud of their marksmanship, and eager to demonstrate their prowess to an adoring public. One such demonstration near Frederick, Maryland, was described in the Pennsylvania Gazette of August 16th, 1775:

> *A clapboard, with a mark the size of a dollar, was put up; they began to fire off hand, and the bystanders were surprised, few shots being made were not close to or in the paper; when they shot for a time in this way, some lay on their backs, some on their breast or side, others ran twenty or thirty steps, and firing, appeared to be equally certain of the mark.*⁹

The Officers of the Rifle Companies

It was no small challenge to find officers who could command these self-confident, independent-minded frontiersmen. They were as likely to challenge authority as they were to follow orders, and they were not about to accept someone's commands just because they carried a sword or wore an officer's insignia. Officers who could successfully lead such men would have to be worthy of their respect, and to lead by example.

The Maryland authorities recognized the challenge of finding qualified officers in their instructions to the Western counties:

> *You will, doubtless, if possible, get experienced officers, and the very best men that can be procured, as well from your affection to the service as for the honor of our province.*¹⁰

Daniel Morgan, who commanded one of the Virginia rifle companies, was the type of leader who could successfully command such troops. Morgan was a powerfully built giant of a man, with a commanding presence and a thundering voice. He had been a hard drinker and a notorious frontier brawler in his youth, driven by raw physical energy and the impulses that often surge through the veins of strong, violent young men. As a teamster, Morgan had earned the nickname "the Old Wagoner," having driven a wagon for the British army during the French and Indian War. While serving there, his fierce independence had gotten the better of him on one occasion, and he had received five hundred lashes on his bare back for being insubordinate to a British officer. He bore those scars like a badge of honor.

Leaders like Morgan did not ask their men to do anything that they wouldn't do themselves. They led "from the front," instead of lurking behind the battle lines in safety and comfort.

Another leader of this kind was Captain Michael Cresap, who commanded one of the Maryland rifle companies, and, while not as well known in history as Daniel Morgan, he was cut from the same mold as "the Old Wagoner." Cresap was the son a rough old frontiersman named Thomas Cresap, who had played a prominent role in the border wars between Maryland and Pennsylvania in the 1720's and 30's,[11] and in the French and Indian War. The Cresap family had a long history as uncompromising warriors.

Although Captain Cresap was battling an unspecified, but serious, health problem, and his business affairs were in some disarray, he accepted the call of his country because he felt honored to be selected for the post, and because he was mindful of upholding his family's proud fighting tradition.[12]

Cresap's leadership style had been developed over years of leading men on the frontier, and was perfectly suited to command riflemen. Young officers like Otho Williams who served under leaders like Cresap had a priceless opportunity to learn the basics of effective military leadership. Cresap's techniques were described by an admirer:

> *...it seems that all who go to war under him do not only pay the most wiling obedience to him as their commander, but, in every instance of distress look up to him as their friend and father. A great part of his time was spent in listening to and relieving their wants, without any apparent sense of fatigue and trouble. When complaints were before him, he determined with kindness and spirit, and on every occasion condescended to please without losing his dignity.*[13]

Congress had decreed that each rifle company would be commanded by a Captain, and that each would have "...three lieutenants, four serjeants, four corporals, a drummer or trumpeter, and sixty-eight privates."[14] Michael Cresap was chosen as Captain of the First Company and Thomas Price was the Captain of the Second Company.[15] Otho Holland Williams was chosen as First Lieutenant under Captain Price, with date of rank June 22nd, 1775.[16]

It was an honor for twenty-six-year-old Otho Holland Williams to be chosen as one of the six men who would serve as Maryland's rifle company lieutenants. Young Williams must surely have held the respect of influential leaders and the community at large, and he undoubtedly met the demanding physical qualifications to be selected for such a rigorous assignment. One Marylander described Williams at the time as "… about six feet high, elegantly formed; his whole appearance and conduct much beyond his years; his manner such as made friends of all who knew him."[17]

A fellow soldier later observed that Williams was "…erect and elegant in form, made for activity rather than strength…,"[18] which may suggest that Williams was more lithe and graceful and less of a dominating physical presence than many of the powerful riflemen that surrounded him. He was also a gifted administrator and writer, and had a depth of humanity and sensitivity that might not be apparent at first to his rugged comrades. While he was strict and formal with people that he did not know well, he had great capacity for building warm and lasting friendships. His letters home would often speak lovingly of home and family, and of his deep love for the land of his childhood in western Maryland.

Lieutenant Williams took his place among the hardy sharpshooters in Captain Price's Second Company, and began his military apprenticeship under strong leaders like Daniel Morgan and Michael Cresap. An observer saw Morgan's Virginians and Price's Marylanders marching a few miles from Frederick, Maryland, and noted their "truly martial" appearance and their "amazingly elated" spirits.[19] The whole country seemed to be caught up in enthusiasm for these troops, and people stood admiringly on the roadsides to applaud as they marched by, offering them beer, cider, buttermilk, apples, cherries and other provisions.[20]

Ordinary citizens were not the only ones swept up with enthusiasm and excitement about the riflemen in these early days of the War. People at the highest reaches of the national government were also impressed with these troops, and believed that such men would make quick work of their British adversaries. Richard Henry Lee wrote admiringly of the riflemen's:

> …*amazing hardihood, their method of living in the woods without carrying provisions with them, the exceeding quickness with which they can march to distant parts, the dexterity to which they have arrived in the use of the Rifle Gun. There is not one of these men who wish a distance less than 200 yards or a larger object than an Orange. Every shot is fatal.*[21]

In a letter to a friend, the prominent Philadelphian James Tilghman alluded to the plan to have these marksmen pay particular attention to picking off enemy officers:

These Riflemen experienced in the Wars with the Indians are compleat Marksmen robust active and bold and are sent for the purpose of taking down the Officers. They will seldom miss their Mark at 200 yards distance.[22]

Throughout the War, Daniel Morgan instructed his men to concentrate on the "epaulets," in other words to concentrate their fire on the officers and non-commissioned officers ("non-coms") of the enemy, whose rank was indicated by the epaulet devices on the shoulders of their uniforms. Morgan and his eminently practical frontiersmen realized that an enemy infantry assault depended on strong leadership from officers and non-coms, and that a very effective way to blunt a British attack was to shoot the leaders.

Captain Price's Second Company left Frederick, Maryland on July 18th, 1775 and arrived in Cambridge, Massachusetts on August 9th,[23] covering 450 miles in just over three weeks, an average of almost twenty-one miles per day along the primitive roads of that time. This impressive feat of endurance and discipline says much about the men in the rifle companies at the outset of the Revolutionary War.

★ ★ ★ ★ ★

The Siege of Boston

When Captain Price's Second Company arrived in Cambridge in early August of 1775, a private named Daniel McCurtin wrote in his diary that there was a "very elegant building" at the College (Harvard,) and several other buildings for the use of students, which made the town appear "very beautiful to the eye."[24] He noted that the men had arrived in good health, a sentiment echoed by Commander-in-Chief George Washington, who noted that "The Troops from the Southward are come in very healthy and in good Order."[25] Private McCurtin added that the troops were also "…much fatigued with our journey here."[26]

General Washington had arrived in the Boston area at the end of June, a few weeks after the Battle of Bunker Hill, and had moved aggressively to establish military order and discipline among the diverse New England regiments that had come in piecemeal over the previous months. He placed Major General Artemus Ward in command of the right wing, south of Boston, which included fortifications at Roxbury and Dorchester; Major General Israel Putnam commanded the center, directly west of Boston; and Major General Charles Lee was in command on the left, between the Mystic River and Willis Creek, shutting off Charlestown Peninsula. Washington's

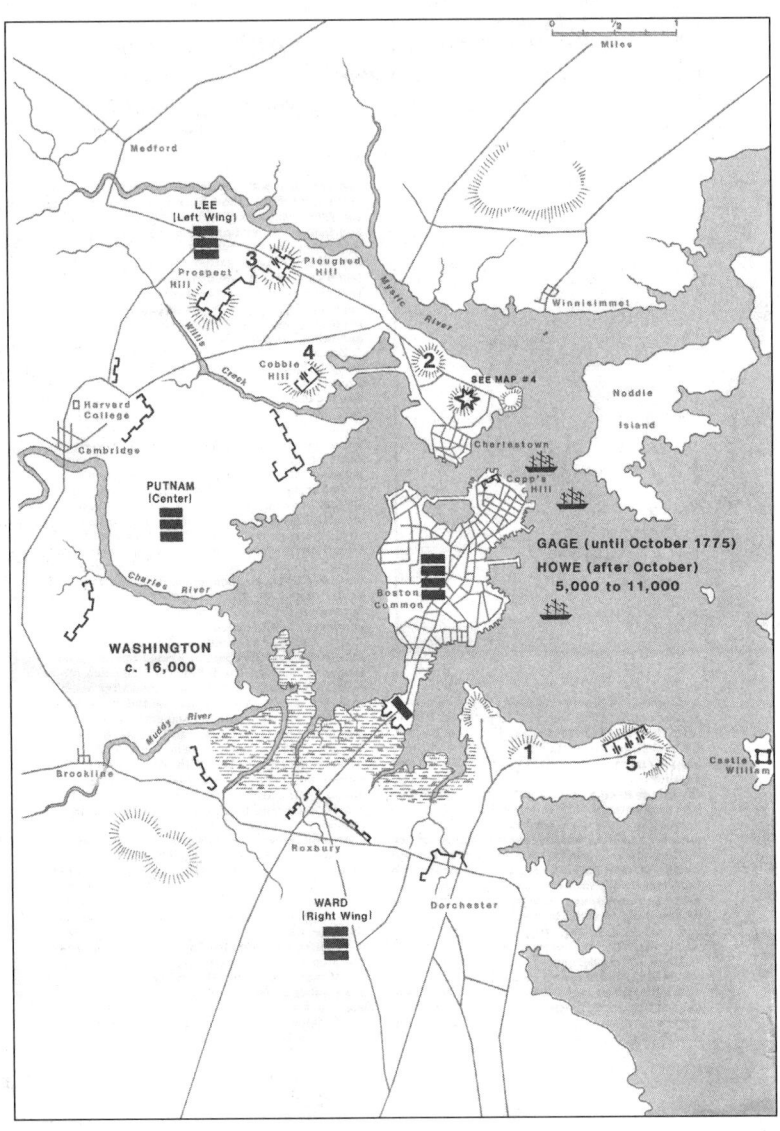

Map 1 - The Siege of Boston

Headquarters retained direct command of the rifle companies and the artillery.[27]

Washington moved Price's and Morgan's rifle companies to Roxbury, in Major General Ward's sector, on August 13th, just five days after their arrival. The next day, Sunday the 14th, Otho Holland Williams and his comrades in The Second Company came under fire for the first time, one private noting that "we had a most amazing shout of cannon thunders which at this time seemed strange to our young soldiers, during this our first alarm. We were fired at with balls, bombs, and Granade shells."[28] Williams and the men would become very accustomed to these steady bombardments over the next seven months.

General Washington had been anxious for his frontiersmen to arrive, and he had specific high-value missions in mind for them. He wanted them to gather intelligence, probe enemy positions, capture high-value British officers, and keep constant pressure on the besieged British army. For example, he had written to Congress in early August that "… I last Saturday Evening ordered some of the Rifle Men down to make a Discovery or bring off a Prisoner."[29] Given the secretive nature of these assignments and the low rank of Otho Williams at the time, it is not possible to detail his exact movements during this period, although we can gather much from the overall manner in which Washington employed the riflemen.

Washington had learned about riflemen during his early experiences on the frontier and in the French and Indian War. He had them report directly to his own headquarters instead of to subordinate commanders, because he felt they would be more effective if he could direct their activities personally. There were initially more riflemen than Congress had authorized, and the Commander-in-Chief dealt with that issue decisively. First, he obtained Congress' permission to pay more soldiers than they had initially authorized. Second, he saw to it that lesser skilled marksmen were weeded out, paid off, and sent home.[30]

The riflemen still loved to demonstrate their skills, and they left an indelible impression on all who witnessed their marksmanship. A Surgeon's Mate with the Massachusetts troops reflected the awe that many people felt when they saw the frontier riflemen up close for the first time:

> …*remarkably stout and hardy men, many of them exceeding six feet in height. They are dressed in white frocks, or rifle-shirts, and round hats. These men are remarkable for the accuracy of their aim; striking a mark with great certainty at two hundred*

> yards distance. At a review, a company of them, while on a quick advance, fired their balls into objects of seven inches diameter, at a distance of two hundred and fifty yards.[31]

In the early days of the siege, inexperienced soldiers might run helter-skelter from artillery shells, as in an incident described by Private Daniel McCurtin:

> *This morning as I was at breakfast in the former dwelling house of Dr. Williams they fired four 32 pounders at the house, one of which rushed through the room and dashed one side out of the chimney, broke 2 partitions and filled our dishes with plastering, ceiling and bricks. Geo. Switcher, Sergeant Torrel and William Johnson were in the room when this happened. Any man may judge whether or no this did not surprise us four young heroes, however as I cannot say for the minds of them who were in company with me, but I know, to the best of my thinking, that I went down two pair of stairs of three strides without a fall and as soon as I was out of doors ran to the Brestwork in great haste, which is our place of safety, without the least concern about my breakfast, to James McCancie's amazement.*[32]

After the excitement of being shot at wore off, the warfare around Boston soon settled into a monotonous siege. British officers remembered with searing clarity the horrible casualties inflicted by American muskets at Bunker Hill, and they would avoid headlong attacks on entrenched American positions for the remainder of the war. They could lob shells at the Americans from their artillery positions in Boston and from their warships in the harbor, but they were never able to bring themselves to mount another serious infantry assault on the American lines. During the early parts of the siege in 1775, the Americans did not have sufficient artillery to bother the British in the city, and therefore Lieutenant Williams and his fellow soldiers became accustomed to a routine of seeking shelter from British bombardments virtually every day, and carrying out intelligence-gathering missions, high-value guard duty, and other assignments.

Riflemen often guarded the troops who were building entrenchments, a task which could also subject every man to the dangers of artillery fire:

> *We stood picquet while our men continued building the fort aforesaid. The firing being too continual, and the work not*

> sufficient to cover our fatigued men, they were obliged to run a trench in the night for the men to cover themselves in the day time from the cruelty of the cannon balls. From this morning unto Thursday they have wrought continually day and night though much exposed to the cannon balls, without the loss of one man or even one wounded.[33]

The continual bombardment and constant danger wore on the spirits of the soldiers, which led some of the less committed men to desert. Private McCurtin disgustedly noted that William Johnson, one of his comrades who had undergone the bombardment at Dr. Williams' house, had run away from the American army and gone, "…just like another noted villain, into Boston."[34]

By August 26th, Private McCurtin wrote that the artillery fire was becoming less intense, and the men were becoming more and more accustomed to the dangers of regular bombardment: "This day nothing very remarkable, only one cannon ball which they fired at us when we were paraded and exercising in an orchard…"[35]

Sometimes British troops deserted to the American camp. McCurtin recorded on August 30th that two British deserters had made their way to the American lines and surrendered to the Marylanders. He recorded that on that same night, the Maryland troops suffered a steady bombardment during a "very long rainy night." By September 2nd, McCurtin also noted ominously that the Marylanders were finding the New England nights to be "very cold."[36][37]

There were periodic lapses of discipline in the Maryland Rifle Companies, as there are in all military units from time to time, and George Washington's army did not hesitate to apply rigorous punishment. The Army's General Orders of September 16th, 1775 record the humiliating treatment administered to one of Captain Price and Lieutenant Williams' sergeants:

> James Finley Serjt in Capt Price's Company of Rifle men, tried by a General Court Martial for "expressing himself disrespectfully of the Continental Association, and drinking Genl Gage's health"--The Court sentence the Prisoner to be deprived of his Arms and Accoutrements, put in a Horse Cart, with a Rope round his neck, and drum'd out of the Army and rendered for-ever incapable of serving in the Continental army.[38]

Lieutenant Williams left a brief commentary on the siege with this statement in a letter home on October 14th:

> ..*no enemy fire on camp since October 6, though one of our floating batteries fired on them in Cambrige recently, the night the play house in Boston opened; cannon burst, wounding 8 or 10 and killing one.*[39]

Captain Michael Cresap continued to suffer poor health in the months since he had arrived in Boston in August with the First Company of Maryland riflemen. Although he had accepted the command with some reluctance because of his health and the state of his personal affairs, he had thrown himself into the task of leading his men on their rapid march to Boston. He also established a strong military culture and set high standards of leadership for his command. After less than two months in the Boston area, he realized that he had to return to Maryland to recover his health. He was granted leave from the Army, and set out to return home to Maryland, leaving Lieutenant Moses Rawlings in command of The First Company of Maryland riflemen. Once one of the most robust of frontiersmen, thirty-three-year-old Cresap had grown steadily weaker, his strength and endurance fatally sapped by nagging illness and the exhausting march to Boston. On his return trip to Maryland, he only made it as far as New York City, where he died of a fever in October 1775. He was honored with an impressive military funeral, prompting one observer to note that he would not begrudge to die if his funeral would be as honorable as Cresap's.[40] Captain Cresap was buried in New York's Trinity Church Yard.[41]

When news of Cresap's death reached Boston, Moses Rawlings was promoted to Captain on October 21st, 1775, and assumed command of First Company of Maryland riflemen.[42]

Lieutenant Williams had arrived in the Boston area in the summer of 1775, and immediately stepped into a world that involved almost daily conflict with enemy troops. Working under good leaders and serving with capable soldiers, his military education had begun. However, life on the American side during the siege of Boston was not all fighting, digging, and dodging cannon balls. On Christmas Eve, December 24th, 1775, it "rained and snowed heavy" all day, but that did not keep Private McCurtin and a friend from walking about three miles from the camp to buy some fruit and fowl for Christmas Day. This Marylander "…never felt so cold in my living days."[43] Christmas Day was a "fine day, though the snow is very high, but shined the whole day, in a clear sun. In the afternoon I enlisted at a fencing school just by our Camps."[44]

Organization of the Continental Army / Promotion to Captain

Congress acted on Washington's recommendation to establish an Army organization of 26 infantry regiments, plus a Rifle Regiment and an Artillery Regiment on November 4th, 1775.[45] This precipitated significant organizational activity, including sending some troops home, declaring some officers unnecessary, and promoting officers who had performed well. Since the men in the Rifle Regiment were enlisted through July 1st, 1776, they did not need to reorganize at this time, but they were given the honor of being designated the First Continental Regiment in recognition that they had been the first troops called into the Continental Army.[46]

While the Maryland rifle companies continued to serve at the siege in Boston, Maryland recognized that it needed to take additional steps to prepare for its defense. On January 1st, 1776, the Maryland Convention resolved that a "...sufficient force be immediately raised and embodied under proper officers, for the defence and protection of the province." 1,444 men, "with proper officers" were to be raised immediately, and the Council of Safety was empowered to order these troops into Virginia, Delaware and Pennsylvania.[47] William Smallwood was named Colonel of this Maryland Battalion and Thomas Price, Captain of the Second Company of Maryland riflemen (Otho Williams' Commanding Officer,) was promoted to Major under Smallwood.[48] Price's promotion was effective on January 3rd, 1776.[49] Otho Holland Williams was promoted to Captain a little more than a month later, on February 5th, 1776,[50] and assumed command of the Second Company of Maryland riflemen.[51]

John Carey, one of Williams' older friends from Frederick, had predicted that the War would "lead to a great rise" in Williams' "station in life."[52] Such a prediction was probably very welcome to an aspiring young officer like Otho Holland Williams. His soldierly qualities had caught the eye of prominent leaders in the army and in the civilian leadership in Maryland.

Victory at Boston; Transfer to New York

On January 25th, 1776, Colonel Henry Knox, commander of the American artillery, arrived in the Boston area with 43 cannon and 14 mortars that his detachment had dragged cross-country through snow and ice from Fort Ticonderoga.[53] The Americans now had sufficient heavy artillery to make life in the city untenable for the British. General Washington soon had his army hard at work placing his newly-acquired big guns where they could do the most damage to the British in and around Boston.

By March 4th, 1776, American artillery dominated Boston from their emplacements on Dorchester Heights, forcing the British to either attack the American positions, or evacuate Boston. The massed artillery fire from the American positions was stronger than anything the riflemen had witnessed up until this time:

> *This night you could see shells, sometimes 7 at a time in the air and as to cannon the continual shaking of the earth by cannonading dried up our wells… This very night as was suspected we entrenched on Dorchester hill, made two strong Forts and seven small breastworks. I cant tell how many men there was on the hill, but this I am certain that there were between 5 & 6 thousand, though I have been informed by authority that there were 11 thousand. This night our Riflemen at Roxbury and 2 Companies from Cambridge went and lay in ambush close by the water side expecting every moment that the Butchers belonging to the Tyrant of Great Britain would be out among us.*"[54]

General Washington anticipated the withdrawal of the British from Boston, and began to plan for the next British move. He concluded that the next likely British target would be New York City, and, accordingly, on March 13th, he began to order his highly valued rifle companies to proceed there "with all possible expedition."[55] The next day, Captain Otho Williams led his Second Company out of the siege lines and in to Cambridge, where they spent the night "in the College among other soldiers."[56] The following day, they began a rapid march toward New York. The British evacuated Boston on St. Patrick's Day, March 17th, 1776, just a few days after Otho Williams and his Second Company had hurried off to help prepare for the defense of New York City.

★ ★ ★ ★ ★

The Fight for New York City
Captain Otho Holland Williams and the Second Maryland Rifle Company

arrived in New York on March 28th, 1776.[57] A few days later, on April 11th, 1776, Williams wrote to his brother Elie that he had been transferred, along with Captain Stephenson to Staten Island, which he called "this beautiful island." Williams thought that many of the island's hills were natural fortifications, and he had heard that Parliament intended to send 25,000 mercenaries to New York to supplement the British army. In this letter, Captain Williams also noted his first direct combat experience of which we have a record, noting that "last Sunday (Easter) the British vessels sent 25 men ashore to get water, with the Savage a ship of war and the James (a Pilate Boat to the Phoenix) for protection." Stephenson's and Williams' troops beat them off and captured "...ten men, a barge, 29 barrels, a standard, a musket, and more small articles." He also noted that he was temporarily in command on Staten Island because his two senior officers were off on other assignments - Stephenson was leaving for Virginia and Rawlings was currently stationed on the Jersey shore.[58]

The same day, Williams wrote a short note to his sister, Mrs. Mercy Stull of Frederick county, Maryland, noting that "Captain Stephenson, who is to deliver this letter, refuses to burden himself with more than one sheet from me, so she must be content with a short note annexed to his letter to their brother Elie." Williams noted that he hoped to be home for a visit before the end of next harvest.[59]

General Washington arrived in New York on April 13th, just a few days after Williams had written home from Staten Island.[60] There was tension in the air around New York, because no one could be certain of the next British moves. Washington kept his troops busy working on defensive positions, while everyone from the lowliest private to the Commander-in-Chief himself speculated on where and when the inevitable blow would fall.

Williams occupied a key position on Staten Island. First, it was fertile farmland, and therefore much sought after as a source of provisions by both the British and American sides. Second, it was also strategically positioned at the entrance to New York Harbor, where British fleet movements could be spotted in time to give early warning to the City. Accordingly, a system of signals was established so that officers in New York could observe signal flags from the heights of the Staten Island hills.

There were many American Loyalists, or "Tories," in the region, and the American army was very concerned with keeping its capabilities, formations, and plans hidden from potential spies. Riflemen on Staten Island came under suspicion when they were accused of accepting bribes to facilitate the passage of spies from the Island to British warships, a problem which General

Washington addressed directly in a letter to the Essex County, New Jersey Committee of Safety on June 17th, 1776.[61] There is no record that anything came of these charges, but such accusations show the tense atmosphere in the area.

Sir William Howe's fleet finally appeared off Sandy Hook in late June,[62] prompting General Washington to report to Congress on June 29th that:

> *For two or three days past three or four Ships have been dropping in and I just now received an Express from an Officer appointed to keep a look out on Staten Island, that forty five arrived at the Hook to day, some say more, and I suppose the whole fleet will be in within a day or two.*[63]

On the 4th of July, while the Declaration of Independence was being signed in Philadelphia, Washington reported once again on the buildup of the British forces around New York:

> *They or at least a part of them are already landed on Staten Island, which is quite contiguous and about 4000 were marching about it yesterday, as I have been advised and are leaving no Acts unessayed, to gain the Inhabitants to their side, who seem but too favourably disposed. It is not unlikely that in a little time they may attempt to cross to the Jersey side, and induce many to join them, either from motives of Interest or fear, unless there is a force to oppose them.*[64]

With the influx of large numbers of British and Hessian troops onto Staten Island, the position of Williams and the riflemen there had become untenable. In August, they were ordered to Fort Lee[65]*, on the New Jersey side of the Hudson.[66]

On August 7th, Washington reported that the British forces had been further augmented by troops returning from the unsuccessful expedition to capture Charleston, South Carolina and by transports that had brought Hessians and Highlanders to Staten Island. He also expected that 12,000 men would arrive from the Banks of Newfoundland very soon, and that "the computed strength of their army will be 30,000 men."[67]

---

*The defense of New York included Forts Washington and Lee, which faced each other across the Hudson River with the objective of preventing British shipping from sailing up the river.

The last ships of the British fleet arrived in the New York area on August 12th, bringing the total strength of the British and Hessian armed force to about 32,000 men.⁶⁸ The actual number of troops was quite close to the estimate that Washington had provided to Congress just a few days earlier, indicating the effectiveness of American intelligence. However, the numbers were daunting. Washington knew that he and his army faced a formidable challenge to defend New York City and its environs.

The Reorganization of the Continental Rifle Troops

By the time General Washington arrived in New York, he had started to worry that he would lose his best rifle companies, including Captain Otho Williams and his company, on July 1st, when their enlistments were due to expire. The Commander-in-Chief expressed his concerns to Congress:

> *As the Time for which the Rifle Men inlisted, will expire on the first of July next, and as the loss of such a valuable and brave body of Men will be of great injury to the Service; I would submit it to the Consideration of Congress whether it would not be best to adopt some method to induce them to continue. They are indeed a very useful Corps, but I need not mention this as their importance is already well known to the Congress. It is necessary they should pay an early attention to this matter, as we know from past experience that Men are very slow in reinlisting.*⁶⁹

General Washington continued to press his concerns about the riflemen with a postscript to his June 8th letter to Congress: "P.S. If Congress have come to any resolution about an allowance to induce men to reinlist, you will please to favor me with it, as the Time the Rifle Regiment is engaged for is just expired."⁷⁰

Congress understood the importance of the riflemen, and officially established the Rifle Regiment on June 27th, 1776, incorporating the three companies of riflemen that remained in the New York area with six new companies to be recruited. Captain Hugh Stevenson was promoted to Colonel and given command of the new regiment. Moses Rawlings was promoted to Lieutenant Colonel and named second-in-command. Otho Holland Williams was promoted to Major, the third senior officer in the Regiment.⁷¹

On the same date that he was being promoted to Major in the Rifle Regiment, the Maryland Convention promoted Otho Holland Williams to Colonel in Maryland's Flying Camp, to command the "...battalion to be raised in Frederick county".[72] Williams responded in a letter written from Frederick Town on July 23rd, 1776:

> *Colonel Stull informs me that at your last convention at Annapolis you did me the very great honour of appointing me a Colonel of the Frederick County Battalion to serve the United States of America in the flying camp until the first day of December next.*
> *Ever since the commencement of the unnatural war waged by a wicked ministry against this Country I have considered it as my indispensable duty to exert my feeble abilities in its defence and entering early into the service have had the good fortune to be so far recommended to the Honorable the Continental Congress as to obtain a commission as a Major of a Battalion of Riflemen to serve the United States three years, and being diffident of my abilities to discharge the duties of a more exalted station at present beg leave to decline the very honorable appointment by which you gentlemen have confer'd an obligation on me ever to be most gratefully remembered and acknowledged, I beg leave in a particular manner to profess my gratitude to those worthy gentlemen by whose recommendations I obtained so respectable an appointment their favorable opinion I trust will always be maintained by a propriety of conduct in Gentlemen.*[73]

It was unusual, indeed, for an officer during the Revolutionary era to turn down a commission as a Colonel and remain a Major. This decision illustrates the thoughtfulness, humility, and soldierly qualities of young Otho Holland Williams. The offer of a promotion to Colonel was also a sign of his growing military reputation.

General Washington continued to press the issue of the retention of the rifle companies, even though he was beset with worries about the growing British power in the New York area and maddeningly unsure of their intentions. The Commander-in-Chief badly needed his riflemen to be with him in the coming campaign, and he dispatched their leader to Philadelphia to discuss matters directly with Congress:

> *I shall communicate to Colonel Stevenson and one of his Field Officers, what you have requested and desire them to repair immediately to Philadelphia. It is an unlucky circumstance, that the term of Inlistment of these three companies and of the Rifle Battalion, should expire at this time, when a hot Campaign is in all probability about to commence.*[74]

It was a source of unending worry to Washington that his riflemen were not reenlisting in large numbers, and a tone of dismay began to appear in his letters to Congress that addressed the subject:

> *Sir: This will be handed you by Colo: Stevenson whom I have ordered, with the Captains of the two Rifle Companies from Maryland to wait on Congress. They will point out such measures as they conceive most likely to advance the raising of the New Battalion and the Persons they think worthy of promotion that have served with them, agreeable to the inclosed List: I am not acquainted with them, but from their report and recommendation, which I doubt not is just, and if Congress will please to enquire of them, they will mention other proper persons for officers.*
> *Only about 40 of the three Old Companies have reinlisted, which I shall form into one for the present and place under an Officer or two, 'till a further and complete Arrangement is made, of the whole Battalion.*[75]

Colonel Hugh Stephenson traveled on to Virginia after his visit to the Continental Congress, and died in his home state during the summer of 1776. The leadership and organization of the Rifle Regiment were matters of immediate importance to General Washington, and he requested the hardy, proven frontiersman, Daniel Morgan, to command this important force. However, Morgan was still on parole after his capture at the Battle of Quebec on December 31st, 1776, and his parole status was a significant complication:

> *As Col: Hugh Stephenson of the Rifle Regiment ordered lately to be raised, is dead, according to the information I have received, I would beg leave to recommend to the particular notice of Congress, Captain Daniel Morgan, just returned among the Prisoners from Canada, as a fit and proper person to succeed to*

the vacancy occasioned by his Death. The present Field Officers of the Regiment cannot claim any right in preference to him, because he ranked above them as a Captain when he first entered the service[76]

John Hancock, the President of Congress, responded to the Commander-in-Chief that they were keeping the position open for Daniel Morgan, in accordance with Washington's request.[77]

However, Morgan was not exchanged until 1777, and could not join the Army to assist in the current campaign for New York.[78] (He eventually declined the appointment.[79]) Command of the riflemen then passed to the capable Lieutenant Colonel Moses Rawlings, whose second-in-command was twenty-eight year old Major Otho Holland Williams.[80]

The Battle of Fort Washington[81]

Once the British had established their base on Staten Island during July and early August, 1776, they began their campaign to take New York, and by early November, 1776, they had largely succeeded, gaining advantage in battles at Long Island August 26th, Kip's Bay on September 15th, Harlem Heights on September 16th and White Plains on October 28th.[82]

At the end of this series of battles, the Americans had been virtually driven out of New York City and its environs. The British held all the territory in the area east of the Hudson River except Fort Washington at the northern tip of Manhattan Island, which stood an imposing 250 feet high above the Hudson River.[83*] This Fort was situated on the eastern end of a line of sunken ships and other obstacles that the Americans had placed in the Hudson River to impede British ships from sailing upriver. Fort Lee was on the New Jersey side of the river, directly across from Fort Washington. The Americans had placed artillery in these two forts to try to prevent British ships from sailing up the river.[84]

The geography of this northern tip of Manhattan (illustrated by the map on page 34) determined its defenses. The area is about three-quarters of a mile wide, and extends northward from New York City and Harlem Heights. It is bounded by the Hudson River on the west, the Harlem River on the east, and Spuyten Duyvil Creek on the north. The borders of both rivers are rocky, with

---

* Fort Washington stood near today's George Washington Bridge and Fort Washington Park, New York City.

one-hundred foot cliffs. Mount Washington (this area is Washington Heights today) rises on the western edge of the island, next to the Hudson River. Fort Washington was built atop this formation, on the highest point in the area. Another hill on the eastern side of the island is named Laurel Hill. Both hills were steep and rugged. A road passed through the narrow valley between the two hills, winding north from New York City towards Kingsbridge, which lay beyond the Harlem River. The area was densely wooded.[85]

The Americans had been working on the defenses in the Fort Washington area since early in the war, and there were thirteen smaller defensive works on the heights around the main fort. There were two completed lines of entrenchments and a third being constructed south of the main positions, facing New York City.[86] The outer entrenchments of the American position stretched over four miles, north to south.

High atop Manhattan Island, and seemingly well-fortified, Fort Washington was thought by the American high command to be a strong position, and one well worth defending. However, it had vulnerabilities that the American leadership did not realize. One British officer observed that the fortifications were "too extensive for the number of troops, as was generally the case with the Americans, who were indefatigable in constructing redoubts."[87] There were other vulnerabilities. Fort Washington had earthen walls, and the hard rock outside the fort made it very difficult to dig defensive trenches. There was no water supply on the hilltop; water had to be carried up from below.[88]

On November 7th, 1776, three British ships maneuvered around the obstructions in the Hudson River and passed successfully through artillery fire from Forts Washington and Lee. It seemed clear that the forts could not stop shipping from moving upriver.[89] It also seemed clear to many observers that Fort Washington should be evacuated immediately, for if it was left as the only remaining American outpost on Manhattan, surrounded by 20,000 British and Hessian troops, it was doomed to fall.

Nonetheless, the American high command was divided on whether or not to evacuate the fort and unite all elements of the army in New Jersey, on the west side of the Hudson River. The American army's Chief Engineer, Israel Putnam, had laid out the lines and thought that the post was impregnable.[90] Washington respected the orders of Congress, which had been to restrict British ships from moving up the Hudson, as well as the decision of a Council of his Generals to try to defend the fort. Still, he tended to think that evacuation was the best decision, but his trusted subordinate, Nathanael Greene, commented that "I cannot conceive the garrison to be in any great danger."[91] Washington allowed Greene's decision to stand. He later explained the reasons for his indecision to his brother John Augustine Washington, noting that he had felt that the fort should be evacuated, but

> ...being determind on by a full Council of General Officers, & receiving a resolution of Congress strongly expressive of their desires, that the Channel of the River (which we had been labouring to stop a long while at this place) might be obstructed, if possible; & knowing that this could not be done unless there were Batteries to protect the Obstruction I did not care to give an absolute Order for withdrawing the Garrison till I could get round & see the Situation of things & then it became too late as the Fort was Invested. I had given it, upon the passing of the last Ships, as my opinion to Genl Greene under whose care it was, that it would be best to evacuate the place—but—as the order was discretionary, & his opinion differed from mine, it unhappyly was delayd too long, to my great grief[92]

Neither Moses Rawlings nor Otho Williams nor the riflemen who served under them were privy to these high-level debates on whether or not to defend the last American bastion on Manhattan. As pawns in this great chess game, they were ordered leave Fort Lee in mid-October, cross the river, and join the garrison at Fort Washington.[93] This decision sent Williams and his comrades directly into harm's way.

Colonel Robert Magaw commanded the 2,800 man garrison that defended the fort. He believed that it was a formidable position, and that his troops could defend it against any conceivable British attack. When the British demanded immediate surrender on November 15th, 1776, Magaw refused, and vowed to defend his position to the last extremity.[94]

When George Washington heard that Magaw had turned down a demand to surrender, he hurried to cross the Hudson from New Jersey to assess the situation himself. Washington's boat was met in the middle of the river by Nathanael Greene and Israel Putnam who were returning by boat from the New York side. They gave the Commander-in-Chief an optimistic report on the morale of the troops and the state of the defenses, and they all returned to New Jersey.[95]

In making his bold pronouncements that he would defend Fort Washington to the last, Magaw did not yet know that one of his key officers, Lieutenant William Demont, had deserted to the British in early November, and provided the British with a complete description of the American defenses. The British would be able to plan their attack with full knowledge of any weak points in the American positions. Demont also provided full detail on some of the arguments and divisions within the American Army, comments that were recorded in the diary of a British officer, Captain Frederick Mackenzie:

> *He says there are great dissentions in the Rebel Army, everybody finding fault with the mode of proceeding, and the inferior officers, even ensigns, insisting that, in such a cause, every man has a right to assist in council and to give his opinion. They are much distressed for clothing. The people from the Southern Colonies declare they will not go into New England, and the others that they will not march to the southward.*[96]

Enlightened by Demont, the British high command devised an effective plan to surround Fort Washington and to launch attacks from three directions supported by naval gunfire from the Hudson River. As part of their preparations, the British daringly drove thirty flatboats, filled to the gunwales with soldiers, up the Hudson past the America sentries, and landed the soldiers in the woods east of the fort where they awaited the coming assault in safety.[97]

British General Lord William Howe sent Hessians under General Knyphausen to the King's Bridge area, across the Harlem River to the northeast of the Fort with orders to attack from the north. Howe ordered General Lord Percy into Harlem, with orders to prepare to attack from the south. Brigadier Matthews, supported by Lord Cornwallis, was ordered to attack from his position east of the Harlem River.[98] The land assaults were to be supported by bombardment from HMS *Pearl* sailing on the Hudson River near the fort.[99]

Altogether, the British had over 13,000 men in position to conduct or support these assaults on Fort Washington,[100] an advantage of more than 4.5-to-1 over Magaw's 2,800 defenders. In addition, the American forces were poorly positioned far out in front of the main fort, defending lines that were two-and-a-half miles long.[101] Moses Rawlings, Otho Williams and their Rifle Regiment defended the northeast sector of the American lines from a small redoubt on the northern tip of Mount Washington,[102]* supported by a battery of three artillery pieces.[103] They would be facing Hessians climbing up the

---

*After the battle, the British named this site Fort Tryon for the British Royal Governor. It is the site of today's Fort Tryon Park.

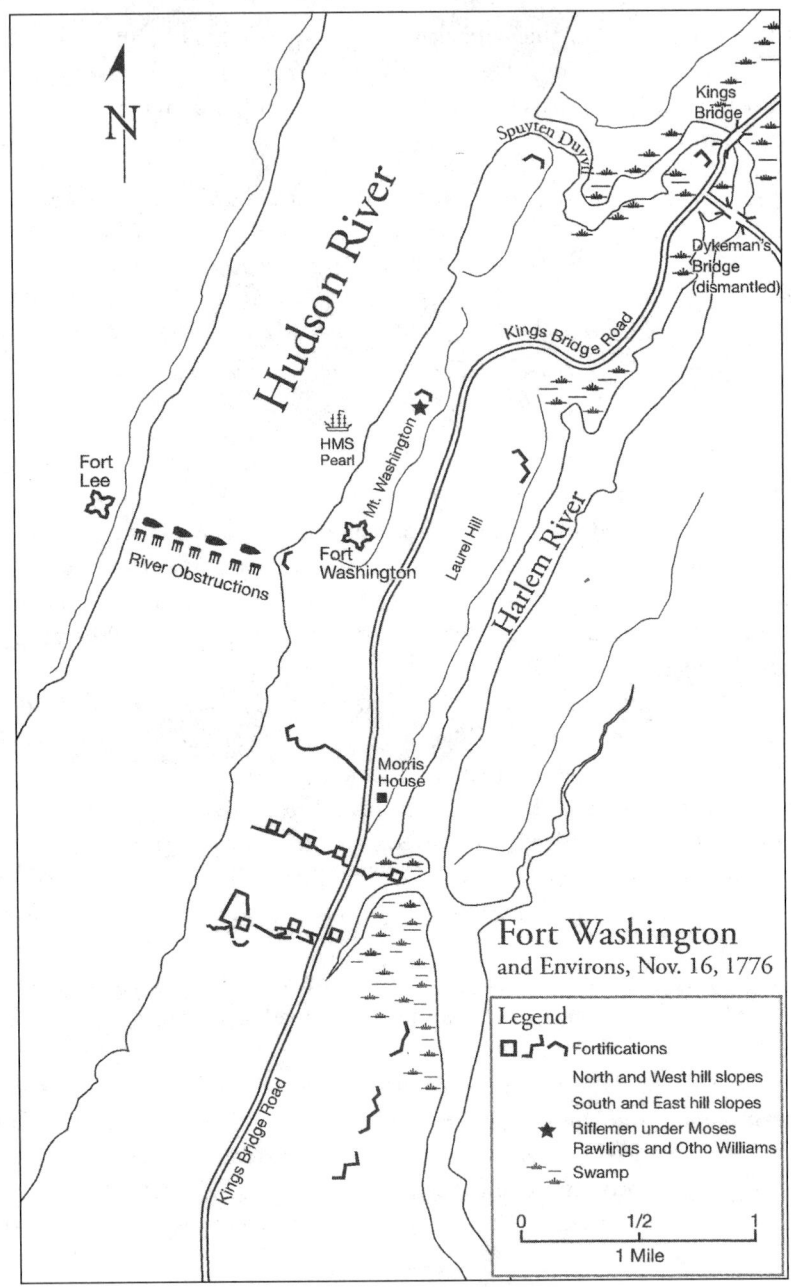

Map 2 - The Battle of Fort Washington

hillside, which was rocky and steep. They had constructed a series of rock breastworks to improve their defenses.[104]

The Hessian troops crossed the Harlem River at five-thirty on the morning of November 16th, 1776, some in flat boats, and some by marching across Kings' Bridge. They were commanded by Lieutenant General Wilhelm von Knyphausen, and were divided into two columns, the right commanded by Colonel Johann Rall[105], and the left, by Major General Martin Conrad Schmidt. They were facing the American riflemen on the heights above, and they were anxious to attack, but the battle plan called for all assaults to commence at the same time. While the Hessians waited, both sides exchanged artillery fire beginning at 7 a.m., but the first infantry attacks were not launched from across the Harlem River until about 10 o'clock in the morning,

The Commander-in-Chief, George Washington, continued to be very concerned about Fort Washington, and he took Generals Greene, Putnam and Hugh Mercer across the river with him to assess the situation on the morning November 16th, the same day that Howe launched his attack. Washington's party heard the sounds of firing almost as soon as their boat set out. When they reached the New York side of the river, they scrambled up a steep slope, where they observed some of the early fighting. Concluding that it was too late to make any changes to the plans for defense and seemingly confident of success, they returned to Fort Lee on the New Jersey side of the river.[106] There has been conjecture by some writers that Washington came very close to being captured by the British that morning.[107]

Soon after the fighting started to their south, the Hessians north of the fort went into action and moved to attack Rawlings, Williams and their riflemen. New to this war, the Hessian officers were anxious to prove their value to their British allies. They were relieved to finally get into the fight.[108]

Rall moved his troops around the right of the American position, and Schmidt moved around their left. Knyphausen led a portion of Rall's command to the attack up the steep hill in the center, but Rawlings' and Williams' riflemen, running from one position to another and supported by their artillery pieces, kept up such an accurate and heavy fire that Knyphausen had to fall back twice to regroup. A Hessian soldier named John Reuber recorded the difficulties of attack in his Journal:

> *...all the regiments marched forward up the hill and were obliged to creep along the rocks, one falling down alive, another being shot dead. We were obliged to drag ourselves by the beech-tree*

> bushes up the height where we could not really stand. At last, however, we got about on the top of the hill, where there were trees and great stones. We had a hard time of it there together. Because they now had no idea of yielding.[109]

Edward J. Lowell, author of the book *The Hessians and the other German Auxiliaries of Great Britain in the Revolutionary War*, provided this description of the Hessian attack:

> The moment for the Hessians to attack had come at last. They waded through a marsh, and climbed the precipitous, rocky hill on which the fort was built. In vain did the riflemen shoot them down. In vain did the artillery rain grape and ball among them. Knyphausen, himself, was continually in the thickest of the fight… 'so that it is wonderful …that he came off without being killed or wounded.'… The ground was so steep in places that the men had to pull themselves up by the bushes[110]

This intense firing continued for about two hours. Rawlings and Williams had positioned their men wisely, and they excelled at this type of fighting. The Hessians had a tough assignment on their hands. The enemy's officers were targeted, and many were either killed outright or mortally wounded. The fighting began to abate when the American rifles grew too hot or were too clogged to fire. Lowell described events when the Hessians finally reached the top of the hill:

> At last they reached the top, where there was a level place. 'Forward, all my grenadiers! cried Rall. The drums beat, the bugles blew, the men shouted Hurrah! Hessians and Americans were mingled in a mass, all rushing wildly towards the fort.[111]

John Adlum, an American soldier in this battle, recalled additional details in the pension application that he submitted many years later:

> Colonel Rawlings was one of the handsomest as well as one of the bravest officers in the army, for he, with Major Williams, with 309 men of their regiment, a picket guard of 100, and a captain's guard of 40 men, repulsed near ten times their number at least twice, and the enemy acknowledged the loss of 600 men.[112]

George Washington learned several days later from a reliable source that "...the Enemy's loss was very considerable, especially in the attack made above the Fort by the Division of Hessians that Marched from Kingsbridge, and where Lieut. Colo Rawlings of the late Colo. Stevenson's Regiment was posted."[113]

Williams and Rawlings, the two senior officers of the rifle troops, had both been badly wounded during the day's fighting.[114] John Adlum remembered being close to Williams when he was wounded, and seeing him being attended by Dr. James McHenry[115*] while under heavy fire from the Hessian lines:[116]
[117]

The riflemen had held out the longest from Howe's simultaneous attacks, but now that their fire had decreased, the American forces were in retreat on all fronts. Men stumbled back to the walls of the main fort, where they quickly realized that there was not enough space for all of them to deploy effectively against the advancing enemy. General Knyphausen sent Magaw a summons to surrender and the Colonel may have decided that further defense was useless and would result in the sacrifice of more of his men. There may also have been other considerations. Historian Christopher Ward felt that "There were more than 2,500 men in the fort, crowded within a space not adequate to receive more than a thousand. Under bombardment it would become a slaughter pen."[118]

There may have also been difficulties in getting the beaten American troops, surrounded by a superior force, to continue the fight. Nathanael Greene reported to Washington two days after the battle that "Col. Magaw could not get the Men to man the lines otherwise he would not have given up the Fort,"[119] a sentiment that Washington shared in a private letter to his brother.[120]

Magaw opened surrender negotiations, but a note soon arrived from George Washington ordering him to hold out until night when his troops could be evacuated. However, Magaw felt that the negotiations were too far along to suspend them, and he surrendered. This was a heavy loss for the American cause. The British had captured two-thousand and eight-hundred men, plus vitally needed arms, artillery and ammunition.[121]

Captain Frederick Mackenzie, who had written of Demont's treason, noted that "The Hessians...were extremely irritated at having lost a good many men in the attack" and killed some of the riflemen after surrender, until

---

*McHenry would serve as Secretary of War under both Presidents Washington and Adams. The Fort in Baltimore, Maryland that bears his name was the scene of the bombardment during the War of 1812.

officers intervened to stop the slaughter.[122]

George Washington witnessed this fighting from his vantage point at Fort Lee, just across the Hudson River. He was devastated by the Fort's surrender, and by the loss of irreplaceable men and materials. He was also infuriated by the brutality of Hessian soldiers.[123]

Along with the anger and devastating sense of loss, Washington experienced another strong emotion – pride in the heroic performance of his riflemen. Rawlings, Williams, and their troops had stoutly resisted the overwhelming Hessian onslaught, and the Commander-in-Chief, a fighting man of uncommon courage himself, was stirred by their spirit. Their reputation spread almost immediately. In the same letter from Greene that reported Magaw's difficulties getting the Americans to man the defenses, he reported to Washington that "the Enimy must have sufferd greatly on the Northside of Fort Washington—Col. Rollings Regiment was Posted there, and behaved with great spirit."[124] Over a year-and-a-half later, Washington still remembered the performance of the riflemen, writing to Congress:

> "...I cannot but feel myself exceedingly interested in favor of these Gentlemen. The conduct of this whole Corps, when Fort Washington was attacked is so generally known and approved, that it is almost unnecessary to add upon the subject. However, I think it but justice to observe, that every representation of that day's transaction gave them the highest credit. They fought with a degree of veteran bravery and tho' but a handful, they maintained their ground a considerable time, notwithstanding the most vigorous efforts to force them. All who were spectators upon the occasion have declared this, and the Enemy themselves have not refused them applause."[125]

In spite of any consolation from the solid performance of the riflemen, the Battle of Fort Washington was a disaster for the American cause. It left a dark stain on Nathanael Greene's military standing, and a blot on the Commander-in-Chief's reputation for leadership and decisiveness. This loss also provided ample fodder for General Washington's growing band of critics in Congress and in the Army.

The men who had defended Fort Washington were subjected to the deep humiliation of a public surrender ceremony:

...all the guns and arms were to be laid down, and when all this was done, Rall's regiment and the old Lossberg, being made to form into two lines facing each other, they were required to march out between the two regiments and deposit their guns and other weapons."[26]

They now faced the unknown rigors of what promised to be a very harsh captivity.

---

1 *Journals of the Continental Congress.* June 14, 1775. Volume 2, Page 89.
2 The fighting was actually on Breed's Hill. Both hills are on what was then Charlestown Neck. Breed's Hill is closer to Boston and 35 feet lower than Bunker Hill. Ref. Symonds, Craig. *A Battlefield Atlas of the American Revolution.* P. 19.
3 See Footnote.
4 Jacob, John J. *Biographical Sketch of the Life of the late Captain Michael Cresap* (hereafter Jacob, Cresap.) Cincinnati, Ohio, 1866. (Reprinted from the Cumberland Edition of 1826, with Notes and Appendix for William Dodge, by Jno. F. Ulhorm, Steam Job Printer, 38 West 3d St.) P. 119.
5 Wright, Robert K., Jr. *The Continental Army* (hereafter Wright, *Continental Army.*) Center Of Military History United States Army, Washington, D. C., 1986. P. 24.
6 Cecere, Michael. *They Are Indeed a Very Useful Corps* (hereafter Cecere, *Useful Corps.*) Heritage Books. Westminster, Maryland. 2006. Pp. 2-3.
7 Ibid. Pp. 1-2.
8 Tiffany, *Sketch.* P. 7.
9 Jacob, *Cresap.* P. 122.
10 Ibid. P. 119.
11 Wilson, Roger B., et. al. *The River and the Ridge. 300 Years of Local History.* Baltimore. 2003.
12 Jacob, *Cresap.* P. 120.
13 Ibid. P. 121.
14 *Journals of the Continental Congress. June 14, 1775.* Volume 2, Page 89.
15 Steuart, Rieman. *A History of the Maryland Line in the Revolutionary War. 1775-1783* (hereafter Steuart, *Maryland Line.*) The Society of the Cincinnati. Towson, Maryland. 1969. P. 1.
16 "*Muster Roll of Captain Thomas Price's Company of Rifle-Men In The Service of the United Colonies.*" Maryland Historical Magazine, September, 1927. Pages 275-281.
17 Tiffany, *Sketch.* P. 4. This statement was attributed to Samuel Smith, who served for a time in the Maryland Line during the Revolutionary War, and was a prominent Baltimore businessman.
18 Lee, Henry. *The Revolutionary War Memoirs of General Henry Lee.* Edited by Robert E. Lee with an Introduction by Charles Royster. (hereafter Lee, Memoirs.) DaCapo Press.. New York. 1998. Pp. 593.
19 Cecere, *Useful Corps.* P. 4. Cecere cites "Danske Dqandridge, "Henry Bedinger to ---Findley," Historic Shepherdstown, (Charlottesville, Va: Michie Co., 1910), Page 95.
20 Ibid. P. 5.
21 Ibid. Pp. 3-4. Cecere cites "James C. Ballagh, ed. Letters of Richard Henry Lee, Vol. I. (New York: Macmillan Co., 1911), 130-131.
22 Bryan, Jennifer A. *"The Horrors of Civil War: The Tilghman Family In the American Revolution.* Article in the Maryland Historical Magazine, Volume 101, No. 1 (Spring 2008.) P. 39. Ms. Bryan cites the letter from James Tilghman to Lady Juliana Penn and William Baker, June 16, 1775, Tilghman Papers, MS 2821, Maryland Historical Society.
23 Balch, Thomas, ed. *Papers Relating Chiefly to the Maryland Line during the Revolution.* (hereafter Balch, *Papers.*) Printed for the Seventy-Six Society. T.K. and P.G. Collins, Printers. Philadelphia. 1857. Pp. 11-12. The section of these papers relating to the march to Boston and the siege around that city is the Diary of Private Daniel McCurtin of Captain Price's Rifle Company.
24 Balch, *Papers*, P. 12.
25 Washington, George. *Letter to Philip J. Schuyler, written at Camp, Cambridge, Mass., August 15, 1775.* The George Washington Papers at the Library of Congress. (hereafter *Washington Papers.*)
26 Balch, *Papers.* P. 12.
27 Wright, *Continental Army.* Pp. 29.
28 Balch, *Papers.* Pp. 12-13.

29 Washington, George. Letter to the Continental Congress. Written at Cambridge on August 4, 1775. . *Washington Papers*.
30 Washington, George. Letter to the Continental Congress. Written at Cambridge on September 21, 1775. *Washington Papers*.
31 Cecere, *Useful Corps*. P. 7. Cerece cites "James Thatcher, M.D., Military Journal of the American Revolution. (Ganesvoort, New York: Corner House Historical Publications, 1998), 31.
32 Balch, *Papers*. P. 13.
33 Ibid. P. 13.
34 Ibid. P. 13.
35 Ibid. P. 14.
36 Ibid. P. 15.
37 In September, 1775 Benedict Arnold led an expedition out of Cambridge to march to and capture Quebec. In Volume 3 his *Life of Nathanael Greene, Major-General of the Army of the Revolution in Three Volumes*. George Washington Greene asserts that Otho Williams was assigned to the regiment of Captain Enos in this expedition, and that the only stain on Otho Williams' military career was that he was among those who left this expedition and returned to Boston, weakening Arnold's command. Arnold continued on the arduous trek through the Maine woods and eventually failed in the attempt to take Quebec. No confirmation of Otho Williams' participation with Arnold on this expedition has been found. The texts *Through A Howling Wilderness* by Thomas A. Desjardin (2006), *Arnold's March from Cambridge to Quebec. A Critical Study Arnold's* by Justin H. Smith (1903,) and *Expedition to Quebec* by John Codman 2nd (1902) all mention a Captain Thomas Williams in Captain Enos's Regiment. It seems likely that George Washington Greene may have confused this Captain Thomas Williams with our subject, Maryland's Otho Williams.
38 Washington, George. General Orders. Head Quarters, Cambridge, September 16, 1775. *Washington Papers*.
39 Williams, Otho Holland. Letter to Dr. Philip Thomas, Fredericktown, Maryland. Written at Camp, Roxbury, Massachusetts. October 14, 1775. *Williams Papers*. Part 1/8. (Item #5.)
40 Jacob, *Cresap*. P. 123.
41 Steuart, *Maryland Line*. P. 70.
42 Ibid. P. 1 and P. 122.
43 Balch, *Papers*, P. 30
44 Ibid. P. 30
45 Wright, *Continental Army*. Pp. 46-47.
46 Ibid. P. 54.
47 Muster Rolls and Other Records of Service of Maryland Troops in the American Revolution. Archives of Maryland Online. Volume 18. (under "Military Records.") Page 4.
48 Ibid. Page 5.
49 Steuart, *Maryland Line*. P. 121.
50 Balch, *Papers*. P. 32.
51 Wright, *Continental Army*. P. 319.
52 Carey, John. Letter to Otho Holland Williams. Written at Frederick Town, October 12, 1775. *Williams Papers*. Part 1/8. (Item #4.)
53 Commager, Henry Steele and Morris, Richard B., eds. *The Spirit of 'Seventy Six. The Story of the American Revolution as told by Participants (hereafter* Commager and Morris.) New York, Evanston, and London. 1958, 1967. P. 174.
54 Balch, *Papers*. P. 33.
55 Washington, George. Letter to the Continental Congress. Written at Cambridge. March 13th, 1776. *Washington Papers*.
56 Balch, *Papers*. P. 35.
57 Ibid. P. 36.
58 Williams, Otho Holland. Letter to Elie Williams, Frederick County, Maryland. April 11th, 1776. *Williams Papers*. Part 1/8. (Item #8.)
59 Williams, Otho Holland. Letter to Mrs. Mercy Stull, Frederick County, Maryland. April 11th, 1776. *Williams Papers*. Part 1/8. (Item #9.)
60 Washington, George. George Washington's Accounts of Expenses for April 1776. (Image 13 of 92.) *Washington Papers*.
61 Washington, George. Letter to the Essex County, New Jersey Committee of Safety. Written at New York, June 17th, 1776. *Washington Papers*.
62 Washington, George. Letter to Continental Congress. Written at New York. June 28th, 1776. (Note 34.) *Washington Papers*.
63 Washington, George. Letter to the Continental Congress. Written at New York, June 29th, 1776. *Washington Papers*.

64 Washington, George. Letter to the Continental Congress. Written at New York, July 4th, 1776. *Washington Papers*.
65 See Footnote.
66 "*The Capture of Colonel Moses Rawlings*," by Dale J. Schmitt. Maryland Historical Magazine, Vol. 71, No. 2, Summer, 1976. P. 206. Schmitt cites "Letter of Henry Bedinger to Rawlings' Heirs, September 29, 1830, Rawlings Papers."
67 Washington, George. Letter to the Continental Congress. Written at Head Quarters, New York. 1 p.m., August 7th, 1776. *Washington Papers*.
68 From note 67 to George Washington's Letter to Congress. Written at New York on July 3rd, 1776. *Washington Papers*.
69 Washington, George. Letter to the Continental Congress. Written at New York, April 22nd, 1776. *Washington Papers*.
70 Washington, George. Letter to the Continental Congress. Written at New York on June 8, 1776. *Washington Papers*.
71 Journals of the Continental Congress. Volume 5. P. 486. June 27, 1776. Library of Congress.
72 Proceedings of the Convention of Maryland for Thursday, June 27, 1776. Proceedings of the Conventions of the Province of Maryland, 1774-1776. Maryland Archives Online. Volume 78, Page 174.
73 Williams, Otho Holland. Letter to the Maryland Council of Safety. Written at Frederick Town, Maryland, July 23rd, 1776. Maryland Archives Online. Volume 12. Pages 104-105.
74 Journal and Correspondence of the Maryland Council of Safety, July 7: December 31, 1776.
Washington, George. Letter to the Continental Congress, written at New York, June 30th, 1776. *Washington Papers*.
75 Washington, George. Letter to the Continental Congress. Written at New York, July 4th, 1776. *Washington Papers*.
76 Washington, George. Letter to Congress. Written at Head Quarters, Harlem Heights. September 28th, 1776. *Washington Papers*.
77 Hancock, John. Letter to George Washington. Written at Philadelphia. October 4th, 1776. Letters of Delegates to Congress: Volume 5 August 16, 1776 - December 31, 1776. Page 305. Journals of the Continental Congress. Library of Congress.
78 Note 42 to entry on letter written by Washington, George. Letter to Congress. Written at Head Quarters, Harlem Heights. September 28th, 1776. *Washington Papers*.
79 Washington, George. Letter to Continental Congress. Written at Headquarters at White Plains. August 21st, 1778. *Washington Papers*.
80 Adlum, John. Pension statement submitted in 1833 (hereafter Adlum, *Pension Statement*.) From Dann, John C., Ed *The Revolution Remembered. Eyewitness Accounts of the War for Independence* (hereafter Dann ed., Accounts.) The University of Chicago Press. Chicago and London. 1980. P. 120
81 Information on the Battle of Fort Washington relies heavily on Reginald Pelham Bolton's" *A History of the Defence and Reduction of Mount Washington*," (hereafter Bolton, *Mount Washington*) which is contained in the Memorial Pamphlet (as Part IV, beginning on page 50) of "*Fort Washington, An Account of the Identification of the Site of Fort Washington, New York City, and the Erection and Dedication of a Monument Thereon Nov. 16, 1901*" by the Empire State Society of the Sons of the American Revolution. New York. 1902.
82 Symonds, Craig L. *Battlefield Atlas of the American Revolution* (hereafter Symonds, *Battlefield Atlas*.). Nautical and Aviation Publishing Company. Baltimore. 1998. Pp. 26-29.
83 See Footnote.
84 Ward, Christopher. (Edited by John Richard Alden.) *The War of the Revolution* (hereafter Ward. *Revolution*.) Skyhorse Publishing. 2011. P. 269.
85 Ibid. P. 268.
86 The defenses of the Fort Washington area are identified in detail on a map on pages 14 and 15 of the commemorative pamphlet *Fort Washington. November 16, 1776. A Memorial from the Empire State Society of the Sons of the American Revolution to the Honorable Mayor and Municipal Assembly of the City of New York, praying for the erection of a suitable monument to mark the site of Fort Washington*. By the Empire State Society of the Sons of the American Revolution. New York. 1898. (hereafter Empire State SAR, *Memorial*.)
87 Fischer, David Hackett. *Washington's Crossing* (hereafter Fischer, Crossing.) P. 111.
88 McCullough, David. *1776 (hereafter* McCullough, 1776.). Simon & Shuster. New York. 2005. P. 237.
89 Ward, *Revolution*. P. 269
90 Ibid. P. 269.
91 Commager and Morris. P. 490.
92 From George Washington to John Augustine Washington, 6–19 November 1776," Founders Online, National Archives (http://founders.archives.gov/documents/Washington/03-07-02-0070 [last update: 2014-09-30]). Source: The Papers of George Washington, Revolutionary War Series, vol. 7, 21 October 1776–5 January 1777, ed. Philander D. Chase. Charlottesville: University Press of Virginia, 1997, pp. 102–106. Note 9 to this entry in the Founders Online is: "The council of war that met on 16 Oct. agreed "that Fort Washington be retained as long as possible," and Congress resolved on 11 Oct "that General Washington be desired, if it be practicable, by every art, and whatever expence, to

obstruct effectually the navigation of the North river, between Fort Washington and Mount Constitution [Fort Lee]" (Journals of the Continental Congress, 6:866)."
93 *"The Capture of Colonel Moses Rawlings,"* by Dale J. Schmitt. Maryland Historical Magazine, Vol. 71, No. 2, Summer, 1976. P. 206. Schmitt cites (1) "Letter of Henry Bedinger to Rawlings' Heirs, September 29, 1830, Rawlings Papers" and "Henry P. Johnston, The Campaign of 1776 around New York and Brooklyn (New York, 1971; originally published 1878, pp. 277-279.)
94 McCullough, *1776*. P. 239.
95 From George Washington to John Hancock, 16 November 1776," Founders Online, National Archives (http://founders.archives.gov/documents/Washington/03-07-02-0118 [last update: 2014-09-30]). Source: *The Papers of George Washington*, Revolutionary War Series, vol. 7, *21 October 1776–5 January 1777*, ed. Philander D. Chase. Charlottesville: University Press of Virginia, 1997, pp. 162–169.
96 Commager and Morris. P. 492.
97 Bolton, *Mount Washington*. P. 87.
98 Ibid, Pp. 89-94.
99 Ibid. P. 114.
100 Fischer, *Crossing*. P. 113.
101 Lowell, Edward J. *The Hessians and the other German Auxiliaries of Great Britain in the Revolutionary War.* (hereafter Lowell, *Hessians*.) New York. 1884. P. 79.
102 See Footnote.
103 Ward, Revolution. P. 271.
104 Bolton, Mount Washington. P. 63.
105 Colonel Johann Rall would command the Hessian troops that George Washington would defeat at Trenton, New Jersey on December 26, 1776. Rall was mortally wounded in that engagement
106 From George Washington to John Hancock, 16 November 1776," Founders Online, National Archives (http://founders.archives.gov/documents/Washington/03-07-02-0118 [last update: 2014-09-30]). Source: The Papers of George Washington, Revolutionary War Series, vol. 7, 21 October 1776–5 January 1777, ed. Philander D. Chase. Charlottesville: University Press of Virginia, 1997, pp. 162–169. Footnote 7. This entry cites a letter from Nathanael Greene to Henry Knox of the day after the battle, November 17, 1776 in the Papers of General Nathanael Greene. I: 351-359.
107 Graydon, Alexander. *Memoirs of a Life, Chiefly Passed In Pennsylvania: Within the Last Sixty Years* (hereafter Graydon, *Memoirs*.) Printed For William Blackwood and T. Cadell, Strand, London. Edinburgh. 1822. Pp. 200-201; Empire State SAR, *Memorial*. P. 22.
108 Lowell, *Hessians*. Pp. 80-81.
109 Journal of Hessian Soldier John Reuber. Commager and Morris. P. 494.
110 Lowell, *Hessians*. Pp. 80-81.
111 Ibid. Pp. 80-81.
112 Adlum, *Pension Statement*. (in Dann ed., *Accounts*.) P. 120
113 Washington, George. Letter to the Continental Congress. Written at Hackensack on November 19, 1776. *Washington Papers*.
114 Bolton, Mount Washington. P. 114.
115 See Footnote.
116 Adlum, *Pension Statement*. P. 120.
The Otho Holland Williams Papers in the Maryland Historical Society contain Williams' Commission to be Major of the Regiment of Rifle
117 Signed by John Hancock, President, and Charles Thomson, Secretary. It is endorsed in the handwriting of Otho Holland Williams with the following statement: "This Commission was stain'd... by the blood... from a wound... received in an action on York Island 16th November 1776 when He was made prisoner."
118 Ward, *Revolution*. P. 274.
119 To George Washington from Major General Nathanael Greene, 18 November 1776," Founders Online, National Archives (http://founders.archives.gov/documents/Washington/03-07-02-0125 [last update: 2014-09-30]). Source: *The Papers of George Washington*, Revolutionary War Series, vol. 7, *21 October 1776–5 January 1777*, ed. Philander D. Chase. Charlottesville: University Press of Virginia, 1997, pp. 175–176.
120 From George Washington to John Augustine Washington, 6–19 November 1776," Founders Online, National Archives (http://founders.archives.gov/documents/Washington/03-07-02-0070 [last update: 2014-09-30]). Source: The Papers of George Washington, Revolutionary War Series, vol. 7, 21 October 1776–5 January 1777, ed. Philander D. Chase. Charlottesville: University Press of Virginia, 1997, pp. 102–106.
121 Empire State SAR, *Memorial*. P. 23.
122 Fischer, *Crossing*. P. 113.
123 Ibid. P. 113.

124 To George Washington from Major General Nathanael Greene, 18 November 1776," Founders Online, National Archives (http://founders.archives.gov/documents/Washington/03-07-02-0125 [last update:2014-10-23]).Source: *The Papers of George Washington*, Revolutionary War Series, vol. 7, 21 October 1776–5 January 1777, ed. Philander D. Chase. Charlottesville: University Press of Virginia, 1997, pp. 175–176.

125 Washington, George. Letter to Continental Congress. Written at Headquarters at White Plains. August 21, 1778. *Washington Papers*.

126 Journal of Hessian Soldier John Reuber. Commager and Morris. P. 494.

CHAPTER 3

FROM PRISONER-OF-WAR
TO ADJUTANT GENERAL OF THE ARMY

Prisoner-of-War

As the guns grew silent at the end of the Battle of Fort Washington, Otho Williams and his fellow prisoners were deeply concerned about how they would be treated in captivity. Hessian soldiers had developed a reputation for brutality, and they had already vented their anger at the American riflemen at Fort Washington by killing several who had been trying to surrender.[1] The immediate danger was that the Hessians might act as they had at Long Island just three months earlier, when they had committed depredations that were described by one American prisoner in a letter home:

> ..they first disarmed me, then plundered me of all I had, watch, buckles, money and sum clothing, after which they abused me by bruising my flesh with the butts of there guns. They knocked me down; I got up and they (kept on) beating me almost all the way to there (camp) where I got shot of them. The next thing I was almost starved to death by them.[2]

British and Hessian officers stopped these brutal acts, but even though the savagery was brought to a halt fairly quickly, the American high command soon began to receive alarming information on the condition of the prisoners. On November 19th, just three days after Fort Washington had surrendered, George Washington wrote to Congress of the "…distressed situation of our Prisoners in New York," which would become more difficult every day "…by the cold, inclement Season that is approaching." Washington wanted blankets and proper clothing for the American prisoners, as well as more humane physical treatment by their captors.[3]

The American soldiers who had been captured at Fort Washington were taken to New York City and distributed to various facilities that the British were using as prisons. Many of the officers were given parole, which gave them the freedom to move about the city.[4] By contrast, the enlisted men were sent to jails such as "The Provost" or several former sugar houses being used to house prisoners. Soon, many unfortunates would be assigned to the prison ships in New York harbor, where the conditions were unimaginably horrible.

Williams enjoyed a reasonably comfortable situation in the early months of his captivity, while he was on parole on Long Island.[5] A fellow prisoner,

Alexander Graydon, recorded that "Flatbush was the place assigned for the officers of our regiment, Col. Shee's and Col. Magaw's. Here also were stationed Cols. Miles, Atlee, Rawlins, and Maj. Williams. The indulgence of arranging ourselves agreeably to our respective circles of acquaintance was granted us by Mr. Loring."[6][7*] One official observer noted that "..the officers on Long Island are boarded out amongst the inhabitants in the most convenient manner, and appear to be very comfortable and healthy."[8] This is confirmed in the *Memoir of Alexander Graydon*, a fellow prisoner of Williams, who noted that his host had permitted Graydon's mother to occupy his part of a house during her stay at Flatbush:

> *This was highly convenient to her, and she became, in some degree, naturalized to her new situation. Her accustomed flow of good spirits returned...She also availed herself of the opportunity of learning from Major Williams the art of making Johnny cakes in the true Maryland fashion*[9]

Williams' interactions with Graydon's mother showed a very gracious young gentleman, and a young man who must have taken some pleasure in domestic chores such as making Johnny cakes .

Commander-in-Chief George Washington wanted Williams returned to his army, and he took a direct interest in his exchange, petitioning British Commissary of Prisoners, Joshua Loring, for Williams' release on January 14th, 1777,[10] and again on February 6th, 1777.[11] Hopes for a quick prisoner exchange were soon crushed, and it seemed that Williams would be a prisoner for an extended period.

During the early months of his captivity, Williams developed a solid friendship with a British Major Ackland, who treated him as a fellow gentleman, and introduced him to the polite society of the British officer corps. This sometimes entailed visits to the "fashionable houses" near the Battery in New York City. On at least one occasion, Ackland bravely defended his American friend from the snubs of his British and Tory hosts.[12]

Captivity grew much worse for Otho Williams on September 6th, 1776,[13] when he was abruptly removed from Long Island, and slammed into the New York City prison called "The Provost"[14] on charges that he had been communicating with the American Army and planning prisoner escapes.[15] At least one observer thought that Williams might have been singled out for this harsh treatment because he had disagreed openly with a titled British

---

*Joshua Loring was the British Commissary General of Prisoners.

officer who had arrogantly insulted some American prisoners.[16]

Life in "The Provost" was miserable, where Williams was:

> ...confined in a room about sixteen feet square that was seldom visited by the breath of heaven, and always remaining in a state of loathsome filth. Among other prisoners, was the celebrated Ethan Allen, and he shared the miserable den, in which Williams was confined. Their only visitors were wretches who came to glut their brutal curiosity, and to torture their victims with loud sentiments of delight in anticipation of seeing them hanged... Their health was much impaired, for their food was of the vilest sort, and scarce enough to keep soul and body together, and to add to these discomforts, the anxiety that preyed upon their minds, was terrible in the extreme.[17]

Ethan Allen gave us a glimpse of his fellow prisoner Otho Holland Williams in his colorfully named *Narrative of Col. Ethan Allen's Captivity, Written by Himself and Now Published for the Information of the Curious in All Nations*:

> A few weeks after my confinement, on like fallacious and wicked pretenses, was brought to the same place[18]* from his parole on Long Island, Major Otho Holland Williams, now a full Col. in the Continental Army. In his character are united the gentleman, officer, soldier, and friend.; he walked through the prison with an air of great disdain; said he 'is this the treatment which gentlemen of the Continental Army are to expect from the rascally British, when in their power?'[19]

A little over three weeks after Williams was imprisoned, the prisoners sent a Memorandum with their complaints to British officials. Although the author of the statement is not known, it rings with language consistent with the writings of Otho Holland Williams.

> Close confined in jail without distinction of rank or character, amongst felons, (a number of whom are under sentence of death,) without their friends being suffered to speak to them, even through the grates. On the scanty allowance of 2 lbs. hard biscuit and 2 lbs. raw pork per man per week, without fuel to dress it. Frequently supplied with water from a pump where

---

*The prison was called The Provost.

all kinds of filth is thrown that can render it obnoxious and unwholesome, (the effects of which are too often felt,) when good water is as easily obtained. Denied the benefit of a hospital, not allowed to send for medicine, nor even a doctor permitted to visit them when in the greatest distress; married men and others who lay at the point of death… Neither pen, ink, or paper allowed, (to prevent their treatment being made public,) the consequence of which, indeed, the prisoners themselves dread, knowing the malignant disposition of their keeper.[20]

John Fell, who kept a journal of his time in the Provost, recorded that the petition was presented on September 26th, 1777, and his entry on September 28th indicates that this "much displeased" the Sergeant, who threatened to lock up the prisoners' rooms. The Sergeant did have his vengeance, as the rooms were indeed locked up on September 29th and 30th.[21]

Williams was still recovering from his wound while he was in the Provost, remembering several years later that "..Dr. McHenry and Dr. Hodge, fellow prisoners with him, used to come and dress his wounds." He also remembered that "…great numbers of dead bodies were dragged in carts past the quarters" where Williams lay as a prisoner. Williams referred to the treatment of the American prisoners as "barbarous."[22] He had been made to ride to the gallows with a rope around his neck, and seated on a coffin, as though being led to his execution.[23]

By the end of December, 1777, Williams' brother Elie was writing alarmingly to the American Board of War about the plight of his brother, and imploring the Board to do everything in its power to obtain Otho's release, or at least to obtain better treatment. It was very galling to his brother that Colonel Williams had not been able to challenge his detention, to face his accusers in an open trial, or even to offer any defense whatever.[24]

Elie's letter to the Board of War stated that he was on his way to camp to provide cash to his brother.[25] A fellow prisoner recorded that when Otho received 40 silver dollars he called a Captain Shepherd and two other prisoners into his room and lent them each ten dollars, which enabled each of them to purchase a shirt, some shoes and other small items. Since Shepherd and the other prisoners so helped were Virginians, some Marylanders felt that Williams' liberality was misplaced.[26]

Williams was released on parole on December 17th, 1777[27] (before the date of Elie's letter to the Board of War) and was finally exchanged and returned to the American ranks on January 16th, 1778,[28] fourteen months to the day after his capture at the Battle of Fort Washington. He was twenty-eight years old. In an interesting twist of fate, he was exchanged for his friend, Major Ackland, who had been captured with "Gentleman Johnny" Burgoyne's army at the Battle of Saratoga.[29] Horatio Gates had taken a direct hand in the discussions that led to Williams' release, and one writer indicated that Gates thus "..proved his friendship."[30] Light Horse Harry Lee recorded that Gates' Adjutant-General James Wilkinson was involved in obtaining Williams' release because Gates was "..personally attached to Major Williams."[31]

Although Williams felt that the British treatment of prisoners had been stern, he noted some acts of kindness in a report to army headquarters on the treatment of prisoners:

> *Before I conclude, permit me to acknowledge to you and the world, that I am much obliged to Daniel Chamier, esq; auditor general, for lending me money; to doctor Richard Huddleton of the seventh British regiment, for several offices of kindness to myself and other prisoners, and that I was treated in a very courteous genteel manner by Major Ackland of the twentieth, for whom I was exchanged.*[32]

In spite of these small acts of kindness, the months that Williams spent as a prisoner in The Provost were demeaning, grueling times for the once robust and hearty young Marylander. He had marched off to War in June 1775, as a strong, fit, and durable young man, but his wound and time in prison had begun to slowly sap his strength and vigor. This change was almost imperceptible at first, but the disease he had acquired during his imprisonment would advance slowly but steadily. Later, it would deprive him of his energy and endurance.[33]

Otho Holland Williams was a mature, determined soldier, completely dedicated to victory in the war against Great Britain. As he left prison, he focused on the future, leaving behind the suffering and discouragement of that painful experience, and ignoring the first faint signs of his disease.

Yet, Williams also experienced the normal human reactions at being released from captivity. His fellow prisoner Alexander Graydon would write in his Memoirs that "Early in the spring, I think, of 1778, I got a letter from Major Williams acquainting me with his releas... It breathed the most extravagant joy; and ...excessive friskiness..."[34]

Promotion to Colonel and Preparation for Command

Otho Williams felt enormous relief to be able to breathe free air again, and he also enjoyed a new, higher military rank. During his imprisonment, he had been promoted to Colonel and given command of the Sixth Maryland Regiment. This was a strong testament to the respect that he had earned for his leadership performance so far in the war. Maryland had recommended him for promotion on December 10th, 1776 (less than a month after the Battle of Fort Washington,)[35] when he was twenty-seven years old.

The Continental Congress approved the final appointment, and on January 16th, 1777, John Hanson, President of the Congress of the United States, wrote to the Board of War recommending that Major Williams be promoted to Colonel. Hanson's support of Williams included high praise for the young Major:

> *I beg leave, in behalf of the committee, to recommend Major Otho Holland Williams, as a gentleman well qualified to succeed Colonel Griffith. His military genius is conspicuous, and his character, as an active, good officer, is so well known and established, that it is altogether unnecessary to say anything in support of it. But his having early stepped forth in the service of his injured country, and marched, as an officer, in the first company that went from this province to the assistance of our army at Boston, where he continued until that place was evacuated by our enemies, and his noble and spirited behavior, on many occasions, particularly at Fort Washington, where he bravely fought and bled in the defence of our invaded rights, and is now bearing the ill-treatment of a haughty, insolent, cruel, brutish, and worse than savage enemy, merits particular notice and attention, and, in the judgment of the committee, entitles him to the promotion.*[36]

Hanson also noted that the officers of the Battalion supported this promotion, and that the appointment would energize a lagging recruiting effort.[37]

Congress conferred the promotion, and noted that Colonel Williams was in command of the Sixth Maryland Regiment as of July 15th, 1777,[38] even though he was still a prisoner-of-war in New York at that time. After he was released from captivity, Williams wrote from Frederick, Maryland, to Maryland Governor Thomas Johnson to thank the Assembly of the State of

Maryland for his appointment, and to request support for his men so that he could prepare them for duty. He lamented the condition of his troops and the number of men present, noting that he had learned that "..there is not above an hundred effective men with Lieutenant-Colonel Ford, and that those are very indifferently clothed." He avowed that "I heartily desire to join the army as soon as possible, but certainly it had better be reinforced by a regiment without a colonel, than by a colonel without a regiment."[39]

Williams had returned to Maryland when he was released from captivity so that he could devote his efforts to recruiting and organizing his new command. The Continental Congress granted him eight thousand dollars to support his recruiting activities.[40]

While Colonel Williams was recuperating and recruiting new troops, the main American army under George Washington was suffering mightily at Valley Forge.

It was a dark hour for the American army as they huddled in this camp in the Pennsylvania countryside. Washington described their situation in gripping terms:

> *To see Men without Cloathes to cover their nakedness, without Blankets to lay on, without Shoes, by which their Marches might be traced by the Blood from their feet, and almost as often without Provisions as with; Marching through frost and Snow, and at Christmas taking up their Winter Quarters within a day's March of the enemy, without a House or Hutt to cover them till they could be built* [41]

Slowly, even in this grueling winter, there were glimmers of hope. On February 6th, 1778, the American envoys in Paris signed a treaty of alliance with France, and the American Revolution would now be officially supported by one of the world's greatest powers. Furthermore, on the frozen fields around Valley Forge, a veteran Prussian warrior, Baron Frederich von Steuben, was beginning to teach new methods of drill, to emphasize precision movements, and to demand unflinching discipline. The practical American troops began to accept and adopt these new procedures, and they began to believe that they would be able to stand toe-to-toe in open combat with the best soldiers the British and Hessians had to offer. By mid-June, 1778, when Williams had joined his regiment in Pennsylvania, there was a new spirit of discipline and confidence in the American army, buoyed by the hard work of the officers and men to master Von Steuben's new procedures.

During this time, George Washington was trying to determine the next move of the British troops that had wintered in Philadelphia. The British high command was disappointed that the occupation of the capital city had not forced the Americans to capitulate, and they were beginning to look for other ways to employ their Army, especially now that France would officially be coming in on the American side. Sir Henry Clinton replaced Sir William Howe as the British Commander-in-Chief in America, and Howe returned to England. Clinton was ordered to evacuate Philadelphia, and he sent the army's baggage, Tory refugees, and Hessian troops to New York by sea, but he had to march his British troops overland through New Jersey because there was not enough room for them on the ships.[42]

Clinton's ten thousand troops crossed the Delaware River at Cooper's Ferry, north of Philadelphia, on June 18th,[43] and once Washington was sure that Clinton intended to march eastward to New York, he led his army across the Delaware River into New Jersey in pursuit. He sent units forward to try to slow the British advance, while the main American army, including Colonel Otho Williams and his Sixth Maryland Regiment, trudged along, several miles behind the forward units. Washington had eventually sent a large enough force forward to warrant assigning the command of those troops to Major General Charles Lee, second in rank only to Washington himself in the American army.

It was brutally hot in New Jersey in these last days of June, 1778, and it was a difficult march for the Americans. Still, they forged ahead and strove to force the British to turn and fight.

On the morning of June 28th, 1778, Lee attacked the British rear guard just north of Monmouth Court House, but the movement was uncoordinated and ineffective. Lee fell back, only to encounter a furious George Washington who stopped Lee's retreat and organized a force to confront the pursuing British. Marylander Lieutenant-Colonel Nathan Ramsey, a friend of Otho Williams, performed heroically during the delaying action, before being seriously wounded and taken prisoner.[44] Many soldiers fainted from the heat and lack of water in the blistering weather. Williams, whose command was held in reserve and not directly involved in the battle, later wrote he had sipped vinegar and water during the battle to overcome the effects of the heat.[45]

Both sides claimed victory in the Battle of Monmouth. The American army felt that it had proved that it could now perform effectively in a stand-up fight with British regulars, and Clinton felt that the British had achieved their objectives, since their army was able to march safely back to New York without further attacks. Otho Williams noted that British deserters and prisoners had made it clear that Sir Henry Clinton was happy to "git snugly off."[46]

A few days later, the American Army celebrated the second anniversary of the Declaration of Independence. They had a sense of achievement in the new-found precision of their units' performance at the Battle of Monmouth. Otho Williams described this celebration for his brother back in Maryland:

> *At 3 o'clock in the afternoon, a cannon was discharged as a signal for the troops to get under arms, half an hour afterwards, the second fire was a signal for the troops to begin their march, and at four the third signal was given, for the troops to be drawn up in two lines, on the west side of the Raritan, which they did in beautiful order. A flag was then hoisted for the feu de joie to begin. Thirteen pieces of artillery were then discharged, and a running fire of small arms went through the lines, beginning at the right of the front line, catching the left, and ending at the right of the second line. The field pieces in intervals of brigades, were discharged in the running fire, thus affording a harmonious and uniform display of music and fire, which was thrice well executed.*[47]

On the next two evenings, General officers, brigade commanders, and many of the field officers dined with the Commander-in-Chief, giving Williams the opportunity to observe up close "..the old warrior in very fine spirits."[48]

The Northern Army on the Defensive around New York

The British army was now essentially bottled up in New York City, and after the Battle of Monmouth, life settled into a predictable military routine for officers like Otho Williams. He had earned a reputation for his role in the fight for Fort Washington, and had exhibited strong leadership and administrative skills. A dedicated soldier, Williams continued to study military science and to prepare for additional responsibilities. He would be given many opportunities to demonstrate his leadership and administrative skills at the highest levels of the army in the coming months.

Though no one knew it then, Monmouth Courthouse was the last major battle of the war in the northern theater.

The Court Martial of Major General Charles Lee

As the American army marched north to encircle New York City after the Battle of Monmouth, Otho Williams and a few other senior officers would remain behind in New Jersey for an assignment that had captured the attention of the country– the court martial of Major General Charles Lee for dereliction of duty at the Battle of Monmouth Courthouse.

Immediately after the battle, the whole American army seemed to realize that things had not gone quite right in the early hours of that brutally hot day. The day after the battle, Otho Williams wrote to a friend that "some neglect render'd the victory incomplete," and that he had heard that "courts of inquiry will be among the consequences." George Washington was sure that Major General Charles Lee was the source of the problem, which he described in a report to Congress a few days after the battle.[50]

On July 6th, Otho Williams wrote to his brother that he would be staying at the Camp at New Brunswick, New Jersey while most of the army marched north because he had been appointed a Member of the Court,[51] which would be sitting initially at Brunswick. The trial had opened on July 4th, 1778. The three formal charges against Lee were: (1) Disobedience of orders, in not attacking the enemy on the 28th of June (2) Misbehavior before the enemy on the same day, by making an unnecessary, disorderly, and shameful retreat, and (3) Disrespect to the Commander-in-Chief, in two letters dated the 1st of July and the 28th of June.[52] Lee pled "Not Guilty" to all charges.

For the next two weeks, the prosecution presented its case, including testimony from various participants in the battle, including the Marquis de Lafayette; Brigadier-Generals Scott, Wayne, and Maxwell; and Marylanders Samuel Smith, James McHenry, and Tench Tillman. Williams and his fellow Court Members were aware that the Commander-in-Chief was infuriated by Charles Lee's conduct, which Washington had expressed in a letter to Lee.[53]

Lee made no effort to endear himself to the Court, and often used caustic language in his presentations. He observed that "Mad Anthony" Wayne, who had served under him at Monmouth, felt that he and he alone knew what was needed in the battle[54] and that Baron von Steuben's testimony should be disregarded because he had been too far removed from the scene to provide any meaningful input to the court (Lee called him a "distant spectator.")[55] Of a witness named Langfrang, Lee tartly commented that " I can assure Monsieur Langfrang, that should he ever honor me with his presence on a similar occasion, I shall think myself justifiable in making use of any means to render the honor as short as possible."[56]

The Court found Lee guilty of all three charges on August 12th, 1778, and he was sentenced to "..be suspended from any command in the armies of the United States of North America, for the term of twelve months."[57] Lee rushed to York, Pennsylvania, where Congress was meeting, and did everything he could to have the verdict overturned, but Congress sustained the Court's decision by a vote of fifteen to seven.[58] Lee's career with the American Army was effectively over. He continued to rail against Washington and his loyal supporters until his death in 1782.[59]

With the completion of the five-and-a-half week trial, Otho Williams returned to his normal duties. Two days after the trial was over, he wrote to his brother Elie from White Plains, New York that he had resumed command of his regiment.[60] His service as a member of the high profile court that tried Charles Lee was further indication of his growing reputation and stature in the army.

★ ★ ★ ★ ★

Baron de Kalb is Placed in Command of the Maryland Continentals

On September 7th, 1778, Baron Johann de Kalb was given command of "Smallwood's and 2nd Maryland,"[61] bringing young Colonel Otho Williams and his fellow Marylanders into frequent contact with one of the outstanding professional soldiers who fought with the American army during the Revolution.

The fifty-seven year old baron had been born to a peasant family in Bavaria, and had spent a lifetime in military service, starting out in the lowest ranks, and rising to prominence fighting for France in the Seven Years' War. Nicholas Rogers of Baltimore, who served as one of the baron's aides, described him in a letter written years after the end of the War:

> Besides his extreme temperance, sobriety and prudence, with his great simplicity of manners which highly fitted him for his undertaking, he had also many of the other qualifications for a soldier, such as patience, long-suffering, strength of constitution, endurance of hunger and thirst, and a cheerful submission, to every inconvenience in lodging ...in size, he was a perfect Ariovistus[62*] being upwards of six feet and fully equal to the fatigues of a soldier. He would often walk twenty or thirty

---

*Ariovistus was a King of the Gauls mentioned in the writings of Julius Caesar.

> *miles a day without sigh, or complaint, and, indeed, often preferred that exercise to riding. His complexion and skin were remarkable, being as fair and fresh as those of a youth.*[63]

During his lifetime of military service, de Kalb had risen to prominence in the French Army. Otho Williams and his Maryland comrades would learn much about soldiering from this experienced leader.

Shortly after de Kalb took command of the Maryland Troops, a controversy raged when Williams and his fellow Colonels Daniel Morgan and William Davies co-signed a letter to the President of Congress that presented "...the honorable Memorial of the Field Officers and Captains now with the Army." The memorial was dated September 13th, 1778 and expressed grievances over such items as lack of half-pay and pensions, medical care, clothing, and other deficiencies. George Washington was not pleased that the officers had by-passed him, and the action of the Colonels seemed threatening enough that Gouveneur Morris made comparisons to the army dictatorship that had formed during the English Civil War.[64]

The letter from Williams, Morgan and Davies was read to the Congress on October 20th, 1778, and it was decided that it would "lie on the table until Congress have fully considered and determined on the report of the committee of arrangement."[65] There is no record that there was ever a direct response to the three Colonels, presumably because Congress incorporated their list of grievances into the many others they had received on that subject. Congress was beleaguered by meager resources, and would continue to struggle with this problem for the rest of the war.

Williams' association with Daniel Morgan in this regard is also noteworthy. Morgan had a fighting reputation second to none, and both he and Williams had been officers in the rifle companies that had been called from the mid-Atlantic states to march to Boston at the beginning of the war. They respected each other as soldiers, would remain friends during the war and thereafter, and would work together effectively on army matters.

Williams sent a report to Commander-in-Chief Washington from Paramus, New Jersey on Monday, September 28th, 1778 that he was "...exceeding sorry to be the Author of bad News...", but that he wanted to be sure that headquarters had an accurate report that the regiment of Colonel Baylor had been surprised, surrounded and captured the previous day, after they had moved from Paramus to Herring Town. About a dozen men had escaped and shown up at Paramus, and Williams stated that one party was being sent out to see if any of the wounded and horses could be recovered. Other units had been sent to scout the movements of the enemy. Williams also explained that he had left his regiment and gone to Paramus for "relieving a Friend from captivity," and had been fortunate to meet with that friend and about forty others who were waiting at Morris Town for "a favourable opportunity to pay their duty at Head Quarters." Williams also reported that Major Fell, commanding at Paramus, had requested consultation on "measures most eligible for him to adopt." Williams provided his advice and was preparing to return to his regiment, as he felt that Major Fell was "active and vigilant."[66]

This letter report to Washington shows that Williams was also an active and vigilant officer. Though technically not having direct line authority at Paramus, he quickly assessed the situation, sent an informative report directly to the Commander-in-Chief, helped to assure the safety of Paramus, and then returned, as previously planned, to his own command.

★ ★ ★ ★ ★

Williams' Position in the New Army Organization

The organization of the Army continued to be a concern of the Congress and the Commander-in-Chief for the remainder of the war. The task of determining rank and precedence among the officer corps seemed unending, and it caused the Army's senior officers to spend many, many hours of laborious investigation into these issues. On February 4th, 1779, Congress resolved:

> *That the Commander in Chief be directed to proceed in such manner as he shall judge expedient, to compleat the arrangement of the army, and to settle the relative rank of officers under the degree of brigadier agreeably to the principles established by an act of Congress on the 24th day of November, 1778…*[67]

Congress followed up this directive on March 9th with a resolution that reduced the number of battalions from 88 to 80, with regiments being eliminated from the New Jersey, Pennsylvania, Virginia, North Carolina, and Georgia quotas.[68] Maryland was still responsible for providing eight battalions.[69] When Washington, Congress, and the state of Maryland had completed their organizational reviews, Otho Holland Williams' position as Colonel of the Sixth Maryland Regiment was confirmed by a commission issued by Congress on June 2nd, 1779, with the notation that his date of rank was January 1st, 1777.[70]

Petition of the Maryland Officers

Washington and Congress spent countless hours dealing with the concerns of the officers and men in the Army, but these issues also had to be addressed by the governments of the individual states. On June 17th, 1779, William Smallwood submitted a petition to the Maryland legislature that laid out the concerns of officers in the Continental service. This petition was signed by many of the Maryland officers, including Otho Holland Williams. This document is a respectful, but direct, expression of grievances over the financial difficulties encountered by these men caused by the rampant depreciation of the Continental currency:

> *We beg leave, most respectfully, to represent to your Excellency and Honors that the several provisions hitherto made by the Legislature for the subsistence of her officers, though liberal at the time of being voted, have by no means been adequate to the exigent expenses of their respective stations... The very great depreciation of the Continental Currency renders it absolutely necessary that some further provision should be made for our support to enable to continue a service in which nothing but a love of Liberty and the rights of mankind can retain us; and we trust that it will be such as will support with decency and dignity the respective ranks which our country has done the honor to confer on us.*[71]

The Maryland legislature re-assembled on July 22nd, and passed an "Act relating to the officers and soldiers of this State in the American army" which attempted to address these grievances. Officers were to receive, every year "four good shirts and a complete uniform" and rations of tea, coffee, chocolate, sugar, rum, soap and tobacco at fixed prices, meted out by the day and month. Officers were awarded $2,000 each for the year 1779 in lieu of the above allowances, and similar provisions were made for non-commissioned officers and privates.[72]

Service as a Sub-Inspector under Baron von Steuben

Baron Von Steuben had dramatically increased the military effectiveness of the American army by developing standard processes for drill, tactics, and discipline and he wrote them in language that the troops could readily master. George Washington supported the Baron with an organization that would help to spread the Baron's training doctrine throughout the army. Moreover, he specified that exceptional officers should be chosen for these vital tasks, noting that "...the Officers of the inspectorship are among the best in the line,"[73] and that "...the Office of Sub-inspector cannot be filled with propriety but by men whose character and abilities will give them influence and ensure their success."[74] To attract these outstanding officers, Washington arranged to have them retain their rank and position in the line regiments.[75]

Otho Holland Williams was named one of the four Sub-Inspectors under Von Steuben in the General Orders of June 24th, 1779.[76] Williams embraced this honor and dove enthusiastically into the work, which Washington defined as "...introducing a regular System of Discipline and Manoeuvres into the Army.[77]

In his description of Otho Holland Williams many years later, Light Horse Harry Lee wrote in his Memoirs that "As a soldier, he may be called a rigid, not cruel, disciplinarian, obeying strictly his superior, he exacted obedience from his inferior."[78] Williams probably had acquired strong instincts for discipline in his upbringing in the Frederick County and Baltimore Clerk's offices, and in his early military service, where he closely observed leaders like Daniel Morgan, Michael Cresap, and Moses Rawlings. He had now served under the experienced leadership of Baron de Kalb for many months, and he undoubtedly learned even more under the guiding hand of Baron von Steuben about precision, discipline, and crisp execution of military maneuvers.

Washington reinforced his strong support for the Sub-Inspector system by recommending to Congress that officers chosen to serve in these roles should receive additional pay as inspectors of thirty dollars a month.[79] He announced in his General Orders of August 17th, 1778 that those amounts of additional pay had been approved.[80] He also requested additional compensation in the form of rations and forage for three horses,[81] which Congress also approved.[82]

Von Steuben's system dramatically improved the military effectiveness of the Continental Army, and Colonel Otho Williams was one of the handpicked officers that introduced these methods. From this point in the war, the Continental troops, including those from Maryland, were as good as any soldiers in the world in their ability to maneuver, fire coordinated volleys on the battlefield, and wield the bayonet with deadly effectiveness. Von Steuben appropriately receives the credit for devising his new system, and Commander-in-Chief Washington provided the support required to make it a success. Those who served under Von Steuben as Sub-Inspectors and Brigade Inspectors led the training and enforced the discipline that made this system work. Williams' service as a Sub-Inspector gave him the reputation as a high ranking officer who could develop discipline and performance in a large body of troops.

This work also brought Williams into frequent contact with officers such as the Baron von Steuben, Nathanael Greene and the Commander-in-Chief himself.

★ ★ ★ ★ ★

Williams' Service as acting Adjutant General

By the end of 1779, the thirty-year-old Colonel Otho Williams had served in the American army in positions of increasing responsibility for four-and-a-half years. He had helped train troops from the very earliest days of the war, and he had led men on the march and in camp, shown his mettle in combat, and spent over a year as a prisoner-of-war. He had also learned to be a very capable administrator.

Otho Williams' performance was rewarded with his appointment on Christmas Day, 1779, as acting Adjutant General of the Army, a position that was essentially the army's Chief Administrative Officer. In this visible and critical post, he would serve in the highest leadership of the army, reporting directly to George Washington. Washington had written that the post of Adjutant General was a position "of the highest trust and importance," and that it must be filled by a "Gentlemen of the first military character."[83] Williams' appointment to this important post was announced in the General Orders for December 25th, 1779, with the explanation that he would serve during the leave of absence of Colonel Alexander Scammel.[84] Since Congress had resolved that an Adjutant General appointed from the line could continue to hold his line position and rank,[85] Colonel Williams retained his position as commander of the Sixth Maryland Regiment while he served temporarily as Adjutant General.

★ ★ ★ ★ ★

The Brutal Winter of 1779-1780

When Williams assumed the duties of Adjutant General on Christmas Day, 1779, the American Army was encamped in winter quarters at Morristown, New Jersey during harsh and frigid weather. Transporting supplies was extremely difficult in the deep snow, frozen roads, and arctic temperatures, and obtaining enough food to keep the army alive was a constant concern during these bitter winter days. In late December and early January, the urgent work of finding food for the army took so much of the Commander-in-Chief's time that he even had to delay responding to correspondents as important as the Board of War, to whom he once wrote that he would have answered them sooner "... had not my whole time and attention been of late engrossed by endeavouring to raise a supply of provision for the Army."[86]

Slowly, the great exertions of Washington and his staff began to produce results. By the end of January, he could write to Congress that "I have now the pleasure to inform Congress, that the situation of the Army for the present, is, and it has been for some days past, comfortable and easy on the score of provision."[87]

★ ★ ★ ★ ★

The acting Adjutant General's Duties

Not only did Colonel Otho Williams enter the office of Adjutant General at a difficult time for the Army, he had to tackle his enormous workload with little support, since two of Colonel Scammel's experienced aides had also taken leave while the Colonel was away. Williams began the work with his characteristic energy and sense of commitment. It is not difficult to envision how his driving work habits and formal sense of military protocol could have created a tense environment in the understaffed office of the Adjutant General. He was consumed by the responsibilities of the office, and had little time for personal activities, even ones as simple as writing letters home to family and friends in his beloved Western Maryland.[88]

The duties of the Adjutant General are described in the "New and Enlarged Military Dictionary" published at the Military Library, near Whitehall, in London, England in 1802:

> *Adjutant General is an officer of distinction, who aids and assists the general in his laborious duty: he forms the several details of duty of the army, with the brigade-majors, and keeps an exact state of each brigade and regiment, with a roll of lieutenant-generals, major-generals, colonels, lieutenant-colonels, and majors. He every day at head quarters receives orders from the general officer of the day, and distributes them to the majors of brigades, from whom he receives the number of men they are to furnish for the duty of the army, and infoms them of any detail which may concern them. On marching days he accompanies the general to the ground of the camp. He makes a daily report of the situation of all the posts placed for the safety of the army,*

and of any changes made in their posts. In a day of battle the adjutant-general sees the infantry drawn up, after which he places himself by the general to receive orders. In a siege he visits the several posts and guards of the trenches, and reports their situation, and how circumstanced: he gives and signs all orders for skirmishing parties (if time permit) and has a serjeant from each brigade to carry any orders which he may have to send.[89]

Williams' heavy workload eventually required that the process for issuing the General Orders be changed so that he did not have to go in person to the Orderly Office every day, with Williams explaining that "...a multiplicity of business in the Adjutant General's office renders it extremely difficult for him to attend at the Orderly Office every day...".[90] To solve this difficulty, he instituted the requirement that the Brigade Majors would report to the Orderly Office each day to obtain and distribute the General Orders. This change placed additional daily responsibility on the Brigade Majors, and these young men bristled at the extra work. They applied to the Commander-in-Chief for relief from the added responsibility.[91] Washington's aide Richard Meade sympathized with Williams' struggles, noting that he was burdened: "...from the immensity of business on his hands, and having only one assistant....".[92] Recognizing the strain of his other duties, the Commander-in-Chief supported Williams, and the General Orders continued to be managed as Williams had instructed. When Colonel Scammel returned with his experienced aides to the post of Adjutant General on April 11th, 1780, the process reverted to the original method since the expedient that Williams had instituted was no longer necessary.[93]

Although the press of business severely limited Williams' time for personal matters, he found time to attend the meeting of the Ancient Free and Accepted Masons serving in the Maryland and Delaware regiments which was held in Morristown on February 7th, 1780. Mordecai Gist represented Maryland and Otho Williams represented Delaware.[94] At the meeting, a resolution was drafted to establish one grand lodge in America, and to have the Grand Masters of the various state lodges nominate a Grand Master for America and send his name to the governing lodge in Europe. This resolution was signed by Mordecai Gist as President of the meeting, and Otho Holland Williams as Secretary.[95]

This was only a brief respite from the press of the heavy duties, which included administration of discipline (including courts martial;) army organization and readiness; prisoner exchange; and military operations.

Even though Williams served as acting Adjutant General for only a few months, his daily tasks involved him in each of these areas during his tenure.

Administration of Discipline

George Washington had learned the value of discipline in his early service in the French and Indian War and on the frontier, and he had a willing subordinate in Colonel Otho Williams. Their stern approach toward officers who did not toe the line is reflected in the General Orders of February 16th, 1780. General Orders were, of course, issued in the name of the Commander-in-Chief, but were prepared by the Adjutant General, who supported stern measures:

> *Frequent delays and neglects have lately happened, to the hindrance of public and essential business, particularly by members of the General Court Martial; The Adjutant General has therefore positive orders to bring the first officer to strict account who shall presume to shew contempt to the court or disrespect to general orders.*[96]

If the officers of the Army were inattentive to some of their duties during this difficult winter, the men in the ranks were even more of a challenge. The tenuous situation of the Army made the troops restless during these hungry months, and many of the officers were home on winter leave, so there was limited supervision and leadership in many units. This resulted in very bad behavior among some of the troops, which was a frequent subject in the General Orders during this period, such as the complaint on December 29th, 1779 that:

> *...the property of the Inhabitants in the vicinity of camp is a prey to the plundering spirit of the soldiery ...To prevent a continuance of these evils the regulations for preserving order in camp and respecting roll calls are to be most rigidly attended to; In addition to these the officers commanding regiments will appoint commissioned officers to visit the men in their huts at different hours of the night, to report all absentees, who are without fail to be brought to immediate trial and punished as they deserve.*[97]

Robbing the local citizenry was not the only type of disciplinary violation committed by the soldiers during these troubled times. Courts martial sat regularly for various violations, including desertion. The General Orders of January 3rd 1780 approved a death sentence for one soldier who had deserted with his arms and accouterments and 100 lashes for another deserter.[98] Another death sentence for desertion was approved on April 2nd.[99]

The American soldiers were apparently incorrigible. Washington was extremely disappointed when he had to return to the subject of their bad behavior a month later in his General Orders of Friday, January 28th, 1780:

> *The General is astonished and mortified to find that notwithstanding the order issued on the 29th. of last month and his exhortation to the officers to prevent it, that the Inhabitants in the vicinity of camp are absolutely a prey to the plundering and licentious spirit of the soldiery. From their daily complaints, and a formal representation of the Magistrates on the subject, a night scarcely passes without gangs of soldiers going out of camp and committing every species of robbery, depredation and the grossest personal Insults. This conduct is intolerable and a disgrace to the army...*[100]

This stern order also directed officers to issue punishment on the spot, authorizing officers of the guard to administer from 100 lashes for straggling and 100 to 500 lashes for robbery or other violent acts.[101]

★ ★ ★ ★ ★

The Court Martial of Benedict Arnold

General Washington and his acting Adjutant General Williams were involved in another aspect of discipline during this period, as Washington forwarded the results of the court martial of Brigadier General Benedict Arnold to Congress for their approval on January 30th, 1780.[102] Arnold was the type of fighting man that Washington instinctively respected, and his combat record up to this point was superb. Badly wounded in the Battle of Saratoga in October, 1777, Arnold had been given command of the troops in Philadelphia, where his expensive tastes and combative personality had earned him powerful enemies. He was charged with various offenses, and acquitted of two, but he was found guilty of giving permission for a ship that was coming from an enemy port to land in Philadelphia; and of the appearance of a conflict of interest by requesting that wagons owned by the public be used to move his personal possessions.

The Court sentenced Arnold to be reprimanded in the Army's General Orders, and Washington complied with an entry on Thursday, April 6th, 1780. The Commander-in-Chief did all he could to soften the blow by recounting his sincere regard for Arnold's prior "distinguished services," but Washington's inherent sense of justice was aroused, and he criticized Arnold with uncompromising language that left no doubt of his disappointment, calling his issuance of an inappropriate permit "peculiarly reprehensible."[103] Arnold's public humiliation was a factor in his future treason.

★ ★ ★ ★ ★

The Combat Readiness of the Army

The combat readiness of the army was an unending concern of the Commander-in-Chief and his acting Adjutant General. Washington's report to his Major Generals and Officers Commanding Brigades of January 22nd, 1780 gave full vent to his concerns about the state of the Army:

> *I am extremely concerned to find by the late reports of the Inspector General, that most of the corps in the Army are in worse order than I had flattered myself. That in general it does not make that progress in order and discipline which might reasonably be expected: that some corps have ever gone backward: and that almost every one has defects and abuses which have existed a considerable time, and ought no longer to be tolerated.*[104]

In his strong, direct enumeration of the Army's organizational deficiencies, the Commander-in-Chief provided necessary information and directed the Army's senior leaders to bring soldiers listed as "sick absent" back to the colors; delete from the rolls names of men who would probably not return to the army; and take "effectual measures to collect those who are improperly absent and who are still recoverable. This is a matter in which I would wish the most rigid exactness to be observed." He also pointed out the inadequate numbers of noncommissioned officers, instances of officers serving in positions not justified by their rank, and many instances where too many officers were absent on furlough.[105] The American Army had much work to do if it was going to be ready for the rigors of campaigning in the Spring and Summer of 1780.

Washington, supported by Otho Williams, felt that one issue that hurt Army morale badly was the disparity in pay between officers from the various states.

George Washington's remarkable leadership was again evident when devising a winning strategy for the Southern campaign. His insightful choice of officers for the mission and his unwavering support for their efforts led to an improbable victory in a little more than a year.

Courtesy of Independence National Historical Park.

Nathanael Greene was Washington's choice to succeed Gates in the South. His adroit application of Washington's instructions led to the ultimate defeat of General Cornwallis at Yorktown. Otho Holland Williams was his Adjutant General and led the Maryland regiments into battle under him.

Courtesy of the National Park Service.

General Horatio Gates, victor at Saratoga and appointed by Congress, lost the Battle of Camden and rode all the way to Charlotte, leaving his troops behind.

Courtesy of National Park Service.

Major General Baron de Kalb was a brave and experienced French officer who volunteered to fight with the Marquis de Lafayette in America in 1777. He led the first troops of the Maryland and Delaware Continental Line south to confront the British at Camden in South Carolina. He was killed in the battle.

Courtesy of the National Park Service.

Colonel Otho Holland Williams led the screening force in the "Race to the Dan" and commanded the Maryland regiments at Guilford Courthouse, Hobkirk's Hill and Eutaw Springs. He was one of Greene's finest field officers.

Courtesy of the National Park Service.

Lt. Colonel "Light Horse" Henry Lee, a resourceful cavalry commander, successfully abetted General Greene's efforts either by fighting as part of his force or by cooperating with partisan leaders, such as Francis Marion, to harass loyalist or regular British units.

Courtesy of the National Park Service.

Lt. Colonel John Eager Howard was an able infantry commander, who let his Maryland regiment at Camden, Cowpens, Guilford Courthouse, Hobkirk's Hill, and Eutaw Springs.

Courtesy of National Park Service.

Lt. Colonel William Washington was a tireless cavalry leader who fought throughout the Southern Campaign. He made a pivotal attack on Tarleton's right flank at Cowpens. In the end he was wounded and captured at Eutaw Springs in September, 1781. He was George Washington's cousin.

Courtesy of the National Park Service.

This is a depiction of the Battle of Guilford Courthouse.

Courtesy of the U.S. Army Center for Military History. Painting by H. Charles McBarron.

Otho Holland Williams attends George Washington's resignation to Congress in Annapolis, December 1783. He is visible between Abiel Foster of New Hampshire and William Emory of Rhode Island who are seated facing George Washington.

Courtesy of United States Capitol, Washington, DC. Painting by Edwin White.

Some of the states offered generous payments to their officers, while others neglected to do so, with the result that officers of the same rank and who were performing essentially the same duties could be receiving markedly different pay. Washington noted that "Nothing can be conceived more chagrining, than for an Officer to see himself destitute of every necessary, while another, not only in the service of the same Government, engaged in defending the same cause, but even in the same regiment and sometimes standing by his side, in the same Company, is decently, if not amply, provided." The Commander-in-Chief wrote Congress in April, 1780 to address this troubling disparity, and to implore Congress to implement a policy that was consistent across the Army.[106] This issue had smoldered for some time, and had been raised by the Maryland officers in a petition to their State Legislature the year before, a petition in which Otho Williams had participated along with many of his fellow Marylanders.[107]

While Congress and the states made many attempts to address this issue during the War, it remained a source of concern.

★ ★ ★ ★ ★

Exchange of Prisoners

Lieutenant Colonel Nathaniel Ramsey was a fellow Maryland officer and friend of Otho Williams who had been captured after performing heroically at the Battle of Monmouth Court House in June, 1778. He wrote to Williams from his captivity in New York City on August 20th, 1779, saying that he was taking advantage of a good opportunity to get a letter to his friends, and asking Williams to relay all pertinent information to his many acquaintances. Ramsay alluded to the Apostle Paul writing a letter from prison, and stated that life in captivity was not all that bad, in that he was healthy and wanted for nothing. Mrs. Ramsay was with him, but was very unhappy that they were not receiving letters from friends.[108]

Four-and-a-half months later, while Williams was still acting Adjutant General, George Washington informed Congress that Ramsay had been permitted to come out of New York on parole with Colonels Matthews, Eli and Magaw. Colonel Magaw had been in command at Fort Washington on November 16th, 1776, when Williams himself had been taken prisoner. These officers carried with them new proposals regarding the exchange of prisoners, but Washington sent them to Congress, as he did not feel authorized to implement the new procedures.[109]

Two weeks later, the officers returned to Morristown with Congress's approval to proceed, and Washington instructed the men to "…communicate to (British) Major General Phillips, I shall be ready to appoint Commissioners to meet Others from the British Commander in Chief at any time and place which may be thought convenient for the final adjustment of the affairs."[110] Unfortunately, there were many delays in negotiating this exchange of prisoners, and Ramsay was still carrying correspondence back and forth between New York and the American Army camp at Morristown on May 4th, 1780.[111] The Commander-in-Chief was still discussing Ramsay's exchange with the Board of War on June 25th.[112] Ramsay was finally exchanged in October 1780,[113] after Williams was no longer acting Adjutant General under Washington.

★ ★ ★ ★ ★

Military Operations

Even in the brutally cold winter of 1779-1780, George Washington never stopped looking for opportunities to strike the British in New York City. He thought he saw an opportunity when the water passage between New Jersey and Staten Island froze solid, providing a possible path for his troops to cross and hit the British camp on Staten Island. Lord Stirling was ordered to lead the attack with a force of 2,500 men, which stepped off on January 15th, 1781. Stirling learned that communications were open between Staten Island and New York, making reinforcements to his British foes possible. Considering the chances of success unfavorable, Stirling ended the mission, and led the attacking force back to the American camps.[114] This is but a minor incident in the history of the war, but it illustrates Washington's aggressiveness, and his incessant attempts to hit the enemy whenever he could. It is also clear indication that Otho Williams was involved in military planning and operations, not only in administrative tasks.

This winter also saw frequent small raids back and forth between the British and Americans, and one such incursion was serious enough for Washington to report to Congress on January 27th that, "I am sorry to inform your Excellency that the Enemy on the night of the 25th surprised our advanced parties which were stationed at Elizabeth Town and New Ark, and made a part of them prisoners…. several people were plundered at New Ark and the Academy burnt; also the Meeting and Town Houses at Elizabeth Town and the House at De Hart's point."[115]

On April 11th, 1780, Colonel Scammel returned from leave and resumed the duties of Adjutant General. Williams had served in that post capably for three-and-a-half months, earning praise for his work in George Washington's General Orders of April 11th:

> *The Commander in Chief requests Colonel Williams to accept his Thanks for the attention assiduity and propriety with which he has conducted the office in the absence of Colonel Scammell.*[116]

By the time that Colonel Scammel returned to duty as Adjutant General, the American high command had begun to formulate strategies to respond to the British decision to move the focus of their activities to the southern states. As Otho Williams returned to his command of the Sixth Maryland Regiment, events were in motion that would transfer the Maryland Line to the south in an effort to reinforce besieged Charleston, South Carolina.

The Decision to Reinforce the South

In early April, 1781, just a few days before Otho Williams was relieved of his duties as acting Adjutant General, General Washington told Congress that in spite of the weakness of his army compared to the British around New York, he had decided to reinforce the South with the Maryland and Delaware Continental regiments, although he wished to have Congress's instructions on this decision.[117] He decided that Major General the Baron de Kalb should have overall command of the force,[118] and he sent de Kalb to Philadelphia to work with the Board of War, Quarter Master, and Commissary General to arrange for transportation and other support.[119] On April 2nd, Washington ordered Brigadier General Mordecai Gist to "..place the Maryland division under your command in the most perfect state of readiness to move at the shortest notice,"[120] and then eight days later he ordered Gist to lead his Maryland Division "to the Southward." Washington urged that the movement be made "as speedily as possible," and reiterated that he wanted "no unavoidable delay."[121] Though Washington was pushing for all possible speed in the movement, he realized that it would be very difficult for these troops to arrive in the South in time to help Charleston. He confided to Baron von Steuben that:

> *Though this detachment cannot in all probability arrive in season to be of any service to Charles Town, it may assist to check the progress of the enemy and save the Carolinas.*[122]

As Otho Williams prepared to lead his troops south, he had achieved much in his military career, but an ominous tone slipped quietly into his life-story when he wrote to his friend Doctor Philip Thomas on September 21st, 1779, that he was sick with fever and rheumatism.[123] This is the first known reference to illness in the young Colonel's correspondence, and it was a quiet harbinger that his once-robust constitution was beginning to suffer from the effects of his harsh captivity and arduous military service.

---

1   Fischer, *Crossing*. P. 113.
2   Gillett, Jonathan. Letter to Eliza Gillett at West Harford. Written at New York. December 2, 1776. Commager and Morris. P. 850.
3   Washington, George. Letter to the Continental Congress. Written at Hackensack. November 19, 1776. *Washington Papers*.
4   Keith, Robert. Statement written on December 19, 1779. Commager and Morris. P. 853.
5   The most complete source of information on Williams' captivity in New York is *A Sketch of the Life and Services of Gen. Otho Holland Williams*, a paper read before the Maryland Historical Society on March 6, 1851 by Osmand Tiffany. The description here is based largely on Tiffany's information.
6   Onderdonk, Henry, Jr. *Revolutionary Incidents Of Suffolk And Kings Counties; With An Account Of The Battle Of Long Island, And The British Prisons And Prison-Ships At New-York* (hereafter Onderdonk, *Incidents*.) Leavitt & Company, 191 Broadway, New York. 1849. P. 173.
7   See Footnote.
8   Boudinot, Elias. Draft Report to General Washington on Conditions in New York. March 2, 1778. Commager and Morris. P. 863.
9   Graydon, *Memoirs*. P. 281.
10 Washington, George. Letter to Joshua Loring. January 14, 1777. *Washington Papers*.
11 Washington, George. Letter to Joshua Loring. February 6, 1777. *Washington Papers*.
12 Osmand Tiffany published a paper on the Life of Otho Holland Williams with the Maryland Historical Society in 1851. According to Tiffany's account, Major Ackland maintained his respect for the Americans for the remainder of his life, and after he had returned to England at the conclusion of the War, he "demanded satisfaction" of a fellow officer who had spoken ill of the Americans. Tiffany recounts that Ackland was killed in the duel. Some credible historians believe that this story may be apocryphal.
13 Dandridge, Danske. *American Prisoners of the Revolution* (hereafter Dandridge, *Prisoners*.). The Michie Company, Printers. Charlottesville, Virginia. 1911. P. 116.
14 Williams was placed in a cell with John Fell, a member of the Council for New Jersey, on September 6, 1777. Ref: *Memorandum in the Provost Jail, N.Y. from April 23, 1777 to January 7, 1778 by John Fell, one of the Council for N. Jersey*. In Onderdonk, *Incidents*. P. 221.
15 Williams, Elie. Letter to the American Board of War. December 29, 1777. *Williams Papers* Part 1/8. (item # 13.)
16 Tiffany, *Sketch*. P. 8.
17 Ibid. Pp. 8-9.
18 See Footnote.
19 Allen, Ethan. *A Narrative of Col. Ethan Allen's Captivity, Written by Himself and Now Published for the Information of the Curious in All Nations*. Published by Thomas & Thomas, from the Press of Charter and Hale. Walpole, New Hampshire. 1807. pp. 131-132.
20 Onderdonk, *Incidents*. P. 226.
21 *Ibid*. P. 222.
22 Williams, Otho. Letter to Dr. Charles McNight dated March 13, 1784. *Williams Papers*. Part 2/8. (Item #242.)
23 Dandridge *Prisoners*. P. 105.
24 Williams, Elie. Letter to the Board of War. Written December 29, 1777. *Williams Papers*. Part 1/8. (item # 13.) The full text of this letter is also in *The Old Martyr's Prison*. By Edward Hagaman Hall (hereafter Hall, *Prison*.). Presented to The Board of Aldermen of the City of New York by The American Scenic and Historic Preservation Society Reprinted from "The City Record" of October 23, 1902. New York *The Old Martyr's Prison*. By Edward Hagaman Hall, P 12.
25 Hall, *Prison*. P. 12.
26 Dandridge, *Prisoners*. P. 18.
27 Onderdonk, *Incidents*. P. 224.

28 Return of Maryland Officers exchanged from the 24th March, 1777. Rolls Of Escaped And Exchanged Prisoners. Records of Maryland Troops in the Continental Service. Military Records. Archives of Maryland Online. Volume 18, page 616.
29 Tiffany, *Sketch*, P. 9.
30 Ibid. P. 9.
31 Lee, *Memoirs*. Pp. 592-3.
32 Gordon, History. (Volume 3.) Pp. 66-67.
33 Peter C. Scheidt, MD, MPH, Professor, George Washington University School of Medicine, has reviewed the available information on Otho Williams' disease. Dr. Scheidt treated a number of tuberculosis cases in his training and his work with the Indian Health Service, US Public Health Service. While Otho Williams lived over two hundred years ago and there is no precise culture or bacteriological identification available, Dr. Scheidt has suggested that from the available information "The symptoms and course are classic for pre-antibiotic tuberculosis"
34 Graydon, *Memoirs*. P. 331.
35 Steuart, *Maryland Line*. P. 21.
36 Hanson, John. Letter to the Board of War. Written at Frederick Town, January 16, 1777. Williams Papers. Part 1/8. (item # 11.) The full text of this letter is included in Scharf, J. Thomas. *History of Maryland from the Earliest Period to the Present Day*. Volume II (1766-1812.) (hereafter Scharf, *Maryland*.) Published by John B. Piet. Baltimore. 1879. Pp. 332-333.
37 Ibid.
38 *Journals of the Continental Congress*, 1774-1789. Tuesday, July 15, 1777. Volume 8, Page 552.
39 Williams, Otho Holland. Letter to Governor Thomas Johnson. Written at Frederick Town on March 16, 1778. *Williams Papers*. Part 1/8. (item # 14.) Excerpts from this letter are quoted in Scharf, *Maryland*. P. 333.
40 Letter from J. Henry to Maryland Governor Johnson. Written at York (Pennsylvania) on April 24, 1778. Archives of Maryland Online. Volume 21, Page 58. *Journal and Correspondence of the Council of Maryland, April 1, 1778 through October 26, 1779*.
41 Washington, George. Letter to John Banister. Written at Valley Forge. April 21, 1778. *Washington Papers*.
42 Symonds, *Battlefield Atlas* P. 61-62.
43 Ibid. P. 65.
44 Williams, Otho. Letter to Dr. Philip Thomas. Written at Camp Monmouth Meeting House, June 29, 1778. *Williams Papers*. Part 1/8. (Item # 15.)
45 Ibid.
46 Ibid.
47 Williams, Otho. Letter to Elie Williams. Written at Camp New Brunswick, July 6, 1778. *Williams Papers*. Part 1/8. (Item #16.)
48 Ibid.
49 Letter to Dr. Philip Thomas. Written at Camp Monmouth Meeting House, June 29, 1778. *Williams Papers*. Part 1/8. (item # 15.)
50 Washington, George. Letter to the Continental Congress. Written at English Town, July 1, 1778. *Washington Papers*.
51 Williams, Otho. Letter to Elie Williams. Written at Camp New Brunswick, July 6, 1778. *Williams Papers*. Part 1/8. (Item #16.)
52 *Proceedings of a General Court Martial, held at Brunswick, in the State of New Jersey By the Order of His Excellency Gen. Washington Commander-in-Chief of the Army of the United States of America, for the Trial of Major-General Lee* (hereafter Charles Lee Court Martial Proceedings). July 4th, 1778. New York. 1864. P. 4.
53 Ibid. P. 115.
54 Ibid. P. 224.
55 Ibid. P. 232.
56 Ibid. P. 232.
57 Ibid. Pp. 238-239.
58 Leckie, Robert. *George Washington's War. The Saga of the American Revolution*. HarperCollins Publishers. New York. 1992. Harper Perenial edition published 1993. New York. Pp. 487.
59 Ibid. P. 489.
60 Williams, Otho. Letter to Elie Williams. Written at Camp White Plains, New York on August 14, 1778. *Williams Papers*. Part 1/8. (item # 19.)
61 Washington, George. General Orders. Written at Head Quarters, White Plains, September 7, 1778. *Washington Papers*.
62 See Footnote.
63 Rogers, Nicholas. Letter to General Henry Lee. Written at New York, 24th January, 1816. Cited in Kapp, Friedrich, "*The Life of John Kalb, Major-General in the Revolutionary Army*," (hererafter Kapp, *Kalb*). Henry Holt and Company. New

York, 1884. Pp 316-317; Kapp added the following note on P. 315 to explain the reason for Rogers' letter to Lee: "When writing his memoirs on the revolution in the South, Henry Lee applied to Rogers for information about Kalb. The above letter was the reply."

64 Williams, Otho Holland; Morgan, Daniel; and Davies, William. Letter to Henry Laurens, Esq., President of Congress. September 22, 1778. This "Memorial" is in the papers of the Continental Congress, No. 41, 7, fols. 191-204. See Notes 49 and 50 to George Washington letter to Gouvernour Morris. Written at Fish-Kill. October 4, 1778. *Washington Papers.*

65 Journals of the Continental Congress, 1774-1789. Volume 12. Pages 1025-26. Tuesday, October 20, 1778.

66 To George Washington from Colonel Otho Holland Williams, 28 September 1778," Founders Online, National Archives (http://founders.archives.gov/documents/Washington/03-17-02-0173, ver. 2014-05-09). Source: The Papers of George Washington, Revolutionary War Series, vol. 17, 15 September–31 October 1778, ed. Philander D. Chase. Charlottesville: University of Virginia Press, 2008, pp. 173–174.

67 Journals of the Continental Congress, 1774-1789. Volume 13. Page 143. Thursday, February 4, 1779.

68 Wright, *Continental Army.* P. 146.

69 Journals of the Continental Congress, 1774-1789.Volume 13. Page 298. Tuesday, March 9, 1779.

70 Resolution of "The United States of America In Congress Assembled, Philadelphia." June 2, 1779. To Otho Holland WILLIAMS. Commission as Colonel of the 6th Maryland Regiment; to take rank as such from January 1, 1777. *Williams Papers.* Part 1/8. (Item #32.)

71 Smallwood, William, et. al. "The Address of the Officers of the Maryland Forces." Petition submitted to the Maryland Legislature. June 17, 1779 Quoted from Scharf, *Maryland.* P. 352.

72 Ibid. P. 353.

73 Washington, George. Letter to the Continental Congress Mustering Committee. Written at Head Quarters, West Point. August 20, 1779. *Washington Papers.*

74 Washington, George. Letter to Francis Barber and John Brooks. Written March 24, 1778. *Washington Papers.*

75 Washington, George. General Orders. Written at Head Quarters, V. Forge, March 28, 1778. *Washington Papers.*

76 Washington, George. General Orders. June 24, 1779. Written at New Windsor. *Washington Papers.*

77 Washington, George. Letter to Peter Scull, written at Head Quarters, Valley Forge, March 19, 1778. *Washington Papers.*

78 Lee, *Memoirs.* P. 593.

79 From George Washington to Henry Laurens, 30 April 1778," Founders Online, National Archives (http://founders.archives.gov/documents/Washington/03-14-02-0612, ver. 2014-05-09). Source: The Papers of George Washington, Revolutionary War Series, vol. 14, 1 March 1778–30 April 1778, ed. David R. Hoth. Charlottesville: University of Virginia Press, 2004, pp. 681–683.

80 Washington, George. General Orders. August 17, 1778, written at Head Quarters, W. Plains. *Washington Papers.*

81 Washington, George. Letter to Congress. Written at New Windsor, July 1, 1779. *Washington Papers.*

82 Washington, George. General Orders. Written at Head Quarters, New Windsor, Wednesday, July 14, 1779. *Washington Papers.*

83 Washington, George. Letter to Continental Congress Conference Committee, January 29, 1778. *Washington Papers.*

84 Washington, George. General Orders. Head Quarters, Morristown, December 25, 1779. *Washington Papers.*

85 Washington, George. General Orders. June 7, 1778. Written at Head Quarters, Valley Forge. *Washington Papers.* Also: Journals of the Continental Congress. Volume 10. P. 543.

86 Washington, George. Letter to the Board of War. Written at Headquarters, Morristown, New Jersey between January 15 - 17, 1780. *Washington Papers.*

87 Washington, George. Letter to Congress. Written at Headquarters, Morristown, January 27, 1780. *Washington Papers.*

88 Perhaps one of the more telling indications of his heavy workload as acting Adjutant General is that the Otho Holland *Williams Papers* in the Maryland Historical Society contain no personal letters written by him during the months that he served in that capacity

89 James, Charles. *New and Enlarged Military Dictionary* (hereafter James, *Military Dictionary*.) Printed for T. Egerton, at the Military Library, near Whitehall. London. 1802. Pp. ACC/ADJ and ADV/AGE. (pages are not numbered in the text; the progression of the definitions is alphabetical.)

90 Washington, George. General Orders. March 10, 1780. Issued at Headquarters, Morristown. *Washington Papers.*

91 Fish, Nicholas. Letter to Tench Tilghman. March 22, 1780. *Washington Papers.*

92 Meade, Richard K. Letter to Nicholas Fish. Written at Headquarters, March 23, 1780. *Washington Papers.*

93 Washington, George. General Orders. April 11, 1780. *Washington Papers.*

94 Announcement of the Meeting of the Ancient Free and Accepted Masons serving in the military lines of Maryland and Delaware. February 5, 1780. *Williams Papers.* Part 1/8 (Item #44.)

95 Convention of Ancient Free and Accepted Masons, Morris Town [N.J.]. To the Right Worshipful The Grand Masters of the Several Lodges in the respective United States. February 7, 1780. *Williams Papers.* Part 1/8, (Item #45.)

96 Washington, George. General Orders. Wednesday, February 16, 1780. Issued at Headquarters, Morristown. *Washington Papers*.
97 Washington, George. General Orders. Wednesday, December 29, 1799. Issued at Headquarters, Morristown. *Washington Papers*.
98 Washington, George. General Orders. Monday, January 3, 1780. Issued at Headquarters, Morristown. *Washington Papers*.
99 Washington, George. General Orders. Sunday, April 2, 1780. Issued at Headquarters, Morristown. *Washington Papers*.
100 Washington, George. General Orders. Friday, January 28, 1780. *Washington Papers*.
101 Ibid.
102 Washington, George. Letter to Congress. Written at Headquarters, Morristown, January 30, 1780. *Washington Papers*.
103 Washington, George. General Orders. Thursday, April 6, 1780. Issued at Headquarters, Morristown. *Washington Papers*.
104 Washington, George. To Continental Army Brigade Commanding Officers. Issued at Head Quarters, Morristown on January 22, 1780. *Washington Papers*.
105 Ibid.
106 Washington, George. Letter to the President of Congress. Written at Head Quarters, Morris Town, April 3, 1780. *Washington Papers*.
107 Smallwood, William, et. al. "The Address of the Officers of the Maryland Forces." Petition submitted to the Maryland Legislature. June 17, 1779 Quoted from Scharf, Maryland. P. 352.
108 Ramsay, Nathaniel. Letter to Otho Holland Williams. August 20, 1779. Written at Flat Bush, New York. Williams Papers. 1/8, (item #35.)
109 Washington, George. Letter to Congress. January 4, 1780. Written at Head Quarters, Morris Town. *Washington Papers*.
110 Washington, George. Letter to Colonels Robert Magaw, George Matthews, and John Ely, and Lieutenant Colonel Nathanael Ramsay. January 19, 1780. Head Quarters, Morris Town. *Washington Papers*.
111 Washington, George. Letter to Governor Thomas Sim Lee of Maryland. Written May 4, 1780 at Head Quarters, Morris Town. *Washington Papers*.
112 Washington, George. Letter to the Continental Congress War Board. Written at Whippeny, June 25, 1780. *Washington Papers*.
113 Steuart, *Maryland Line*. P. 121.
114 Washington, George. Letter to the Continental Congress. January 18, 1780. Written at Head Quarters, Morris Town. *Washington Papers*.
115 Washington, George. Letter to Congress. January 27, 1780. Written at Head Quarters, Morris Town. *Washington Papers*.
116 Washington, George. General Orders. Head Quarters, Morristown, April 11, 1780. *Washington Papers*.
117 Washington, George. Letter to the President of Congress. Written at Head Quarters, Morris Town. April 2, 1780. *Washington Papers*.
118 Washington, George. Letter to Nathanael Greene. Written at Head Quarters, Morris Town on April 2, 1780. *Washington Papers*.
119 Washington, George. Letter to Baron De Kalb. Written at Head Quarters, Morris Town, April 2, 1780. *Washington Papers*.
120 Washington, George. Letter to Brigadier General Mordecai Gist. April 2, 1780. Written at Head Quarters, Morris Town. *Washington Papers*.
121 Washington, George. Letter to Brigadier General Mordecai Gist. April 10, 1780. Written at Head Quarters, Morris Town. *Washington Papers*.
122 Washington, George. Letter to Baron Steuben. Written at Morris Town, April 2, 1780, *Washington Papers*.
123 Williams, Otho. Letter to Dr. Philip Thomas. September 21, 1779. *Williams Papers*. Part 1/ 8. (Item #36.)

CHAPTER 4

TRANSFER TO THE SOUTH; SOUTHERN TERRAIN

Otho Williams described the departure of the Maryland and Delaware troops for the South in writing that he intended for future publication:

> *On the 16th day of April 1780, the quotas of Maryland and Delaware troops, about fourteen hundred infantry, marched under the orders of the Baron De Kalb, from cantonments near Morristown in New Jersey, for the head of the Chesapeake Bay. They embarked the 3rd day of May, at the head of Elk River, and arrived at Petersburgh in Virginia, early in June.*[1]

De Kalb chose Colonel Otho Williams to be the Deputy Adjutant General[2] of his little corps, undoubtedly seeking to capitalize on the experience the Colonel had gained while serving in that role for the Commander-in-Chief. A de Kalb biographer notes that Williams stood "high in Kalb's confidence and esteem," and calls Williams "one of the ablest officers of the Revolution."[3]

From this time until the end of his war service, Williams would hold the simultaneous positions of Deputy Adjutant General of the southern army and commander of an operational unit, initially the Sixth Maryland Regiment. General Washington defended this practice of having Williams serve in these dual roles when Baron von Steuben questioned how anyone could be effective while serving simultaneously in two such important positions, and without hurting the opportunities for other valuable officers. Washington noted that:

> *You mention the case of Colo. Williams, who acts as Dy. Adjt. General to the southern Army. The Regiment to which that Gentleman belongs is with that Army, and therefore he can occasionally put himself at the head of it without interfering with or giving umbrage to any other Officer.*[4]

The troops started their southward trip by marching from Morristown, New Jersey, to Philadelphia, Pennsylvania, where de Kalb had been working on the logistics of the operation since April 8th. He directed them to Head of Elk at the northern end of the Chesapeake Bay, where the infantry embarked on boats bound for Virginia, while the artillery, ammunition, and baggage traveled on land.[5] De Kalb himself did not leave Philadelphia until May 13th, when he had finally completed all the necessary administrative details. He stopped at Annapolis, Maryland to receive money from the Maryland government, and arrived at Richmond, Virginia on May 22nd, where he expected to join the troops. Discovering that Virginia Governor Thomas Jefferson had changed the location of the rendezvous to Petersburg, he proceeded there, arriving on May 23rd, just in time to supervise the unloading of the last transports as they were arriving from their trip down the Bay.[6]

The further south that de Kalb traveled, the more he became discouraged with the support he was receiving from the Virginia and North Carolina governments, in spite of the fact that their assistance had been requested well in advance, by no less a figure than the Commander-in-Chief of the American Army. General Washington had written to Governor Richard Caswell of North Carolina and Governor John Rutledge of South Carolina before the troops had left New Jersey:

> *Your Excellency will have received I presume before this, a transcript of an Act of Congress of the 25th of February, calling on the several States for specific quantities of provision, Rum, and Forage for the Army....I beg leave to add that it appears to me essential, that a part of the flour and forage should be collected as soon as it can be done, at proper Stages on the usual route through the State for the marching of Troops to or from the more Northern ones...*[7]

De Kalb grew increasingly frustrated as state governments failed to provide the requested material support, and he was further discouraged when he did not receive the wagons that he had been promised. This made it necessary for his troops to carry much of the army's baggage and supplies on their backs, in spite of the increasingly hot weather. De Kalb vented the frustrations of a European military mindset in a private letter to a friend in Philadelphia:

> *I meet with no support, no integrity, and no virtue in the State of Virginia, and place my sole reliance on the French fleet and army, which are coming to our relief. For my part, I expect a most toilsome campaign, having been detained by the non-arrival of my wagons.*[8]

On June 6th, de Kalb learned that the British had captured Charleston several weeks earlier (on May 12th.) He promptly reported this finding to the Board of War, and announced his intention to "...be on the defensive until reinforcement, and further orders and directions either from your Board, Congress, or the Commander in Chief."[9]

De Kalb inched further southward, crossing from Virginia into North Carolina on June 20th.[10] On this same date Colonel Otho Williams, who must have been given permission to be away from his command during this part of the march, was striving to catch up with the Army, writing to his brother Elie from Fredericksburg, Virginia that he had intended to leave Fredericksburg a day earlier, but had stayed over to dine with General George Weedon and his friends. He reported that he had sent his baggage and a barrel of good flour ahead, and that he would set off the next day to rejoin the Army, although he was not sure exactly where its headquarters were located at the present time. Williams told his brother that he had sent him a letter two days earlier with news of the "unlucky state" of Abraham Buford's cavalry detachment in a region of north-central South Carolina called the Waxhaws, where British troops under the command of Colonel Banastre Tarleton had cut down Americans on May 29th, reportedly after they had surrendered, although "no official account has come yet." Williams was familiar with the military situation in the North, reporting that "Gen. Kniphausen commands, in person, a force of 5,000 men and is trying to force Gen. Washington into a general action before the arrival of the French fleet." He reported that "..the cavalry with 2500 Virginia militia and the Maryland Division will make up the Southern Army, till the 5,000 men now being raised by this State (Virginia) join them in a few months."[11] These numbers indicate that Williams was anticipating that the southern army would reach a size of approximately 9,000 troops, a number which would prove to be far too optimistic.

Further ahead on the road southward, Baron de Kalb bared his troubles in an anguished letter to his wife:

> *Here I am at last, considerably south, suffering from intolerable heat, the worst of quarters, and the most voracious of insects of every hue and form. The most disagreeable of the latter is what is commonly called the tick, a kind of strong black flea, which makes its way under the skin, and by its bite produces the most painful irritation and inflammation, which lasts a number of days. My whole body is covered with these stings.*[12]

Remarking on another aspect of the weather, De Kalb mentioned that "Of the violence of the thunderstorms in this part of the world the Europeans cannot form any idea."[13]

De Kalb was having difficulty adjusting to the environment in the southern states, and the burden of this command weighed heavily on him, an anguish which he shared openly in his letters to his wife:

> *I would fain be rid of my command, than which there can be nothing more annoying or difficult. My current position makes me doubly anxious to return to you as soon as possible.*[14]

A Description of the Southern Theater

De Kalb's letters home make clear that he realized that the Southern Theater was going to be dramatically different from the northern states where he had served for the past three years, and radically different from anything he had ever experienced in Europe. Another northerner who would join the southern army in the future would one day write:

> *Nothing but blood and slaughter prevail here, and the operations are in a country little short of a wilderness.*[15]

Any strategy that would successfully defend the southern states from the invading British would depend on the ability to understand southern geography; cope with the topography, climate, and everyday challenges of feeding the army; and learn how to deal with friend and foe in the partisan warfare that characterized parts of the region. Whichever army, British or American, that could maintain a strong presence in the region would encourage their friends, dishearten their foes, and strengthen their chances for victory.

Understanding the war in the South requires some familiarity with the geography of the region, the nature of the population, and the capabilities of the contending forces.

The Environment
Topography

The map shows the terrain, waterways, fording places, settlements, mills, forts, and battlefields that would play important roles in the fighting between June, 1780 and September, 1781.

The map (page 77) shows an area about 280 miles east-to-west, and 350 miles north-to-south, encompassing portions of the states of Georgia,

South Carolina, North Carolina and Virginia. The low, flat area from the Atlantic Ocean to about 100 miles inland is called the Coastal Plain, often referred to as the "Low Country." The terrain then begins a gradual rise in a region called the Piedmont, which becomes rolling foothills, and eventually the Appalachian Mountains. Revolutionary War writers sometimes used the phrase "upper route" to describe a movement in the high ground of the Piedmont or the mountains.

★ ★ ★ ★ ★

The Rivers

The great rivers of this region start in the mountains as narrow, rushing streams, which plunge down the mountain sides in a generally easterly or southeasterly direction. The northernmost river on the map, the Dan, continues its easterly course until it joins the east-flowing Roanoke River. The other rivers shown - the Neuse, Haw, Deep, Yadkin, Catawba, Broad, and Savannah - eventually take up a southeasterly direction as they flow oceanward. As the map shows, many of these rivers flow into a river of another name for their final journey to the sea: the Haw and Deep Rivers flow into the Cape Fear; the Yadkin flows into the Pee Dee; the Catawba flows into the Wateree, which flows into the Santee; the Broad and the Saluda become the Congaree, which also flows into the Santee.

The boundary between the Piedmont and the Coastal Plain is called the "fall line," to indicate the area where the rivers flow down over the last waterfalls and onto the Coastal Plain. A boat moving inland from the ocean would encounter a fairly level river until it reached the fall line, where waterfalls, rapids and rising terrain would stop shipment by water. This required goods going inland to be taken off the boats and loaded onto wagons or pack horses for the trip onto higher ground. Similarly, hunters, trappers, and farmers bringing their goods down from the upper regions could unload here, and move their goods onto boats for an easier journey to the coastal cities. Today's U.S. Routes 1 and 95 roughly follow the fall line as they traverse the region.

Since the fall line was essentially the head of navigation for these rivers, cities were often founded there, as a transition point for traffic between the Coastal Plain and the inland regions. Petersburg, Virginia; Cheraw and Camden, South Carolina; and Augusta, Georgia are some of the cities of the region that are located on the fall line.

When new land was settled, early inhabitants often clung to the riverbanks, preferring to establish their settlements where they would have

Map 3 - The Southern Theater-Operations in the South

easy transportation to other areas via the waterways. In 1780, the interior regions of the southern states still had that tendency, as described by Henry Lee in his noteworthy Memoirs:

> *You must know that only on the rivers is there the least attention to agriculture among these people, unless high up in the country. The settlements on the river are rich and populous; the intermediate lands barren and unsettled. Therefore the motions of the army must be from river to river, striking at the head of navigation, and receiving by boats the produce.*[16]

Rivers were essential transportation routes during the Revolutionary War. Even the most fully developed roads in the region were little more than cart paths, which could turn rapidly to mud and become virtually impassable when it rained. The fastest way to move supplies was by water, and the British tried to supply their armies using the rivers as highways from the ocean into the interior. In South Carolina, they built a chain of forts inland from the Santee River – Forts Watson, Motte, Granby, and Ninety-Six[17]*– to protect the boat traffic that carried much needed supplies to British outposts in the countryside.

Since the rivers were so important to communications and transportation, military leaders had to consider control of the rivers in all their planning. For example, when the British decided to march north into North Carolina, they detached a force to take the port of Wilmington, which permitted them to off-load supplies there from their ocean-going vessels, and send boats up the Cape Fear River to supply their army.

The rivers could be highways for troops and supplies, but they could also be formidable barriers to an army that was marching overland. All the rivers were dotted with various fording places, where the normal watercourses were shallow enough that people could wade across during periods of low flow. These fords were key strategic locations for any army trying to advance or to escape from a pursuing enemy. There were some places where the rivers were not quite fordable, but were suitable for a ferry, and enterprising people established ferries at these locations. Knowledge of the fords and ferries, and the ability to control these key crossing points could be vital to winning or losing any engagement. Thus Irwin's Ferry and Boyd's Ferry on the Dan River;

---

*The picturesque name "Ninety-six" is derived from the fact that the settlement was ninety-six miles from Keowee, a Cherokee settlement.

Trading Ford on the Yadkin River; and Beatty's Ford and Cowan's Ford on the Catawba all play important roles in the war in the South.

On a map, it might appear that crossing a fording place was an inconsequential activity, no more challenging than crossing a river on a modern highway bridge today. However, a river crossing in the eighteenth century could be a formidable challenge, as described in some detail by an early civilian historian of the Revolutionary War, Benson J. Lossing, when he was traveling in the South to gather information for his book:

> *We pushed on towards the South Fork of the Catawba…I was told that the ford was marked by a row of rocks, occurring at short intervals across the stream; but when I reached the bank, few of them could be seen above the surface of the swift and swollen stream. The distance across is about two hundred and fifty yards, and the whole stream flows in a single channel.…I resolved to venture alone, relying upon the few rocks visible for indications of the safest place for a passage… Twice the wheels ran upon rocks, and the wagon was almost overturned, the water being, in the mean while, far over the hubs; and when within a few yards of the southern shore, we crossed a narrow channel, so deep that my horse kept his feet with difficulty, and the wagon, having a tight body, floated for a moment. The next instant we struck firm ground. I breathed freer as we ascended the bank, and with a thankful heart rode on…*[18]

Lossing told his story about crossing this ford in peacetime. He did not have to hold his firelock and ammunition high above his head to keep them dry, and there were no soldiers on the opposite shore firing at him trying to prevent his crossing. And yet, Lossing breathed a great relief when he reached the far shore of the Catawba River safely. Soldiers crossing such fording places would have a much more difficult time if they were opposed by armed enemies on the opposite shore. Lossing described the scene as it would have been when British troops crossed Cowan's Ford on the Catawba River during the War:

> *The current was rapid, the stream in many places waist-deep, and almost five hundred yards wide, yet the brave Britons, led on by General O'Hara, plunged into the stream, and in the face of a severe fire from Captain Graham's riflemen, who were posted at the ford, pressed forward to the opposite bank…*

The British reserved their fire until they had gained the shore, and, then, pouring a few volleys into the ranks of Graham, soon dispersed them.[19]

In other words, to cross this river, British troops would have to wade some five hundred yards through deep, fast-running water, probably holding their muskets and ammunition high above their heads to keep them dry, and in the face of heavy fire from deadly accurate colonial rifles. The American troops that crossed these streams in such difficult circumstances were also often being pressured from behind by British troops who were aggressively pursuing them. When troops were in mid-stream, they were virtually defenseless against attacks from either ahead or behind. Moving army units safely across a river in 1780 or 1781 was no small challenge.

Southern rivers could be formidable barriers under normal conditions, but they were also susceptible to enormous changes in width and depth, depending on the torrential rains that could come and go with little warning. An American General reported in one letter that, "The Pedee rose 25 feet the last week in 30 hours."[20] A fleeing army might rest safe behind an impassable river that stood between it and the enemy, but when the rain subsided, it was only a matter of time until the water level receded, and the pursuers could cross over.

An astute General would quickly realize the vital importance of these streams, rivers and crossings in this Southern Theater. An army's survival might depend on knowing how to use the watercourses as avenues of attack or retreat.

One American leader who instinctively understood the importance of the southern rivers was Commander-in-Chief George Washington, whose great estate, Mount Vernon, fronted on the Potomac River. Washington had himself experienced many adventures on that river in his youth, ranging from its upper reaches in the mountains to its passage by his beloved Virginia home. Washington had lived much of his life on and near the great rivers, and he was personally familiar with how they could be highways or barriers for an army traveling cross-country.

Washington had exploited the Delaware River brilliantly during the Trenton and Princeton campaigns of 1776/1777 - first as a defensive moat that kept his little army safe from assault, and then as a highway for his own attacks on Hessian and British outposts. This man knew that wise use of the rivers could provide a decisive military advantage, and in a letter to Governor

Thomas Jefferson of Virginia, he demonstrated his clear understanding of ways to exploit the mighty rivers:

> *Should the enemy continue in the lower parts of Virginia, they will have every advantage by being able to move up and down the Rivers in small parties, while it will be out of our power to molest them for want of the means of suddenly transporting ourselves across those Rivers to come at them. This might be in a very great degree obviated and they kept in check, if we had a number of ... flat boats upon travelling carriages attending the Army collected to watch their motions. We could then move across from River to River with more rapidity than they could go down one and up another, and none of their detachments would be ever secure by having the Water between them and us. Major Genl. Greene is perfectly acquainted with the kind of Boats I have mentioned, and with the mode of fixing them. He will give the proper directions for having them constructed, should your Excellency approve the plan.*[21]

Any astute commander in the South would pay heed to such thoughtful advice.

Climate

The weather and environment in the southern states also offered new challenges to Otho Williams and his comrades who were marching down from the North. As Baron de Kalb had described to his wife, violent rainstorms could flare up with little notice, turning the roads into quagmires, turning the rivers into raging torrents, and greatly expanding the size of river swamps. During the hot summer months, armies often marched in the evenings and at night to avoid the discomfort of brutally hot and humid days.

During hot weather, low lying regions teemed with insects, which were viewed only as a nuisance, since their links to diseases such as malaria and yellow fever were not yet understood at the time. Soldiers from the northern states were particularly susceptible to these ravages, as were those from England, Scotland, Ireland, and Germany.

The heat and the constant campaigning could wreck even a vigorous constitution. Lord Rawdon, a young, energetic and effective British officer entered the Southern Theater in 1780 in perfect health, and sailed for home only fifteen months later, exhausted and ill from his exertions and exposure to the southern climate. This young warrior was all of twenty-seven years old.[22]

Another British soldier left this dismal assessment of how difficult it was to march in the summer heat in the South, and how some of his comrades lost their lives not to combat, but to the perils of life on the march:

> *During renewed successions of forced marches, under the rage of a burning sun, and in a climate, at that season, peculiarly inimical to man, they were frequently, when sinking under the most excessive fatigue, not only destitute of every comfort, but almost of every necessary which seems essential to his existence... Above fifty men, in this last expedition, sunk under the vigour of their exertions, and perished through mere fatigue.*[23]

Food

The British army tried to keep its troops supplied from the sea, and to avoid dependence on the countryside for food and forage. Even with their ample resources and comparatively sophisticated design, these systems were sometimes stretched beyond their limits, which forced the British to live off the countryside, as was common for the American troops. Some regions in this theater were sparsely settled and infertile, where there had never been ample supplies to feed an army. All regions became increasingly destitute as the war continued, with many once-prosperous areas being depleted by the voracious consumption and constant movement of the opposing forces.

A British officer described the difficulties encountered by his men:

> *During the greater part of the time, they were totally destitute of bread, and the country afforded no vegetables for a substitute. Salt at length failed; and their only resources were water, and the wild cattle which they found in the woods...*[24]

American troops were usually less well supplied than the British, and were constantly short of food, clothing and ammunition, requiring that the officers of the American Army were usually preoccupied with finding enough food for their men to eat. On several occasions, commanders would place their troops where it was easy to find food rather than in an optimum military disposition.

The troops often lived hand-to-mouth, and had to scavenge the countryside to find even meager rations. Marylander John Eager Howard remembered in later years that money "…became useless in procuring any thing whatever for the army, and recourse was had to other means for subsistence."[25] Otho Holland Williams would one day write that "…we seldom encamped where there was any thing to purchase."[26]

The *Memoirs* of Light Horse Harry Lee give insight into the American army's supply problems, and some of their innovative solutions for finding rations:

> *We had often experienced in the course of the campaign want of food, and had sometimes seriously suffered from the scantiness of our supplies, rendered more pinching by their quality;… Of meat, we had literally none; for the few meager cattle brought to camp as beef would not afford more than one or two ounces per man.*
>
> *Frogs abounded in some neighboring ponds, and on them chiefly did the light troops subsist. They became in great demand from their nutritiousness and, after conquering the existing prejudice, were diligently sought after. Even the alligator was used by a few; and, very probably, had the army been much longer detained upon that ground, might have rivaled the frog in the estimation of our epicures.*[27]

★ ★ ★ ★ ★

Population

De Kalb, Williams, Howard and their 1,400 Continental troops were entering a region that was much less densely populated than the northern states where they had been fighting. The only city of any real size in the South was Charleston, with about 11,000 inhabitants. The only other settlements with populations of any significance were the coastal cities of Wilmington, North Carolina; Georgetown, South Carolina; and Savannah, Georgia.

Inland villages typically contained only a few houses and inhabitants. The important village of Charlotte was described as:

> *…standing on elevated ground, contained about twenty houses, built on two streets crossing each other at right angles. The court-house constructed of stone,*[28] *stood at the intersection of the two streets.*[29]

Since there were only a few settlements of any size, the flour mills that dotted the countryside often served as the places where people gathered to exchange goods and news, a function that would later be served in more populous regions by country stores and post offices.[30] The mills themselves and the roads that led to them were important landmarks. They were also logical places to store grain, and were often the object of armies searching for food.

The populace in some of the regions tended to have very pronounced loyalties to one side or the other. In the Ninety-Six region of South Carolina, where the British built one of their strong garrisons, the prevailing sentiment was Loyalist, or Tory – terms that described those who remained loyal to the Crown. The area around Hillsborough, North Carolina, was also known to be Loyalist, even though the town was the capital of the state.

On the other hand, in the region around Charlotte most people were Whigs, or pro-Revolution. A British officer remembered the particular virulence of the Whigs in the Charlotte area:

> *The town and environs abounded with inveterate enemies...It was evident, and it had been frequently mentioned to the King's officers, that the counties of Mecklenburg and Rohan were more hostile to England than any other in America. The vigilance and animosity of these surrounding districts checked the exertions of the well-effected, and totally destroyed all communication between the King's troops and Loyalists in the other parts of the province. No British commander could obtain any information in that position which would facilitate his designs or guide his future conduct...The foraging parties were every day harassed by the inhabitants, who did not remain at home to receive payment for the produce of their plantations, but generally fired from covert places to annoy the British detachments.*[31]

★ ★ ★ ★ ★

The Nature of the War in the South
"Tarleton's Quarter"

As Otho Williams and his Maryland troops were arriving in the South, news of some fighting at a region called the Waxhaws in South Carolina touched off a controversy that would affect the nature of the War in the South for its duration.

An aggressive young British commander named Banastre Tarleton led a fast-moving light unit in hot pursuit of an American force commanded by Colonel Abraham Buford. When Tarleton caught up with Buford, the

American commander made the tactical mistake of holding his fire too long, which permitted Tarleton and his men to fall upon the Americans with deadly effectiveness. Overwhelmed, the Americans gave signs of their intent to surrender. While it is hard to discern exactly what happened in the next few moments from records that are over two hundred years old,[32*] the word went forth from this site that the British had brutally struck unarmed Americans after they had surrendered. This story spread across the southern states, and brought white-hot intensity to many people's hatred of the British.

"Tarleton's Quarter" became a watchword that meant that there would be no leniency for men who surrendered on the Revolutionary War battlefields in the South. For the remainder of the War, American and British soldiers went into battle expecting "Tarleton's Quarter," or very brutal treatment if they surrendered. Soldiers on both sides felt that surrender could lead to extremely harsh treatment as a prisoner, and they would fight hard to avoid capture in the coming conflict.

★ ★ ★ ★ ★

Backwoods Fighting Tactics

Brutal tactics did not start or end with Tarleton's victory at the Waxhaws. Before and during the Revolutionary War, the countryside of Georgia, South Carolina, and North Carolina was often the scene of bitter, uncompromising warfare between different groups of combatants. Intense hatreds seethed within various segments of society, and vengeance was often unleashed with devastating effect. Senior British and American commanders soon learned that the strong presence of regular military forces was necessary to pacify many areas, and to keep the demons of partisan fighting at bay, or at least under some control.

In the mid-eighteenth century, colonists had witnessed some brutal warfare between settlers and various native american tribes, such as the Cherokee and Catawba nations, who were being pushed off their land. Indian war parties had attacked isolated settlements, killed the men, burned the crops and homesteads, and taken the women and children captive. American frontiersmen had also conducted merciless raids on the tribes, and many

---

*Another view of this encounter has been published by Dr. Jim Piecuch in the book *"The Blood Be Upon Your Head: Tarleton and the Myth of Buford's Massacre*. Lugoff, South Carolina. The Southern Campaigns of the American Revolution Press. 2010.

backwoodsmen had learned their fighting skills in this hard, uncompromising warfare, where rifle and hatchet were wielded with deadly effectiveness. Several prominent American military leaders in the South during the Revolutionary War had received their first experience of warfare in these brutal frontier encounters, including Henry Laurens, Francis Marion, William Moultrie, Benjamin Huger, and Andrew Pickens[33] – all names that we will hear again as our story develops.

The British army preyed on the southern frontiersmen's dread of Indian warriors. Their envoys maintained frequent contact with the tribes, and supplied them with regular gifts and other inducements to provide information or stir up trouble. Trouble on the home front sometimes caused American militiamen to leave the army and go home to defend their families.

The historian Benson Lossing traveled extensively in the South in the late 1840s and interviewed as many remaining eye-witnesses of the war as he could find. He kept a detailed catalog of many stories that had been passed down orally about the conflict, and he was convinced that he had identified the moment when all the brutality started - right after the British attacked Charleston in 1776:

> ...the Cherokees commenced a series of massacres upon the western frontiers of the province. Already a few stockade forts had been erected in that section, and to these the terrified borderers fled for safety. Colonel Williamson, of the district of Ninety-Six, who was charged with the defense of the upper country, raised about five hundred true men, and in his first skirmish with the Indians, in which he took some prisoners, discovered thirteen white men, Tories, disguised as savages, and wielding their tomahawk and scalping knife.
> The indignation excited against these men extended to their class, and this discovery was the beginning of these bloody scenes between bands of Whigs and Tories, which characterized many districts of South Carolina. The domestic feuds which ensued were pregnant with horrid results.[34]

The merciless warfare between the native tribes and the settlers was a continual backdrop to the war in the South. In 1781, the British induced the Cherokees to attack several settlements in the Ninety-Six region, where they massacred the residents and burned their houses. The Americans retaliated:

General Pickens, with a party of militia, penetrated the Cherokee country, and in the space of fourteen days he burned thirteen of their villages, killed more than forty of the Indians, and took nearly seventy of them prisoners. They sued for peace, promised never to listen to the British again, and from that time they remained quiet.[35]

★ ★ ★ ★ ★

Ruffians

Partisan bands from both sides regularly wreaked havoc on the population. The stories about one notable Tory example, Thomas "Burntfoot" Brown, and his inveterate Whig foe, Elijah Clark, illustrate the ugly nature of this warfare.

Thomas Brown[36] had been born in England to a prosperous family, and grew up as a loyal Englishman, proud of his country's heritage and obedient to his King. In the early 1770's, he emigrated to Georgia, and established himself as a gentleman planter near the town of Augusta.

He was proud of his loyalty to crown and country, and his intense pro-British sentiments became well known in the community. On August 2nd, 1775, Brown was attacked by a rough crowd, which fractured his skull, ripped off his clothes, and tarred and feathered him. The hot tar caused burns all over his body and eventually resulted in the loss of two toes.

Brown was understandably enraged by the treatment he had received, and his hatred drove him to become a forceful, vengeful leader of Georgia's backcountry Loyalists. He developed excellent working relationships with native American allies, particularly the Creeks and Cherokees, and built a network of pro-British friends from the Carolinas to Florida. The British gave him the rank of Lieutenant Colonel, and he selected and trained a mounted Loyalist group, which he led with devastating effectiveness.

Many Georgian partisans hated Brown, and he was reputed to have committed untold atrocities during the course of the war. He was reputed to have had thirteen prisoners hung from the staircase of a Tory fortress, and to have turned some other prisoners over to Indians for torture.[37]

When Brown and his fellow troops were captured at the siege of Augusta, Georgia in 1781, Elijah Clarke and his band of Georgian partisans were determined to inflict merciless vengeance on their prisoners. Earlier in the siege, one of the Tory outposts had surrendered, and Clarke's forces had been able to murder several of the prisoners, including their commander, before the regular troops could regain control over the situation. Clarke and his Georgians would have liked nothing better than to than to take out their vengeance on Brown, but Light Horse Harry Lee put Brown under an armed guard to guarantee his safety, and later noted this incident as an example of how the South "...often sank into barbarity."[38]

The Revolution in the South is known for the brutality of the opponents in the region. Propagandists were active on both sides during the war, and they were not above embellishing these stories to rally support their own point of view. While the facts in many cases are clouded by each side's tendency to spin tales and use such events for propaganda, it seems undeniable that horrible acts were committed by both sides

Otho Williams once observed that "… murders are committed daily by pretended Whigs and reputed Tories."[39]

Henry Lee's Memoir of the Revolution in the South recounted another particularly brutal act by a band of Tories:

> *Among the many murders and burning of house perpetrated by this banditti, that of Colonel Kobb was particularly atrocious. A party of them, led by a Captain Jones, surprised the colonel on a visit to his family. He defended his house, until he was induced, by the promise of personal safety, to surrender as a prisoner of war; when he was immediately murdered in the presence of his wife and children, and his house burnt.*[40]

William Richardson Davie, an effective partisan leader from North Carolina who eventually served as commissary officer of the southern army, noted that the British would burn the plantation house whenever they gained possession of property owned by patriots.[41]

A patriot militiaman left a record of the slaughter of some troops who had become prisoners of the Americans:

> *We went to where six were standing together. Some discussion taking place, I heard some of our men cry out, 'Remember Buford,' and the prisoners were immediately hewed to pieces with broadswords.*[42]

The victors at the Battle of King's Mountain invoked stern justice on some of their prisoners:

> *On the morning after the battle (Oct. 8, 1780), a court-martial was held, and several of the Tory prisoners were found*

guilty of murder and other high crimes. Colonel Cleveland had previously declared that if certain persons, who were the chief marauders, and who had forfeited their lives, should fall into his hands, he would hang them. Ten of these men were suspended upon a tulip-tree, which is yet standing...[43]

Otho Williams wrote the following postscript to a letter:

Yesterday the famous Major Gray, the infamous spy and notorious horse thief, lost his mulatto Head. It is exhibited at Cheraw Hill, a terror to Tories.[44]

Deserters

The presence of deserters in both armies also contributed to the brutality that characterized some parts of the War in the South. During the course of the fighting, men from both armies switched sides at various times, and for various reasons. When soldiers became prisoners, they were often given the opportunity to sign up to serve with their captors. It was a "marriage of convenience." The captors needed troops, and the prisoners were hoping for improved treatment, and, perhaps, a future opportunity to escape and return to their original unit. There were other myriad reasons for desertion, from the desire to have some rum or decent rations, to a genuine desire to support the cause of the other side.

Whatever the reasons, desertion was a major issue for both sides. The commander of the American army at the end of the war, Nathanael Greene, was reported to have said that:

At the close of the war, we fought the enemy with British soldiers, and they fought us with those of America.[45]

Soldiers who had taken up arms against their former comrades did not expect gentle treatment if they were captured. A sergeant in the Delaware Line recorded that on May 1st, 1781, the Americans hanged five deserters who had been taken prisoner at the Battle of Hobkirk's Hill. They hanged five more on May 17th, and three more on May 19th.[46] This same sergeant recorded another instance of hanging a deserter, and the method that the officers used to advertise this punishment and maximize its impact on the men:

> *On the twenty-fifth instant was tried and found guilty one Solomon Slocum, of the Second Maryland Battalion, for desertion to the enemy, joining with them, and coming in as a spy into our camp, when agreeable to his sentence, he was hanged on a tree by the roadside in full view of all who passed by.*[47]

Spying and deceit could reach into the inner circle of the highest officials. In one instance:

> *A man named William Peters, who was steward to General Greene and his wife, was confined to the provost under sentence of death for corresponding with the enemy by letters, some of the letters being found about him, which specified that he was to recruit a number of men on our service for the enemy.*[48]

In Banastre Tarleton's *History of the Campaigns of 1780 and 1781 in the Southern Provinces of North America*, he notes that when American prisoners were found to have violated parole and taken up arms against the British, they were, "upon a full conviction of their guilt," publicly executed.[49]

★ ★ ★ ★ ★

British Forces

The British forces were professional soldiers, led by officers from the upper classes of society. There were British Army units made up of soldiers from the British Isles (often called "redcoats" for their distinctive jackets,) as well as German mercenaries and American Provincial units called "Loyalist" or "Tory" commands. On May 1st, 1780, the British Army in South Carolina consisted of 7,041 British, Scottish and Irish troops; 3,018 Germans; and 2,788 Provincials, for a total of 12,847 men.[50] For the most part, British units performed well on the march and in battle throughout the time of Otho Williams' service in the South. It was hard to imagine a more formidable challenge for the Americans.

The British army units were inured to hard service by intense training and discipline. New troops typically spent the first six months of their enlistment in four one-hour sessions of drill a day, where they learned how to march in column and in line, shift rapidly from one formation to the other, and handle their weapons.[51] It was important for each soldier to master the rote method of loading and firing their muskets, which went as follows:

> *Each soldier took a paper cartridge, containing powder and ball, from the cartridge box on his belt, tipped a little powder into the flashpan about the trigger and, holding the musket butt down on the road, poured the remainder of the contents of the cartridge down the barrel. Then, taking the ramrod from its holder on the gun, he rammed the powder tight. It was a cumbersome operation, but British troops were well drilled in the use of muskets. All of them could fire three rounds a minute...*[52]

The muzzle loading muskets used by both sides in the Revolutionary War were notoriously inaccurate, particularly beyond 100 yards. This fact dictated the infantry tactics of the day, which were to march in line abreast to within 100 yards of the enemy, halt, and fire one or more volleys. Well trained troops also knew how to coordinate volleys between the first, second and third lines, or between various units along the line, so that a constant sheet of fire was maintained. In this manner, the enemy was kept under constant fire, since some parts of the line were firing at all times, while other sections were reloading.

The British were trained to finish the affair by going straight at the enemy with their deadly sixteen inch bayonets, firmly attached to the end of their muskets. The British were masters at choreographing their assaults to appear as terrifying as possible to their inexperienced foes. The long lines of impeccably dressed soldiers, marching in step to the relentless pounding of loud drums, bayonets glinting in the sun, battle flags snapping in the breeze, bagpipes skirling when the Scottish troops were engaged - the sights and sounds of an assault by British regulars were frightening. This war would show several instances where inexperienced American troops would simply turn and run in terror when they encountered this imposing sight.

Britain's disciplined troops could keep moving steadily forward, even when they were marching over difficult terrain, facing cannon fire, and being pummeled by enemy musket volleys. When someone in the front rank went down, the gap was quickly filled by a man from the next rank, so that the attack appeared to go on apace. One British officer of a later time left a riveting view of what it was like to participate in such an assault:

> *Gaps were made in the different companies, only to be filled up next moment. And still the line advanced...not a sound to be heard save now and then a suppressed shriek of pain as someone*

> *was freshly wounded followed by a sharp word of command, 'Close up' and 'mind your dressing.' I saw a shrapnel shell burst right in the face of one of the Companies of the right wing. It tore a wide gap and the men near it involuntarily turned away from the fire and smoke. I called out, 'Don't turn, men, don't turn,' and was at once answered, 'never fear Mister Barter, sir, we ain't agoing to turn.*[53]

This same officer also lived to experience the feelings of pride and exhilaration when the enemy turned and ran:

> *...they (i.e. the enemy) could not stand it, their line wavered and undulated, many began firing with their firelocks at their hips and at last as we were closing on them, the whole turned and ran for dear life...*[54]

The ultimate goal of the traditional British bayonet assault was to smash the enemy line, and cause their disordered, frightened foe to drop their muskets and run. Certain elements high in the British government were confident that this would be the outcome of every encounter in their rebellious colonies. The First Lord of the Admiralty, Lord Sandwich, had said of the Americans:

> *They are raw undisciplined cowardly men...Believe me my Lords, the very sound of cannon would carry them off...as fast as their feet could carry them.*[55]

British Colonel James Grant, who had served in the Americas, said that "...they would never dare to face an English Army."[56] At the start of the War, many British officers agreed with Sandwich and Grant that they would win every single engagement as long as they could lure the Americans into a stand-up fight.

The German troops that fought with the British were mercenaries hired by the Crown to try to help supply the needs for more men when recruiting efforts in the British Isles fell short. The German units were tough, disciplined professionals like the British.

The term "Provincial Units" described professional units made up of American colonists who maintained their loyalty to the King, and fought for the British side. Some of these were well trained, disciplined units. They often had good leaders. However, since they were not from the "home country," they were given secondary status in the British hierarchy, even to the point of being paid less than their British counterparts. Some of the Provincial Units that fought in the South with distinction were two regiments of DeLancey's New York Volunteers.[57]

There were also militia units on the British side, made up of Southerners who remained loyal to the Crown. These units typically did not perform well during the war, and produced no great, memorable partisan leaders like the American "Swamp Fox," Francis Marion, or "The Gamecock," Thomas Sumter, or "The Elder," Andrew Pickens.

★ ★ ★ ★ ★

American Forces

Although there were variations in the composition and assignments of patriot militia, most of them were bands of men from a specific locality who were called up for temporary service by state governments. Their terms of service could sometimes be a few days or a few months. The men were likely to head home at almost any time for any of a number of reasons, such as to help with planting or harvesting, or to help defend their homes. These "citizen soldiers" in the South were very inclined to follow officers that they respected. Strong leaders like Daniel Morgan, Francis Marion, Andrew Pickens, Thomas Sumter, William Davidson, and Edward Stevens could draw large numbers of volunteers, forge them into effective fighting units, and keep them under arms long enough to help achieve important objectives.

Militia duties included guarding depots, protecting supply wagons, or manning defensive positions. There were times when an imminent battle drew out large numbers of militia who had a desire to fight the hated British, but they might fade away again just as quickly when they saw that the danger to their local communities had passed. The constant ebb and flow of militia troops was a recurring problem for American leaders, who might not know from one day to the next how many troops were in their command. Sometimes militia troops were still arriving the night before a battle, which posed serious challenges for the leaders who were trying to hurry them to their proper position in the battle formation.

The battlefield performance of militia units varied greatly. There were times when militiamen stood their ground and performed as well as professional troops. There were other times when entire regiments of militia simply broke and ran at the first sight of a British attack. In most of the cases where the militia performed well, the ranks included former regulars and the leaders were experienced, respected officers.

Generals Washington and Greene had developed distrust for the militia, and expressed a strong preference for regular troops. Their mistrust was based on experience. For example, during one particularly dangerous and stressful period in the war, when the Americans were under tremendous pressure and desperately needed every man they could find, some militia simply ignored this crisis. Nathanael Greene wrote:

> *The North Carolina militia have all deserted us, except about 80 men. Majors and captains are among the deserters.*[58]

However, many Continental officers and soldiers did not give due credit to the contributions of militia, who had left hearth and home behind to take up arms against the British. Without reinforcements from militia troops, the American armies in the south did not have enough men to meet the British in battle on an equal footing. The American side owed much to the numerous men who were not trained as professional soldiers, but still answered the call to fight for their country.

The frontiersmen in militia units from the backcountry were a breed unto themselves. Fiercely independent and content to be left alone to pursue their own lives, these ferocious fighters would band together when it suited their interests, and would serve only under officers that they respected.

Another kind of militia were the partisan units led by men like Francis Marion, for whom war was a full-time calling. Marion was an endlessly innovative soldier, who found ways to pester the British forces constantly, yet he was always able to pull away quickly to safety if the fighting became too costly. Moving constantly, changing his base of operations frequently, lurking in the swamps and woods beyond the reach of any foe, Marion was an extremely valuable source of information for his commander, and a perpetual thorn in the side of every British officer in the region.

There were many small bands like Marion's that roamed the southern countryside, usually within a day's ride of their own homes. Every single British supply train and every single British messenger knew that they could be ambushed at any moment by these pesky guerilla units.

Continental Troops

Officers like Otho Williams had learned how to teach troops to march, maneuver, and fight. The men in the American Continental Army that they trained were as close to professional soldiers as any units that the states produced during the war. They reported to General Washington, who reported to the Continental Congress. This reporting relations ship made the Continental army the first truly national organization in American history.

Washington knew from experience that he needed highly trained, disciplined troops, so he lobbied Congress long and hard to authorize additional Continental units. He often expressed his belief that militia units were not up to the task of head-on confrontations with British professionals, as in the following excerpt from a circular letter to the state governors:

> *I solemnly declare I never was witness to a single instance that can countenance an opinion of Militia or raw troops being fit for the real business of fighting. I have found them useful as light parties to skirmish the Woods, but incapable of making or sustaining a serious attack. This firmness is only acquired by habit of discipline and service…I mean not to detract from the merit of the Militia; their zeal and spirit upon a variety of occasions have intitled them to the highest applause; but it is of the greatest importance we should learn to estimate them rightly. We may expect everything from ours that Militia is capable of, but we must not expect from any, service for which Regulars alone are fit.*[59]

Many units in the Continental Army developed into fine combat units during the course of this war, and they did it largely by hard work and study. George Washington urged the leaders under his command to take care of their troops and to devote as much time as possible to studying the profession of arms. Early in the war, he set out this objective in General Orders:

> *Officers, attentive to their duty, will find abundant employment, in training and disciplining their men--providing for them-- and seeing that they appear neat, clean and soldier-like--Nor will any thing redound more to their honor--afford them more solid amusement--or better answer the end of their appointment, than to devote the vacant moments, they may have, to the study of Military authors.*[60][61]

The men in Washington's army heeded this direction, which we know from their performance in battle as the war progressed, but also more directly from the observations of a professional Hessian officer, Johann Ewald, who published the diary that he maintained during the war. Ewald was deeply impressed with what his American adversaries had accomplished:

> ...the Americans have trained a great many excellent officers who very often shame and excell (sic.) our experienced officers, who consider it sinful to read a book or to think of learning anything during the war. For the love of justice and in praise of this nation, I must admit that when we examined a haversack of the enemy, which contained only two shirts, we also found the most excellent military books translated into their language. For example, Turpin, Jenny, Grandmaison, La Croix, Tielke's Field Engineer, and the Instructions of the great Frederick to his generals I have found more than one hundred times. Moreover, several among their officers had designed excellent small handbooks[62] and distributed them in the army. Upon reading these books, I have exhorted our gentlemen many times to read and emulate these people, who only two years before were hunters, lawyers, physicians, clergymen, tradesmen, innkeepers, shoemakers, and tailors.[63]

Military men like George Washington and the Hessian Johann Ewald knew the difference in combat capability between Continental troops (or "Regulars") and Militia from their battlefield performance, but civilians in the war zone also learned that there were important differences in the behavior of these two types of soldiers. The residents of Salem, North Carolina left a lasting testimony to the discipline of Continental troops when they wrote to a senior American commander complaining about the depredations committed repeatedly by militia, and pleading for a return of the much better behaved regulars:

> ...the great Excesses at all Times committed by the Militia both here & at the old Town called Bethabara and within a few Days past, since the regular Troops (departed?), the Hospital & the magazine of Ammunition were gone from hence, the renewed Excess of some Georgia & South Carolina People traveling thro' here the Robberies committed in our Neighbourhood, the unreasonable Treatment we just now receive of a couple of hundred militia of another County...; with horrid Imprecations, striking the people, ... & threatening not to leave this place before they have killed a Number of us, besides many Pretences

> to pick a Quarrell or invade Peoples Properties. The exemplary good order always observed by the Regulars which were here quartered, together with the express Declarations of General Smallwood Colonell (sic.) White & others, make us bold to hope, that your Excellency will condescend to send a few of Your Regulars here to protect the Place with such further Instructions as Your Excellency in your Wisdom shall think proper, and if it could be, in the same Time to grant us a Protection in Writing.[64]

The Hessian officer Johann Ewald, who had commented on how conscientiously young American officers had studied the military profession, left another remarkable tribute to the American Continental troops with the following observation at the end of the War:

> Concerning the American army, one should not think that it can be compared to a motley crowd of farmers. The so-called Continental, or standing, regiments are under good discipline and drill in the English style as well as the English themselves. I have seen the Rhode Island Regiment march and perform several mountings of the guard which left nothing to criticize. The men were complete masters of their legs, carried their weapons well, held their heads straight, faced right without moving an eye, and wheeled so excellently without their officers having to shout much, that the regiment looked like it was dressed in line with a string... I have seen many soldiers of this army without shoe, with tattered breeches and uniforms patched with all sorts of colored cloth, without neckband and only the lid of a hat, who marched and stood their guard as proudly as the best uniformed soldier in the world, despite the raw weather and hard rain in October. But he keeps his piece clean and shining, and powders his hair as white as possible with provisions flour when on grand parades...from this one can perceive what an enthusiasm— which these poor fellows call 'Liberty' – can do![65]

It is clear from these testimonies that Otho Williams had the privilege to lead tough, disciplined men in the Continental Line, soldiers who had who been given the best training the American Army could provide. There were others on the American side whose primary duties were to conduct raids, gather intelligence, protect supply lines, and stand guard over fixed positions.

Many of those troops would join the colors for only a few days or weeks at a time, and then return home to help with the planting or the harvest, or attend to other important personal matters, but Williams and his fellow Continentals were in this fight to the finish. If these Continental troops could stand up to formidable attacks of British professionals, there was hope that independence could eventually be won.

Otho Holland Williams learned the profession of arms in an army led by George Washington, whose influence on a young officer's knowledge of strategy and tactics was important. In the same letter in which he suggested books for Colonel William Woodford and his officers to read, he laid down some philosophies of leadership that must have influenced the development of young officers like Williams:

> *The best general advice I can give, and which I am sure you stand in no need of, is to be strict in your discipline; that is, to require nothing unreasonable of your officers and men, but see that whatever is required be punctually complied with. Reward and punish every man according to his merit, without partiality or prejudice; hear his complaints; if well founded, redress them; if otherwise, discourage them, in order to prevent frivolous ones. Discourage vice in every shape, and impress upon the mind of every man, from the first to the lowest, the importance of the cause, and what it is they are contending for. For ever keep in view the necessity of guarding against surprises. In all your marches, at times, at least, even when there is no possible danger, move with front, rear, and flank guards, that they may be familiarized to the use; and be regular in your encampments, appointing necessary guards for the security of your camp. In short, whether you expect an enemy or not, this should be practised; otherwise your attempts will be confused and awkward, when necessary. Be plain and precise in your orders, and keep copies of them to refer to, that no mistakes may happen. Be easy and condescending in your deportment to your officers, but not too familiar, lest you subject yourself to a want of that respect, which is necessary to support a proper command.*[66]

Soldiering in the South

Williams wrote home shortly after his arrival in the South to describe the challenges of that service:

> *The affairs of our little southern army are much deranged, and we find ourselves under very considerable embarrassments in our present position; the want of provisions is an inconvenience we have often experienced, but we have never been in a country so unwilling to supply us as at present. By military authority, we collect a kind of casual subsistence that can scarcely be called our daily bread. The fatigue of campaigning in this country is almost inconceivable. I have slept, when I have had time to sleep, in my clothes. I seldom divest myself of my sword, boots or coat; my horse is constantly saddled, and we eat when provisions are to be got, and we have nothing else to do… I find myself so capable of sustaining the fatigue, and by my good fortune (the favor of Providence) I have so often escaped the danger, that I am contented to do my duty, and submit myself to that fate which Heaven ordains.*[67]

The fighting in the South would be a formidable test of soldiering.

---

1 Williams, Otho Holland. "Narrative of Col. Otho Williams." Found Appendix B of William Johnson's Life and Correspondence of Nathanael Greene, Vol. I. (hereafter Williams, Narrative (in Johnson, *Greene*.)) P. 485.
2 Williams would serve as "Deputy" Adjutant General subsequently under DeKalb, Horatio Gates and Nathanael Greene. He carried out the duties of Adjutant General for each of these commands, but the term "Deputy" indicated that in addition to reporting operationally to DeKalb, Gates, or Greene directly, he also had an administrative reporting relationship to the Adjutant General of the Army, who reported to Commander-in-Chief George Washington
3 Kapp, *Kalb*. P. 207 and endnote 92 on P. 273.
4 Washington, George. Letter to Baron von Steuben. Written at Philadelphia, February 8, 1782. *Washington Papers*.
5 Kapp, *Kalb*. P. 195.
6 Ibid. P. 196.
7 Washington, George. Letter to Governor Richard Caswell. Written April 7, 1780 at Head Quarters, Morris Town. Washington sent a very similar letter to Governor John Rutledge on April 15th, 1780, the day before the Maryland and Delaware troops left Morristown. *Washington Papers*.
8 Kapp, *Kalb*. P. 198. Kapp cites "Diary of Christopher Marshall in Philadelphia (MS.), communicated by William Duane, Esq. of that city."
9 Ibid. P. 199.
10 Ibid. P. 199.
11 Williams, Otho Holland. Letter to his brother, Elie Williams. Written at Fredericksburg, Virginia, June 20, 1780. *Williams Papers*. Part 1/8. (Item # 48.)
12 De Kalb, Johann. Letter to his wife. Written at Goshen, North Carolina, June 21, 1780. Cited in Kapp, *Kalb*. P. 200.
13 Ibid. P. 200.
14 Ibid. P. 201.
15 Greene, Nathanael. Letter to his wife. Greene. *Life of Greene, (Volume III.)* P.208.
16 Lee, *Memoirs*. P. 36.

17 See Footnote.
18 Lossing, Benson J. *Pictorial Field-Book of the Revolution* (hereafter Lossing, *Field-Book*.) Harper Brothers. New York. 1850. P. 422.
19 Ibid. Pp. 392-393.
20 Greene, Nathanael. Letter to General Daniel Morgan. Written at Camp on Pedee, S.C. January 19th, 1781. *Greene Papers*. 7:147.
21 Washington, George. Letter to Governor Thomas Jefferson of Virginia. Written at Head Quarters, Passaic Falls. November 8, 1780. *Washington Papers*.
22 Pancake, John S. *This Destructive War. The British Campaign in the Carolinas, 1780-1782.* (hereafter Pancake, *This Destructive War.*) The University of Alabama Press. Tuscaloosa and London. Pp. 215-216.
23 Tarleton, *History*. P. 523.
24 Ibid. P. 523.
25 Saffell, W.T.R. *Records of the Revolutionary War Containing the Military and Financial Correspondence of Distinguished Officers*. Third Edition. 1894. P. 102.
26 Ibid. P. 105.
27 Lee, *Memoirs*. P. 386.
28 The Charlotte Museum of History has constructed a diorama of Charlotte as it appeared in 1780, including the courthouse, which is depicted as a log cabin mounted on brick pillars, challenging Lee's memory that the Courthouse was built of stone. There is a drawing of this courthouse between pages 40 and 41 of *General Joseph Graham and his Papers on North Carolina Revolutionary History William A. Graham*. Published for the Author by Edwards & Broughton. Raleigh. 1904.
29 Lee, *Memoirs*. P. 196.
30 Graham, William A. "The Battle of Ramseur's Mill." In "The North Carolina Booklet. Great Events in North Carolina History, Vol. 4, No.2." (June 1904). E. M. Uzzell and Company, Printers and Binders. Raleigh: North Carolina Society Daughters of the Revolution, 1904. 1st ed. P. 6. Cited in Sherman, William Thomas. *Calendar and Record of the Revolutionary War in the South: 1780-1781. Ninth Edition*. 2014 P. 16.
31 Tarleton, *History*. P. 163.
32 See Footnote.
33 Lossing, *Field-Book*. P. 440.
34 Lossing, Benson J. *Pictorial Field-Book of the Revolution, Volume 2* (hereafter Lossing *Field-Book, Volume 2.*). New York. Harper & Brothers Publishers. 1852. P. 647.
35 Ibid. P. 648.
36 Buchanan, John. The Road to Guilford Courthouse (hereafter Buchanan, *Road to Guilford Courthouse*.) John Wiley & Sons, Inc. New York et. al. 1997. pp. 95-100 is the source for the most of the information herein on Thomas Brown (sometimes spelled "Browne" in the various references.); Buchanan cites Edward J. Cashin's biography of Brown (*The King's Ranger - Thomas Brown and the American Revolution On The Southern Frontier*. University of Georgia. Athens 1999.)
37 Ibid. P. 192.
38 Lee, *Memoirs*. P. 357.
39 Williams, Otho Holland. Letter to Elie Williams. Written at Camp before Ninety-Six, South Carolina. June 12, 1781. *Williams Papers*. Part 1/8. (Item # 106.)
40 Lee, *Memoirs*. P. 553.
41 Davie, William Richardson. *Recollections of Colonel William R. Davie*. In Commager and Morris. P. 1138.
42 Pension application of Moses Hall W10105. Southern Campaigns Revolutionary War Pension Statements & Rosters. http://revwarapps.org/
43 Lossing, *Field Book. Volume 2*. P. 635.
44 Williams, Otho Holland. Letter to General Daniel Morgan. Written at Camp P.D., 25th January, 1781. In Myers, T. Bailey, Ed. *Cowpens Papers. Being Correspondence of General Morgan and the Prominent Actors. From the Collection of Theodorus Bailey Myers. Contributed to the Centennial Celebration* (hereafter Myers, *Cowpens Papers.*) The News and Courier. Charleston, South Carolina. May 11th, 1881. P. 33.
45 Pancake, *This Destructive War*. P. 217
46 Seymour, William, Sergeant Major, Delaware Regiment. "*Journal of the Southern Expedition, 1780-1783*," (hereafter Seymour, *Journal*) published in the Pennsylvania Magazine of History and Biography, 7 (1883): 286-98, 377-94. P. 383.
47 Ibid. P. 379.
48 Ibid. P. 389.
49 Tarleton, *History*. P. 160.
50 Smith, Page. *A New Age Now Begins: A People's History of the American Revolution*. Vol. 2. P. 1392 Cited in Sherman, William Thomas. Calendar and Record of the Revolutionary War in the South: 1780-1781. Ninth Edition. 2014. P. 644.
51 Holmes, Richard. *Redcoat. The British Soldier in the Age of Horse and Musket* (hereafter Holmes, *Redcoat*.) Harper

Collins Publishers. London. 2001. P. 165.
52 Pearson, Michael. *Those Damned Rebels. The American Revolution As Seen Through British Eyes* (hereafter Pearson, *Rebels*.) First Da Capo Press Edition. 2000. P. 69.
53 Holmes. *Redcoat*. p. 219-220.
54 Ibid. Pp. 220.
55 Pearson, *Rebels*. P. 57.
56 Ibid. P. 57.
57 Pancake, *This Destructive War*. P. 54.
58 Greene, Nathanael. Letter to Colonel Otho Holland Williams. Written at Col. William Moore's, N.C. February 13, 1781. *Greene Papers*. 7:285.
59 Washington, George. Letter to Meshech Weare, et al, October 18, 1780, Circular Letter on Continental Army. *Washington Papers*.
60 Washington, George. General Orders. Head-Quarters, Morristown, May 8, 1777. *Washington Papers*.; in a letter to Colonel William Woodford, written at Cambridge, Massachusetts on November 10, 1775, Washington mentioned five books that "As to the manual exercise, the evolutions and manoeuvres of a regiment, with other knowledge necessary to the soldier, you will acquire them from those authors, who have treated upon these subjects," and then names Humphrey Bland, A Treatise of Military Discipline (9th ed., London, 1762); Lancelot Théodore, comte de Turpin de Crissé, An Essay on the Art of War, translated by Capt. Joseph Otway (London, 1761); Roger Stevenson, Military Instructions for Officers Detached in the Field (Philadelphia, 1775); Captaine de Jeney, The Partisan: or, The Art of Making War in Detachment, translated by J. Berkenhout (London, 1760); and William Young, Manœuvres, or Practical Observations on the Art of War (London, 1771, all of which were among the books in Washington's personal library. From George Washington to Colonel William Woodford, 10 November 1775," Founders Online, National Archives (http://founders.archives.gov/documents/Washington/03-02-02-0320, ver. 2014-05-09). Source: The Papers of George Washington, Revolutionary War Series, vol. 2, 16 September 1775–31 December 1775, ed. Philander D. Chase. Charlottesville: University Press of Virginia, 1987, pp. 346–347.
61 George Washington's personal library included books that he specifically recommended to his officers, including" Humphrey Bland, *A Treatise of Military Discipline* (9th ed., London, 1762); Lancelot Théodore, comte de Turpin de Crissé, *An Essay on the Art of War*, translated by Capt. Joseph Otway (London, 1761); Roger Stevenson, *Military Instructions for Officers Detached in the Field* (Philadelphia, 1775); Captaine de Jeney, *The Partisan: or, The Art of Making War in Detachment*, translated by J. Berkenhout (London, 1760); and William Young, *Manœuvres, or Practical Observations on the Art of War* (London, 1771). Ref: Note 3 to letter from George Washington to William Woodford, November 10, 1775. In Founders Online Series from the National Archives.
62 The Society of the Cincinnati Library in Washington, D.C. holds eight pages of hand-written notes in the writing of Otho Holland Williams, folded, apparently, to fit into a pocket or carrier of some sort. The contents are copied from "Military Institutions of Vegetius in five books, translated from the original Latin. With a preface and notes. By Lieutenant John Clarke," printed in London, 1767.
63 Ewald, Johann. *Diary of the American War: A Hessian Journal*. (hereafter Ewald, Diary.) Translated and edited by Joseph P. Tustin. Yale University Press, New Haven and London, 1979. P. 108.
64 Letter from the Residents of Salem, North Carolina to Nathanael Greene. February 8, 1781. *Greene Papers*. 7:260-261.
65 Ewald, *Diary*. Pp. 340-341.
66 From George Washington to Colonel William Woodford, 10 November 1775. Founders Online, National Archieves (http://founders.archives.gov/documents/Washington/03-02-02-0320, ver. 2014-05-09). Source: The Papers of George Washington, Revolutionary War Series, vol. 2, 16 September 1775-31 December 1775, ed. Philander D. Chase, Charlottevsville: University Press of Virginia 1987, pp.346-347.
67 Tiffany, *Sketch*. P. 14.

CHAPTER 5

THE BATTLE OF CAMDEN
REBUILDING THE ARMY[1]

Colonel Otho Williams marched south with Maryland and Delaware troops who were tough professional soldiers, signed up for long enlistments, not just for the few weeks or months that were typical of militia callups. Williams and his men were in this fight for the duration.

Many of the Maryland troops had spent the winter of 1777/78 in Wilmington, Delaware, and then marched to Valley Forge the following spring, where they were trained in the techniques that Baron von Steuben had developed. These men were accustomed to a daily life of drill and discipline, and they were some of the best trained soldiers in the American Army.

By the time that Williams was ordered to the Carolinas with his regiment in 1780, the officers in this Continental force had become seasoned military leaders. At the start of the war, many officers had been awarded their positions based on family or political connections, but over time, the harsh realities of combat and military life largely weeded out men who did not meet the demanding standards imposed by the Commander-in-Chief. Washington and his staff tried very hard to ensure that performance was the main consideration for promotion, and they tried to bypass officers who showed little commitment or ability. Congress was, of course, subject to politics and could, particularly early in the war, urge Washington to promote well-connected people from members' constituencies, or foreign officers who had impressed them. Even when Williams went to the Carolinas, it was still possible to hold a high military position based on political considerations or European rank, but military competence was increasingly the standard that determined promotion in the Army. Writing long after the war, historian George Washington Greene, grandson of Nathanael Greene who had been Otho Williams' commander, noted the following in his biographical sketch of Williams:

> *Beginning his military career with no advantage of military training, his rare intelligence led him directly to the true sources, and gave him a clear perception of the fundamental principles of the science.*[2]

As he entered the campaign in the South, Otho Williams had been in the army for almost six years, and had gained worthwhile experience in combat, leadership and army administration. He was serving with very capable troops of the Continental Line, men had who been given the best training that the American army could provide. If they could hold their own against their professional British foes, the war might be won.

Horatio Gates is Appointed to Command the Southern Army

While Baron de Kalb, Otho Williams, and their men were struggling to find enough food and keep moving further south, Congress was working to provide the southern army with a new commander. The capture of General Lincoln and his entire force at Charleston had left the foreigner de Kalb in command of the only remaining Continental Army in the South, and there was a consensus that an American should command in the southern theater. Congress had a favorite for the post, Major General Horatio Gates, whose reputation stood very high with many of the legislators, largely because of his impressive victory at the Battle of Saratoga in 1777.

Saratoga had been a turning point for the American cause, and this victory gave France the confidence to enter into a formal alliance with the Americans. Gates, who had been in command, was given credit for the victory, but he had benefited greatly from the astute selection of a defensive position before he had arrived, and to the battlefield heroics of men like Benedict Arnold and Daniel Morgan. Congress had made Gates Chairman of the Board of War, a position in which he had significant influence in all military matters.

Even though Washington retained his post as Commander-in-Chief, the lines of authority between Washington and Gates were somewhat blurred. Washington was not sure whether or not to expect Gates to join the main army around New York for the 1780 campaign, and he humbled himself to write Gates directly to discover his intentions:

> *Sir: As the opening of the campaign is fast approaching, and it is time to form a general disposition of the Army with a view to it, it is essential I should know, as soon as possible, what General Officers will be present. For this purpose, I am to request you will inform me, without delay, whether the situation of your private affairs will permit you to take the field this campaign or not, and if you do take the field, when we may hope to see you at Camp.*[3]

While Washington pondered whether or not Gates would be rejoining him for the summer campaign, Gates' allies in Congress were working to obtain the southern command for him. On June 6th, Congressman John Armstrong, Sr., the father of one of Gates' aides, wrote from Philadelphia that "… your call to the field may be Set down as Certain, but the time when, & the place where, as uncertain; it may be in a fortnight, and yet may not be until the Fall."[4]

On June 13th, less than two weeks after Washington had asked Gates if he intended to return to the northern army, Congress resolved unanimously that "Major General Gates immediately repair to and take command in the southern department,"[5] a decision that was made without consulting the Commander-in-Chief. Gates' orders were written with great deference to the hero of Saratoga, and were dispatched by Samuel Huntington, the President of Congress, that very day:

> *Enclosed you will receive the Orders of Congress of this Day, to take the Command in the southern Department......You are doubtless informed that the Continental Troops of the Delaware and Maryland Lines under Baron De Kalb are gone to the southward, and it is probable a considerable Body of Militia from North Carolina & Virginia are assembled and collecting to cover the Country from the ravages of the Enemy.*
> *As Congress are unable without further Information to give any particular Orders, your own Prudence & Experience will dictate the most proper Measures to be adopted as Circumstances shall appear".*[6]

Huntington's assurance that a "considerable Body of Militia from North Carolina & Virginia" was assembling may have given Gates the impression that he was going to be enthusiastically supported by the people, troops and governments of the South.

The day after Gates' appointment, Congress endorsed the recommendations of the Board of War to give him substantial power over the organization and operation of the southern army, again with no direct involvement by Commander-in-Chief Washington. Congress was doing all in its power to give General Gates all the tools he needed to succeed, decreeing:

> *That Major General Gates be and he is hereby authorised and empowered to take such measures, from time to time, for the defence of the southern states as he shall think most proper: and it is earnestly recommended to the governments of the said states to give every assistance in their power for carrying such measures into execution.*[7]

Gates, who was at his home Traveler's Rest in Virginia during these negotiations, was represented in Philadelphia by his aide, John Armstrong, Jr., and his aide's father, Congressman John Armstrong, Sr. The two Armstrongs worked directly with the Board of War and Congress to obtain all possible support for Gates' efforts. Armstrong, Sr. added a postscript to his June 15th letter to Gates that he was worried that his son's delicate constitution would not permit him to serve in the warm climate in the south.[8] Young Armstrong may have been a good soldier and a competent aide, but Gates must also have considered his father's position as a Congressman when he made the decision to keep the young man close by his side.

Gates' appointment was ardently supported by many in Congress who believed that affairs in the South would take a positive turn under such an accomplished soldier. The sentiments that Georgia Representative Richard Howly[9]* expressed in a July 28th letter to Gates are representative of the support enjoyed by the new southern Commander:

> *Its with a high Degree of Satisfaction, I consider your appointment to the command of the Southern department. The gloom thrown over our affairs in that quarter, by the heavy losses we Sustained in Charlestown, must give way to the consideration, of having an officer called forth to the general direction; whose zeal and abilities are competent, to the management of the most hazardous matters. Whilst I congratulate my country on the Principle, I wish you with great ardency Success in the Event, and as it will be the business of Congress to afford you all necessary and possible Support. I must consider it as an indispensable Duty on me, from a knowledge of the Department you are engaged in, to give you Every information, that may be useful in the attainment of your object.*[10]

Meantime, George Washington was sensitive to the effort to have Gate bypass him as Commander-in-Chief and report directly to Congress. Characteristically, he proceeded carefully, confiding to Virginia Congressman Joseph Jones:

> *Considering the delicate situation in which I stand with respect to General Gates, I feel an unwillingness to give any opinion*

---

*Howly was elected to Congress from Georgia on January 11th, 1780 and served through September, 1781.

> *(even in a confidential way) in a matter in which he is concerned, lest my Sentiments (being known) should have unfavourable interpretation ascribed to them by illiberal Minds.*[11]

Although Washington and his supporters kept largely silent as Horatio Gates prepared to march south, the new southern commander was inundated with praise from his many ardent supporters. A lonely pessimistic voice stands out in the din, that of Gates' old friend and neighbor, the disgraced Major General Charles Lee, who cautioned "take care, lest your Northern laurels turn to Southern willows."[12]

In spite of Charles Lee's warning, Gates seemed to be very enthusiastic for the task ahead, as he expressed in a letter to Benjamin Lincoln, who had been forced to surrender Charleston to the British:

> *I wish to save the Southern States. I wish to recover the territories we have lost. I wish to restore you to your Command, and to reinstate you to the Dignity, to which your Virtues, and your Perseverance, have so justly entitled you*[13]

The Board of War supported Gates by recalling to active duty officers whom he felt would be of value to his command, and on Friday, June 16th, 1780, Congress called on General George Weedon and Colonel Daniel Morgan to serve with the southern army. Weedon had been permitted to retire on August 18th, 1778, with the proviso that he could be called back to the service if "the difficulties he then laboured under should be removed."[14]* Morgan had resigned on July 18th, 1779 when he was not given command of the light infantry. Congress had decided to grant him a furlough instead of allowing him to resign, so that he could be called back to the Army if needed.[15] Morgan had played an indispensable role in Gates' successful Saratoga campaign, and the new Commander of the southern army wisely sought to have this veteran warrior at his side once again.

★ ★ ★ ★ ★

Gates Takes Command

As Gates moved south to join his command, he communicated to Baron

---

*Weedon did not join the Southern army but held a command in the Virginia militia, where he served effectively in the decisive Yorktown campaign of 1781.

de Kalb that he was on his way, and the Baron replied respectfully and with a sense of relief:

> *I am happy by your arrival, for I have struggled with a good many difficulties for provisions ever since I arrived in this State;… The design I had to move nearer the enemy to drive them from Peedee River, a plentiful country, has been defeated by the impossibility of subsisting on the road, and no immediate supplies to be depended on in the first instances after a difficult march.*[16]

Gates replied from Hillsborough, North Carolina, where he was working to obtain supplies and other support for the Army:

> *I am astonished at your distress and difficulties, and have ever since my arrival here upon last Tuesday been endeavoring to alleviate them.*[17]

Gates added that "I think all my writing business will be finished to-day; if so, I shall set out tomorrow for camp, and hope to be with you on Saturday,"[18] and he sent Major Armstrong[19] on to announce his approach.

The new commander arrived at the American camp at Deep River on Tuesday, July 25th, and assumed command of the Southern army on that date.[20] He was received with decorum and respect by the veteran professional soldier de Kalb, and the ceremonies included a salute fired by the Army's little artillery unit. Gates was equally gracious to de Kalb, and showed him the respect of approving his standing orders.[21]

Gates acted energetically for the next few weeks, immediately issuing the order for the troops to be "in readiness to march at a moment's warning," This order "…was a matter of great astonishment to those who knew the real situation of the troops."[22] The new commander had been briefed by de Kalb on the destitute condition of the men, yet Gates must have been confident somehow that a forward movement would alleviate the army's distress.

The reasons for this confidence are not entirely clear. He may have naively accepted the assurances of the Virginia and North Carolina governments that they would provide material support to his army, or he may have expected that he could obtain provisions by moving forward and merging his force with General Caswell's North Carolina militia. It also seems possible that he may have simply thought that the region in which the army was camped was depleted of resources, and that more could be obtained by forging ahead.

De Kalb's biographer surmised 100 years later that Gates had "evidently wanted to distinguish himself by a quick and energetic advance,"[23] and it does seem possible that the General's supreme self-confidence was part of what spurred him on. He was apparently so intent on moving further south that he was undeterred by the fact that he had to leave two brass cannons and some baggage behind for lack of horses.[24]

Colonel Otho Williams and de Kalb were two of the many officers who felt that any movement forward was ill-advised at this time, especially since Gates had specified that the Army would march on the direct route to Camden, South Carolina, a path that was thought to be through a barren region where supplies would be very scanty, at best. Men who knew the area better than Gates felt that it would be better to swing west through Salisbury and Charlotte, thereby passing through a land that was comparatively rich in provisions and populated by ardent supporters of the American cause.

Gates got his army underway, but his commanders were uneasy with that decision. Williams and Gates were acquaintances,[25] and de Kalb prompted Williams to urge Gates to change his mind on the timing and the path of the march into South Carolina. Williams wrote in his *Narrative* that he tried every conceivable argument to convince Gates to redirect the movement,[26*, 27] and the general finally agreed to confer with his commanders when the march halted for the noon meal. Williams noted that "the writer don't know" if such a conference actually took place, but the march resumed in its direct southward path toward Camden after the noonday break, through a region that Williams said was even more barren than had been advertised.[28]

The land may have been as sterile and unproductive as Williams wrote in his *Narrative*, but the troops marched 18 miles on July 27th, 18 miles on July 28th, and 18 miles on July 29th, according to the reliable *Journal* of Robert Kirkwood.[29] After resting at Smiths Mill during torrential thunder storms for the next two days,[30] they resumed their march on August 1st, marching 10 miles that day, and then 18 on August 2nd, 18 on August 3rd, and 17 on August 4th. Altogether, from the time that the men set out from Deep River on July 27th until they reached the vicinity of Camden, South Carolina on August 15th, they marched 189 miles in 20 calendar days, an average of 13.5

---

*Williams wrote his *Narrative* after the actual events, and seems to have yielded somewhat to the natural human tendency to show his own actions positively.

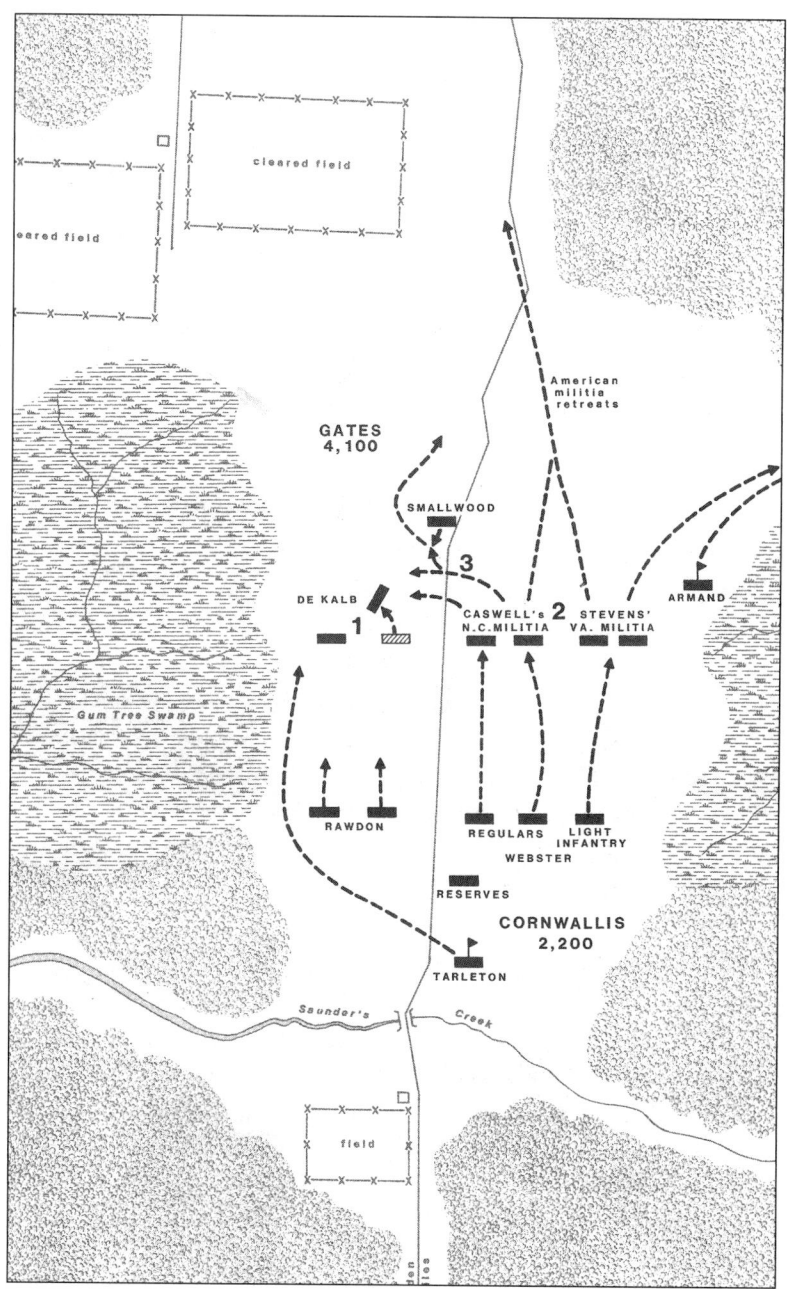

Map 4 - The Battle of Camden

miles a day for the 14 days they marched (there were no marches on July 30th or 31st, when there was a "terrific thunderstorm"[31], or on August 5th, 7th, 9th, or 14th.)[32] There were undoubtedly serious supply problems during this campaign, but the case may have been overstated in Williams' after-the-fact *Narrative*, in the pleading letters of southern army commanders, and in the writing of early historians, references that seem inclined to characterize the army as famished and desperately in want of supplies.[33]

Still, it was a difficult march, as described by Seargant Major William Seymour of the Delaware Continentals:

> *This is a poor barren part of the country. The inhabitants are chiefly of a Scotch extraction, living in mean cottages, and are much disaffected, being great enemies to their country.*[34]

One of the methods that Gates apparently used to encourage the soldiers to keep moving forward was to promise them that plenteous provisions would be growing in the fields up ahead on the Pee Dee River, and Williams stated that when they arrived there on August 1st:

> *...the preceding crop of corn (the principle article of produce) was exhausted, and the new grain, although luxuriant and fine, was unfit for use. Many of the soldiery, urged by necessity, plucked the green ears and boiled them with the lean beef, which was collected in the woods, made for themselves a repast, not unpalatable to be sure, but which was attended with painful effects. Green peaches also were substituted for bread and had similar consequences.*[35]

Williams added that some of the officers used their hair powder to thicken their soup.[36]

Robert Kirkwood and his Delaware troops crossed the Pee Dee River on August 1st,[37] and he must have been with a forward screening force, as Williams stated that the army crossed that river in bateau on August 3rd.[38] Lieutenant Colonel Charles Porterfield, a respected officer, met the army on the south bank of the Pee Dee, and Colonel Francis Marion, who had been with the army, was dispatched by Gates to gather intelligence on the British.[39] Some corn was obtained and ground at May's Mill, and the troops were given a meal, after which, Williams later wrote, "all was again content, cheerfulness, and mirth. It was astonishing as it was pleasing to observe the transition."[40] Napoleon was right. An army marches on its stomach.

On August 6th, Gates accepted Major Armstrong's illness and announced in his General Orders that "Colonel Williams, Inspector of the Maryland Division, having obligingly accepted to act as Deputy Adjutant General of the southern army during the illness of Major Armstrong, he is be obeyed as such, and all orders coming from Col Williams as Depy Adjutant Genl are to be obeyed."[41]

Gates was apparently well aware that the troops had been unhappy with their limited rations, and he felt that he had to justify his actions to his Adjutant General, so he explained his motivations to Williams for proceeding on the path he had chosen: (1) he needed to overtake the North Carolina militia commanded by the elusive General Caswell so that he could merge the two forces (2) that the Governor of North Carolina had informed him that substantial supplies of provisions had been forwarded to Caswell, and (3) that having started on the direct route, a return to Deep River and a swing to the west would be viewed by the populace as a retreat.[42][43]

Gates was apparently surprised that the North Carolina government had not provided the supplies that he had been promised earlier, and he wrote in a very concerned and disappointed tone to Governor Nash on August 3rd:

> *The distress this army has suffered and still continues to suffer for want of provisions has perhaps destroyed the finest opportunity that could be presented of driving in the enemy's advanced posts, in all likelihood even unto Charleston... I'm astonished that I have not intelligence of any flour coming to me from the interior part of the State. Your Excellency cannot believe this miserable country, already ravaged by the enemy and gleaned by the militia under Generals Caswell and Rutherford, can afford a handful to me... I am anxious that this letter should find your Excellency and the Executive Council at Hillsboro, exerting all your authority and influence to supply your almost famished troops.*[44]

To add to Gates' vexations, General Caswell of the North Carolina militia was sending him conflicting reports, some of which seemed to assume that Caswell was Gates' equal, an attitude which Adjutant General Williams found inappropriate. On August 5th, Caswell reported that he was about to attack a fortified British post on Lynch's Creek. This motivated Gates to urge his force to move even faster, because he had little faith that Caswell could competently execute such an attack. The very next day, Caswell submitted another report, this time expressing worry that he might be attacked by the same British force that he had said he was going to attack only a day earlier.[45] It seems understandable that Gates wanted to overtake this apparently unpredictable militia commander and to exercise experienced military leadership over Caswell's troops.

General Gates and Colonel Otho Williams rode to General Caswell's camp on the afternoon of August 6th, and, while they were received graciously enough, and "regaled with wine and other novelties, exquisitely grateful and pleasingly exhilarating." The guests saw that the militia camp was haphazard and poorly organized, and that "tables, chairs, bedsteads, benches, and many other articles of heavy and cumbrous household stuff, were scattered before the tent doors in great disorder."[46] De Kalb's biographer noted that Gates and Williams found the officers of Caswell's command "living in abundance,"[47] which would possibly explain what had happened to some of the provisions that the government of North Carolina had gathered to send the Continental Army.

Gates forced a junction between his Continentals and the North Carolina militia the next day, August 7th, and Caswell seemed to accept his subordinate position graciously enough. In Williams' words, "The Baron De Kalb commanded the right wing of the army, composed of the regular troops, and General Caswell the left, of militia."[48] This logical system of organization - having the militia under one commander and the Continentals under another – may have set the stage for problems at any upcoming battle.

The forces of de Kalb and Caswell merged at about noon on the 7th, and Gates led them off that very afternoon toward the enemy's position on Lynch's Creek. Colonel Williams and Lieutenant Colonel Ford of the Maryland Continentals, who was officer of the day, inspected the American camp and found crisp military procedures in effect among the Maryland and Delaware Continentals, and extremely lax procedures in the militia camp. Perhaps fortunately, the British had evacuated their position on Lynch's Creek, and fallen back to a better position closer to Camden. Gates was apparently buoyed by the retreat of the small British detachment, and Williams noted that "General Gates saw himself master of the field."[49]

Gates was now in the presence of the enemy, but his scouts had not provided accurate information on the size and disposition of the force, nor on the approach of British reinforcements to the area. As he moved forward toward a possible clash with the British, Gates ordered that a number of wagons carry all the army's heavy baggage to Charlotte, with as many of the women and children that could be induced to leave,[50*] but a large number of the women would not leave their men. In addition to bonds of affection, they felt safer under the protection of the army, and better assured that they would have enough to eat.[51]

General Gates advanced forward toward Little Lynch's Creek, but when he arrived there he found the British in a strong position. On August 11th, he maneuvered the American army to the right[52], using Maryland Continental Colonel Josias Hall and a detachment of 300 men to shield his left flank and then become a rear guard after the Army had passed. The British commander, Lord Rawdon, pulled all his troops back into Camden,[53] where he dug in to await the arrival of Lord Cornwallis, who was marching with reinforcements from Charleston.

Gates' men lay on their arms all night on August 12th/13th,[54] so that they would be ready to move in an instant if they were attacked by the nearby British forces. The Americans marched 16 miles to Rugeley's Mill[55] on August 13th,[56] where they were joined on the 14th by General Edward Stevens and a contingent of Virginia militia.[57] The Virginia troops were a welcome addition, but they had been on a grueling march, and had worn themselves out trying to catch up with the Army. John Eager Howard of Maryland later wrote that:

> ...*the heat was so oppressive they could not march in the day, and therefore they had for several nights made forced marches to come up with us, which broke the spirits* of the *men*.[58]

On the 15th, an inhabitant of Camden entered the American camp, and, acting in a friendly manner, promised to return to the town and collect good intelligence for the Americans. Williams and his fellow officers were suspicious that the man was spying for the British, but Gates apparently accepted his word and allowed him to return to the city in good graces.[59]

Williams grumbled in his *Narrative* that Stevens and the Virginians had apparently traveled to join Gates using out-of-the-way routes, so their arrival was not widely known, which was viewed as a missed opportunity to "spirit up" American supporters in the region. Williams also noted that Stevens' only significant addition to the army's provisions was a supply of molasses,

---

*Both armies had a number of women and children that followed them. They often helped with chores such as washing clothes and cooking. Some were family members, and some were not.

and, with post-campaign twenty-twenty vision, he observed that Gates might have been very wise to wait right here for additional troops and supplies to come in. Gates was still acting aggressively, and on August 15th he issued General Orders that directed his army to move out at 10 o'clock that night. The troops were to "...observe the profoundest silence upon the march; and any soldier who offers to fire without the command of his officer, must be instantly put to death."[60]

When Gates had completed writing this order and given it to his Adjutant General, Otho Williams, to distribute, he also mentioned that he had seven thousand troops now under his command, a figure which Williams immediately questioned, according to his *Narrative*. He called the general officers to a council with Gates in Rugeley's Barn to review Gates' orders, and he directed them to provide accurate returns of the actual number of troops in their commands. Since he was not required to attend the council, Williams made hurried visits to the various commands and gathered their reports of the number of men that were present. He completed his rounds quickly, and returned to the council meeting just as it was breaking up, where he reported that there were "exactly three thousand and fifty-two" rank and file who were present and fit for duty. Gates had just heard the alarming news that his force was only 43% of what he had thought it had been, but he still remarked, "...these are enough for our purpose." The Commanding General further pointed out that there were thirteen general officers in the council, and that none had objected to his aggressive General Orders.[61]

Williams' *Narrative* maintained that there was widespread opposition to Gates' aggressiveness, but that all the opposition was stated in private, not in the open forum of the council of general officers. Williams wrote that Colonel Armand, the cavalry leader who was to lead the advance and scout ahead for enemy contacts, was particularly upset with Gates' orders, because he felt that they took away some of the cavalryman's prerogatives, and he also objected because "cavalry had never been put in the front of a line of battle in the dark." In spite of the consternation in the ranks of the generals, the army marched off as ordered, and no one appears to have openly challenged Gates' orders.[62]

It was standard practice before a battle to give the men a ration of rum to fortify them for the rigors of combat. Since no spirits were available, someone suggested that the molasses that Stevens had brought might be an acceptable substitute. This was done, and the troops had a dessert made of molasses mixed with mush or dumplings, which acted like a laxative. As a result the troops were "breaking ranks all night" as they moved forward into the unknown dangers ahead.[63]

★ ★ ★ ★ ★

Gates and George Washington

Gates may have felt that he was in a powerful position now, and well on his way to a second glorious victory that would add to the laurels he had won at Saratoga. He had been active and aggressive since assuming the command of the southern army, and he was clearly acting on his own initiative. Commander-in-Chief George Washington worried and wondered what was transpiring "to the southward," since Gates apparently made no effort to keep him informed, as Washington had requested when he was appointed to the southern command. Washington's letter of August 12 expresses his concern:

> *In mine of the 18th July I desired you to make frequent communications of the situation of affairs to the Southward. I cannot forbear repeating my wish on this subject, as circumstances may require a sudden alteration of our present plans; and should the transference of the whole or a part of the force of our Allies to the southward be deemed eligible, it will be necessary that we should be acquainted before hand with your strength, expectations and resources; and with the number, position and circumstances of the Enemy. You may depend upon every intelligence from me, which can in any way affect or be interesting to the operations in your quarter.*[64]

In addition to offering Gates whatever intelligence he had that might be helpful to the southern commander, Washington also detached an experienced military engineer, Colonel Thaddeus Kosciusko, from his command and sent him to help Gates. Washington noted that he parted with Kosciusko reluctantly, and that he had "… experienced great satisfaction from his general conduct, and particularly from the attention and zeal with which he has prosecuted the Works committed to his charge at West Point."[65]

Prelude to Battle

Colonel Thomas Sumter of South Carolina was a very independent militia commander who was respected for his knowledge of the country and his reputed capabilities to collect accurate intelligence on the enemy, but he was difficult to work with.[66] He had learned that the British were sending a significant supply of stores to Camden from Charleston, and he proposed to capture much needed ammunition, clothing, and other supplies from this detachment. Stressing the importance of this raid, Sumter asked Gates for infantry and artillery reinforcements, and Gates complied with Sumter's request, apparently confident that he had enough troops at hand to meet any contingency. Otho Williams wrote in his *Narrative* that:

> *The general ordered a detachment of one hundred regular infantry and a party of artillery, with two brass fieldpieces, under Lieutenant Colonel Woolford, to join Colonel Sumter, and act under his command.*[67]

The intelligence that Sumter had been providing to Gates may have been the basis for his confidence, as Sumter had told him that:

> *…they (the British) meant to make no great opposition at Camden, but that all their preparations were mere amusements, by which they expected to gain time to remove their sick and wounded.*[68]

Sumter ended this note with words that may have assured Gates even more: "The next of your favours I am honored with I hope will be from Santee or Camden."[69]

At about 2 a.m. on August 16th, Colonel Armand's cavalry made contact with the British, and had a brief encounter in which some of Armand's troopers were wounded. They retreated rapidly, throwing the First Maryland Regiment temporarily into disorder. In this melee, the brave Lieutenant Colonel Charles Porterfield of Virginia was severely wounded. Light Horse Harry Lee wrote that Porterfield was an officer "…whose promise of future greatness had endeared him to the whole army. Wounded in his brave stand in the morning, when our dragoons basely fled, he was taken off the field, never more to draw his sword."[70]

Both the British and the Americans took a few prisoners in this early skirmish, and Williams was startled to learn from one British captive that Lord Cornwallis had arrived from Charleston to reinforce Lord Rawdon. Williams rushed to Gates with the alarming news that over three thousand British regulars were forming a line of battle just five or six hundred yards in front of the Americans. Instead of enjoying superiority in numbers, the Americans were now up against a roughly equivalent force of British professionals.

Gates was astonished at this news, and immediately directed Williams to convene a Council of War. When Williams called on Baron de Kalb to tell him of the meeting, the Baron showed good military sense by asking, "…has the General given you orders to retreat the army?"[71]

When Gates met with his general officers, he informed them that they faced the combined forces of Rawdon and Cornwallis, and asked, "Gentlemen, what is best to be done?" There was silence for a few moments, and finally General Edward Stevens (whom Williams called "the gallant Stevens") of the Virginia militia said, "Gentlemen, is it not too late now to do anything but fight?" Williams recorded that no other officer spoke, and that Gates ordered them to return to their commands.[72]

Since Gates had decided to stand and fight, the American army spent the rest of the night filing into position for the next day's battle. The Maryland and Delaware regiments of regulars under de Kalb were placed on the right; the North Carolina militia under General Caswell took up their position in the center of the American line, and the Virginia militia under General Edward Stevens filed off to take up their positions on the left.

The troops spent a tense night, with the crackle of intermittent gunfire sounding in the darkness ahead, as the forward units of both armies probed and skirmished, trying to discover what lay in front of them.[73]

Gates formed his line of battle, which Colonel Christian Senf, Gates' Chief Engineer described as follows The Second Maryland Brigade (about 400 men) under Brigadier General Mordecai Gist was stationed on the right of the road leading to Camden, with two field pieces on his right. General de Kalb took station with this element of his command. There was an "almost impassable" swamp and Gregs Quarter Creek to the right of these units. On the left of Gist's Brigade in the main road were two field pieces and three brigades of North Carolina Militia of 1200 men under the Brigadiers Rutherford, Graidery, & Butler. To their left were two field pieces, and then the Virginia Militia of 700 men under Brigadier General Stevens, and then the Light Infantry of about 300 men under Colonel Porterfield. Colonel Armand with about 60 cavalry was in the rear of the Light Infantry to support the left. The First Maryland Brigade of about 400 men under Brigadier General Smallwood stood in the rear of the Line across the road, as a Corps of Reserve.[74]

★ ★ ★ ★ ★

The Battle of Camden

At dawn on August 16th, 1780, Adjutant General Otho Williams and artilleryman Captain Anthony Singleton saw the British marching toward the American lines. Singleton and Williams discussed the situation, and Williams ordered the American artillery to fire on the deploying enemy, hoping to disrupt them while they were shifting from their column formation into a line-abreast for battle. Williams quickly rode to General Gates and suggested that Stevens should strike the British right before they were able to complete their attack formation. Gates replied tersely, "Sir that's right, let it be done."[75] [76]

Williams undoubtedly relied on his early experience as a leader of riflemen when he took about forty-five volunteers from Stevens' ranks, and slid into the trees ahead of the British right, intending to pepper the deploying British ranks with several volleys that would delay the attack. Cornwallis spotted Williams' attempt on his right, and hurried his deployment. The British were in line and ready to attack before Williams' fire could significantly slow their efforts.[77]

The British moved forward aggressively, impressively arrayed in bright uniforms, perfectly aligned, and with all the panoply of an 18th century infantry attack. It was too much for the militia. The British advance quickly overwhelmed these troops on the American left, and:

> ...threw the whole body of the militia into such a panic that they generally threw down their loaded arms and fled in the utmost consternation. The unworthy example of the Virginians was almost instantly followed by the North Carolinians.[78]

A North Carolina militiaman named George Watts left a remarkable account of the militia panic at Camden when he submitted his pension application many years later. The memories of many old soldiers often tend to make their youthful military actions seem more noble than they actually were, and to try to associate themselves with important events and acts of valor. Watts, on the other hand, is brutally honest and his remarks give unique insight into a panic such as occurred at Camden:

> I well remember everything that occurred...I remember I was among the nearest to the enemy; that a man named John Summers was my file leader; that we had orders to wait for the word to commence firing; that the militia were in front and in a feeble condition at the time. They were fatigued. The weather was warm excessively. They had been fed a short time previously on molasses entirely.
> I can state on oath that I believe my gun was the first gun fired, notwithstanding the orders, for we were close to the enemy, who

> *appeared to maneuver in contempt of us, and I fired without thinking, except that I might prevent the man opposite from killing me.*
>
> *The discharge and loud roar soon became general from one end of the lines to the other. Amongst other things, I confess I was amongst the first that fled. The cause of that I cannot tell, except that everyone I saw was about to do the same. There was no effort to rally, no encouragement to fight. Officers and men joined in the flight. I threw away my gun, and, reflecting I might be punished for being found without arms, I picked up a drum, which gave forth such sounds when touched by twigs I cast it away.*
>
> *When we had gone, we heard the roar of guns still, but we knew not why. Had we known, we might have returned.*[79]

Although the Continental troops on the American right stayed in formation and presented an unbroken front, the final outcome of the battle had already been decided in these first few minutes. When the left and center of the American line melted away, British victory was inevitable.

Otho Williams saw it all from a front-row seat, and stated that "the writer avers it of his own knowledge, having seen and observed every part of the army, from left to right, during the action," and he wrote that "…a great majority of the militia, (at least two-thirds of the army) fled without firing a shot."[80]

Williams wrote of the sense of fear and panic that gripped men like Garret Watts and spread like wildfire through the ranks of the Virginia and North Carolina militia:

> *He who has never seen the effect of a panic upon a multitude can have but an imperfect idea of such a thing. The best disciplined troops have been enervated and made cowards by it. Armies have been routed by it, even where no enemy appeared to furnish an excuse. Like electricity, it operates instantaneously - like sympathy, it is irresistible where it touches.*[81]

Even after their Virginia and North Carolina comrades on the left broke and ran, the far right of the American line stood firm, displaying the courage and discipline that would become the hallmarks of the Maryland and Delaware Continentals.

> *The regular troops, who had the keen edge of sensibility rubbed off by strict discipline and hard service, saw the confusion with but little emotion. They engaged seriously in the affair; and, notwithstanding some irregularity, which was created by the militia breaking, pell mell, through the second line, order was restored there - time enough to give the enemy a severe check, which abated the fury of their assault, and obliged them to assume a more deliberate manner of acting.*[82]

The Continentals on the American right put up a stiff resistance, and even drove their adversaries back several times in the early fighting:

Williams's first-hand account of the heavy fighting on the right continued:

> *The second Maryland brigade, including the battalion of Delawares, on the right, were engaged with the enemy's left, which they opposed with very great firmness. They even advanced upon them, and had taken a number of prisoners, when their companions of the first Brigade (which formed the second line) being greatly outflanked, were obliged to give ground.*[83]

The obstinate fight on the right ebbed and flowed. At one juncture, the First Maryland Brigade began to waver, but

> *...Colonel Gunby, Major Anderson, and a number of other brave officers, assisted by the Deputy Adjutant General (Author's note: this was Otho Holland William) and Major Jones, one of Smallwood's aides, rallied the brigade, and renewed the contest. Again they were obliged to give way - and were again rallied - the second brigade still warmly engaged - the distance between the two brigades did not exceed two hundred yards...*[84]

As this brutal combat continued, Williams crossed the battlefield to communicate with the First Maryland, less than two hundred yards away from where he was engaged with the Second Maryland. The First Maryland, which had been positioned as the army's reserve unit behind the front lines, thought they should retreat but they could not obtain permission because their Commanding Officer, Brigadier General Smallwood, was not to be found. Williams wanted to be sure that the Maryland units were coordinated if they did decide to retreat, and he called on his own regiment, the Sixth Maryland, to stand firm, but Lieutenant Colonel Ford, a trusted officer said

"They have done all that can be expected of them. We are outnumbered and outflanked. See the enemy charge bayonets."[85]

With no further opposition from the fleeing militia on their right, the British were able to concentrate their whole force on the two Continental Brigades, and their overwhelming superiority took its toll. The American right disintegrated:

> *The enemy having collected their corps, and directing their whole force against these two devoted brigades, a tremendous fire of musketry was, for some time, kept up on both sides, with equal perseverance and obstinacy, until Lord Cornwallis perceiving there was no cavalry opposed to him, pushed forward his dragoons - and his infantry charging at the same moment, with fixed bayonets, put an end to the contest. His victory was complete.*[86]

The only chance to survive and escape capture was to run for the woods and swamps, either alone or in small groups. In the words of Light Horse Harry Lee (who was not present at this battle):

> *The pursuit was continued with keenness, and none were saved but those who penetrated the swamps which had been deemed impassable. The road was heaped with the dead and wounded. Arms, artillery, horses and baggage, were strewed in every direction; and the whole adjacent country presented evidences of the signal defeat.*[87]

General Gates was swept away by the rush of retreating militia. The troops that had been with Sumter on his raid returned and reported the success of their mission, but this news was little consolation in the face of the obvious disaster before him. Gates stopped a few miles from the battlefield, hoping to gather some semblance of military formation, but unsuccessful there, he moved on to Charlotte. Discouraged also with prospects at Charlotte, Gates then moved on to Hillsborough in hopes of finding men and resources to use as the foundation for a new fighting force

Cornwallis could barely suppress his glee when he wrote Loyalist Lieutenant Colonel J. Harris Cruger two days after the battle, in a report that also showed that Gates had commanded an army with a sizeable baggage train:

> *I have the pleasure to inform you, that on the morning of the 16th I attacked and totally defeated General Gates's army; above 1000 were killed and wounded, and about 800 taken prisoners. We are in possession of eight pieces of brass cannon – all they had in the field – all their ammunition waggons, a great number of arms, and 130 baggage waggons; in short, there never was a more complete victory.*[88]

In describing the outcome of the battle in his history of the war in the south, Light Horse Harry Lee confirmed the heavy losses among the valuable Continental troops:

> *Our loss was very heavy. More than a third of the continental troops were killed and wounded; and of the wounded one hundred and seventy were made prisoners. The regiment of Delaware was nearly annihilated; and lieutenant colonel Vaughn and major Patton being taken, its remnant, less than two companies, was placed under the orders of Kirkwood, senior captain.*[89]

In his *Narrative*, Otho Williams described his activities during the battle, from the time that he ordered the opening artillery salvos until the last stand, when his own Sixth Maryland Regiment had been part of the sturdy resistance on the right. He had helped to rally Smallwood's First Maryland Brigade when it began to falter under the weight of British assaults, and he had personally crossed the two hundred yards of open ground between Smallwood's and Gist's Maryland units to urge his own Sixth to continue their brave fight. Even though his Deputy Commander, Lieutenant Colonel Benjamin Ford, had assured him that the troops had already given their all, they continued to offer a firm resistance in the face of infantry and cavalry assaults, as Lord Cornwallis sensed his advantage and moved his entire force in for the kill. Baron de Kalb was in the thick of the fight until eleven wounds brought him down and he was taken by the British. The brave Maryland and Delaware troops were finally forced to succumb to superior numbers.

In a letter that Williams wrote to his sister some three months after the battle, he noted that he was very pleased with the battlefield performance of his horse Liberty, who acted bravely during the conflict, including one moment when a British platoon directed its fire at Williams. Fortunately, he was able to move quickly when he saw the order being given, and neither Williams nor his horse was hit, although three balls penetrated his coat.[90]

When Light Horse Harry Lee studied the battle and penned his *Memoirs* many years later, he left glowing praise for his friend Otho Williams:

> *Colonel Williams, adjutant general, was conspicuous throughout the action; cheerfully risking his valuable life out of his station, performing his assumed duties with precision and effect, and volunteering his person wherever danger called.*[91]

Williams' battlefield heroics were noted in the record of the Battle of Camden from its earliest reports. The Adjutant General of the Continental Army, Alexander Scammel wrote from army headquarters in New Jersey to congratulate Williams on his "glorious laurels."[92]

August 16th, 1780 was a disastrous day for the American cause, but a discerning observer might see a glimmer of hope coming out of Camden. The Maryland and Delaware Continentals had stood their ground for a considerable time, and inflicted serious casualties on front-line British troops before they were defeated by superior numbers.

The basic issue for the American army at Camden was that only the Continental troops had been trained to stand up to a British frontal assault, and they were deployed where they could not stiffen the whole line. A large percentage of the American forces had been militia, who did not live under daily military discipline and who might simply leave the army at any time, no matter how ardently their officers begged them to stay. In the fighting in North and South Carolina, it was always difficult to cobble together a large enough force to confront the British head on, and even when the American commanders had enough men, they were never sure how long they would stay with the army. It would remain for the experienced and innovative General Daniel Morgan, now making his way from his home in Virginia toward the southern army, to devise a system that would meld the strengths of militia and the Continentals into a winning battlefield formation.

George Washington used the Battle of Camden as his principal example for comparing the disciplined performance of Continental troops to the unreliability of militia when he sent a circular letter to several states in October, 1780:

> *The late Battle of Campden is a melancholy comment upon this doctrine. The Militia fled at the first fire, and left the Continental troops surrounded on every side and overpowered by numbers to combat for safety instead of Victory. The enemy themselves have witnessed to their Valor.*[93]

Experienced officers such as George Washington and Otho Williams understood the advantages of trained, disciplined troops like the Maryland and Delaware Continentals, commanded by men like John Eager Howard, John Gunby, and Robert Kirkwood. While the American high command continually sought ways to employ militia as effectively as possible, they felt that the only sure path to victory was to invest time and effort to recruit and train substantial numbers of regular troops, a goal that was not achieved during this war.

Meanwhile, Samuel Huntington, President of Congress, passed a summary of Gates' report of the battle on to George Washington:

> *I have this Day received from General Gates Despatches, containing the disagreeable Intelligence of the total Defeat of the Army under his Command; Copies of which are enclosed. A most unhappy Event, and unexpected immediately after the Intelligence we had just received of the several Advantages gained by our Troops in that quarter. We have no particular Account of the Numbers killed or taken. Report saith that Generals Smallwood & Gist and Colonel Armand are among the slain, and that Baron de Kalb is wounded & a Prisoner. We wish for more particular Intelligence than General Gates's Letter before it is published by Authority.*[94]

Congress took the time to express their official appreciation for the performance of the Maryland troops at the Battle of Camden. The President of Congress, Samuel Huntington, wrote to the commanders of the two Maryland regiments, William Smallwood and Mordecai Gist that:

> *Notwithstanding the Event of the Action near Cambden the 16 of August last, I have the Pleasure to present you with the Thanks of Congress expressed in the Copy of their Act enclosed of the 14 Instant to yourself in particular and the brave Officers & Troops who distinguished themselves by their Bravery & Valour on that Occasion.*[95]

Colonel Otho Williams was not mentioned in the reports of the battle, but his actions in this campaign were those of an experienced and effective combat officer and army administrator.

The Aftermath of Camden
The Retreat

Despite any faint glimmers of hope that were kindled by the performance of the Maryland and Delaware troops, there was no hiding the fact that the Battle of Camden was a very serious setback. Gloom pervaded the American side in the South after this crushing defeat. Charleston had fallen to the British in May of 1780, and here at Camden, only three months later, the last sizable American army in the South had been routed, with the loss of precious wagons, artillery, ammunition and supplies. The tattered remnants of the defeated American army retreated into North Carolina in a desperate attempt to survive, while citizens throughout the South began to prepare for a future ruled by a strong British army and its Tory allies

John Jacob was with the little band of men that clustered around John Eager Howard, and escaped from Camden to fight another day:

> *After this battle no poor fellows were in a more destitute and suffering condition. The baggage wagons that were with the army were all taken, all our clothes were lost, very few of the officers having a second shirt…Neither had we food of any kind; we lived on watermelons, peaches, etc. from the night of the 15th of August to the night of the 17th or 18th, I do not recollect which…*[96]

While what was left of the American army struggled to evade capture and find some safe place to regroup, Lord Cornwallis basked in the warm glow of complete victory. His Lordship and his army had always been very confident of their ability to defeat the Americans in direct combat, and Camden seemed to validate that confidence in every particular. The picture of fleeing militia was implanted firmly in the minds of the British officers and men. In the coming battles, Cornwallis and his troops would expect the American line to collapse at the first hint of a well-directed bayonet attack.

Cornwallis also believed that he had beaten the best general the Americans had to offer, the "Hero of Saratoga," Horatio Gates. North Carolina and Virginia seemed to be his for the taking. As the sun set on August 16th, 1781, it certainly seemed that the southern states would now be easy pickings for the very confident British army.

Only a small remnant of the Continental army remained together in any semblance of military order, and parts of the North Carolina countryside that had once been bastions of support for the American cause now began to exhibit loyalist tendencies. Even the irrepressible American partisan warrior Francis Marion had to report to Gates that some of the men who had fought under him in the past had joined the other side.[97] Things were so bad that some militiamen who had been heading for Camden to assist the American army changed sides when they learned the outcome of the battle, and turned on the American troops. Otho Williams described what it was like for the retreating Americans to meet the former friends who had shifted their allegiance:

> ...they met many of their insidious friends, armed, and advancing to join the American army; but learning its fate from the refugees, they acted decidedly in concert with the victors; and, captivating some, plundering others, and maltreating all the fugitives they met, returned, exultingly, home.[98]

Charles Stedman, who served in the British army, left a gripping eyewitness description of the road that led from the battlefield to Charlotte, North Carolina:

> The number of dead horses, broken wagons, and baggage, scattered on the road, formed a perfect scene of horror and confusion: Arms knapsacks, and accoutrements found were innumerable; such was the terror and dismay of the Americans.[99]

John Eager Howard and a small number of the survivors of Camden arrived at the first stopping-off-point, Charlotte, on the 19th, having covered sixty miles in the three days since the battle. They lived on "watermelons, peaches, etc." along the way.[100]

Adjutant General Otho Williams had reached Charlotte before Howard, and began to organize a further retreat to Salisbury. His description of that retreat also carries a tone of darkness and despair:

> By noon a very lengthy line of march occupied the road from Charlotte to Salisbury. It consisted of the wretched remnant of the late southern army; a great number of distressed whig families, and the whole tribe of Catawba Indians (about three hundred in number, about fifty of sixty of whom were warriors, but indifferently armed); ....Those officers and men, who were recently wounded, and had resolution to undertake the fatigue, were differently transported; some in wagons, some in litters, and some on horseback - their sufferings were indescribable. The

THE BATTLE OF CAMDEN; REBUILDING THE ARMY

> *distresses of the women and children, who fled from Charlotte and its neighborhood; the nakedness of the Indians, and the number of their infants and aged persons; and the disorder of the whole line of march, conspired to render it as scene too picturesque and complicated to describe. A just representation would exhibit an image of compound wretchedness - care, anxiety, pain, poverty, hurry, confusion, humiliation, and dejection would be characteristic traits in the mortifying picture.*[101]

But even in the midst of all this gloom and despair, Williams could catch a few glimmers of hope:

> *The fertility of the country between Charlotte and Salisbury - the hospitality of the inhabitants - and the numbers of their habitants on the route, afforded, in many instances, that relief which was requisite to preserve life; besides a liberal supply of provisions for all this cavalcade.*[102]

General Smallwood started to pull some small units together at Salisbury, and to select officers to command them. Otho Williams was among the Maryland officers who chose to move on to Hillsborough, rather than remain with their fellow Marylander, Smallwood:

> *General Smallwood halted his party at Salisbury - selected about one hundred and fifty effective men - and sent the remainder, perhaps fifty or sixty more, over the Yadkin River, with the wagons, women, & c.*
> *The effectives he officered according to his pleasure, and permitted the field officers, particularly those who had not formerly belonged to his brigade, to proceed to Hillsboro - Hall, Williams, and Howard, were of the number who availed themselves, at their leisure, of this permission.*[103]

The Death of Baron de Kalb

In the midst of this cruel warfare, Lord Cornwallis had the opportunity to display the profession of arms in a better light when Baron de Kalb died from his wounds a few days after the Battle of Camden. The Baron, an associate of the Marquis de Lafayette, was known for his distinguished military career in Europe and for gallant service in the American War. Because of his

European background and stature, and perhaps also because of their common bond as Masons,[104] Cornwallis insured that the Baron was treated with the greatest respect. A letter from de Kalb's loyal aide, DuBuysson, written at Hillsborough on September 2nd, 1780, provided a view of the Camden Battle and information on de Kalb's final days and burial:

> *The Baron De Kalb...withstood with the greatest bravery, coolness and intrepidity, with the brave Marylanders alone, the furious charge of the whole British army; but superior bravery was obliged at length to yield to superior numbers, and the baron, having had his horse killed under him, fell into the hands of the enemy, pierced with eight wounds of bayonets and three musket balls....Lord Cornwallis and Rawdon treated us with the greatest civility. The baron, dying of his wounds two days after the action, was buried with all the honors of war, and his funeral attended by all the officers of the British army*[105]

Cornwallis Moves into North Carolina

Lord Cornwallis moved from Camden toward Charlotte on September 8th, a little more than three weeks after the battle. His Lordship led the main army personally, while his trusted cavalry leader, Lieutenant Colonel Banastre Tarleton, led the British Legion and light infantry as a screening force. Major Patrick Ferguson commanded a force of Tories that operated further to the West, protecting Cornwallis's left flank as he advanced into North Carolina.[106]

Cornwallis' advance created havoc among supporters of the Revolution around Charlotte. The roads leading north out of Charlotte were clogged with retreating families, their wagons piled high with movable earthly possessions. The presence of a British Army gave strength to local Loyalists, just as the presence of a successful American Army would have given succor to the Patriots. This phenomenon consistently played a role in the decision-making of both the British and the American commanders, as they maneuvered across the southern landscape. Ultimate victory depended upon control of the countryside, and the Army that could maintain a presence in any local area would win the confidence of the people. Army commanders on both sides of this war hated to leave the impression that they were abandoning any territory, which was a strong consideration in the strategic planning on both sides.

THE BATTLE OF CAMDEN; REBUILDING THE ARMY

Otho Williams' *Narrative* left a graphic picture of the bitter fruits for Patriot sympathizers when a British army was in the region:

> ...inhabitants of the country who had ever been in arms, or were even suspected of disloyalty; some who were accused of having received protections, and violated the conditions, were hung without any form of trial. Prompt punishments, for supposed crimes, were inflicted at the will of superior officers in the different British garrisons, and every measure was adopted, which the arrogance of power could devise, to subjugate the minds, as well as the privileges of the people.[107]

The Search for a Scapegoat

Congress decided to order an official inquiry into Horatio Gates' performance at the Battle of Camden, which Otho Williams believed was because "...letters which were addressed to Congress, respecting the overthrow of his whole army, were so vague and unsatisfactory; and others which were written, were so disingenuous..."[108] Williams also revealed much of his private thinking on the Battle of Camden in a letter to Alexander Hamilton two weeks after the battle:

> Our retreat was the most mortifying that could have happened. Those who escaped the dangers of the field, knew not where to find protection: the wounded found no relief from the inhabitants, who were immediately in arms against us; and many of our fugitive officers and men were disarmed by those faithless villains, who had flattered us with promises of joining us against the enemy.[109]
>
> General Gates used the utmost expedition in getting from the lost field to this place. As this step is unaccountable to me, you must expect to know the reason another time, and from better authority. ...The General is extremely mortified at the disappointment his hopes have met with; and I think it ungenerous to oppress dejected spirits by a premature censure.
>
> The legislature of this State is now sitting at this place, and devising means of defending the country...From the best accounts I can get, Lord Cornwallis had with him, on the day of battle, the seventy-first, sixty-third, thirty-third, and twenty-

> third British regiments; a corps of Hessians, Tarlton's Legion, and some new levies, amounting to about three thousand men. Our numbers were very little greater; and our force will not be imagined so great, by those who are informed of our long march in a barren country, with very little other subsistence than a short allowance of fresh beef, green corn, apples, and peaches. As soon as I recover from a relaxation of spirits, which is all my present complaint, I will write you again, and inform you that we are resolved not to despair, but bear our fortunes like veterans in the South.... Present my most respectful compliments to the General, whom I love; to all my friends at Head Quarters and in camp...[109]

Williams was in a ticklish situation with respect to Horatio Gates. They were acquaintances, and Gates had intervened personally to try to help the younger man when he had been a prisoner-of-war. When young John Armstrong was not able to carry out the duties of Deputy Adjutant General of the southern army, Gates turned to Williams, who had experience in the role. This assignment brought Williams into constant contact with Gates, and, as shown in his *Narrative*, Williams did not always agree with his commander's decisions, although he appears to have done all in his power to carry out Gates' orders faithfully. Williams was also sympathetic to the older man, whose son had recently died. The path that Williams laid out for his conduct was to try to stick to statements of fact, gather information, and be guarded in his statements until the court martial was held. Williams had previous experience with such a high level inquiry as a member of the court that had tried Major General Charles Lee after the Battle of Monmouth in 1778, and he was proceeding carefully and wisely in anticipation of being an important witness in the expected trial. Williams shared his concerns with Daniel Morgan:

> Doctr. Brown who is just arrived and resumes, or continues his post in the Hospl. Department, Informs me that Major Giles told him that he told Genl. Gates I had, as well as others, censured his Conduct in the action of Camden - The letters I wrote on the Subject contain'd matters of Fact. - I always expected to be called on as Evidence upon an Enquiry into the Genls. Conduct, Therefore avoided giving my opinion....I'm conscious of having conducted myself with the strictest propriety

> *in that affair, and I shall say upon Oath when required all and no more, than what I have at different times mentioned to the General; and I have said much less to others - You are particularly acquainted with my Private sentiments on the Subject. I hope you will believe I have at no time been inconsistant, whatever (torn page) may have been put upon my Letters (torn page) whatever information Majr. Giles might have recd. on the Subject. I shall quiet the Old Gentlemans doubts by letter, for in whatever Light his conduct may appear to the World I always rather pitied than condemned his misfortunes -*[110]

While Williams maintained a sense of delicacy and restraint regarding his written observations about Horatio Gates, Alexander Hamilton (who said of Gates, "I am his enemy") criticized the defeated General harshly in a letter to Congressman James Duane of New York:[111]

> *Did anyone ever hear of such a disposition or such a flight? His best troops placed on the side strongest by nature, his worst on the weakest by nature, and his attack made with these. Tis impossible to give a more complete picture of military absurdity. It is equally against the maxims of war and common sense. We see the consequences. His left ran away, and left his right uncovered... But was there ever an instance of a general running away, as Gates has done, from his whole army? And was there ever so precipitate a flight? One hundred and eighty miles in three days and a half. It does admirable credit to the activity of a man at his time of life. But it disgraces the general and the soldier.*[112]

Gates had sent his first report to Congress four days after the battle, but then waited a full ten days, until August 30th, to send a report directly to Commander-in-Chief Washington.[113] Washington was adept at making his points with the pen, and he cleverly chided Gates for not reporting to him earlier:

> *I have received your several favors of the 30th of August, 3rd and 15th September... The first account, which I received of the unfortunate affair near Campden, was by a Copy of your letter of the 20th August, from Hillsboro, to the president of Congress.*[114]

Washington graciously added some positive statements about the American performance at Camden, and provided some wise advice on the path that Gates should now pursue.

> *The behavior of the Continental Troops does them infinite honor. The accounts, which the Enemy give of the action, shew that their Victory was dearly bought. Under present circumstances, the System which you are pursuing seems extremely proper. It would answer no good purpose to take a position near the enemy, while you are so far inferior in force. If they can be kept in check, by the light irregular troops under Colo. Sumter and other active Officers, they will gain nothing by the time which must be necessarily spent by you, in collecting and arranging the new Army, forming Magazines and replacing the Stores which were lost in the Action.*[115]

Washington's inherent graciousness shines through in this letter to the defeated and disgraced Horatio Gates. The Commander-in-Chief had himself suffered setbacks during the war, and he was the butt of criticism from many in Congress and the army. Soldiers like Charles Lee and a number of members of Congress left a written trail of their criticisms, and many have felt then and since that Horatio Gates had taken part in the effort to make the case against the tall Virginian. Washington loyalists like Alexander Hamilton were ready to pillory Gates, and send him off in disgrace and dishonor after Camden,[116] but in the aftermath of that great battlefield disaster, Washington treated Gates with dignity, and acted the part of a patient, thoughtful, professional leader.

Most important of all, Washington did not let one defeat throw him into despair or hopelessness. After Camden, he immediately sought ways to reinforce the South, and to do everything that he could to turn the tide against Cornwallis.

Gates was strongly criticized from many quarters for his performance at the Battle of Camden, but, he also had support from some unexpected sources. Nathanael Greene wrote to Dr. Benjamin Rush on August 8th, 1781 that "General Gates left this Country under a heavy load; and I can assure you he did not deserve it."[117] Otho Williams noted in his *Narrative* that he visited the Camden battlefield with Greene, and that Greene "approved" Gates' actions.[118]

In the end, there was to be no court martial of Horatio Gates for the disastrous defeat of August 16th, 1780. On August 14th, 1782, almost exactly two years after the battle, Congress repealed the resolution that called for an inquiry into Gates' conduct at the Battle of Camden, and he rejoined the Continental Army shortly thereafter.[119]

Rebuilding the Army

Eight days after their defeat at Camden, on August 16th, 1780, the remnants of the beaten American army left Salisbury, North Carolina and continued their retreat toward Hillsborough, where General Gates had established his headquarters. They arrived at Hillsborough on September 6th.[120] North Carolina's governor and state legislature were located at Hillsborough, and the town had historically served as a stores depot and a rendezvous point for militia. Gates hoped that the British would advance slowly into North Carolina, so that the Americans would have time to rebuild an effective fighting force.

General Gates and his officers decided to organize his much-reduced army into one lone regiment, which would be commanded by Colonel Otho Williams, with John Eager Howard as second-in-command. The regiment, which amounted to only 700 or 800 men, would consist of two battalions, commanded by Majors Harman and Anderson.[121] Howard, Williams and their officers and non-commissioned officers set about promptly to restore discipline and order, and to prepare the troops for future operations.

Since the force was so small, there was a surplus of officers, and those who were not needed in the ranks were sent home on recruiting duty.[122]

Williams Commands the Continentals

Colonel Williams kept a Brigade and Regimental Order Book for this period, with the first entry on September 13th, 1780, which established the crisp, disciplined tone that Williams wanted to impose on his command:

> *Colonel Williams being appointed to the Command of the Troops of Maryland and Delaware which are to be formed into One Regiment of two Battalions and two Light Infantry Companies, agreeable to General Orders of Yesterday, calls upon all Officers who have appointments in the said Regiment to give the most assiduous Attention to their respective duties. The*

> *Troops are to be assembled with as much Expedition as possible. The Companies formed & the Orderly Serjeants named, the Muster Rolls made out, and the men Armed. Majors Anderson and Hardman will attend particularly to the Execution of this order and prepare their Battalions to parade at 6 o'clock this afternoon.*[123]

One of Williams' first acts was to move his troops out of the town of Hillsborough because the inhabitants had begun to "...experience and complain of the inconveniences of having soldiers billeted among them; and the officers were equally sensible of the difficulty of restraining the licentiousness of the soldiers, when not immediately under their observation." Williams moved the men to a vacant farm outside of town, where the army built wigwams out of "...fence rails, poles, and corn tops."[124] From these crude beginnings, Williams and his officers set out to restore the fighting trim of the Maryland and Delaware Continentals.

His new responsibilities gave Williams the opportunity to employ all the military leadership skills that he had learned under George Washington, Baron von Steuben, and Baron de Kalb. He was a strict disciplinarian, and he believed that the measures he imposed were having a beneficial effect:

> *The usual camp-guards and centinels being posted, no person could come into, or go out of camp without a permit. Parade duties were regularly attended, as well by officers as soldiers, and discipline, not only began to be perfectly restored, but even gave an air of stability and confidence to the regiment, which all their rags could not disguise. In this encampment no circumstance of want or distress was admitted as an excuse for relaxing from the strictest discipline, to which the soldiers the more cheerfully submitted, as they saw their officers constantly occupied in procuring for them whatever was attainable in their situation.*
>
> *Absolutely without pay; almost destitute of clothing; often with only a half ration, and never with a whole one (without substituting one article for another) not a soldier was heard to murmur, after the third or fourth day of their being encamped. Instead of meeting and conferring in small sullen squads, as they had formerly done, they filled up the intervals from duty with manly exercises and field sports; in short the officers had very*

> *soon the entire confidence of the men, who divested themselves of all unnecessary care, and devoted themselves to duty and pasttime, within the limits assigned them.*[125]

It is much more interesting to read about military strategy or battles than it is to review the often mind-numbing routine of daily military life, but for every hour that Otho Williams spent in combat, he spent weeks and months drilling troops, teaching essential fighting skills, and worrying about how to feed the men or to give them a chance to rest. He led countless marches across the countryside in the heat of summer and the cold of winter. He tirelessly supervised daily camp life, and demanded disciplined behavior from his officers and men at all times. This seemingly dull, unending, routine work was essential preparation for these young Revolutionary soldiers. Williams was the type of officer that attended to every detail that would prepare his men for combat, as illustrated by this entry in his General Orders:

> *The Commanding Officers of Corps will please to order their Arms to be put in the best possible order to have the flints taken out, and wooden knockers put in and practice the Firing motions twice a Day.*[126]

If these men were like virtually all others in the history of warfare, many of the soldiers undoubtedly complained about that order, but the benefit of such rigor and attention to detail would pay dividends in future battles.

Moreover, Williams and his deputy Lieutenant Colonel John Eager Howard used the full weight of military justice to enforce their authority. The first of many courts martial during this period was on September 16th, just three days after Williams assumed command:

> *The Court Martial appointed for the Tryal of Isaac alias Patrick Coleman of the first Company in the 2nd Battalion, suspected of stealing a Rifle, after hearing the Evidence are of opinion he is Guilty of stealing a Rifle and do sentence him to receive Fifty lashes on his bare back. The sentence is approved and ordered to be in Execution at Retreat.*[127]

On September 19th, a Court Martial of which Captain Robert Kirkwood was President found Levin Culver, Stephen Culver, Thomas Chatman and George Baumgartner guilty of desertion, and sentenced each of these men to receive 100 lashes. Richard Duvall was sentenced to 50 lashes for selling a mare that did not belong to him, and 50 lashes were ordered for Augustin

Carnes, for attempting to sell his musket.

Colonel Williams continued to apply discipline, and he did not spare the rod when punishment was judged to be appropriate:

> *The Commandant approves each and all of the aforegoing Sentences and orders the punishments to be inflicted this afternoon at Retreat. The Colonel is determined not to pardon, nor mitigate the punishment due to so treacherous and scandalous crimes as Desertion and directs that these sentences against those who are found Guilty to be properly executed.*[128]

The public punishment of September 19th was not a one-time affair, but rather the work of discipline and punishment was a regular part of daily camp life. Courts martial sat on September 20th, 21st, and 29th; October 13th, 14th, 16th, 25th, 28th, and 31st; November 6th, 7th and 10th; and January 7th, 12th, and 16th. The courts typically met in the morning, and sentenced several soldiers to receive 50 or 100 lashes that afternoon, at Retreat.[129] It was common for the troops to witness severe whippings of their comrades for breaches of discipline.

The weight of Otho Williams' responsibilities during this period would have been enormous if his only task had been to command the Maryland and Delaware troops, but he also continued to serve as the southern army's Deputy Adjutant General, and to serve General Gates in other areas of army administration, as well. In a letter home on September 23rd, he complained that Gates was using him in almost every department of the army, and that while he would like to decline his extra duties, Gates would not permit him to do so. Williams insisted that he was "...more interested in his own regiment than in anything else... because its discipline and its military achievements were the soundest basis for his own reputation." He reported that he had not yet been able to obtain tents, blankets or shoes for his men, but they were generally well armed and increasing in numbers, since many escaped captives were coming in.[130]

In spite of his heavy daily workload, Williams had the responsibility to inform the main army's Adjutant General of activities in the South. This required him to send periodic reports to Colonel Alexander Scammel,[131]* General Washington's Adjutant General with the main army. Williams

---

*This is the same Alexander Scammel in whose place Williams served temporarily as Acting Adjutant General from December 1779 to April 1780, under General Washington.

reported that he was weighed down by his many responsibilities and by the loss of many of the Army's papers during the retreat from Camden. He explained that it was extremely difficult to find accurate records of which men had been killed or captured, and that he had therefore reported a large number simply as "missing."[132] He had been able to design appropriate forms for compiling this information, but his nature as a perfectionist left him displeased that he was unable to provide complete and precise data. Williams also maintained correspondence with Baron von Steuben, keeping him informed of the status of the southern army, providing detailed requests for assistance, and asking for advice on the role of the Inspectors Department.[133]

Williams' workload was enormous, and he carried out his Adjutant General duties without an assistant. Slowly, Gates realized that his Adjutant General was overburdened, and relieved him of a portion of his duties.[134]

Cornwallis Advances to Charlotte

While the American army was trying to regain its fighting strength at Hillsborough, Lord Cornwallis was moving his army into North Carolina toward Charlotte, where he planned to set up headquarters. His first taste of what was in store for his army in that region was young William Richardson Davie's determined stand at the Charlotte courthouse on September 26th, 1780. Davie's small force held off the advance elements of Cornwallis' army for a time, inflicting casualties before he skillfully withdrew his men out of harm's way. Davie and militia General William Davidson would control the countryside around Charlotte during Cornwallis' time there.[135] Partisan groups mercilessly harassed British foraging parties and couriers, and it seemed to the British as though the entire countryside had risen against them. Cornwallis' position in Charlotte became more tenuous when American riflemen defeated Patrick Ferguson and his Loyalist militia at the Battle of King's Mountain on October 7th, 1781.[136*]

---

*Osmand Tiffany's very useful manuscript "A Sketch of the Life and Services of Gen. Otho Holland Williams," contains a regrettable error that Otho Williams took part in the Battle of King's Mountain, which he did not.

Daniel Morgan Joins the Southern Army[137]

While Cornwallis was occupying Charlotte, the American army at Hillsborough received an important addition when Daniel Morgan, the experienced commander of light troops, rode into camp and reported for duty in late September.[138] Morgan, known by the nickname "The Old Wagoner," had served under Gates at Saratoga, and had played an important role in that important victory. General Gates had worked hard to lure The Old Wagoner out of his self-imposed retirement, and to have him promoted to Brigadier General, providing a just reward for Morgan's prior service and giving him the authority and prestige to deal effectively with other senior officers.

Gates' experience at Saratoga had taught him the value of fast-moving light troops - units that were unencumbered by baggage, wagons, and other accoutrements of war - and he realized the value that such a unit could provide in the southern theater. While working to bring Morgan to his southern army, Gates had written to Samuel Huntington, President of Congress, that he intended to place Morgan "…at the Head of a Select Corps from whose services I expect the most brilliant success."[139]

Daniel Morgan was a bear of a man, with a tempestuous history that went back to the Virginia frontier, where he was known in his youth for hard-drinking, brawling, and general mayhem. During the French and Indian War, he had driven a wagon in support of General Edward Braddock's disastrous campaign to try to take Fort Duquesne (current day Pittsburgh, Pennsylvania), and had received five hundred lashes from the British for striking an officer who had reprimanded him. Morgan hated the British, and he would use that story and the scars on his back to help inspire his troops, explaining that had taken the worst punishment that the British army could impose and lived to fight another day. He assured his men that he knew how to deal with this enemy, and that if the troops would stick with him, he would show them the way to victory, as he had done at Saratoga

After joining a rifle company and serving at the siege of Boston in 1775, Morgan had been chosen to accompany Benedict Arnold on his arduous march through the Maine backwoods and the attack on Quebec, Canada. He performed heroically on the march and in the final assault on Quebec on New Year's Eve, 1775, where he and his men were captured after putting up a magnificent fight.

When he was exchanged for a British officer and released, Morgan rejoined the main American army commanded by George Washington. When the British General Burgoyne invaded New York from Canada in 1777, Washington sent Morgan to join the army under General Gates at Saratoga,

New York. Morgan added further luster to his military reputation with his fine performance on the Saratoga battlefields - Freeman's Farm on September 19th, 1777 and Bemis Heights on October 7th, 1777.[140] A hallmark of Morgan's troops was their unerring ability to spot the officers in the British ranks, and bring them down with deadly accurate rifle fire. Morgan called this going after the enemy's "epaulets."

Morgan was only one man, but he brought aggressiveness and a fiery brand of leadership that became very important to the southern command. After his arrival, Gates implemented his vision and formed a unit of light troops, starting with three companies of light infantry, two commanded by Captains Brooks and Bruin of Maryland, respectively, and one commanded by Captain Robert Kirkwood of Delaware.[141] Lieutenant Colonel John Eager Howard, Otho Williams' second-in-command, was chosen to lead these infantry units.
[142] [143]

Gates and Morgan wasted no time getting the light troops on the road. Morgan marched his command out of Hillsborough on October 8th, and arrived at Salisbury on October 15th, a 95-mile march.[144] Morgan was in the saddle again, commanding troops, but he had to inform Gates that "I have been very sick since I left Hillsborough, but have got well except a very sore mouth."[145]

Morgan's light infantry needed cavalry to round out its capabilities, so William Washington and his cavalry were detached to serve under Morgan. Washington was a distant relative of the Commander-in-Chief, and he had fought in the north at Long Island, Trenton, and Princeton during 1776/1777. He was sent south in 1779 to help in the defense of Charleston. He and his command had managed to escape from Charleston, and they had joined up with Gates' army in early November. Gates also assigned Morgan three companies of riflemen which he combined with Howard's light infantry and Washington's cavalry into a force that began to be called the "Flying Army."

Cornwallis Retreats to South Carolina

Lord Cornwallis had spent uncomfortable weeks in Charlotte, where he was continually harassed by a population in arms, and he had been astonished by Ferguson's defeat. His Lordship finally decided that he could not safely remain in Charlotte, and on October 14th, one week after the Battle of King's Mountain, he began a difficult retreat to Winnsboro, South Carolina, which he reached on October 29th.[146] [147]

When General Gates learned that Cornwallis was retreating back into South Carolina, he was greatly relieved that he would not have to try to defend North Carolina with his meager force. The beleaguered Americans were slowly starting to receive supplies and reinforcements from Virginia and the northern states, and now that they were free from the pressure of Cornwallis' army, they would have more time to build their strength.

While news of King's Mountain and Cornwallis' retreat was certainly encouraging, Otho Williams and his little command continued to face almost insurmountable difficulties as they struggled to keep the body and soul of the army alive. These were enormously difficult times for the Maryland and Delaware troops and for their leaders. The fact that these units were able to stay together and retain some form of military capability is a testament to the grit, determination, and leadership ability of Otho Williams and the men around him.

★ ★ ★ ★ ★

Gates Marches from Hillsborough to Charlotte

Morgan had led the Flying Army out of Salisbury on October 18th, and he moved closer to Charlotte in easy marches, arriving at New Providence, 14 miles from Charlotte, a week later, on October 25th.[148] On November 4th, he led his troops south out of Charlotte toward Camden "to reconnoiter the enemy's lines and procure forage…" They reached Ruegely's Mill, thirteen miles from Camden, and then returned to their camp at New Providence on November 9th.[149] Seeing that Cornwallis had retreated back to South Carolina, Gates carefully pondered his next move. Otho Williams confided this information to his friend Daniel Morgan: "The Genl. Has been in some suspence, however I believe he is now determined to move westward." Williams added a personal note to Morgan at the bottom of this letter, congratulating him on his recent promotion by Congress, making his "best compliments," and signing it "Otho" instead of his usual formal signature in army-related letters, "O.H. Williams."[150]

Gates finally decided to march toward Charlotte. In his *Narrative*, Williams emphasized that the fighting spirit and enthusiasm of the men had been restored by their time in Hillsborough.

> *A laboratory was erected, and employed mending arms; and the residue of the clothing, &c. was distributed. Each man in the brigade was supplied with one new shirt, a short coat, a pair of woolen overalls, a pair of shoes, and a hat or a cap. The*

dividend of blankets was very inadequate to the occasion — they were apportioned to the companies and every other practicable provision was made to prepare the brigade for the field. The officers exerted themselves, and the soldiers were emulous who should be the first in readiness to march. Even the convalescents were impatient of being left behind — so generally had the martial spirit revived in the soldiery.[151]

Even though he felt that the time at Hillsborough had been good for the army, Williams felt no remorse about leaving, writing to Daniel Morgan that "Tomorrow we leave this Dirty, disagreeable hole Hillsborough."[152]

Williams commanded the Brigade when it left Hillsborough on November 2nd, and his orders were to find a good spot near Salisbury where he would wait for a few days for General Gates to join him.[153] He wrote to Gates on November 11th, expressing discouragement that his troops had not been able to find adequate food and forage in the area, and acknowledging that he had received Gates' notification that he would join the army the night of the 11th.

In a November 11th letter to Gates, Williams reported that he had been too ill to leave his quarters since he had arrived near Salisbury, but that he was still doing all he could to gather needed supplies.[154] On November 24th, Williams wrote to his brother Elie that he had a cold which had taken "its old seat in my breast," and that since General Gates had agreed to leave him in good quarters in Salisbury for a few days, he was feeling better. Now that he had regained his health, he intended to rejoin his command, which was camped near Charlotte. Williams also gave evidence that he was feeling better by reporting that he had been deer-hunting the past three or four mornings.[155]

General Gates decided that Charlotte was the best place for his troops to spend the winter, so the men built huts[156] and prepared to live there until spring. Gates' plan was that Morgan and the Flying Army would stay in the field, serving as a screening force and advance guard for the troops in Charlotte.[157]

The American army had come a long way in the three-and-a-half months since the defeat at Camden. In these months of hard work and Spartan surroundings, the little army under Gates had not won any memorable victory which would inspire the populace or impress future historians. The few men they had were short of every necessity, but they had managed to keep a sense of military organization and discipline. They had survived, regrouped, and reorganized, and now they were even beginning to make a few aggressive moves in the direction of the enemy. The Americans had made an important comeback in these few months. Badly bloodied at Camden, the army had bounced off the canvas and was preparing to fight again.

A sergeant in the Delaware Continentals left a soldier's tribute to his comrades from Maryland:

> ..the manly fortitude of the Maryland Line was very great, being obliged to march and do duty barefoot, being all the winter the chief part of them wanting coats and shoes, which they bore with the greatest patience imaginable, for which their praise should never be forgotten; and indeed in all the hardships which they had undergone they never seemed to frown.[158]

The Appointment of Nathanael Greene to the Southern Command

Shortly after the Battle of Camden, Alexander Hamilton had penned some prescient observations, when he questioned whether or not Congress would choose a new commander for the South:

> But what will be done by Congress? Will he (Gates) be changed or not? If he is changed, for God's sake overcome prejudice, and send Greene. You know my opinion of him. I stake my reputation on the events, give him but fair play.[159]

The crushing defeat at the Battle of Camden had severely eroded Congressional confidence in Horatio Gates, and they asked the man that they had ignored when they appointed Gates, Commander-in-Chief George Washington, to name a new commander of the southern army. On October 14th, while Williams, Gates and the southern army had been trying to regain their combat readiness in Hillsborough, Washington chose his trusted lieutenant, Nathanael Greene for the southern command, a choice that Alexander Hamilton and many others in the army undoubtedly endorsed. Greene left the Northern army promptly, and began his journey south to take charge of his forces.[160]

On October 22nd, Washington wrote to inform Gates that Congress had directed that a Court of Inquiry be convened to investigate his performance at Camden, and that he had chosen Greene to serve in his place until the inquiry was completed. Washington added his characteristic assurances that Gates would be given the fairest possible hearing.[161]

In the wake of the disaster at Camden, Congress had worked hard to support the southern army, and had done what it could from Philadelphia to request others to support American strategy in the South. Its resolution of September 7th, 1780 addressed a wide range of topics, including forwarding and storing provisions, drafting troops, providing weapons, equipping cavalry, and sending cavalry reinforcements from the northern army.[162] These directives, issued from far-off Philadelphia, tried to rally resources for the support of the southern army, but the tangible results fell far short of the goal. One fortunate outcome, however, was Washington's decision to detach Light Horse Harry Lee and his Legion from the northern army and send it south to join the fight against the British. This efficient and well-led force of cavalry and light infantry would play an important role in the coming campaign.

The President of Congress sent Green his orders on the next day, October 31st, authorizing him to "…organize & employ the Army under your Command in the Manner you shall judge most proper, subject to the Controul of the Commander in Chief," and conveying wishes"…that your Command may be attended with desired Success, to the Satisfaction of your Country and your personal Honor."[163]

Congress was doing is best to send men and materiel to reinforce the southern army, but of all its efforts, perhaps the most important reinforcement would come in the person of one man, Nathanael Greene, the new commander.

Greene was a former Quaker and the manager of an ironworks, but he had earned George Washington's trust through many shared experiences during the war, including Greene's disastrous decision to try to defend Fort Washington in November, 1776, which had led to the capture and imprisonment of the entire defending force, including Otho Williams. Greene's record was not perfect, and his resume did not include a brilliant victory such as Gates could claim for Saratoga. But Greene was accustomed to operating with scant resources, and to dealing with enormous obstacles. He would do all that perseverance, diligence, tireless energy, high intelligence, strategic vision and hard work could accomplish.

Otho Williams looked forward to the arrival of Nathanael Greene, and hoped that he would be happy under his command.[164]

1   Otho Holland Williams started to write a history of the Revolutionary War, and his narrative on the early phases of the campaign of 1780/1781 is included as Appendix B to Volume I of Judge William Johnson's *Sketches of the Life and Correspondence of Nathanael Greene, Major General of the Armies of the United States in the War of the Revolution*, which was published in Charleston, South Carolina in 1822. Williams personally witnessed most of the incidents he described, and he was an excellent writer, with a gift for compelling narrative. While he sometimes seems to have succumbed moderately to a very human tendency to present his own actions in a favorable light, his inclination in that regard is mild compared to many other writers. His Narrative is referred to extensively herein.
2   Greene, Life of Greene. (Volume III.) P. 109.
3   Washington, George. Letter to Horatio Gates. Written at Head Quarters, Morris Town, June 4, 1780. *Washington Papers*.
4   Armstrong, John, Sr. Letter to Horatio Gates. Written at Philadelphia, June 6, 1780. Letters of Delegates to Congress, Volume 15, pages 258-259. Library of Congress.
5   Journals of the Continental Congress. Tuesday, June 13, 1780. Volume 17, page 508. Library of Congress.
6   Huntington, Samuel, President of Congress. Letter to Horatio Gates. Written at Philadelphia, June 13, 1780. Letters of Delegates to Congress. Volume 15, page 312. Library of Congress.
7   Journals of the Continental Congress. Wednesday, June 14, 1780. Volume 17, pages 510-511. Library of Congress.
8   Armstrong, John, Sr. Letter to Horatio Gates. Written at Philadelphia, June 15, 1780. Letters of Delegates to Congress, Volume 15, pages 319-320. Library of Congress.
9   See Footnote.
10 Howly, Richard. Letter to Horatio Gates. Written at Philadelphia, July 28, 1780. Letters of Delegates to Congress, Volume 15, pages 517-518. Library of Congress.
11 Washington, George. Letter to Joseph Jones. Written at Headquarters, Bergen County. July 22, 1780. *Washington Papers*.
12 Kapp, *Kalb*. P. 204. Kapp cites "Washington Irving's Life of Washington, 8vo Edition, IV, 75."
13 Gates, Horatio. Letter to General Benjamin Lincoln. Written at Fredericksburgh, 4th July, 1780. Magazine of American History, Volume V, No. 4. 1880. p. 283. This is included with article by John Austin Stevens, "The Southern Campaign, 1780. Gates at Camden" (hereafter Stevens, *Gates at Camden*.)
14 See Footnote.
15 Journals of the Continental Congress. Friday, June 16, 1780. Volume 17, Pp. 518-519.
16 De Kalb, Johann. Letter to Horatio Gates. Written at camp on Deep River, North Carolina, July 16, 1780. Cited in Kapp, *Kalb*. Pp. 204-205.
17 Gates, Horatio. Letter to Baron de Kalb. Written at Hillsborough, North Carolina, July 20, 1780. Cited in Kapp, Kalb,. P. 206.
18 Ibid.
19 This is John Armstrong, Jr., the son of Congressman John Armstrong, Sr., as mentioned previously. Otho Williams notes in his *Narrative of the Campaign of 1780* that Gates intended to have the younger Armstrong act as deputy adjutant general, but that he was "prevented by sickness." Williams retained the post.
20 Kirkwood, Robert. *The Journal and Order Book of Captain Robert Kirkwood of the Delaware Regiment of the Continental Line*. (Edited by Reverend Joseph Brown Turner.) (hereafter Kirkwood, *Journal*.) The Historical Society of Delaware. Wilmington, 1910. P. 10.
21 Williams, *Narrative* (in Johnson, Greene.) P. 486.
22 Ibid. P. 486.
23 Kapp, *Kalb*. P. 207.
24 Williams, *Narrative* (in Johnson, Greene.) P. 487.
25 At the start of the War, Williams' and Gates's homes in Western Maryland and Northern Virginia (now West Virginia) were no more than 40 miles apart. John Carey wrote to Williams in 1775 asking him to pass information on to Gates (Chapter 2.) Also, as noted earlier, Gates took an active role in helping to obtain Williams' exchange when he was a prisoner of war.
26 See Footnote.
27 Williams wrote his *Narrative* after the actual events, and it seems reasonable to assume that he yielded somewhat to the natural human tendency to describe his own actions in a good light.
28 Williams, *Narrative* (in Johnson, *Greene*.) P. 487.
29 Kirkwood, *Journal*. P. 10.
30 Kapp, *Kalb*. P. 211.
31 Ibid. P. 211.
32 Kirkwood, *Journal*. Pp. 10-11.
33 The American Army would march on this same route to Camden nine months later, in April 1781, and no one seems to have written then that the Army should have followed the western route through Salisbury and Charlotte. In fact, this

description of the route was written by Sergeant-Major Williams Seymour of the Delaware Regiment of Continentals to describe the later march, which he pointed out was on the same route that Gates had taken in July/August, 1780. The lack of ardent criticism at the later date may suggest either that the route wasn't as bad as feared, or that the writers of the criticism, including Williams, were trying to demonstrate that their own military instincts had been superior to those of Gates, and that they were trying to distance themselves from association with the failures of the campaign.

34 Seymour, *Journal*. P. 380.
35 Williams, *Narrative* (in Johnson, *Greene*.) P. 487.
36 Ibid. P. 487.
37 Kirkwood, *Journal*. P. 10.
38 Williams, *Narrative* (in Johnson, *Greene*.) P. 488.
39 Ibid. P. 488.
40 Ibid. P. 488.
41 Gates, Horatio. General Orders. Issued at Head Quarters. Deep Creek. 6 August 1780. Stevens, Gates at *Camden*. p. 315.
42 Williams, *Narrative* (in Johnson, *Greene*.) Pp. 488-489.
43 In documenting these discussions after the fact, Williams was aware that he might be called to testify under oath on these matters, and he stated that he had attempted to document the details as accurately as he could remember them. He inserted in his *Narrative* (on page 490) that "…A regard to facts, to which the writer thinks he may possibly hereafter be called to testify on oath, obliges him to state them faithfully as they occurred, or were communicated to him; preserving the memory of authorities, as well as incidents, in order to (*render*) a correct statement of the circumstances, about which he may be interrogated." This statement seems to imply that this portion of Williams' Narrative was written fairly soon after the battle, when he still expected that there would be a court martial of Horatio Gates to which he would be called to testify. William Gordon, author of *The History Of The Rise, Progress, And Establishment, Of The Independence Of The United States Of America* said in a note to Volume 3 on page 450 that "recourse has been had to the detail of facts written by the deputy adjutant general, Col. Otho H. Williams…" This text was published in 1788, so the Williams Narrative had to be written before that time.
44 Gates, Horatio. Letter to Governor Nash of North Carolina. Written on August 3, 1780. Kapp, *Kalb*. P. 213.
45 Williams, *Narrative* (in Johnson, *Greene*.) P. 489.
46 Ibid. P. 489.
47 Kapp, *Kalb*. P. 217.
48 Williams, *Narrative* (in Johnson, *Greene*.) P. 490.
49 Ibid. P. 490.
50 See Footnote.
51 Williams, *Narrative* (in Johnson, *Greene*.) P. 491.
52 De Kalb's biographer is very critical of Gates, and states that "Had he possessed sufficient military shrewdness, he would have turned Lord Rawdon's flank by a forced march up the creek, and entered Camden unopposed." (Kapp, *Kalb*. Pages 219 and 220.) As with much after-the-fact commentary on military operations, this assessment may have overlooked many realities of the actual situation. For example, if Gates had proceeded as Kapp suggested, he might have been trapped in Camden by the combined forces of Rawdon and Cornwallis, which would hardly have been seen as "military shrewdness."
53 Williams, *Narrative* (in Johnson, *Greene*) p. 491.
54 Kirkwood, *Journal*. P. 11.
55 Kirkwood called this Mill, "Ridgleys Mill." In his Narrative (page 491 in William Johnson's, of William Johnson's Life and Correspondence of Nathanael Greene, vol. I.) Otho Williams spelled it "Rugley's Mills," and noted that the site was also called "Clermont."
56 Kirkwood, *Journal*, p. 11.
57 Williams, *Narrative* (in Johnson, *Greene*.) P. 491.
58 Lee, *Memoirs*. P. 191. This is a "Note from Colonel Howard" at the bottom of page 191.
59 Williams, *Narrative* (in Johnson, *Greene*.) P. 491.
60 Ibid. P. 493.
61 Ibid. P. 493.
62 Ibid. P. 493.
63 Ibid. P. 494.
64 Washington, George. Letter to Horatio Gates. Written at Head Quarters, Orange Town, August 12th, 1780. *Washington Papers*.
65 Ibid.
66 Davie, William R. Recollection of a Conversation between General Nathanael Greene and Colonel William R. Davie. Greene Papers. 8:225. (Davie remembered that Greene had said "Sumter refuses to obey my orders.")
67 Williams, *Narrative* (in Johnson, Greene.) P. 492.

68 Stevens, *Gates ta Camden*. P. 266.
69 Ibid. P. 266.
70 Lee, *Memoirs*. P. 186
71 Williams, *Narrative* (in Johnson, *Greene*.) P. 495.
72 Ibid. Pp. 494-495.
73 Ibid. P. 495.
74 Stevens, *Gates at Camden*. p. 275-277.
75 Williams, *Narrative* (in Johnson, *Greene*.) P.495.
76 This seems characteristic of Gates's orders that are recorded from the time he took command - showing a strange passivity and total willingness to accept the recommendations of subordinates without question, challenge or elaboration. Whatever his style or meaning, this was the last order he would give this day.
77 Banastre Tarleton criticized the American army for "attempting to make an alteration in the disposition the instant the two armies were going to engage,' which he said the British noticed and capitalized on by a launching a "sudden and skillful attack," which "threw the American left wing into a state of confusion from which it never recovered." Ref: Tarleton, *History*. P. 113.
78 Williams, *Narrative* (in Johnson, *Greene*.) P. 495.
79 Watts, Garret. Pension Application. From The Revolution Remembered. Dann, ed., *Accounts*. Pp. 194-195.
80 Williams, *Narrative* (in Johnson, *Greene*.) P.496.
81 Ibid. P. 496.
82 Ibid. P. 496.
83 Ibid. P. 496.
84 Ibid. P. 496.
85 Ibid. P. 496.
86 Ibid. P. 496.
87 Lee, *Memoirs*. 184-185.
88 Cornwallis, Charles. Letter to Lieutenant Colonel J. Harris Cruger, written at Camden, South Carolina, August 18th, 1780. Ross, Charles, Esq., Ed. *Correspondence of Charles, First Marquis Cornwallis. In Three Volumes. Vol. I. Second Edition* (hereafter Ross, *Cornwallis Correspondence*.). John Murray, Albemarle Street. London. 1859. P. 56.
89 Lee, *Memoirs*. P. 185.
90 Williams, Otho. Letter to his sister Mrs. John Stull. Written at Salisbury, North Carolina, November 24, 1780. *Williams Paper*s. Part 1/8. (Item # 69.)
91 Lee, *Memoirs*. P 186.
92 Scammel, Alexander. Letter to Otho Holland Williams, written at Head Quarters, Totowa, New Jersey. October 19, 1780. *Williams Papers*. Part 1/8. (Item # 59.)
93 Washington, George. Letter to Meshech Weare, et al, October 18, 1780, Circular Letter on Continental Army. Washington Papers. (Meshech Weare was the presiding officer of New Hampshire's Governor's Council from 1776 to 1784. Ref: National Governors Association web site: http://www.nga.org)
94 Huntington, Samuel, President of Congress. Letter to George Washington. Written at Philadelphia, August 31st, 1780. Letters of Delegates to Congress, Volume 15, pages 639-640. Library of Congress
95 Huntington, Samuel, President of Congress. Letters to William Smallwood and Mordecai Gist. Written at Philadelphia, October 18th,1780. Letters of Delegates to Congress, Volume 16, pages 222-223. Library of Congress
96 Jacob, *Cresap*. P. 25.
97 Treacy, M.F. *Prelude to Yorktown* (hereafter Treacy, *Prelude*.) The University of North Carolina Press. Chapel Hill. P. 43.
98 Williams, *Narrative* (in Johnson, *Greene*.) P. 497.
99 Stedman, Charles. *History of the Origins, Progress and Termination of the American War, Vol. II*. (hereafter Stedman, *History*.) Printed for the Author and Sold by J. Murray, Fleet-Street; J. Debrett, Piccadilly; And J. Kerby, Corner of Wigmore-Street, Cavendish-Square. London. 1794. P. 210.
100 Jacob, *Cresap*. P. 25.
101 Williams, *Narrative* (in Johnson, *Greene*.) P. 501-502.
102 Ibid. Pp. 501-502
103 Ibid. P. 502.
104 Lumpkin, Henry. *From Savannah to Yorktown, The American Revolution in the South*. Columbia, South Carolina, 1981. Pp. 65-66.
105 Zucker, Adolf Eduard. *General De Kalb, Lafayette's Mentor*. (Volume 53 in the University of North Carolina studies in the Germanic Languages and literatures.) University of North Carolina Press. Chapel Hill. 1966. Pp. 227-228.
106 Commager and Morris. P. 1135.
107 Williams, *Narrative* (in Johnson, *Greene*.) P. 503-504.
108 Ibid. Pp. 509-510.

109 Williams, Otho. Letter to Alexander Hamilton. Written at Hillsborough, North Carolina on August 30, 1780. Hawks, F. L., Ed. *Official And Other Papers Of The Late Major-General Alexander Hamilton: Compiled Chiefly From The Originals In The Possession Of Mrs. Hamilton*. Vol. I. Wiley & Putnam. New York and London. 1842. Pp. 424-427. Also in National Archives, Founders Onlline.
110 Williams, Otho Holland. Letter to unidentified recipient, January 3, 1781. Written at Camp Hicks Creek. January 3, 1781. In Myers, *Cowpens Papers*. P. 14. (Note: The Myers Collection at the New York Public Library indicates that Williams wrote this letter to Daniel Morgan, and that seems consistent with its contents.)
111 James Duane was elected to Congress from New York July 28, 1774, and served through early November, 1783. Ref: Library of Congress. American Memory. Letters of Delegates to Congress: Volume 25 March 1, 1788 December 31, 1789. List of Delegates.
112 Hamilton, Alexander. Letter to James Duane. September 6th, 1780. Commager and Morris, p. 1135.
113 Gates apparently realized his oversight by September 27th, when he wrote to Congress, requesting that they forward his report to Washington, so that it might never be "insinuated" that he was "guilty of the smallest Neglect to the exalted Character, who so eminently fills that Station." (From the notes accompanying Samuel Huntington's letter to George Washington of October 9th, 1780 in the Letters to Delegates of Congress, Volume 16, page 170. Library of Congress.)
114 Washington, George. Letter to Horatio Gates. Written at Head quarters near Passaic Falls, October 8, 1780. *Washington Papers*.
115 Ibid.
116 Letter from Alexander Hamilton to James Duane. September 6th, 1780. In Commager and Morris. P. 1135.
117 Greene, Nathanael. Letter to Dr. Benjamin Rush. Written at Head Quarters High Hills Santee, South Carolina. August 8th, 1781. *Greene Papers*. 9:149
118 Williams, *Narrative* (in Johnson, *Greene*.) P. 499.
119 *Greene Papers*. 9:426. Note 5.
120 Seymour, *Journal*. P. 289.
121 Higginbotham, Don. *Daniel Morgan. Revolutionary Rifleman* (hereafter *Higginbotham, Morgan*.). University of North Carolina Press. Chapel Hill. 1961. p. 107 states that the force was 700 men. Seymour, William, Sergeant Major, Delaware Regiment. *"Journal of the Southern Expedition, 1780-1783* P. 289, states that it was 800."
122 Lee, *Memoirs*. P. 208.
123 Williams, Otho. *Brigade and Regimental Orders. O. H. Williams, Comm*. September 13, 1780 - February 10, 1781. Maryland Historical Society Manuscript Collection. MS 768. Entry for September 13th, 1780.
124 Williams, *Narrative* (in Johnson, *Greene*.). P. 505.
125 Ibid. P. 505-506.
126 Williams, Otho. *Brigade and Regimental Orders. O. H. Williams, Comm*. September 13, 1780 - February 10, 1781. Maryland Historical Society Manuscript Collection. MS 768. Entry for January 22, 1781.
127 Williams, Otho. *Brigade and Regimental Orders. O. H. Williams, Comm*. September 13, 1780 - February 10, 1781. Maryland Historical Society Manuscript Collection. MS 768. Entry for September 1st, 1780.
128 Williams, Otho. *Brigade and Regimental Orders. O. H. Williams, Comm*. September 13, 1780 - February 10, 1781. Maryland Historical Society Manuscript Collection. MS 768. Entry for September 19th, 1780.
129 Williams, Otho. *Brigade and Regimental Orders. O. H. Williams, Comm*. September 13, 1780 - February 10, 1781. Maryland Historical Society Manuscript Collection. MS 768.
130 Williams, Otho. Letter to Col. John Stull, written near Hillsborough on September 23, 1780. *Williams Papers*. Part 1/8. (Item # 53.)
131 See Footnote.
132 Williams, Otho. Letter to Colonel Alexander Scammel, Adjutant General of the Army. Written at Camp, Hillsborough, North Carolina. October 12, 1780. *Williams Papers*. Part 1/8 (Item # 57.)
133 Williams, Otho. Letter to Baron von Steuben, Written at Hillsborough, North Carolina. October 12, 1780. *Williams Papers*. Part 1/8 (Item # 58.)
134 Williams, Otho. Letter to Colonel Alexander Scammel, Adjutant General of the Army. Written at Camp, Hillsborough, North Carolina. October 12th, 1780. *Williams Papers*. Part 1/8. (Iitem # 57.)
135 Buchanan, *Road to Guilford Courthouse*. Pp.188-190.
136 See Footnote.
137 Higginbotham, *Morgan* is the basis for this description of Morgan and his career.
138 Higginbotham, *Morgan*. P.107.
139 Gates, Horatio. Letter to Samuel Huntington, President of Congress. Written at Fredericksburg, Va. July 4, 1780. Stevens, *Gates at Camden* p. 282.
140 Symonds, *Battlefield Atlas*. Pages 47 and 51.
141 Seymour, *Journal*. P.290.
142 Williams, *Narrative* (in Johnson, *Greene*.) P.508.
143 Williams' and Seymour's narratives disagree on some details. Seymour states that there were three companies, and

Williams states that there were four. Seymour states that the unit marched for Salisbury on October 7th, and Williams states that the plan to form the light unit "commenced on October 19." Seymour does not identify Howard as the battalion commander.

144 Kirkwood, *Journal*. P.12.

145 Morgan Daniel. Letter to Horatio Gates. Written at Salisbury, North Carolina, October 20, 1780. From the Theodorus Bailey Collection, New York Public Library.

146 Buchanan, *Road to Guilford Court House*. P. 243.

147 Otho Williams thought that Cornwallis retreated "without any known adequate cause." He pointed out that while partisan raids like those led by William Richardson Davie were annoying, still the British commander could "go where he pleased." Williams seemed perplexed by Cornwallis' decision to go back to South Carolina, concluding that "His lordship had been fatigued by the insolence of the volunteers, and chose to retire to a camp of repose." Williams, *Narrative* (in Johnson, *Greene*.) page 508.

148 Kirkwood, *Journal*. P.12. (Kirkwood also reported that Daniel Morgan received his commission as a Brigadier General from Congress while his command was at New Providence.)

149 Seymour, *Journal*. P.290. Dates are confirmed in Kirkwood, *Journal*. P.12. The quote is from Seymour. Seymour said they marched to Hanging Rock near Camden; Kirkwood said they marched to "Ridgey's Mill."

150 Williams, Otho Holland. Letter to Daniel Morgan, October 31st, 1780. Written at "Camp Hillsborough." From the Theodorus Bailey Myers Collection, New York Public Library. (The New York Public Library has "MY 1068 stamped on this document.)

151 Williams, *Narrative* (Johnson, *Greene*.) P. 508-509.

152 Williams, Otho Holland. Letter to Daniel Morgan, October 31st, 1780. Written at "Camp Hillsborough." From the Theodorus Bailey Myers Collection, New York Public Library. (The New York Public Library has "MY 1068 stamped on this document.)

153 Williams, Otho. Letter to William Smallwood, written at Salisbury, North Carolina. November 8, 1780. *Williams Papers*. Part 1/8. (Item # 64.)

154 Williams, Otho. Letter to Horatio Gates. Written at Salisbury, North Carolina. November 11, 1780. *Williams Papers*. Part 1/8. (Item # 66.)

155 Williams, Otho. Letter to Elie Williams. Written at Salisbury, North Carolina. November 24, 1780. *Williams Papers*. Part 1/8. (Item # 70.)

156 Kirkwood, *Journal*. P. 12.

157 Williams, *Narrative* (in Johnson, *Greene*.) P. 508.

158 Seymour, *Journal*. P.292.

159 Hamilton, Alexander. Letter to James Duane. September 6th, 1780. Commager and Morris, p. 1135.

160 Ward, *Revolution* P. 749.

161 Washington, George. Letter to Horatio Gates. Written at Headquarters, "Prackness.: October 22, 1780. *Washington Papers*.

162 Journals of the Continental Congress. Thursday, September 7, 1780. Volume 18. Pages 809-810. Library of Congress

163 Huntington, Samuel, President of Congress. Letter to Nathanael Greene. Written at Philadelphia, October 31, 1780. Letters of Delegates to Congress, Volume 16, pages 293-294. Library of Congress.

164 Williams, Otho. Letter to Elie Williams. Written at Salisbury, North Carolina. November 24th, 1780. Williams Papers. Part 1/8. (Item # 70.)

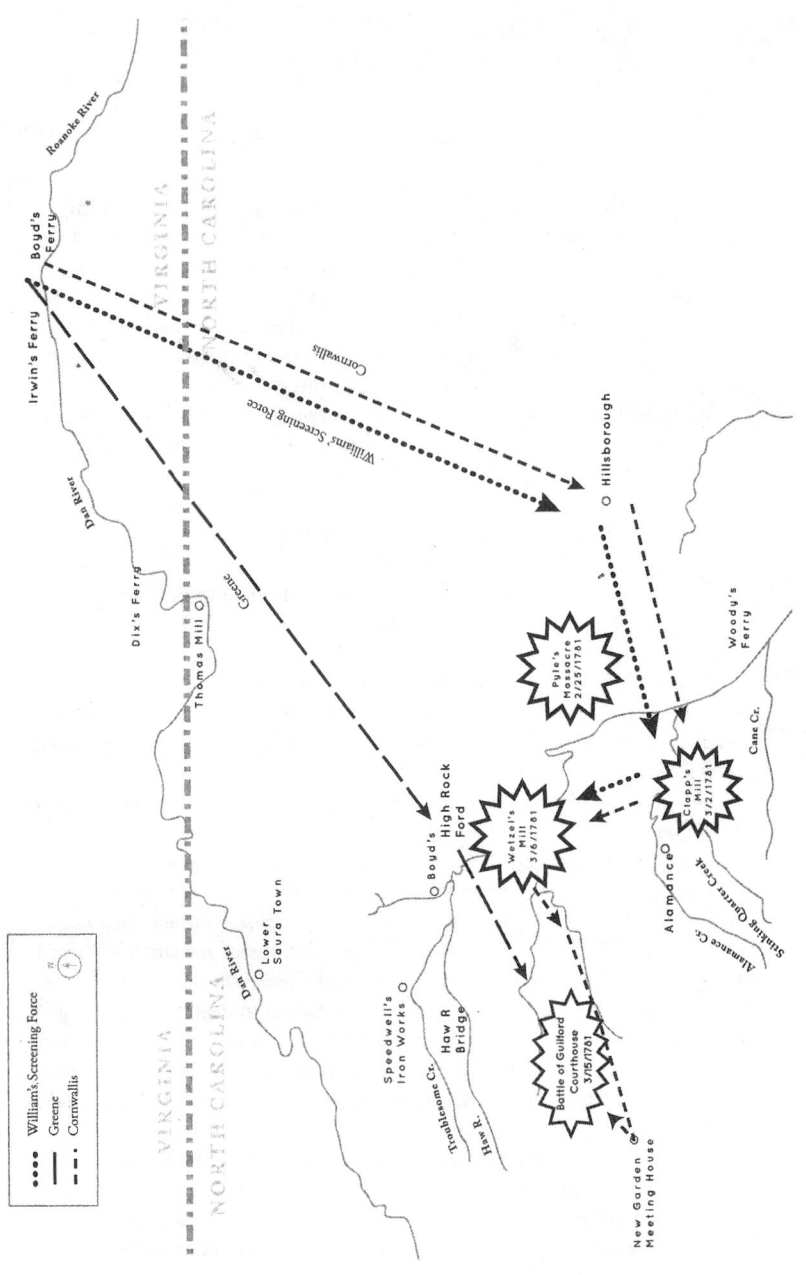

Map 5 - Maneuvers before the Battle of Guilford Courthouse

CHAPTER 6

GREENE TAKES COMMAND OF THE SOUTHERN ARMY

"the Boats were secured on the other side, and the ford had become impassable"[1]

Nathanael Greene remained in Philadelphia from October 27th through November 3rd, 1780,[2] working with Congress to prepare for his new command in the South. After he left Philadelphia, he traveled to the army's camp at Charlotte, North Carolina, stopping off at Annapolis, Maryland and Richmond, Virginia to garner support for his army from the state legislatures that were meeting in those state capitals.[3] He arrived in Charlotte on December 4th,[4] and relieved General Gates on December 6th.[5]

The change of command could have been a contentious affair if Greene and Gates had acted out any of the bitter sentiments that must surely have been present under the surface. Greene was intensely loyal to his mentor George Washington, and he believed that Gates had worked to undermine the Commander-in-Chief. Gates may have looked on the younger man as a novice who had contributed to a series of disasters, including the most egregious example of the Battle of Fort Washington. Instead, both men rose to the occasion, displaying dignity, decorum, and mutual respect, which prompted Otho Williams to record that "…the officers who were present, had an elegant lesson of propriety exhibited on a most delicate and interesting occasion."[6]

Greene respected Williams' capabilities, and Williams referred to his commander as "the judicious and gallant General Greene."[7] These two soldiers were friends, and they were totally committed to the cause of American independence. Their ability to work together would now do much to determine the outcome of the war in the South.

Williams' Retrospective on Horatio Gates

With Greene now in command, Gates prepared to return to his home in western Virginia, and he would depart with his reputation under a heavy cloud. Otho Williams wrote sympathetically of his former commander, and he felt badly for his friend, whose distress was driven by his performance on the Camden battlefield and by the personal tragedy of his son's untimely death:

> *None but an unfortunate soldier, and a father left childless, could assimilate his feelings, to those of this unhappy gentleman - yet many sympathized with him, remembered his former public services, wished for the return of tranquility to his afflicted mind, and hoped, even for a restoration of his honours.*[8]

Williams wrote privately to his family that he was sorry for the "good old man."[9]

Nathanael Greene eventually made a thorough study of the Camden campaign, which included a tour of the battlefield with Otho Williams. Greene used his efforts to convince "influential characters" to prevail on Congress to withdraw their demand to court martial Gates. Greene had as much reason as anyone to want to pillory Gates, but his own evaluation was that the older man was as much a victim of ill fortune and the performance of untrained militia as he was of damning mistakes. Assisted by Greene's interventions, Gates was eventually restored to his position under Washington with the Northern Army.[10]

Greene's Strategy for the South

After Nathanael Greene arrived in the South, he reported his plans to the Commander-in-Chief:

> *My first object will be to equip a flying Army to consist of about eight hundred horse and one thousand Infantry. This force with the occasional aid of the Militia will serve to confine the enemy in their limits and render it difficult for them to subsist in the interior country. I see little prospect of getting a force to contend with the enemy upon equal grounds and therefore must make the most of a kind of partizan war untill we can levy and equip a larger force...*[11]

Washington's answer included a reiteration of his recommendation to build portable boats as part of a strategy to use the rivers of the South to thwart enemy intentions:

> *...I would recommend the Building of a number of flat bottomed Boats of as large a construction as can be conveniently*

> *transported on Carriages; this I conceive might be of great utility, by furnishing the means to take advantage of the Enemys situation by crossing those Rivers which would otherwise be impassable…*[12]

Washington's foresight in emphasizing the importance of boats and river crossings would stand the southern army in good stead in future operations.[13]

Nathanael Greene had a voracious appetite for information, and he sent men scurrying in all directions to learn any detail, however small, that might help his army. On December 1st, just a few days before he was to take command, he had written to General Stevens of Virginia with specific instructions on how to collect information about the rivers. His exhaustive preparation for any eventuality would also serve this army well.

> *Lieutenant-colonel Carrington is exploring the Dan River, in order to perform transportation up the Roanoke as high as the upper Sauratown, and I want you to appoint a good and intelligent officer with three privates to go up the Yadkin as far as Hughes Creek to explore carefully the river, the depth of water, the current, and the rocks, and every other obstruction that will impede the business of transportation.*[14]

Greene understood the importance of the rivers to his forthcoming operations. He would soon be writing to Washington that "We had secured all the boats, and the river was so high that the enemy could not follow us."[15]

Greene Divides His Army; the "Camp of Repose"

Otho Williams was proud of the force of some 700 Continentals that he and John Eager Howard had salvaged from the wreckage after the Battle of Camden, and he knew how far they had come since the disastrous days right after the battle. However, Nathanael Greene looked at the men with a fresh set of eyes, and realized very quickly that he commanded a small, undernourished, poorly equipped Army. Greene wrote that:

> *The appearance of the troops was wretched beyond description, and their distress, on account of provisions, was little less than*

> *their sufferings for want of clothing and other necessities. General Gates had lost the confidence of the officers, and the troops all their discipline, and (they have been) so addicted to plundering that they were a terror to the inhabitants...*[16]

Greene would ultimately need a larger force if he was going to be able to confront the British on the battlefield, but even with the pressing need for more troops, he took the unusual step of sending a cavalry unit back to Virginia that did not meet standards, as he described in a December 14th letter to Virginia Governor Thomas Jefferson:

> *Lieut. Read who commands Major Nelsons corps of horse in the Majors absence; and who will have the honor to deliver this has orders to proceed to Virginia with his command: it being the opinion of Col. Washington that they are altogether unfit for further service until they are cloathed. General Smallwood is also of the same opinion, who from necessity has paid particular attention to their wants, in consequence of dayly complaints. Thirteen of them deserted in a body a day or two before I arrivd at the Army. Their sufferings and discontent is so great, that Genl. Smallwood and my self are of opinion, they had best be sent home to be cloathed, as they can be of no use here; and only serve to consume provision and forage, already grown exceeding scarce, by the amazing consumption of the numerous Militia horse, that have been in the field this Campaign. Indeed not a man unfit for actual duty for want of cloathing ought to be sent to this Army; the difficulty of obtaining subsistence is great, and the fatigue and hardships excessive...*[17]

In Otho Williams' role as Adjutant General of the southern army, he was responsible for compiling the returns that showed how many men were present and fit for duty. After Greene arrived and took command, Williams struggled to give the new Commanding General an accurate count of his force. On December 18th, he forwarded to Greene a report on the Maryland and Delaware troops, with the specific terms of enlistment for each Marylander (all the Delaware troops were signed up for the duration of the War.) The Virginia troops were "so deranged" that getting an accurate count was impossible. He was able to forward a weekly return of Colonel Buford's detachment, including the terms of their enlistments, but he had not yet received the returns from William Washington's cavalry or the artillery.[18]

By December 29th, Williams and Greene had compiled the best possible accounting of their force, which Greene described in a letter to the Marquis de Lafayette, in which he reported that his whole army consisted of 2,307 men; 1,482 of whom were present and fit for duty; 547 were absent, and 128 were detached on extra service. These, with 90 cavalry and 60 artillerymen, completed the entire roll of the southern army. Of these men, only 949 were Continentals; all the rest were militia. Greene lamented that his " whole force fit for duty that (were) properly clothed and properly equipt (did) not amount to 800 men."[19]

The "Camp of Repose"

Greene decided that the Charlotte area did not have sufficient resources to feed his men for the winter, so he decided to divide his army into two major divisions, and to send them to different areas to make it easier for them to find food and forage. He had sent Thaddeus Kosciusko to seek the best possible location for a winter camp, and Kosciusko had chosen Cheraw, South Carolina. Cheraw was off of Cornwallis' direct path into North Carolina. It was easy to defend, and provisions were more available than in Charlotte. Greene decided to send Morgan's Flying Army to the west while he marched his main force eastward to Cheraw.

Greene was a voracious reader, and he was well versed in the military classics. He surely understood that his decision to divide his force in the face of a superior enemy went against long established military maxims, but Greene really had very little choice in the matter. He was forced to locate his army where the men could find enough food, and this largely self-trained General was not afraid to defy tradition.

Colonel Williams marched toward Cheraw with General Greene and the main southern army in late December, 1780. They had a difficult journey, as Williams described to his friend Daniel Morgan:

> We arrived here the 26th. Inst. after a very tedious and disagreeable march owing to the badness of the roads and the poor and weak states of our teams.[20]

He described the strategic situation to his brother Elie back in Western Maryland:

> *Gen. [Daniel] Morgan with the Light Infantry and some Light Dragoons is detached to the west of the Catawba River to act as occasion may demand; Gen. [Nathanael] Greene, with the remainder of the army, is on the east of the Pee Dee River in a Camp of repose, a secure position to rest and rediscipline his men and to await supplies; there is a great deal to be done, for we are actually in want of almost every essential thing... But we have very good hopes of Tents and some articles of Cloathing.*[21]

Nathanael Greene described the camp to his wife, including the living arrangements with the Adjutant General, his good friend, Otho Williams:

> *I am posted in the wilderness on a great river, endeavoring to reform the army and improve its discipline. The weather is mild and the climate moderate, so that we all live in Markees without the least inconvenience. Col Williams lives with me, and we have many agreeable moments in recapitulating the pleasures and diversions of Morristown. Good God how happy we were and how little we seem'd to know it.*[22]

Williams would share with his family that he was "much attached" to Greene personally,[23] and how much he respected Greene's diligence, intelligence, and energy:

> *We are at present in a Camp of Repose and the General is exerting himself and every Body else to put his little Army in a better condition.*[24]

While the units commanded by Morgan and Greene were separated, General Greene was concerned about the safety of Morgan's detachment, and anxious for frequent updates on their situation ("Do not be sparing of your expresses but let me know as often as possible of your situation.") He also instructed Morgan to join the main force at Cheraw if the British turned east to attack Greene, Williams and the main force at their "camp of repose."[25]

The Commanding General also tried to anticipate any eventuality, including the most likely moves by their British opponent, and he told Morgan that he thought that:

> *...probably they mean to form a junction, and attempt to give a blow to a part of our force while we are divided and most probably that blow will be aimed at you, as our position in the*

> *Centre of a Wilderness is less susceptible than your Camp - I know your discretion renders all caution from me unnecessary, but my Friendship will plead an excuse for the impertinence of wishing you to run no risque of a Defeat.*[26]

Greene's Adjutant General Otho Williams was also corresponding regularly with Morgan during this nervous time, and his writing sometimes took on a little flair that was not usually found in the Commanding General's direct language:

> *May your Laurells flourish when your Locks fade, and an Age of Peace reward your toils in War - My Love to every Fellow Soldier, and Adieu-*[27]

Williams also received some kind sentiments from even so hard-bitten a warrior as Daniel Morgan, and the Adjutant thanked The Old Wagoner appropriately:

> *I thank you for your obliging sentiments in my favor and will endeavour always to deserve them by a conduct consistent with the high Ideas you have of moral rectitude and propriety.*[28]

On the other hand, Colonel Williams rarely permitted friendship or pleasantries to interfere with duty:

> *Genl. Greene desires you will please to fwd. returns of your Command. Lt. Col. Howard will please to make a Distinct return of the Light Infy. and mark all Casualties minutely that they may be entered in our Muster Rolls. - I have wrote Coll. Washington for a Special return of Cavalry called for by the Honble Board of War.*[29]

Williams also found time at Cheraw to write to Mr. John Dunlap, a Pennsylvania newspaperman that he felt had been unfair to the southern army, expressing the sentiment that Dunlap's paper, *The Pennsylvania Packet*, had been saying that the army "…is stronger and in better circumstances than it is…", and that, in fact, the army was weak and starving. Williams emphasized that this was a personal letter, not an official one, but he expressed concern that over-stating the army's strength might make the populace overconfident.[30]

Shortly after Williams sent this letter, an important reinforcement arrived at Greene's camp at Cheraw when Light Horse Harry Lee and his Legion rode into camp in early January. These troops were in "excellent condition." General Greene sent Lee and his Legion off almost immediately to support Francis Marion in an effort to capture Georgetown, South Carolina,[31] the first of many ventures that this command and its leader would participate in during the coming campaigns. Lee and Otho Williams formed an effective military partnership, and became friends for life.

Williams' Duties as Adjutant General

Doing the administrative work for an underfed, undermanned army was a thankless and unending task. In a letter to the Inspector General, Baron von Steuben, on November 12th, Williams forwarded a list of the troops in the southern army, with additional details such as information on clothing, arms, and accoutrements. He also forwarded the muster rolls for October to the Inspector General, the Board of War, and the governors of states from which the various units originated.[32]

On December 24th, 1780, Baron von Steuben wrote to Nathanael Greene, requesting that he have his Adjutant General (Williams) send in "at once" a return of all the troops from Virginia with the Army, as well as a full listing of all the officers from Virginia and the horses with the two cavalry regiments.[33]

Greene and Williams sometimes even had to apologize to each other for abbreviated correspondence due of shortages of paper or ink. On January 13th, 1781, Williams confided to von Steuben that he sometimes had "much trouble with the officers" of the southern army in carrying out his duties as Adjutant General because he was not sustained in that post by his superiors. He had served in the role successively under Baron de Kalb, Gates, and Greene. Gates had wanted to replace him with Major Armstrong, but because the major was ill for an extended period, Gates had retained Williams in the post. Williams also noted that he could serve more forcefully in his additional duties as Deputy Inspector General if he were officially confirmed in the post, which would also remove any concern that he would be replaced in the role if Greene were to be relieved.[34] On February 4th, an aide of von Steuben wrote to Williams saying that "application will be made to Congress" for the appointment that Williams requested. Enclosed with this letter was a copy of Congress's Resolve regarding the Department of the Inspector General,[35] which Williams had requested to insure that he understood fully all the duties for which he was responsible.³⁶ No record of Congress making the official appointment has been found.

On January 20th, Williams had the unpleasant task of forwarding to Baron Von Steuben a report that was not sufficiently complete on the status of the cavalry, but it was the best information that he had been able to gather from the officers commanding the southern army's cavalry detachments. To improve the quality of his reports, Williams had now gone so far as to obtain General Green's permission to employ an officer in the first cavalry regiment to work full time on assembling accurate returns, and he would shortly be sending instructions to William Washington to do the same.³⁷

Morgan's Victory at Cowpens and the Race to the Dan
Williams wrote to his brother Elie on January 14th, 1781 that the British were marching toward Morgan's Flying Army,³⁸ and that he continued to be very worried about Morgan and his men. The cloud of concern lifted nine days later, when Morgan's aide Major Edward Giles rode into the camp at Cheraw and delivered the electrifying news that six days earlier, on January 17th, Morgan had won an overwhelming victory over British Lieutenant Colonel Banastre Tarleton at Cowpens in South Carolina.³⁹

Williams wrote to his friend Dr. James McHenry that same day, reporting that the American victory at Cowpens was complete, and that the British had suffered a number of indignities... "two elegant Standards were taken," ... the Legion must wear their Coats without facings," and... "the Band of Music of the Legion is ours and the 71st lost their Bagpipes."⁴⁰ It was a tremendous victory, and it gave a much needed boost to American hopes in the south. At the Battle of King's Mountain three months earlier, frontiersmen had employed traditional hit and run tactics and deadly accurate rifle fire to surround and shatter Patrick Ferguson's command. At Cowpens, on the other hand, the Continental infantry under John Eager Howard had met British infantry head-on and beat them at their own game of stand-up volleys and bayonet charges. The training that Baron von Steuben had begun in the frigid hills of Valley Forge three winters earlier had paid off handsomely for Howard's men. As a Sub-Inspector under Von Steuben, Williams had played an important role in instilling the strict discipline, rigorous military routine, and continual practice of key combat skills that had contributed so significantly to the victory at Cowpens. The Continental Line from Maryland

and Delaware now felt that they could stand up to any attack that the British could deliver.

Williams wrote to his friend Morgan with characteristic rhetorical flourish as soon as he heard about the victory at Cowpens:

> *I rejoice exceedingly at your success. - The advantages you have gained are important, and do great Honor to your little Corps. I am particularly happy that so great a share of the Glory is due to the Officers and men of the Light Infantry… Next to the happiness which a man feels at his own good fortune is that which attends his Friends. I am much pleased that you have plucked the Laurells from the brows of the hitherto fortunate Tarlton, than if he has fallen by the hands of Lucifer - Vengeance Is not sweet if it is not taken as we have it - I am delighted that the accumulated Honors of a young partisan sho'd. be plundered by my Old Friend.*[41]

There was joy in the American camp and across the southern countryside at the news from Cowpens, but to his everlasting credit, Daniel Morgan did not sit on his laurels and wait for the accolades to roll in. With superb military intuition, the Old Wagoner realized that he had beaten only a detachment of the British army, and that his forward position left him dangerously exposed to Cornwallis' much larger force. Morgan also understood that he held a prize that Cornwallis would desperately try to retake, the hundreds of British soldiers who had become prisoners-of-war. Morgan quickly attended to the wounded of both sides and gathered up the spoils of victory. Then he marched his main force away from Cowpens almost immediately, preparing to send his prisoners off to Virginia[42] and to hurry his little Flying Army north and out of harm's way.

Initially Cornwallis' force moved ponderously, and his lordship was very frustrated by his inability to overtake Morgan. He decided to burn most of his wagons and heavy baggage so that his troops could move more quickly. As Morgan reported to Greene on January 29th, "…An express Just arrived who informs they have burnd their waggons and loaded their men very heavy."[43] Cornwallis' explanation revealed how badly he missed the light troops that he had lost at Cowpens:

> *…as the loss of my light troops, could only be remedied by the activity of the whole Corps, I employed a halt of two days in collecting some flour and in destroying superfluous baggage and*

*all my Waggons except those loaded with Hospital Stores, Salt & Ammunition, and four [wagons], reserved empty in readiness for sick or wounded.*⁴⁴

When Greene heard that Cornwallis has burned his baggage, he was heard to say, "Then he is ours."⁴⁵ On January 30th, he wrote to his second-in-command General Isaac Huger: "I am not without hopes of ruining Lord Cornwallis, if he persists in his mad scheme of pushing through the country."⁴⁶

Greene was concerned for the safety of the Flying Army, but he was also increasingly alarmed at Morgan's reports of his own deteriorating physical condition due to sciatica and other ailments. He decided to join Morgan's little force and help with the challenges of eluding Cornwallis' superior column. Greene left Brigadier General Huger and Colonel Otho Williams in command at Cheraw on January 28th, and then galloped cross-country with only a small personal guard to seek a rendezvous with the Old Wagoner. Greene sent word back to Huger and Williams to move the main army north to a spot where they could form a junction with Greene, Morgan and the Flying Army. This would unite Greene's command once again, and prepare them for any eventuality. In the meantime, Greene completed his 150 mile ride in three days, catching up with Morgan at Sherill's Ford on the Catawba River on January 30th. He sent General Huger detailed instructions from there:

*I have just arrivd at this place where General Morgan is posted with his light troops. The Enemy lay on the other side of the Catabaw about 18 miles below this. All the fords between this and Charlotte are occupied by the Militia under General Davidson. The Enemy appear determined to cross and from different accounts have in contemplation visiting Salisbury.... I beg you to hasten your march towards Salisbury as fast as possible.*⁴⁷

Greene met Morgan and his troops on the east side of the swollen Catawba River, which was protecting them from Cornwallis, who was west of the river and unable to cross. Although Greene and Morgan were safe for the moment, the river level was starting to fall, and it was only a matter of time before Cornwallis could move his army across and resume his pursuit. Greene quickly overrode Morgan's recommendation to march west into the mountains, and assured him that he would assume any responsibility for any disaster that would befall the Flying Army. Morgan and Greene led their soldiers off toward the Yadkin River, leaving the Catawba fords behind them to be defended by militia under the command of the trusted North Carolina militia Brigadier General, William Davidson. The next day, February 1st, the British forced their way across the Catawba River fords. Davidson was killed at the very outset of the skirmish,[48] and General Cornwallis moved his army across with little difficulty.

While Morgan and Greene were deftly staying ahead of Cornwallis in the hills of western North Carolina, Otho Williams and Isaac Huger were slogging northward from Cheraw with the goal of joining up with their comrades at the first convenient point. Williams and Huger had sent the weakest horses with the wagons and baggage off to the comparative safety of Hillsborough, North Carolina, but the troops still faced a very difficult march. It was a logistical nightmare, where the men were:

> ...some times without meat, often without flour, and always without spirituous liquors. Notwithstanding the wintry season, and their having little clothing, they were daily reduced to the necessity of fording deep creeks, and of remaining wet without any change of raiment, till the heat of their bodies and occasional fires in the woods, dried their tattered rags. Their route lay through a barren country, which scarcely afforded necessaries for a few straggling inhabitants. They were retarded by heavy rains, broken bridges, bad roads, and poor horses.[49]

Summarizing these difficulties, Huger wrote to Greene on February 1st that: "...the poorness of the horses, the badness of the harness, heavy roads and deep Creeks subjected me to great inconvenience and delay."[50]

Cornwallis and his troops were experiencing the same difficulties, which General Charles O'Hara described to the Duke of Grafton:

> In the most barren, inhospitable part of North America, opposed to the most savage, inveterate, perfidious, cruel enemy with zeal and bayonets only, it was resolved to follow Greene's army to the end of the world.[51]

Revolutionary War historian William Gordon used words believed to have been originally penned by Otho Holland Williams to describe the ordeal facing the armies:

Though the toils and sufferings of the Americans exceeded, those of the royal army were far from trifling. The British had in common with the others bad roads, heavy rains, a want of cover, deep creeks and rivers through which to pass in the depth of winter: but then they were well supplied in the articles of shoes and clothes.[52][53]

Daniel Morgan went on ahead of Greene, and arrived at Guilford Courthouse on February 6th, where he reported to the Commanding General that he had been " much indisposed with pains &c." and to " add to misfortunes, am violently attack'd with the piles," and that he could barely ride.[54]

On February 7th, Morgan reported to Greene that he thought that the British would arrive at Guilford Courthouse the next day. After reporting that he was unable to ride because of various ailments, he painted a dire picture of the tactical situation and urged Greene to rush to Guilford Courthouse: "The enemy is within seven or eight miles of this place."[55]

On February 9th, Greene convened a Council of War with his most senior officers - General Huger, General Morgan, and Colonel Otho Williams. The Council reviewed the Army's perilous situation and debated whether or not to make a stand against Cornwallis at Guilford Courthouse. Huger, Morgan, and Williams determined unanimously that:

...we ought to avoid a general Action at all Events, and that the Army ought to retreat immediately over the Roanoke (Dan) River.[56][57]*

Greene decided to form a screening force to shield his Army from the onrushing Cornwallis. He described its purpose in a letter to George Washington:

I have formed a light army composed of the cavalry of the 1 & 3d Regts and the Legion amounting to 240, a detachment of 280 Infantry under Lt Col. [John Eager] Howard, the Infantry of Lt Col Lee's Legion and 60 Virga Rifle Men making in their whole 700 Men which will be ordered with the Militia

---

*The American Army would be marching toward the Dan River. The name of this river changes to the Roanoke River further to the east.

> *to harrass the enemy in their advance, check their progress and if possible give us an opportunity to retire without a general action.*[58]

Greene also informed the Commander-in-Chief that "General Morgan is so unwell that he has left the Army."[59]

Greene understandably wanted the veteran Morgan to command his fast-moving screening force and fend off the British. The Commanding General of the southern army and many other people tried to prevail on The Old Wagoner to remain in the field, but Morgan claimed that sciatica and possibly other ailments had seriously eroded his ability to carry out his duties. Greene reluctantly agreed to release him, making sure to emphasize that he was expected to return to the Army when he was healthy again, and that his leave was granted "until he recovers his health."[60]

Morgan's departure left an opening in the command of Greene's light forces, and he turned to Colonel Otho Holland Williams of the Maryland Line to fill that vital role.

> *The capital expedient resorted to on this occasion, to secure the unmolested retreat of the American army, was that of detaching seven hundred light troops, under Colonel Williams, to cover its retreat. Both officers and men of this detachment, were of the elite of the American army.*[61]

Williams described his role, somewhat immodestly, to historian David Ramsay, describing the command as "seven hundred of the flower of the American Army," and the process of his selection:

> *Unfortunately the gallant Gl. Morgan was attacked with a fit of rheumatism which obliged him to quit the field. The command of the Light Troops was committed to Col. W... commandant of the Maryland Line & A.G. of the So. Army, in whose abilities the G. was pleased to put confidence.*[62]

Recognizing that his remarks about his own service might manifest a self-aggrandizing tone, Williams added that:

> *Dr. R... will have the goodness to pardon me if I betray a design of perpetuating my own name - The above is the fact tho' it does not amount to so handsome a compliment as the Doctor has made me in the page following that which is quoted.*[63]

Williams Commands the Screening Force on the Retreat to the Dan

General Cornwallis crossed the Yadkin River on February 9th, and reached Salem (today's Winston-Salem) on February 10th. He was now only twenty-five miles from the American troops at Guilford Courthouse, and His Lordship was in an excellent position to catch Greene and bring him to battle.

The British commander was determined to swoop down on the Americans as quickly as he could, and Greene was equally determined to scamper off safely into Virginia before he could be caught. The next few days would come to be called "The Race to the Dan," a military campaign that would showcase the leadership qualities of Otho Williams.[64]* Cornwallis had been told by spies that there were not enough boats on the Dan River for Greene to be able to cross at the wide, deep lower fords, so be believed that Greene would have to move to the west and cross at the upper fords. Accordingly, when Cornwallis and his troops reached Salem, he felt that he was in an excellent position to cut Greene off from the upper fords. However, Greene and Williams lured Cornwallis into believing that he had Greene's army in his grasp, but Greene and the main force were actually marching rapidly toward the lower fords where boats awaited to aid their crossing, while Williams positioned his screening force to make Cornwallis think that it was Greene's entire army.

To achieve this deception, Generals Greene and Huger marched off to the northeast toward Boyd's and Irwin's Ferries, while Williams led the screening force northwest toward the British to distract the enemy and shield Greene's retreat. For the next few days, Otho Williams and his men were in an extremely perilous situation. Their job was to keep between Cornwallis's much larger force and Greene, to protect the main American army from being detected and attacked, and to avoid heavy combat. It was an extremely demanding assignment that required speed of movement, constant alertness and rapid response to any threat, twenty-four hours a day.

Light Horse Harry Lee described the daily rigors that Williams and his troops endured as they carried out his perilous mission:

> *Throughout the night, the corps of Williams held a respectable distance, to thwart, as far as was practicable, the nocturnal assault. The duty, severe in the day, became more so at night; for*

---

*The description of the Race to the Dan in the following paragraphs is based on John Buchanan's *The Road to Guilford Courthouse*, pages 354-365.

> *numerous patrols and strong pickets were necessarily furnished by the light troops, not only for their own safety, but to prevent the enemy from placing himself, by a circuitous march, between Williams and Greene. Such a manoeuvre would have been fatal to the American army; and, to render it impossible, half of the troops were alternately appropriated every night to duty; so that each man, during the retreat, was entitled to but six hours' repose in forty-eight... Williams always pressed forward with the utmost dispatch in the morning, to gain such a distance in front as would secure breakfast to his soldiers, their only meal during this rapid and hazardous retreat. So fatigued was officer and soldier, and so much more operative is weariness than hunger, that each man not placed on duty surrendered himself to repose as soon as the night position was taken.*[65]

Lee described additional privations of the American army:

> *The shoes were generally worn out, the body clothes much tattered, and not more than a blanket for four men. The light corps was rather better off, but among their officers there was not a blanket for every three; so that among those whose hour admitted rest, it was an established rule, that at every fire, one should, in routine, keep upon his legs to preserve the fire in vigor. The tents were never used by the corps under Williams during the retreat. The heat of the fires was the only protection from rain, and sometimes snow; it kept the circumjacent ground and air dry, while imparting warmth to the body. Provisions were not to be found in abundance, so swift was our progress. The single meal allowed us was always scanty, though good in quality and very nutritious, being bacon and corn meal.*[66]

Williams later wrote a brief note about shoes for the troops in the comments that he provided to Doctor David Ramsay about the history that he was writing. A focus on shoe leather may have seemed a trivial detail to some observers, but the soldier in the field was well aware that this was a crucial factor in the screening force's ability to survive:

> *Pack horses which had been sent from Guilford to Hillsboro to bring shoes arrived (without which the troops could no longer sustain the fatigue they were exposed to) & fortunately met the*

> Army at this crisis and the General for want of time was obliged to employ the moments necessary for refreshment in seeing those articles delivered to the men who were animated by his activity and always cheerful.⁶⁷

On Sunday, February 11th, Williams wrote a hurried report to Greene that showed the nature of the constant skirmishing between the van of Cornwallis' army and the American Screening force:

> Uncertain of the Enemy's motions I waited for information at Bruces till one Hour ago. I sent 2 parties of Dragoons & some Country men different roads for intelligence. Accident informed me the Enemy were within six or Eight miles of my Quarters. I detach'd Coll Lee with a Troop of Dragoons & put the rest of the Light Troops in Motion to Cross the Haw River at a Bridge. Coll Lee met the Enemy's advance, s{tood} a Charge and Captured 3 or 4 Men whom I send you. They Say Ld Cornwallis & the whole British Army preceeded by Coll Tarltons Legion is close in our rear.⁶⁸

Greene informed Williams of the actions he was taking to get the Army's baggage to safety:

> It is very evident the enemy intend to push us in crossing the river. The night before last, as soon as I got your letter, I sent off the baggage and stores, with orders to cross as fast as they got to the river. I will endeavour to avoid him. The Cavalry wait to Cover. Coll Lee & the Infantry are Crossing the Bridge..... You have the flower of the army, don't expose the men too much, lest our situation should grow more critical⁶⁹

The pressure on Williams was enormous. He was very concerned that Cornwallis would catch up with Greene's force before it could cross the Dan River. He sometimes visualized a desperate last stand to protect the main Southern army, and he tried to calculate the time and distance required for Greene and his troops to reach the safety of Virginia:

> I conclude you march'd as far to day as you cod and if your Army can make but Eleven miles in a Day you will not be able to pass the ferry in less than two Days more. In less time than that we will be dri{ven in} to your Camp or I must risque the Troops I've

> the Honor to command and in doing that I risque every thing. You know the consequence it will be to the Army and every body knows retreating Troops must suffer in the consequences however hardy they may be in their Opposition...[70]

A few minutes later, Williams had a sinking feeling when he saw campfires up ahead, which he immediately assumed belonged to Greene and the main army. If Greene was so close by, Williams would have no choice but to turn his little force around and throw it against Cornwallis in a desperate attempt to protect the main army. He felt a tremendous sense of relief when he discovered that Greene and his force had left the area hours before, and had left the fires burning for Williams and his men. Cornwallis was pressing them so closely, however, that Williams and his troops did not have the time to stop and enjoy the warmth or cook a meal.[71]

At 4 a.m. on February 14th, Greene instructed Williams to follow the route of the main Army, and also described how minimal sleep, the press of Cornwallis' pursuit, and the potential for spies lurking at every corner had put his army under tremendous stress:

> Follow our route, as a division of our force may encourage the enemy to push us further than they will dare to do, if we are together. I have not slept four hours since you left me, so great has been my solicitude to prepare for the worst. I have great reason to believe, that one of Tarleton's officers was in our camp the night before last.[72]

At 2 p.m. on the 14th, Greene reported to Williams the encouraging news that "The greater part of our waggons are over, and the troops are crossing."[73] Two-and-a-half hours later, at 5:30 p.m., Greene was finally able to invite Williams and the screening force to rejoin the main army that had gathered safely on the north side of the Dan River:

> All our troops are over, and the stage is clear. The infantry will cross here, the horse below. Major Hardman has posted his party in readiness on this [the south] side, and the infantry and artillery are posted on the other, and I am ready to receive and give you a hearty welcome.[74]

Word of this message spread like wildfire through Williams' 700 man force, and they let out a loud cheer of relief and joy, which was heard around the countryside. The British troops closest to Williams were led by General

O'Hara, and when they heard the ruckus, they knew right away that their quarry had escaped.⁷⁵

Williams and the screening force were fourteen miles from the lower Dan crossings when they received Greene's invitation to join him in Virginia, and they set out immediately, with Light Horse Harry Lee remaining behind as a rear guard. Williams and most of the screening force chewed up the fourteen miles in just a few hours, and crossed the Dan by evening. Lee reached the river with the last units between eight and nine p.m., and crossed, the men in the boats and the horses swimming alongside. The last boatload included Light Horse Harry Lee and Greene's indefatigable quartermaster-general, Edward Carrington.⁷⁶

During the two weeks between January 29th, when he left the camp at Cheraw, and February 14th, when the screening force crossed the Dan River, Williams was under constant stress, never knowing when he would have to meet the enemy in mortal combat. After he was given command of the screening force on February 10th, he was in daily contact with the British, and was burdened by the responsibility of protecting the main army from disaster. Greene, who labored under similar difficulties, described his own exhaustion from the ordeal in a letter to Thomas Jefferson:

> *I have not time to enter into a farther detail of matters, being pressed on every side with a multiplicity of business, and almost fatigued to death have had a retreat to conduct for upwards of 200 miles Manouvering constantly in the face of the enemy to give time for the Militia to turn out and to get off our Stores. In addition to the common difficulties incident to all retreats we have had several large rivers to cross and the enemy at our heels before we could get over.*⁷⁷

But with all the challenges, the American army was safe on the north side of the Dan River, and Lord Cornwallis could only gaze across those waters longingly, for there were no boats for miles around to ferry the British cross. A deeply frustrated Charles Cornwallis described his disappointment in a letter to his superiors in England:

> *…with heavy rains, bad roads, and the passage of many deep creeks, and bridges destroyed by the enemy's light troops, rendered all our exertions vain, for upon our arrival at Boyd's Ferry on the 15th, we learned that his rear-guard had got over the night before, his baggage and main body having passed the preceding*

day at that and a neighbouring ferry, where more flats had been collected than had been represented to me as possible."[78]

Years later, when Banastre Tarleton wrote his *History of the Campaigns of 1780 and 1781*, he paid tribute to the performance of Greene, Williams and the entire American army during this grueling campaign:

Every measure of the Americans, during their march from the Catawba to Virginia was judiciously designed and vigorously executed.[79]

Nathanael Greene left a lasting testament to his friend Otho Williams, the commander of the screening force in his February 15th letter to Commander in Chief George Washington:

…I found it necessary to form as strong a covering party as possible, which was commanded by Col. Williams who had orders to keep as near the enemy as he could without exposing the party too much and retard their march all in his power. His conduct upon the occasion does him the highest honor.[80]

★ ★ ★ ★ ★

Respite in Virginia; Re-Entry to North Carolina

Williams must have been exhausted from the ordeal of the past few weeks, but he found time to write to his brother Elie on February 15th, the day after the Army had crossed the Dan, to bemoan the weak state of Greene's army, with shortages of supplies and troops. At that time, he was concerned that Greene might have to retreat further over the Bannister and Stanton Rivers.[81]

A few days later, on February 21st, he reported to Elie that Cornwallis had not tried to cross the Dan River, but instead had retreated toward Hillsborough, North Carolina,[82] which would take the pressure off until the armies chose to grapple with each other again.

In the short time that Williams and his troops were able to rest and refit north of the Dan River, Williams took the opportunity to report to Nathanael Greene that he had been suffering physically during the difficult military actions of the past few weeks. He reported that the "Rheumatism: in his breast, neck, and shoulders had been exceedingly painful," and that riding had been almost unbearable. He had been able to find some relief by bathing his feet and getting a good, warm night's sleep, and he hoped that his improving health and the improving prospects of the Army would enable him to participate in the "Glories of a successful Campaign." Williams and Greene must have discussed the possibility that Williams' health was so bad that he might have to step down from his command, since he wrote to Greene that, with prospects for success so promising, he would be reluctant to "relinquish the Honor of a command" which Greene had "so obligingly bestow'd" on him.[83] Williams' superb performance in command of the screening force during the Race to the Dan is even more impressive when his poor health is taken into account. He was a very determined and capable soldier, totally committed to his assigned mission, in spite of all difficulties.

The next few days formed a happy interlude in the history of the southern army, which Light Horse Harry Lee, who personally witnessed these events, described warmly as providing '...wholesome and abundant supplies of food in the rich and friendly country of Halifax."[84] Lee elaborated:

> *In the camp of Greene, joy beamed in every face; and as if every man was conscious of having done his duty, the subsequent days to the reunion of the army on the north of the Dan were spent in mutual gratulations; with the rehearsal of the hopes and fears which agitated every breast during the retreat; interspersed with the many simple but interesting anecdotes with which every tongue was sprung.*[85]

By contrast, Lord Cornwallis and the British troops were forced to march through territory that had been picked clean of all manner of provisions, and they were more than 150 miles from their closest supply bases at Camden, South Carolina and Wilmington, North Carolina. Cornwallis attempted to attract recruits from the Tories of North Carolina, but he was very disappointed in the results. He had been told that there were many strong British sympathizers in the area, but he was forced to conclude that "Their numbers are not so great as had been represented and their friendship was only passive."[86]

Cornwallis was learning from hard experience that it was not going to be easy to control the formidable North Carolina landscape, or to win decisive battles against the pesky, fast-moving Americans. He described some of the difficulties in a letter to Lord Germain:

> *The immense extent of this country, cut with numberless rivers and creeks, and the total want of internal navigation, will*

> *make it very difficult to reduce this province to obedience by a direct attack upon it.*[87]

The conquest of the southern states may have looked like a fairly easy matter to the British High Command when they devised this campaign in far-off London and New York, but Cornwallis and his men were learning the very painful lesson that actual conditions on the ground were a lot tougher than the idealized situation that remote British planners had expected. Cornwallis was also faced with an adversary in Nathanael Greene who would use every small advantage to its maximum benefit.

Cornwallis had stretched his supply lines to the breaking point when he had chased Greene across North Carolina. After Greene crossed the Dan into Virginia, the British Army retreated almost immediately to Hillsborough, North Carolina to search for food and forage. The Hillsborough area provided some modest provisions, but the British troops had to be extremely aggressive to find food, and they often had to use force to take what they needed from the local farmers and merchants. As a result, the British troops quickly wore out their welcome with the local populace.

The Commissary General of the British Army, Charles Stedman left this record of one foraging expedition into Hillsborough:

> *...such was the situation of the British army, that the author with a file of men, was obliged to go from house to house, throughout the town, to take provisions from the inhabitants, many of whom were greatly distressed by this measure, which could be justified only by extreme necessity*[88]

Greene had the pleasure of seeing his Army eating well and enjoying a little rest during this interlude north of the Dan River, but he would also have been very pleased a month later, when he read praise from his mentor, the Commander-in-Chief, for the success of his retreat into Virginia:

> *You may be assured that your retreat before Cornwallis is highly applauded by all ranks, and reflects much honor on your military abilities.*[89]

★ ★ ★ ★ ★

Greene Reenters North Carolina

Nathanael Greene wanted to prevent Cornwallis from controlling North Carolina, and he was determined to pursue that objective actively. While the

American army was enjoying its first restful encampment in weeks, Greene thought, talked, and wrote constantly about ways to bedevil and defeat the British.

Greene's first move was to send Henry Lee and his Legion back into North Carolina. Lee crossed the Dan River on February 19th, and reported the next day that he was camped within twenty five miles of Hillsborough, where Cornwallis had established his headquarters. Lee had sent a detachment toward Hillsborough to gather intelligence, especially Cornwallis' next intended move. At this juncture, Lee thought it was possible that the British might fall back toward Cross Creek, North Carolina.[90]

The next day, February 21st, Greene informed Andrew Pickens that "Lt Col Lee with his Legion is in full pursuit. Col Williams with the light Infantry is also on the march," and also that "the army will cross the river in the Morning, with a considerable reinforcement of Militia. If we can get up with the enemy, I have no doubt of giving a good account of them."[91]

Otho Williams had crossed the Dan and entered the "no man's land" between the British and American armies. Continuing in command of the screening force, he had the responsibility to find and develop intelligence on the enemy; to protect Greene's army from surprise; and to probe the enemy's defenses while keeping his own command safe from attack. As had been the case in the retreat to the Dan just a week earlier, he was supported by outstanding officers – William Washington, Henry Lee and John Eager Howard among them – but the ultimate responsibility fell upon the shoulders of Otho Williams. The frequent communication between Williams, Greene and Lee during these tense days is an indication of how quickly things were developing as they worked together to find Cornwallis' army and bring it to battle.

Lee soon reported that Cornwallis and his army had arrived in Hillsborough on the evening of February 20th, and that Lee was moving his Legion closer to the enemy. He was also expecting to make contact with militia General Andrew Pickens,[92] a proven fighter who was in command of a unit of South Carolina and Georgia militia.

Otho Williams reported to Greene from inside North Carolina at 8 a.m. on February 22nd that he had delayed his march to wait for a delivery of beef cattle, as his men were out of provisions. Ever mindful of the need to feed an army on the march, Williams advised Greene that if he proceeded on the path that the British had just taken, the surroundings would have been picked bare of provisions. Williams recommended an alternate route for Greene where, "if intelligence justifies it," Greene could proceed through a fertile and untouched farming area.[93] At 4 p.m. that afternoon, Williams had to clarify for Greene the marching route he had recommended for the main army. He also reported that his location offered only scant provisions of corn, which had to be ground that night.[94]

On February 23rd, Lee reported to Greene that he was probing for intelligence at Hillsborough, and that he was disgusted with the attitudes of the people of the region. When Cornwallis had established his headquarters in the town, the British general had asked for volunteers, and Lee said that people had swarmed to town to take the oath of allegiance, and would have served under British arms if Lee and Pickens had not entered the area. Lee also passed on the encouraging news that the British troops needed shoes and that their cavalry was "exceedingly fatigued."[95]

Food and forage were not the only items in short supply. On February 25th, Greene sent a note to Williams that was written on the back of a letter from Henry Lee to Greene, with the notation, "Pray Excuse; paper is Very Scarce."[96] Williams responded by moving his troops where they would shield Greene's men more effectively; he also sent two reports from Mr. James Bruff, who had been "very inquisitive and active" in gaining information on the enemy. Bruff had provided information that the British were leaving Hillsborough, and Williams was sending John Eager Howard in that direction.[97] Other practical matters included information that Williams was marching to his destination on an indirect route so that he could obtain some food that Bruff had collected for them; he had sent for flour from Ramsey's Mill, but the Hyco River was so high that the waterwheel was "drown'd." Because of the deepness of the river, Williams warned that Greene would not be able to cross the river at Ramsey's Mill.[98]

The letter that Greene had written on the back of contained the report that Lee had routed a Tory cavalry force under Colonel Pyle in an encounter that had a devastating effect on Tory morale and recruitment. At the start of the engagement, Pyle and his troops had mistaken Lee and his Legion for Tarleton and his troops. Lee, supported by militia under the command of the able Andrew Pickens in the nearby woods, intended to use this subterfuge to maneuver his cavalry past Pyle, but when some troops in the rear ranks discovered that they were facing adversaries, firing broke out and the situation quickly degenerated into a short, brutal encounter in which Lee reported "the greatest part of them were left on the field dead & wounded."[99] The American commanders Greene and Pickens were pleased with the results of the encounter, Pickens noting that decimation of Pyle's militia "… has knocked up Toryism altogether in this part."[100]

Another record of this incident stated that six Tory prisoners were hacked to death with broadswords by militiamen to chants of "Remember Buford."[101] American families and fighting men had not forgotten Tarleton's reported atrocities at Waxhaw, South Carolina the previous May. Brutality was never very far under the surface in this war in the South.

Nathanael Greene did not dwell on any of the unsavory aspects of Lee's victory over Pyle. To him, the main importance of the encounter was its impact on Tory morale, and he looked on the incident with cold, hard realism: "It has had a very happy effect on those disaffected Persons, of which there are too many in this Country."[102]

Greene had recrossed the Dan with the main army on February 22nd, intent on re-taking North Carolina. He once again detached Otho Williams and his light screening force to shield the main force from the enemy. Henry Lee's Memoirs recalled their operations:

> *After our repassage of the Dan, Washington and his horse were again placed in the van, and with Howard and Lee, led by Williams, played that arduous game of marches, countermarches, and manoeuvres, which greatly contributed to baffle the skillful display of talents and enterprises exhibited by Lord Cornwallis in his persevering attempt to force Greene, at the head of an inferior army, to battle, or to cut him off from his approaching re-enforcements and supplies.*[103]

Greene moved the main army to a new camp almost daily, and the screening force of Williams, Washington, Howard and Lee maneuvered ceaselessly over the next few weeks to provide a shield to Greene's main force. They also did what they could to harass and nettle Cornwallis and his troops as much possible.

It was tense, unending warfare. Once again, Williams and his comrades endured skirmishes, raids, and ambushes at all hours of the day and night. They were always under arms, always at the ready, always looking and listening with strained senses to keep their units out of harm's way.

Greene described his approach in a letter to his friend Joseph Reed:

> *It was certain I could not fight him (Cornwallis) in a general action without almost certain ruin. To skirmish with him was my only chance. Those happened dayly, and the enemy suffered considerably. But our militia coming out principally upon the*

footing of volunteers, they fell off dayly after every skirmish, and went home to tell the news....In this situation, with an inferior force, I kept constantly in the neighbourhood of Lord Cornwallis...[104]

★ ★ ★ ★ ★

The Skirmish at Clapp's Mill[105*]

At 8 p.m. the evening of March 1st, Williams wrote to Greene that he had located Cornwallis three miles from his infantry camp on Alamance Creek, and that he intended to launch an attack at 4 a.m., trusting that "...if we make a brisk, unexpected attack and are aided by Providence our advantage may be considerable and of great consequence to your future operations." Williams added that he was determined "...to commence hostilities as early as possible"[106] Henry Lee also wrote to Greene on March 1st, revealing that he disagreed with Williams and thought that the attack should hold off until the British had broken camp and were on the march.[107]

Williams' planned attack did not come off as he had hoped. He had sent orders to Andrew Pickens to send a troop of mounted militia to reconnoiter the British position, an assignment which Pickens gave to Joseph Graham.[108] Graham went forward in accordance with his orders, and it was "nearly dark" when he was ascending the hill up from the Alamance when he encountered William Washington and his troops. Washington advised Graham not to proceed, saying that there was a "skygale ahead," pointing toward the light given off by the fires of the British camp, "which appeared as if the woods were on fire." Graham and Washington rode together back to the camp of Andrew Pickens, who approved their decision to return.[109]

Otho Williams was unhappy with Graham's decision to abort his mission, and he wrote to Light Horse Harry Lee at 3 a.m. on March 2nd:

> *You will please advance with the legion in time to be here about daybreak, as I wish to form the van to-morrow. The fatigue your horse has suffered, induced me to employ the mounted militia on detached service, and to obtain intelligence. But I can no*

---

*The narrative of Joseph Graham, who participated in this skirmish, is the primary reference herein for the Clapp's Mill affair. It is published in Graham, William A. *General Joseph Graham and his Papers on North Carolina Revolutionary History*. Raleigh. Edwards & Broughton. Raleigh 1904. Pp. 329-340.

longer depend on their cautious observations, and equivocal intelligence; besides, I want an officer in the front, capable of catching a sudden opportunity, if an advantage can be taken of the enemy. He may make one incautious step.[110]

Lee was in Pickens' camp early the next morning, requesting that some militia cavalrymen join him on his mission. Many volunteered. Forty were chosen to accompany Lee, and he placed them under the command of Captains Graham and Simmons. Lee led them forward, and soon after they crossed the Alamance, they joined some riflemen under Colonel William Preston, the cavalry of Lee's Legion under Major Rudolph, and some Catawba Indians. Lee deployed his forward troops as follows: (1) Units of twenty combined riflemen and cavalrymen in front, 100 yards to the right and left of the road, the left commanded by Captain Graham, the right by Captain Simmons. (2) Six Catawba Indians and four of Lee's cavalrymen in the main road across from Graham and Simmons, and (3) Major Dickson with two hundred mounted infantry In the rear of Simmons on the right of the road, aligned with Major Rudolph's command across the road.[111]

An alarm spread through the American ranks when they heard British fifes and drums beating up ahead, but they soon discerned that this was only a changing of the guard. Two of Lee's troopers rushed a British prisoner to Lee, who interrogated him and sent him to the rear. The next line of American troops was composed of veterans under proven leaders, Captains Kirkwood and Oldham, who came into sight marching up the road from the Alamance. With these dispositions completed, the entire command under Lee moved forward slowly.[112] The main body of Williams' force was deployed on the other side of the Alamance, with William Washington supporting the rear.[113]

The forward troops marched "upwards of a mile", and the units on either side of the road had to march through fences and fields. They came upon a house and double barn, in front of which was a thick wood, extending across the road to Clapp's plantation. The Indians ran forward and fired. The riflemen under Graham and Simmons could see the British up ahead in formation, and began to fire. Major Dickson and Colonel Preston had their men dismount, tie their horses to a fence, and move toward the enemy. Major Rudolph deployed the Legion cavalry in line behind the double barn. The American lines advanced, and a heavy fire began on both sides. The Catawba Indians immediately fled, and the heavy fire from the British lines caused bark and twigs to fly dangerously among the Americans. After firing three rounds the American front line became panic-stricken and retreated without orders. Lee tried to rally the militia without success, and then ordered Graham to try to cover the retreat. Rudolph led Lee's cavalry calmly, and in compact order, back toward the Alamance. The British pursued, but their advance soon felt the fire from Kirkwood's and Oldham's infantry, who were on high ground, which enabled them to fire over the heads of the retreating Americans and into the advancing British troops. The British cavalry halted, and waited for their infantry to come forward in support.[114]

Williams and Lee then took command of the line of regulars, with Williams commanding on the left and Lee on the right.[115] They tried desperately to rally the militia, but as soon as they moved one group into position and moved to rally another, the first group would melt away. Major Dickinson, according to Joseph Graham who was in this fight, "with his characteristic coolness and decision" recommended to Williams that if he would direct the militia to form on "the next rise, beyond that hollow," that the militia would hold formation. Williams accepted the recommendation, and the American line was soon restored and firm. Firing soon ceased, and the Americans marched off unmolested. After a mile or two, they reached the Alamance, crossed the ford, and were reunited with Williams' main force, which included William Washington's cavalry. Joseph Graham's narrative of these events sounds quite relieved to have reached this line of support:

> *our retreat was effected with difficulty; retreated about one mile to the ford, on Big Alamance, where Col Otho Williams, the regulars under his command, and Washington's cavalry were drawn up to support us.*[116]

Graham was impressed with the disposition of the troops, noting that Colonel Williams had completed those arrangements "before he came on to battle." They stood in formation for about a half hour, and then marched back five or six miles, when the different corps separated.[117]

The enemy that these troops had faced was Banastre Tarleton's "whole corps" of the cavalry, a few mounted infantry, a light company of the Guards, and one hundred and fifty of Colonel Webster's men."[118] One substantive estimate is that Tarleton commanded 404 men of Cornwallis' total command of 2,213, while Otho Williams had 2,039 men, of which Lee commanded about 700 in the forward ranks.[119]

Williams' reported the incident to Greene on March 2nd:

> *Lt Col Lee advanced very slowly and with great circumspection. Several intelligent officers were out, but the people here will speak nothing but German which few of us understand, therefore we co(uld) not find the Enemy without some Risque. Lee advanc'd one Mile from our Camp where his Flank was Fired upon. The mounted Rifle men had not time to dismount and did not return the fire so brisk as I expected. However those on Foot and the Infantry of the Legion were making a handsome defence when I order'd a gradual retreat which was well enough effected considering the irregularity of our order. I believe very few fell on either side. We have 10 or 12 wounded.*[120]

This skirmish at Clapp's Mill was a small affair in the grand scheme of the competition between Greene and Cornwallis,[121] but it reveals much about the military character of Otho Williams. Williams was on his own, several miles removed from Greene. His decisions alone would decide the fate of his detachment. In this situation, he aggressively sought out direct confrontation with the enemy, but he did so in a formation that enabled him to gather direct information about his enemy's strength and location, while still moving forward cautiously. He deployed small flanking parties that were ready to protect his main lines, and each line was supported by troops behind them who could help immediately if a strong enemy appeared. Williams had stationed his forces in the same general formation that Daniel Morgan had pioneered at Cowpens – militia in front to slow the enemy's advance, and the Continentals, under Williams' direct command, in the rear to receive the brunt of any attack.

Williams rode to the front-lines to engage directly in the fight. We do not know exactly when he left his main force behind the Alamance and rode forward to the line of Continentals under Kirkwood and Oldham, but it seems reasonable that he heard the firing up ahead and rode forward to take command of the defense and to plan the next movements of his force. This would mean that Williams was a soldier who would "ride to the sound of the guns," but he also exhibited considerable prudence in his tactical decisions – sending Lee forward "with great circumspection," and ordering a "gradual retreat." In short, at Clapp's Mill, Otho Williams exhibited the steady hand and clear thinking of an experienced combat commander.

Williams was not alone in wanting to hit Cornwallis. If anything, Nathanael Greene wanted even more ardently to draw the British into a battle. As we have seen earlier, Williams could become irritable when he was tired and under heavy stress, and a few days after the affair at Clapp's Mill, he protested to his commander because he felt that Greene and his staff were urging him to attack the enemy once too often:

> *I am always mindful of your orders to attack the Enemy when any opportunity offers. The repe(ti)tion of this order imply's how solicitous you are to have it done & Major Burnet mention'd it as your very particular desire in his letter of this Day. Perhaps I am to construe those frequent intimations as sufficiently expressive. Whenever an Opportunity offers I will embrace it if I can be justified by the circumstances, or the opinion of the principal Officers serving with me; if any thing more is expected I wod thank you to be explicit.*[122]

Williams' obvious sense of irritation may have been heightened by the fact that he had previously enjoyed frequent, direct contact with his friend Greene, and he was now being asked to respond to orders from subordinate members of the staff. Communications with Major Burnet may have been particularly irksome, as Greene once described him as "cross."[123]

Having vented his feelings to his friend, Williams assumed a calmer, apologetic tone in a note to Greene two days later:

> *Ever proud of your Esteem, I was perhaps too tenacious of your approbation, and therefore suspiciously interrogated Major Burnett respecting your sentiments of my Conduct. Conscious of having done everything in my power, I was only apprehensive that there might appear to you a seeming delay in our passing the river... I regard your Friendship as invaluable and than(k) you for the obliging manner in which you have expressed it. I will endeavour to deserve it by rectitude of Conduct wch alone can secure the Esteem of men of Sense and Merit.*[124]

Williams was not the only soldier in Greene's army who could become irritable. While officers and men in the Continental service were signed up for long enlistments and were accustomed to strict discipline, many others chafed under the routines of military service that are associated with regular soldiering. The capable and independent riflemen from the frontier regions were accustomed to expressing themselves very directly, and were particular about the officers under whom they served. In late, February, Williams had requested that Greene send someone (preferably Major David Campbell, if he was available) to command the riflemen who were joining his command, as Williams does not "understand them perfectly,"[125] a somewhat surprising statement, since Williams had served in a rifle unit himself in the earliest days of the War.

A few days later Colonel William Morgan was sent by Virginia Militia General Edward Stevens to command Williams' riflemen, but the riflemen refused to serve under him. Otho Williams noted that "It is difficult to manage them, and I have had hints that they do not expect to go farther than Hillsborough unless upon an occasion, the advantage or necessity of which they will judge." Fortunately for Williams, the riflemen apparently agreed to serve under the universally respected Andrew Pickens.[126]

Williams had another encounter with the militia when he and Light Horse Harry Lee met with all of the militia officers under Preston and Pickens the day after the Skirmish at Clapp's Mill. Lee and Williams asked these leaders to send every third man home with their horse because they found it difficult to change positions in combat without first taking care to find and protect their horses. Williams and Lee suggested that half their number organized as infantry would be much more helpful than all of them mounted. The militia officers were unanimous that their men would never accept sending horses home.[127] Such discussions led many militia officers and men to question how much respect Otho Williams had for their service. From Williams' perspective, the militia riflemen who supported Greene's army brought invaluable military skills with them, but managing them effectively was a continuous challenge.

★ ★ ★ ★ ★

Weitzel's Mill[128]

Lord Cornwallis continued to probe the American screening force and to search for ways to bring General Greene to battle before he received reinforcements from Virginia. His Lordship found it very difficult to obtain information about his enemy's location and movements, which he attributed to "timid friends and inveterate rebels."[129] Cornwallis could also just as easily have noted that his lack of information and inability to attack Greene were largely due to the actions of the screening force commanded by Colonel Otho Williams. Light Horse Harry Lee, who reported to Otho Williams, would have added that the superiority of the American cavalry continually thwarted British efforts to find and attack Greene or to obtain actionable intelligence.[130]

On March 5th, Cornwallis was finally able to gain some useful information on his enemy's whereabouts,[131] when he learned that Williams' screening force was "...posted carelessly at separate plantations for the convenience of subsisting."[132] Williams' command was strung out south and east of Reedy Fork, where they could "...conveniently interrupt the British parties while collecting provisions and forage."[133] Cornwallis decided to try to exploit the dispersion of Williams' screening force. If the British could move quickly, they might be able to separate Greene from Williams by establishing a position at Weitzel's Mill, which stood between the two American forces. The British commander felt that if he could split the American Army, he might defeat Williams, and then attack Greene.[134]

Williams was unaware that Cornwallis was preparing to take advantage of his separation from Greene. He wrote to his commander early on the morning of March 6th from "Martin Boons 7 miles east Col Paselys"[135] that he had moved his force three miles the previous evening, and that the British army was seven miles off, in the same position it had occupied previously. Williams added that "While Lord Cornwallis keeps his present position, like a bear with his stern in a corner, I cannot Attack him but tooth and nail. We have two days provisions and are ready for action." Williams sounded as though he wanted to move aggressively, but he would soon be surprised to learn that Cornwallis was trying to steal a march on him.[136]

Cornwallis' entire Army was in motion at 3 a.m. on March 6th,[137] headed toward Weitzel's Mill. The secrecy of the British movement was aided by a heavy morning fog, which helped to hide their movement from any observers. Cornwallis sent Tarleton and his Legion, supported by Lieutenant-Colonel James Webster and his infantry, to move ahead as quickly as they could toward Weitzel's Mill.[138]

After crossing the Alamance, Tarleton charged down the road toward Reedy Fork. He was close to stealing a march on Williams. Fortunately for the Americans, Tarleton was discovered by what Williams called one of his "reconnoitering Officers,"[139] which Joseph Graham[140]* identified as a patrol from William Washington's troops.[141] Williams put his troops "instantly

---

*Joseph Graham is the same the North Carolina militia cavalry officer who had fought at Clapp's Mill. His thorough and well written papers are an extremely valuable resource on the encounters in which he was involved.

in motion." Just as Williams and his troops were setting out, two prisoners informed him that Cornwallis was marching on a parallel road to his left, and was headed for Weitzel's Mill.[142]

Williams sent out flanking parties to slow the British advance, and he ordered the cavalry led by William Washington and Henry Lee to delay the British while he pushed forward as quickly as he could. The American troops closest to Tarleton were commanded by an impressive soldier, Colonel William Campbell,[143] one of the heroes of King's Mountain. Lee reported that "some remissness of the guards" and the morning fog allowed the British to surprise Campbell, but that "the alertness of the light troops soon recovered the momentary disadvantage." Lee recorded that his Legion advanced to support Campbell, and their combined force stunted the British attack, and then held them back as the Americans gradually withdrew up the road.[144] Joseph Graham does not mention Lee specifically in this phase of the engagement, merely noting that:

> *All were soon in motion, each pushing into the road to gain the British front, which some did with difficulty. The British advanced with such celerity that some small parties, who endeavored to reach their front, fell on their flanks. A scattering fire was continually kept up, either on the flanks or in front; as their rule was, whenever they saw their adversaries, to fire upon them, without halting, and press on in as compact an order as such rapid movements would admit.*[145]

Cornwallis had specifically picked two aggressive and fast-moving officers, Tarleton and Webster, to lead his attack, and he was ready to support them with additional infantry and artillery whenever they needed it. He was impatient for success, and ready to probe any weak point in the American defenses or apply more force when they were standing firm.

Joseph Graham described the running combat that occurred as all parties raced for the Mill:

> *Colonel Tarleton and Corps were within one hundred yards of the front of their infantry, and though so many opportunities offered for attacking scattering parties of militia coming in on the flanks, he never attempted to charge or pursue them. The appearance of Washington and Lee before him, must have prevented him from improving such advantages as*

frequently offered in the course of the day. Washington and Lee superintended the rear alternately in person...[146]

William Campbell and his riflemen were also part of the group that skirmished with Tarleton along the road, as Otho Williams reported that Campbell had, "in concert with Lt Col Washington served as a covering to the retireing troops..."[147] Graham reported that there was fighting all along the road, and that "on the first sight of any force within his reach in front, the enemy, without halting, fired a platoon and kept steadily forward." Graham also recorded that "when we came within a short distance of Whitsell's Mill on the Reedy Fork of Haw River, Colonel Williams galloped ahead in haste and selected a position for battle."[148] The screening force would fight from defensive positions personally selected by Williams.

The American troops reached Reedy Fork in the early afternoon, comfortably ahead of the British, and began crossing, protected by Campbell and Washington, who artfully delayed the British advance. To further delay Webster and Tarleton, Williams placed Colonel William Preston of Virginia and a party of riflemen in a good defensive position on wooded ground, where they could block the British advance and cover the Americans while they crossed Reedy Fork. The British poured a "brisk" fire onto Preston's troops, which the riflemen returned "with great spirit."[149]

The main American force crossed the Fork and took up their designated positions:

> *The main body of the militia passed first after the horses and waggons, and formed on the opposite side of the water; then the regular infantry under lieut. Col. Howard; after that Lee's legion and cavalry. Campbell and Washington filed off about half a mile from the mill, crossed and rejoined the rest on the other side of the creek.*[150]

Joseph Graham described the action of Preston and his riflemen:

> *As the enemy approached, the two companies of riflemen began to fire. The enemy halted, the first time it had done so in twelve miles, and immediately began to deploy...The riflemen kept up a severe fire, retreating from tree to tree to the flanks of our second line. When the enemy approached this, a brisk fire commenced on both sides. From the state of the atmosphere, they became enveloped in smoke; the fire had lasted but a short time, when*

> the militia were seen running down the hill from under the
> smoke. The ford was crowded, many passing the watercourse at
> other places. Some, it was said, were drowned.[151]

As Preston and his riflemen rushed across the creek, they were pursued by the British infantry, who proceeded with "great precipitation."[152]

Williams had placed 350 Continental infantry under John Eager Howard and some militia directly across from the ford, with Washington's cavalry and a small force of militia cavalry under Joseph Graham 100 yards to their right and Lee's cavalry (under Rudolph) 100 yards to their left. Lee himself had been assisting Preston in his efforts to delay the oncoming British.[153]

Joseph Graham described this phase of the fight in terms that give great insight into the discipline and combat prowess of the Continental troops of Greene's Southern army and of the leadership and discipline of officers like Otho Williams and John Eager Howard. Their tireless routine of requiring their troops to practice the procedures for loading and firing their weapons every day paid off handsomely in critical moments like this:

> The next object presented was the British pushing forward from
> under the smoke in disorder. Upon which the Regulars under
> Colonel Williams and the militia under him on the north side
> of the water began a brisk fire over the heads of the retreating
> militia, which caused the advancing foe to halt and repair his
> line, which was done in a short time.
> The fire of Williams' Regulars, their front about thirty poles
> long,[154]* was, while it continued, equal to anything that had been
> seen in the war, for they were under excellent discipline.[155]

These well directed, coordinated, disciplined volleys blunted the force of the British advance, and gave the Americans a brief respite to adjust their defenses. The British Lieutenant Colonel Webster retired to the south of the creek and regrouped for another attack.

In their second attack, the British were supported by the artillery pieces that Cornwallis had deployed on a hill that overlooked the Mill, a development which "dismayed the militia so manifestly, that Williams gave them orders to retire; and then followed with Howard's battalion, flanked by a company

---

*A pole is 16.5 feet, so the Continental formation was, according to Graham, about 165 yards long.

of Delaware infantry and the infantry of the legion, the whole covered by Washington's cavalry. The cavalry of the legion covered the baggage and ammunition wagons, which accidentally took a different route."[156]

Lieutenant Colonel Webster had personally led the main British assault across the center ford. When Light Horse Harry Lee wrote his *Memoirs* long after the war, he remembered that Webster had come under fire from an abandoned schoolhouse, where Lee had stationed twenty-five hand-picked riflemen, all of whom were superb marksmen and had served at King's Mountain. Webster's horse had to struggle through the deep water, so the riflemen should have had a very easy target. Lee alleged that the riflemen fired either thirty-two or thirty-three rounds at Webster, but did not hit him or his horse even once, which stunned everyone who saw these crack shots miss such an open and slow-moving target.[157][158]

As he was moving away from the scene of the fighting, Williams ordered Captain Joseph Graham to take a half-dozen of his men and find General Greene to give him a verbal report, since Williams did not have the leisure to write at this moment. Graham was directed "to inform the General of the dispositions made at the mill and the result of the battle."

> You may tell him but two of our Regulars are killed and three wounded, and from the best I can learn, not more than twenty or twenty-five of the militia. You move with Colonel Washington. Say that the militia, though scattered at first are generally collected, and joined us again; that the last seen of the enemy was about a mile on this side of the battle-field. He was then returning. But chiefly I wish the General to send me word whether it is his will that I file off to the right at a place he mentioned. Tell him I shall keep along this road until I receive orders.[159]

Graham also recalled what happened when he reached Greene, which gives an insightful glance into the mind of the Commanding General while his screening force commander was fighting not too far away:

> The party proceeded, and in travelling three or four miles overtook the army with General Greene on the march. The General himself was near the rear, in much solicitude. He had heard the firing and was anxious to know the result. After hearing the relation, he asked many questions, and then ordered one of his aids to bring the map, dismounted, and

he and the aid got astride of a log and spread the map, each hand holding a corner. After examination, it was decided that Colonel Williams' cavalry and all the light troops should file off at the place proposed, which led to Carthey's Bridge, on Troublesome Creek, which they crossed about midnight and encamped. General Greene continued his march by the direct road to Troublesome Iron Works, some distance above Colonel Williams. He got there about dark, and continued at this place until he moved on to the battle at Guilford Court-House.[160]

Williams was able to supplement Graham's oral report to Greene with his own written description the next day, March 7th, in a letter which described his retreat and subsequent actions:

The ground on this side being very unfavourable I waited only 'till Col Preston cross'd and then order'd the Troops to retire. The Enemy pursued some distance but receiving several severe checks from small covering parties and being cow'd by our Cavalry He tho't proper to halt. We continued to retire about five miles where we Encamped and were refreshing ourselves when Major Burnett deliver'd the instructions from you which induced me to cross the Haw River and take post there. Our loss is very inconsiderable, very few were kill'd & most of our wounded were brought off. The Party I detach'd Yesterday morning is arrived safe. The Enemy Encamped last night between Whitsel Mill and High Rock.[161]

In Nathanael Greene's view, the affair at Weitzel's Mill was a minor incident, as he described in his report a few days later to Commander-in-Chief George Washington:

On the 6th the British moved down towards High Rock, either with a view to intercept our Stores, or cut off the Light Infantry from the main Body of the Army then advanced near seven Miles but they were handsomely opposed and suffered considerably without effecting any thing.[162]

Greene expressed complete satisfaction with Otho Williams' performance at Weitzel's Mill in a letter to a friend written twelve days after the skirmish:

> *In this situation with an inferior force, I kept constantly in the neighbourhood of Lord Cornwallis, until the 6th when he made a rapid push at our Light Infantry, commanded by Col. Williams, who very judiciously avoided the blow...*[163]

Weitzel's Mill Controversies

The historical record of the skirmish at Weitzel's Mill is muddled, particularly as it regards the performance of Otho Williams. Nathanael Greene praised Williams' performance in private correspondence and official reports that he wrote very soon after the event, however there were various militia units and leaders who expressed dissatisfaction with some of Williams' command decisions. Additionally, years later, William Richardson Davie, a very distinguished Revolutionary officer from North Carolina, would write a damning critique of Williams for his actions on March 6th, 1781.

Many of the militia who had joined Greene and Williams had been in a surly mood, even before the skirmish began. On the day before the Weitzel's Mill affair, the highly regarded militia general Andrew Pickens had written Greene about the unhappiness in his command:

> *The South Carolinians and Georgians are truly in a miserable plight, not one to be met with a second shirt and I have been informed by them, necessity compels them to return towards the South. The services of those Men, they having most of them been out from the time Charlestown was taken and the distress they are now in prevents my insisting on their stay. If it was possible and agreeable to you, I could wish likewise to return, altho I would serve my Country in any part, but I look on it I am capable of doing more good there than here.*[164]

On March 8th, two days after the affair at Weitzel's Mill and at a time when a major battle with Cornwallis seemed imminent, Greene ordered Pickens to lead his Georgia and South Carolina troops to South Carolina.[165] It seems amazing that a proven veteran combat leader like Andrew Pickens would march away from the army and head south when a major battle against Cornwallis was in the immediate offing, but the army's leaders were convinced that these troops would not remain in the service unless they returned south.

Pickens had also recounted that militiamen throughout Greene's command had been unhappy with the plans that Williams and Light Horse Harry Lee had discussed with them about taking away their horses, and were deserting as a result.[166] Light Horse Harry had gone one step further, and wanted to have a consolidated mounted force. Moreover, his troops needed some good mounts to replace some of theirs which had been ridden very hard in recent campaigns.[167] Too many horses stretched the slender logistics of Greene's army even further, and it had made sense to the senior army leadership to send excess horses away. One observer at Salem on March 4th reported that 150 horses passed through, "returning from the army for lack of forage," and another at Bethabara reported that "One party after another came from the army with riderless horses. It was said that these were all Colonel Preston's horses and about fifty of his men."[168]

The Virginia militiamen who remained to serve under William Preston at Weitzel's Mill were also extremely unhappy with their experience with the army, and they, too, headed for home. Preston wrote to Governor Thomas Jefferson of Virginia that after their defeat in the delaying action at Weitzel's Mill, "…no arguments that could be made use of by myself, or the other officers, could induce the remaining few to remain another week…"[169] Major Charles Magill, Jefferson's representative on Greene's staff, reported to the Governor that

> *On the late skirmishes, of which an account was given in my last, the Riflemen complained, that the burthen and heat of the Day was entirely thrown on them, and that they were to be made a sacrifice by the Regular Officers to screen their own troops; full of this idea the greater number left the Light Troops. Some rejoined their Regiments with the main Body, and others thought it a plausible excuse for their return home.*[170]

Greene could hardly have been encouraged by the fact that important groups of militia had decided to go home in the immediate aftermath of the fight at Weitzel's Mill.

Captain Joseph Graham, a militia cavalryman, provided a balanced view of the complaints of some of his fellow militiamen:

> *The whole way from the battle, three or four miles, the broken militia were coming in on each flank, sometimes in squads of twenty or thirty, sometimes singly. They were much dissatisfied with the place that had been assigned them by the Continental officers, not allowing them, as they stated, an equal chance with the Regulars; having had to cross the Reedy Fork under the whole fire of the enemy in order of battle. It might be stated in defence*

> *of the officers that they were really so situated that it became necessary to risk the sacrifice of one part of their command to save the rest, and though the life of one man is as dear to him as that of another, yet the loss to the cause of three or four of militiamen whose term of service would expire in a week or two was not as great as the loss of one regular, who was well trained, and engaged to serve during the war. But this was a kind of logic they were unwilling to admit. When it was discovered that the enemy were going back, Lee's cavalry fell in the rear of the militia, who were collecting fast, and following Williams; Lee himself taking much pains to convince the militia officers of the necessity there was for making the arrangements adopted for the battle.*[171]

The level of controversy surrounding the skirmish at Weitzel's Mill was stoked further in later years when, as noted earlier, William Richardson Davie criticized Williams for his performance. Davie was a proven warrior. He had served as Commissary General of the southern army, and his duties had brought him into daily contact with Nathanael Greene. Davie was therefore in an excellent position to know the thoughts that were being discussed around Army Headquarters at the time, and his observations must be considered highly credible.

Davie's surviving writing on Weitzel's Mill appears in Gordon's *History of the Rise Progress and Establishment of the Independence of the United States*. It is a scathing critique of Williams:

> *From the minute detail of the affairs at Whitsill's mill, Mr Gordon I suppose recd the relation from Col Williams; I was not present, being with the main Army; and can only say that Colo Williams was reproached for suffering so important a movement of the Enemy to take place without observing it, 'till he had scarce time to escape himself, altho' he commanded a party of observation, and the salvation of the Army depended upon his vigilance – this seems to be confessed in Gordons account, altho' it is unintelligible from the minutiae with which he had crowded the relation. Genl Greene was at that moment more exposed than he had ever been.*[172]

If Greene and others criticized Williams at the time, as Davie related, the criticism was verbal, and did not make its way into contemporaneous documents. As we have seen, twelve days after the event, Greene told a private correspondent that Williams had "...very judiciously avoided the blow..."[173] at Weitzel's Mill. In his report to George Washington, Greene had minimized the impact of the affair, and had offered no criticism of Williams. When he met with Joseph Graham after the skirmish and pulled out his map to determine his next moves, there is no record of any adverse comments regarding Williams.

Davie is a highly credible source, and his criticisms of Williams' record at the Weitzel's Mill affair and on other occasions deserve careful evaluation. Perhaps Davie is correct that Greene was very unhappy with the performance of his friend Otho Williams, but if Greene expressed this anger aloud, he did not put it down in his official or private writings, either at the time or later.

Davie's tone in this and other comments about Williams is quite negative, and one wonders if there may have been underlying reasons for his apparent dislike of the Deputy Adjutant General. Perhaps Davie resented the obvious close friendship between Williams and Greene, or perhaps the officers from North and South Carolina felt that the Maryland leaders had received unfair preferment for praise or promotions. It is also possible that disagreements over the various written histories may have been a source of contention between the men. For example, Davie may have been offended by statements in Williams' *Narrative*, such as his comment about the effectiveness of Davie's cavalry raids on Cornwallis after the Battle of Camden:

> *Major Davie, with his mounted volunteers, equipped as dragoons, sometimes intercepted his convoys of provisions — sometimes disturbed his pickets — and even once or twice, insulted the van of his army on its march. These, however, were feeble and ineffectual resistances; his lordship could go where he pleased.*[174]

Such a comment would undoubtedly have been hurtful to the pride of such an accomplished soldier as Davie, who wrote that his exploit in attacking Cornwallis in Charlotte:

> *...furnishes a very striking instance of the bravery and importance of the American Militia; few examples can be shewn of any troops who in one action changed their position twice in good order although pressed by a much superior body of Infantry and charged three times by thrice their number of*

Cavalry, unsupported & in the presence of the enemys whole army and finally retreating in perfect order.[175]

This statement also firmly establishes Davie's pride in the capabilities and performance of the militia troops with whom he served, and Williams was reputed to have little confidence in or respect for militia. It seems conceivable that Davie's attitude toward Williams was influenced by the disaffection that existed between some militia officers, which Davie had been, and regular officers like Williams.

Regarding Williams' feelings toward Davie, Williams wrote that Davie was "...an active and spirited young gentleman..." in the notes that he sent to historian David Ramsay in February, 1782,[176] and as an "an enterprising and gallant young man" in his *Narrative of the Campaign of 1780*.[177] The root causes of Davie's obvious irritation with Williams are difficult to pin down, and would not appear to have been prompted by any insult proffered by the Marylander. On the contrary, Williams appears to have given Davie high praise the few times he mentioned him in surviving documents.

In the grand scheme of the story of the Revolutionary War, Weitzel's Mill is hardly a footnote. Williams chose to downplay the importance of this affair in all his subsequent writings. For example, he wrote to Historian David Ramsay in early 1782 that:

> *Attempts of this sort occasioned two reencounters between the British Army and the Light Infantry commanded by Col Williams, one on the 2nd of March at Allamance - the other on the 6th at Whitsall's Mill on Reedy Fork - Lord Cornwallis has made the latter a matter of importance by an official letter to the minister - Col Williams' report to Genl Greene & the Generals information will set that affair in a true light. The following is an extract of a genl order issued the 8th Mar: 'The Genl returns his thanks to Col. Williams commanding the light Troops for the judicious maneuver in which he conducted the retreat on the 6th and is happy to hear of the good order and regularity which prevailed upon the occasion.*[178]

The affair at Weitzel's Mill occurred because Williams' command was strung out among several plantations, which gave Cornwallis an excellent opportunity to cut him off from Greene and fight the two parts of Greene's army piecemeal. However, it seems that Williams did not have much choice in the matter because he had to feed his troops, and no single location would have provided sufficient provisions for the entire force. And however justified criticism of Williams' dispositions and alertness may be, the fact is that he and his men were able to respond effectively on that foggy morning of March 6th, 1781. Lee's and William Washington's cavalry, Campbell's and Preston's riflemen, and John Eager Howard's Continentals all had a hand in holding off the British advance that day, and the entire screening force was able to march away, unmolested, at the end of the fight.

Bad luck and unexpected events also played some role at Weitzel's Mill, as they always do in combat. Lee recorded that the sentries at Campbell's camp were inattentive, and allowed the British to get very close to their camp before they were spotted.[179] Such lapses and the morning fog contributed greatly to Cornwallis' ability to achieve the initial surprise.

Williams and his men seem to have responded well to these early mistakes, and to have quickly mounted a resistance that successfully thwarted the British advance. The American troops were directed to good defensive positions on Reedy Fork Creek, and they fought well from those positions. The Americans, as usual, were faster afoot, and out-marched their British foes all day long.

Williams was criticized by the militia for ordering Colonel Preston and his riflemen to serve as a blocking force. This seems to have been a perfectly sensible military decision, but when the riflemen suffered significant casualties that day, they complained that they had been sacrificed so that Williams could save his precious Continentals. Williams did belong to the group of regular officers that was skeptical of militia troops, and he was not a man to hide such an attitude. This may well have been a factor in the animosity between Preston's Virginians and the commander of the screening force. The Virginians may have sincerely believed that Williams valued them less than the Continental troops, and that he was therefore less concerned with their safety than he was with that of the Continentals. Joseph Graham's narrative supports this thinking.

Nathanael Greene had an eye for talent, and he was a demanding taskmaster. He would support Otho Williams in many ways for as long as he lived, praising him often in official reports, maintaining a friendly personal correspondence, and supporting his friend's advancement in the Army. Greene relied heavily on Williams in council, on the march, and in combat for the rest of his time with the Army.

Whatever faults he might have found in his Adjutant General's performance on March 6th, Greene reported to Commander-in-Chief George Washington that the British had been "…handsomely opposed and suffered considerably without effecting any thing."[180] Perhaps that is the appropriate final judgment on the events of March 6th, 1781 at Weitzel's Mill.

The Screening force is Disbanded

Two days after the affair at Weitzel's Mill, Otho Williams submitted a recommendation to Greene for a reorganization of the Army, which Greene "permitted him to do…"[181] Williams had apparently discussed his plans with Light Horse Harry Lee, who knew of his intention to leave command of the screening force and rejoin the main army.[182]

While the details of Williams' recommendation to Greene are lost, the Commander of the southern army rearranged his screening force just three days after the affair at Weitzel's Mill, as he described in a letter to Lee:

> *The Light Infantry is dissolvd, and the Army will take upon itself an entire new formation. Col Williams will join the line. And I propose in lieu of the light Infantry two parties of observation, one to be commanded by you, and the other by Lt Col Washington. You are to attend to the enemies movement upon the left wing and Washington upon the right.*[183]

Not all of Greene's motives in making this change are clear, but he wrote to Governor Thomas Jefferson of Virginia that he could now be more aggressive because he had a much larger force.[184] It is possible that Greene had always looked on the screening force as a defensive unit, designed primarily to protect the Army from a pursuing foe, rather than as an offensive force that could scout ahead, gather intelligence, and pave the way for the army to advance. This defensive mindset is certainly consistent with the way that Greene and Williams used the screening force during the Race to the Dan. The new arrangement under Lee and William Washington would not include any Continental infantry, which seems to indicate that Greene wanted speed of movement from his new "parties of observation," but he did not feel that he needed massed infantry firepower from these units. Williams' use of combined forces of riflemen and cavalry to guard the right and left of his front line at Clapp's Mill may have been an early indication of his thinking on the best arrangement of forces.

Given the timing and nature of the reorganization, the historian may ask other questions. Was Greene prompted to make this change because he was dissatisfied with the performance of Williams and the screening force at Weitzel's Mill? Was Greene swayed by the complaints from the militia that Williams had sacrificed them to protect the Continentals? Was Williams exhausted from the rigorous demands of commanding the Screening Force? Did his deteriorating health make it essential that he be given a less demanding assignment?

We have further insight into these questions from a report of Major Charles Magill, the representative of Governor Thomas Jefferson of Virginia on Greene's staff, in describing the formation of the Corps of Observation:

> *A new Arrangement of the Light Infantry has taken place, more to the satisfaction, I hope, of the Militia. Colo Washington, supported by a body of Riflemen under the command of Colo Campbell, commands on the right, and Colo Lee, supported by Colo Preston upon the left of the Line. The infantry belonging to the Maryland and Virginia Lines, draughted for the Light Corps, are to rejoin their Regiments. ...Colo Williams, an excellent officer who Commanded the Corps, immediately declined the command, and in order to give more satisfaction. Genl Greene made the Judicious arrangement above recited.*[185]

Magill's report seems to indicate that the riflemen's discontent was focused on Colonel Otho Williams, who they thought had ordered them into harm's way to protect the Continental Line. Lee, on the other hand, had personally supported Preston's riflemen at Weitzel's Mill.[186] Since their new assignment was to work under Lee and Washington, and not under Williams, and that approach gave "more satisfaction," it appears that Williams was the officer that the riflemen resented. Magill's observation that the "excellent officer" Williams declined the command to provide a more satisfactory overall arrangement is indicative of Williams' tendency to do what he could to support Greene with minimum disruption to good order and discipline.

Shortly after this reorganization, Williams wrote to his brother Elie that the army had been rearranged, and that Otho would now be "free of dangerous duty..." Williams noted the change from a light corps to "parties of observation," and commented to his brother that he had been mentioned often in the general orders of General Greene.[187]

After the affair at Weitzel's Mill, Greene and Cornwallis continued to march and countermarch, and feel each other out in the vicinity of a small country hamlet named Guilford Courthouse.

Cornwallis did not receive the support from the populace that he had anticipated, and he was concerned about the welfare of his men...

> ...*on account of the sufferings of the Army from the want of supplies of every kind. At the same time I was determined to fight the Rebel Army if it approached me, being convinced that it would be impossible to succeed in that great object of our arduous Campaign—the calling forth the numerous loyalists of North Carolina—whilst a doubt remained on their minds of the superiority of our Arms. With these views, I had moved to the Quaker Meeting House in the fork of Deep River, on the 13th, and on the 14th.*[188]

By the night of March 14th, Greene knew that his force had grown large enough to take on Cornwallis' Army. He placed his men in positions near the Courthouse on ground that he had chosen carefully, and prepared to offer Lord Cornwallis the battle that His Lordship had been seeking. Cornwallis and his army were camped just twelve miles away, at Deep River Friends Meeting House,[189] and when the British scouts told their commander where Greene was positioned, he determined to attack the next day.

The months of retreat, maneuver and evasive tactics were over for these two armies. The day for battle had finally come.

---

1   Cornwallis, Charles. Cornwallis, Charles. Letter to Lord Germain. Written at Guilford. March 17th, 1781. In Stevens, Benjamin Franklin, ed. *The Campaign in Virginia 1781. An Exact Reprint of Six Rare Pamphlets on the Clinton-Cornwallis Controversy. Volume I.* (hereafter Stevens, *Campaign in Virginia*.) London. 1888. P. 359.
2   Committee of Congress. Letter to Nathanael Greene. Note (2.) Written at Philadelphia, November 27th, 1780. Letters of Delegates to Congress, Volume 16, page 388. Library of Congress.
3   Treacy, *Prelude*. Pp 56-57.
4   Williams, *Narrative* (in Johnson, Greene.) P. 509.
5   Seymour, *Journal*. P. 291. The date of the change of command is confirmed in Kirkwood, *Journal*. P. 13.
6   Williams, *Narrative* (in Johnson, Greene.) P. 510.
7   Ibid. P. 499.
8   Ibid. P. 510.
9   Williams, Otho. Letter to Elie Williams. Written at Salisbury, North Carolina. November 24th, 1780. *Williams Papers*. Part 1/8. (Item # 70.)
10 Williams, *Narrative* (in Johnson, Greene.) P. 510.
11 To George Washington from Nathanael Greene, 31 October 1780," Founders Online, National Archives (http://founders.archives.gov/documents/Washington/99-01-02-03758 [last update: 2015-03-20]). Source: this is an Early Access document from The Papers of George Washington. IT IS NOT AN AUTHORITATIVE FINAL VERSION
12 Washington, George. Letter to Nathanael Greene. Written at Head Quarters near Passaic Falls, November 8th, 1780. *Washington Papers*.
13 Greene ordered Thaddeus Kosciuszko to build these boats, and he directed General Isaac Huger to "let as many of the Boats follow the Army as are complete." From Greene, Nathanael. Letter to General Isaac Huger. Written at Sherrard's Ford, N.C. January 30th, 1781. *Greene Papers*. 7:219-221. (Letter text and Note 4.) There does not appear to be documentation of the actual use of these boats. It is interesting that the British would take two boats, mounted on carriages, with them to "facilitate the passage of any waters" when they marched into Virginia a few months hence. It seems conceivable that they adopted this innovation because they learned of it from the Americans. (Ref: Tarleton. *History*. P. 293.)
14 Greene, Nathanael. Letter to General Stevens. Written at Salisbury, North Carolina, December 1st, 1780. Quoted in Nathanael Greene, *Major-General In The Army Of The Revolution, Volume 3* by George Washington Greene, P. 66.
15 Greene, Nathanael. Letter to George Washington. Written at Camp Guilford Courthouse. February 9th, 1781. *Greene Papers*. 7:268.

16 Greene, Nathanael. Letter to Joseph Reed. Written at Camp on the Peedee. January 9th, 1781. Commager and Morris. P. 1152.
17 To Thomas Jefferson from Nathanael Greene, 14th December 1780," Founders Online, National Archives (http://founders.archives.gov/documents/Jefferson/01-04-02-0254, ver. 2014-05-09). Source: *The Papers of Thomas Jefferson, vol. 4, 1 October 1780–24 February 1781*, ed. Julian P. Boyd. Princeton: Princeton University Press, 1951, pp. 206–207.
18 Williams, Otho. Letter to Nathanael Greene. Written at Camp Charlotte. December 1st, 1780. *Williams Papers*. Part 1/8. (Item # 73.)
19 Greene, Nathanael. Letter to the Marquis de Lafayette. December 29th, 1780. Quoted in *Nathanael Greene, Major-General In The Army Of The Revolution, Volume 3* by George Washington Greene, P. 70.
20 Greene, Nathanael. Letter to Daniel Morgan, December 29th, 1780 from "Camp at the Cheraw." *Greene Papers*. 7:22.
21 Williams, Otho. Letter to Elie Williams. Written at South Carolina Camp Pee Dee River. December 31st, 1780. *Williams Papers*. Part 1/8. (Item # 76.)
22 Greene, Nathanael. Letter to Catherine Greene. December 29th, 1780. Written at "Camp on the Pedee. *Greene Papers*. 7: 16.
23 Williams, Otho Holland. Letter to Elie Williams. Written at Camp Hicks Creek, S.C. January 14th, 1781. in *Williams Papers*. Part 1/8. (Item # 82.)
24 Williams, Otho Holland. Letter to Daniel Morgan, December 30th, 1780. Written at "Camp Hicks Creek." Myers, *Cowpens Papers*. P. 11.
25 Greene, Nathanael. Letter to Daniel Morgan, December 29th, 1780 from "Camp at the Cheraw on the East Side of Peedee." *Greene Papers*. 7:22.
26 Williams, Otho Holland. Letter to Daniel Morgan, December 30th, 1780 from Camp at Hicks Creek on P.D. Myers, *Cowpens Papers*. P. 12.
27 Ibid. P. 12.
28 Williams, Otho Holland. Letter to Daniel Morgan, January 13th, 1781. Written at "Camp Hicks Creek." Myers, *Cowpens Papers*. P. 18.
29 Williams, Otho Holland. Addendum to a letter to Daniel Morgan, December 30th, 1780. Written at "Camp Hicks Creek." Myers, *Cowpens Papers*. P. 12.
30 Williams, Otho. Letter to John Dunlap. Written at Camp on Hicks Creek on the Pee Dee River, South Carolina. December 31st, 1780. *Williams Papers*. Part 1/8. (Item # 77.)
31 *Greene Papers*. 7:104. Note 2 to letter from Nathanael Greene to Colonel Henry Lee, Jr. Written at Camp on the Pee Dee, South Carolina. January 12th, 1781.
32 Williams, Otho. Letter to Baron von Steuben. Written at Camp, Salisbury, N.C. November 12th, 1780. *Williams Papers*. Part 1/8. (Item # 67.)
33 Von Steuben, Baron. Letter to Nathanael Greene. December 24th, 1780. *Williams Papers*. Part 1/8. (Item # 74.)
34 Williams, Otho Holland. Letter to Baron von Steuben. Written at Camp, Hicks Creek, S.C. January 13th, 1781. *Williams Papers*. Part 1/8. (Item # 79.)
35 Walker, Benjamin. Letter to Otho Holland Williams. February 4th, 1781. *Williams Papers* Part 1/8. (Item # 88.)
36 No document has been found that confirms Williams' appointment as Inspector General of the southern army, although he did keep in his papers the Congressional directives regarding additional pay and allowances for members of the Inspector's Department. Ref: Calendar of the General Otho Holland Williams Papers at the Maryland Historical Society, 1744-1839 MS.908 (Part 1/8. Items 71 and 72.)
37 Williams, Otho Holland. Letter to Baron von Steuben. Written at Camp Hicks Creek, S.C. January 20th, 1781. *Williams* Part 1/8. (Iitem # 83.)
38 Williams, Otho Holland. Letter to Elie Williams. Written at Camp Hicks Creek, S.C. on January 14th, 1781. *Williams Papers*. Part 1/8. (Item # 82.)
39 Williams, Otho Holland. Extracts from the Notebook. Written at Hicks Creek on Pee Dee River, January 23rd, 1781. *Williams Papers*. Part 1/8. (Item # 84.)
40 Williams, Otho Holland. Letter to Dr. James McHenry. Written at Hicks Creek, South Carolina, January 23rd, 1781. *Williams Papers*. Part 1/8. (Item # 85.)
41 Williams, Otho Holland. Letter to Daniel Morgan, January 25th, 1781. Written at "Camp P. D." Myers, *Cowpens Papers*. P. 33.
42 Morgan sent the British prisoners to Virginia under the guard of militia who were returning home after the battle. Although some British prisoners escaped and returned to Cornwallis' army, most were sent to prisoner-of-war camps in Winchester, Virginia or in Maryland. Ref: Babits, Lawrence E. *A Devil of a Whipping. The Battle of Cowpens*. P. 144.
43 Morgan, Daniel. Letter to Nathanael Greene. Written at Beattie's Ford, North Carolina. January 29th, 1781. *Greene Papers*. P. 215.
44 Cornwallis, Charles. Letter to George Germain. March 17th, 1781. In Note 2 to Daniel Morgan letter to Nathanael Greene. Written at Beaties Ford, N.C. 29th January, 1781. *Greene Papers*. 7:216.
45 Ward, *Revolution*. P. 766.

46 Greene, Nathanael. Letter to General Isaac Huger. Written at Sherrard's Ford, N.C. January 30th, 1781. *Greene Papers*. 7:220.
47 Ibid. 7: 219-220.
48 Gordon, *History*. Volume IV. Pp. 38-39.
49 Ibid. Pp. 41-42.
50 Huger, Isaac. Letter to Nathanael Greene. Written at Mask's Ferry, North Carolina. February 1st, 1781. *Greene Papers*. 7:232.
51 Sherman, William Thomas. Calendar and Record of the Revolutionary War in the South: 1780-1781. Fourth Edition. (http://www.americanrevolution.org/south.pdf) Sherman cites Wickwire, Franklin and Mary. Cornwallis: The American Adventure. Houghton Mifflin Co., Boston, 1970. P. 278. (O'Hara to Duke of Grafton, Apr. 20, 1781, Grafton Papers Ac. 423/191.)
52 Gordon, *History. Vol. IV*. Pp. 41.42.
53 From the style and nature of this writing, William Thomas Sherman, who maintains the comprehensive web site "Calendar and Record of the Revolutionary War in the South: 1780-1781" believes that these words were originally written by Otho Holland Williams. Sherman quotes the author Gordon, as follows: "The advantage of col. O. H. Williams's official papers, of private letters, and of subsequent conversation with gen. Greene, for the purpose of information, has occasioned a variation in diverse parts of the above narrative from Dr. Ramsay and others." Calendar of the Revolution &c., 4th edition, .page 305. In the preface to his first edition, Gordon had stated that he had been "...indulged by the late Generals Washington, Gates, Greene, Lincoln, and Otho Williams with a liberal examination of their papers, both of a public and private nature." (Gordon, William, D.D. *The History of the Rise Progress and Establishment of the Independence of the United States of America, Including an Account of the Late War Volume I*. Charles Dilly in the Poultry and James Buckland in Pater-Noster-Row, London, 1788. page 10.) This supposition is further strengthened by an Otho Holland Williams letter to Governor Henry Lee of Virginia in 1792, in which Williams noted that he recognized "whole pages" of Williams' narrative in Gordon's book. (Williams, Otho Holland. Letter to Governor Henry Lee of Virginia. Written at Baltimore, March 15th, 1792. Calendar of the Otho Holland Williams Papers in the Manuscript Collections of the Maryland Historical Society. MS 908.(Part 4 of 8, item #688.)
54 Morgan, Daniel. Letter to Nathanael Greene. Written at Guilford Courthouse, North Carolina. February 6th, 1781. *Greene Papers*. 7:254.
55 Morgan, Daniel. Letter to Nathanael Greene. Written at Guilford Courthouse, North Carolina. February 8th, 1781. *Greene Papers*. 7:256.
56 Proceedings of a Council of War held at Guilford Courthouse, February 9th, 1781. *Greene Papers*. 7:262.
57 See Footnote
58 Greene, Nathanael. Letter to George Washington. Written at Camp Guilford Courthouse, North Carolina. February 9th, 1781. *Greene Papers*. 7:268.
59 Ibid.
60 Greene, Nathanael. Letter to Daniel Morgan. Written at Camp, Guilford Court House. 10th February, 1781. *Greene Papers*. 7:271.
61 Johnson, *Greene*. P. 429.
62 Williams, Otho Holland. "*Some Notes & Remarks on His History of the War in South Carolina*" sent to Historian David Ramsay. Forwarded with a letter to Ramsay, written at Camp at Pon Pon, Quarters at Mr. Hayne's. 2nd February, 1782. *Williams Papers*. Part 1/ 8. (Item #139 is the letter; Item 140 is the enclosure with Williams' comments on Ramsay's text.)
63 Ibid.
64 See Footnote.
65 Lee, *Memoirs*. Pp. 238-239.
66 Ibid. Footnote on P. 248.
67 Williams, Otho Holland. "*Some Notes & Remarks on His History of the War in South Carolina*" sent to Historian David Ramsay. Forwarded with a letter to Ramsay, written at Camp at Pon Pon, Quarters at Mr. Hayne's. 2nd February, 1782. Williams Papers. Part 1/8. (Item #139 is the letter; Item 140 is the enclosure with Williams' comments on Ramsay's text.)
68 Williams, Otho Holland. Letter to Nathanael Greene. Written at John Rhodes', North Carolina. Sunday, February 11th at 3 o'clock. *Greene Papers*. 7:283.
69 Greene, Nathanael. Letter to Colonel Otho Holland Williams. Written at Col. William Moore's, North Carolina. February 13th, 1781. *Greene Papers*. 7:285.
70 Williams, Otho Holland. Letter to Nathanael Greene. Written at Colonel Moore's, North Carolina. February 13th, 1781 at 7 P.M. *Greene Papers*. 7:286.
71 Note 5 to Otho Holland Williams' letter of 7 P.M., February 13th, 1781 to Nathanael Greene. *Greene Papers*. 7:286-287.
72 Greene, Nathanael. Letter to Otho Holland Williams. Written at 4 A.M. February 14th, 1781. *Greene Papers*. 7:287.

73 Greene, Nathanael. Letter to Otho Holland Williams. Written at Irwin's Ferry, Virginia at 2 P.M. February 14th, 1781. *Greene Papers.* 7:287.
74 Greene, Nathanael. Letter to Otho Holland Williams. Written at Irwin's Ferry, Virginia at 1/2 past five o'clock. February 14th, 1781. *Greene Papers.* 7:287.
75 Buchanan, *Road to Guilford Courthouse.* P 358.
76 Lee, *Memoirs.* Pp 246-247.
77 To Thomas Jefferson from Nathanael Greene, 15th February 1781," Founders Online, National Archives (http://founders.archives.gov/documents/Jefferson/01-04-02-0775, ver. 2014-05-09). Source: *The Papers of Thomas Jefferson, vol. 4, 1 October 1780–24th February 1781*, ed. Julian P. Boyd. Princeton: Princeton University Press, 1951, pp. 615–616.
78 Cornwallis, Charles. Letter to Lord George Germain. Written at Guilford. March 17th 1781. *Correspondence of Charles, First Marquis Cornwallis. Vol. I.* p. 505.
79 Tarleston, Banastre. *History of the Campaigns of 1780 and 1781.* Pp. 235-236.
80 Greene, Nathanael. Letter to George Washington. Written at Camp Irwin's Ferry on the Dan River. February 15th, 1781. *Greene Papers.* 7: 293.
81 Williams, Otho Holland. Letter to Elie Williams. Written at Irvin's Ferry, Dan River, Virginia. February 15th, 1781. *Williams Papers.* Part 1/8. (Items# 91.)
82 Williams, Otho Holland. Letter to Elie Williams. Written at Irvins Ferry, Dan River, Virginia. February 21st, 1781. *Williams Papers.* Part 1/8. (Item # 92.)
83 Williams, Otho Holland. Letter to Nathanael Greene. 18th February, 1781. Written at "Col Woodens, Va." *Greene Papers.* 7:315.
84 Lee, *Memoirs.* P. 249.
85 Ibid. P. 251.
86 Cornwallis, Charles. Letter to Lord Germain. Written at Wilmington, North Carolina. April 18th, 1781. Ross, *Cornwallis Correspondence.* 1. P. 89.
87 Ibid. P. 88.
88 Stedman. *History.* 2. P. 335.
89 Washington, George. Letter to Nathanael Greene. Written at Headquarters, New Windsor. March 21st, 1781. *Washington Papers.*
90 Lee, Henry. Letter to Nathanael Greene. Written at Legion Camp Hycotee River, N.C. 20th February, 1781. *Greene Papers.* 7:324.
91 Greene, Nathanael. Letter to Andrew Pickens. Written at Camp Irvins Ferry (Va.) Feb 21st. 1781. *Greene Papers.* 7:327.
92 Lee, Henry. Letter to Nathanael Greene. Written at Hycotee Creek, N.C. 21st February, 1781. *Greene Papers.* 7:330.
93 Williams, Otho Holland. Letter to Nathanael Greene. Written at Wiley's , N.C. 22nd February, 1781. *Greene Papers.* 7:334.
94 Williams, Otho Holland. Letter to Nathanael Greene. Written at Raney's Mill, N.C. 22nd February, 1781. *Greene Papers.* 7:334.
95 Lee, Henry. Letter to Nathanael Greene. Written at Brownins farm near Hyco-Creek, N.C. 23rd February, 1781. *Greene Papers.* 7:336.
96 Greene, Nathanael. Letter to Otho Holland Williams. 25th February, 1781. *Greene Papers.* 7: 348.
97 Williams and Howard had bad information about Cornwallis' location. The British remained in Hillsborough, and Howard marched to within two miles of the town before discovering that fact. When he realized the error, he reversed his march and moved quickly back toward his comrades. Ref: Note 3 to letter from Otho Holland Williams to Nathanael Greene. Written at Mitchells Mill, N.C. 26th February, 1781. *Greene Papers.* 7:360.
98 Williams, Otho Holland. Letter to Nathanael Greene. Written at Widow Grier's, N.C. 25th February, 1781. *Greene Papers.* 7:349-350.
99 Lee, Henry. Letter to Nathanael Greene. Written near William O'Neal's Plantation, Orange County, N.C. 25th February, 1781. *Greene Paper*s. 7:348.
100 Pickens, Andrew. Letter to Nathanael Greene. Written at Camp Rippey's, N.C. 26th February, 1781. *Greene Papers.* 7:358.
101 Buchanan, *Guilford Courthouse.* P. 364.
102 Greene, Nathanael Letter to Governor Thomas Jefferson of Virginia Written at High Rock Ford, N.C. 28th February, 1781. *Greene Papers.* 7:367.
103 Lee, *Memoirs.* P. 588.
104 Greene, Nathanael. Letter to President Joseph Reed of Pennsylvania. Written from Camp Near the Iron Works, March 18th, 1781. *Greene Papers.* 7:449.
105 See Footnote.
106 Williams, Otho Holland. Letter to Nathanael Greene. Written at Allamance, N.C. March 1st, 1781, 8 O'Clock PM. *Greene Papers.* 7:378-379.

107 Lee, Henry. Letter to Nathanael Greene. Written at Allamance County, N.C., March 1st, 1781. *Greene Papers.* 7:379.
108 Note 2 to letter from Otho H. Williams to Nathanael Greene. Written at Alamance, N.C., 1st March, 1781. 8 o'clock PM. *Greene Papers.* 7:379.
109 Graham, William A. *General Joseph Graham and his Papers on North Carolina Revolutionary History.* (hereafter Graham, *Papers.*) Edwards & Broughton. Raleigh. 1904. P. 329.
110 Lee, Henry, IV. *The Campaign of 1781 in the Carolinas; with Remarks Historical and Critical on Johnson's Life of Greene.* Published by E. Littell. William Brown, Printer. Philadelphia. 1824. P. 158.
111 Graham, Papers. P. 330. Separately, Graham drew a map of the dispositions at Clapp's Mill. That map shows the front line as described above, but for the second line shows "Lee's Horse" in the road with units under "Colo Preston" to the right of the road and "Major Dickson" to the left of the road. Behind that line are "Captain Kirkwood & Oldham's Regulars," deployed just after the Alamance crossing. Behind the Alamance are "Colo O. Williams" and "Washington," (William Washington's cavalry.) Ref: Map by Joseph Graham in *Prelude to Guilford Courthouse.* By Robert Dunkerly. In Southern Campaigns of the Revolutionary War. Volume 3, Number 3. March 2006. P. 39.
112 Graham, *Papers.* P. 330.
113 Map by Joseph Graham in *Prelude to Guilford Courthouse.* By Robert Dunkerly. In Southern Campaigns of the Revolutionary War. Volume 3, Number 3. March 2006. P. 39.
114 Graham, *Papers.* P. 333.
115 Graham's narrative does not state specifically when Williams left his main force, crossed the Alamance, and joined the forward units. His appearance with Oldham and Kirkwood as the British were approaching suggests that he probably heard the sound of the firing up ahead and rode forward to ascertain the situation and prepare his command for the appropriate next moves.
116 Graham, *Papers.* P. 52.
117 Ibid. Pp. 333-334.
118 Tarleton, Banastre. A History of the Campaigns of 1780 and 1781. P. 241.
119 Bright Jeffrey G and Dunaway, Stewart E. *Like A Bear with his Stern in a Corner. The NC Campaign during the American Revolution.* Self-Published. LaVergne, Tennessee. P. 62.
120 Williams, Otho. Report to Nathanael Greene. Written at Alamance, March 2nd, 1781. From *Greene Papers.* 7:381.
121 On March 10th, 1718, Nathanael Greene included one sentence about Clapp's Mil in his letter report to George Washington. "on the 2d Lieutt Colo Lee with a detachment of Rifle-Men attacked the advanced of the British Army under Colo Tarlton near Alamance, and killed and wounded, by report, about thirty of them." *Greene Papers.* 7:422.
122 Williams, Otho Holland. Letter to Nathanael Greene. March 4th, 1781. Written at "Wm Shaffers on Stony Creek e miles N.E. Col Pasleys. *Greene Papers.* 7:394.
123 Greene, Nathanael. Letter to Otho Holland Williams. June 6th 1782. *Papers of General Nathanael Greene.* 11: 300.
124 Williams, Otho Holland. Letter to Nathanael Greene. March 6th, 1781. Written at "Martin Boons 7 miles East Col Pasleys." *Greene Papers.* 7: 406-407.
125 Williams, Otho Holland. Letter to Nathanael Greene. Written at Widow Grier's, North Carolina. 25th February, 1781. *Greene Papers.* 7:350.
126 Williams, Otho Holland. Letter to Nathanael Greene. Written at Mitchell's Mill, N.C. 26th February, 1781. *Greene Papers.* 7:360.
127 Graham, *Papers.* P. 334.
128 There are a wide variety of spellings of the name of this mill in the literature. Henry Lee, Tarleton and Cornwallis called it "Wetzel's." Gordon called it "Whitsill's." Otho Williams called it "Whitsel's." This text uses the spelling employed by most current authors, "Weitzel's."
129 Cornwallis, Charles. Letter to Lord Germain. Written at Guilford. March 17th, 1781. From Tarleton, *History.* P. 273.
130 Lee, *Memoirs.* P. 265. (Characteristically, Lee added a footnote that begins with "No country in the world affords better riders than the United States, especially the States south of Pennsylvania…"
131 Tarleton, *History.* P. 244.
132 Cornwallis, Charles. Letter to Lord Germain. Written at Guilford. March 17th, 1781. From Tarleton, *History.* P. 274.
133 Lee, *Memoirs.* P. 265.
134 In her superbly written *Prelude to Yorktown*, M.F. Treacy asserts that there was a large quantity of cornmeal at Weitzel's Mill, and that Greene's wagons had been sent there to carry it to his camp. Ms. Treacy's reference for this information is the 1881 text *King's Mountain and Its Heroes*, by Lyman C. Draper, LLD, page 392, where Draper states that "The main object was to protect the mill as long as possible, and to enable Greene's provision wagons to load with flour and meal, and get off with the needed supply, which they barely effected." This is an interesting and plausible addition to the story of Weitzel's Mill. However, other references are not as clear on this point (for example, Greene stated in his report to George Washington that the British moved "…either with a view to intercept our Stores, or cut off the Light Infantry from the

main Body of the Army.") Otho Williams makes no mention whatever of provision wagons in his report of the skirmish to Greene, written on March 7th, the day after the fighting. Apparently, the first authors that include the story of the provision wagons were Draper in 1881 and Treacy in 1963. In his text *The American Revolution in the Southern Colonies* published in 2000, David Lee Russell states that "…Williams was able to hold off a storming party led by James Webster and the troops of the 23rd Regiment until the valuable wagons of meal escaped." (page 227.) Mr. Russell cites Treacy often, and may possibly have used her writing as his source for this conclusion. Documents written by Nathanael Greene and Otho Williams at the time do not mention these wagons. The earliest authors did not, and the 1881 Draper text appears to be the oldest one that emphasizes this point. Accordingly we mention the wagons as a plausible addition to the story of Weitzel's Mill, but incorporate it as a footnote and not an element of our main text.

135 Since this letter is dated March 6th, the day of the skirmish at Weitzel's Mill, and it gives no indication of Cornwallis' pending attack, it must have been written very early in the morning, before Williams knew of the movement of the British troops, which Lee said began at 3a.m.)

136 Williams, Otho Holland. Letter to Nathanael Greene. Written at Martin Boons 7 miles east of Col Paselys. 6th March, 1781. *Greene Papers*. 7:406-407.

137 Lee, *Memoirs*. P. 265.

138 Tarleton, *History*. P.244.

139 Williams, Otho Holland. Letter to Nathanael Greene. March 7th, 1781. Written at "Camp near the Old Bridge on Haw River." *Greene Papers*. 7:407-408.

140 See Footnote.

141 Graham, *Papers*. P. 342.

142 Williams, Otho Holland. Letter to Nathanael Greene. March 7th, 1781. Written at "Camp near the Old Bridge on Haw River." *Greene Papers*. 7:407-408.

143 Joseph Graham identifies the commander of the troops closest to Tarleton as "Colonel Clark," and states later that "Williams, Pickens, Clark, Preston, Lee and Washington were all moving in their front." It seems probable that Graham misidentified Colonel William Campbell, instead calling him "Colonel Clark."

144 Lee, *Memoirs*. P. 265.

145 Graham, *Papers*. Pp. 342-343

146 Ibid. 342-343.

147 Williams, Otho Holland. Letter to Nathanael Greene. Written at Camp near the Old Bridge at Haw River. 7th March, 1781. *Greene Papers*. 7:407.

148 Graham, *Papers*. P. 343.

149 Williams, Otho Holland. Letter to Nathanael Greene. March 7th, 1781. Written at "Camp near the Old Bridge on Haw River." *Greene Papers*. 7:407-408.

150 Gordon, *History*. Volume IV. P. 51

151 Graham, *Papers*. P. 344.

152 Gordon, *History Volume IV*. P. 51.

153 Graham, *Papers*. Pp. 343-344.

154 A pole is 16.5 feet, so the Continental formation was, according to Graham, about 165 yards long.

155 Ibid. P. 344

156 Gordon, *History*. Volume IV. P.52.

157 Lee, *Memoirs*. Pp. 266-267.

158 Although the story of the riflemen firing at and missing British officer James Webster has been repeated may times, the author has not found contemporary documentation of the event. It seems remarkable that so many accomplished marksmen would miss such an easy target, although the uncertainty of combat, smoke hovering over the battle space and other possible factors might explain such an occurrence.

159 Graham, *Papers*, Pp. 346-347.

160 Ibid. P. 347.

161 Williams, Otho Holland. Letter to Nathanael Greene. March 7th, 1781. Written at "Camp near the Old Bridge on Haw River." *Greene Papers*. 7:407-408.

162 Greene, Nathanael. Letter to George Washington. March 10th, 1781. Written at "Head Quarters, Iron Works, North Carolina." *Greene Papers*. 7:422.

163 Greene, Nathanael. Letter to Joseph Reed, President of the Pennsylvania Council. March 18th, 1781. Written at "Camp near the Iron Works." *Greene Papers*. 7:449.

164 Pickens, Andrew. Letter to Nathanael Greene. Written at Camp Shearers, N.C ., 5th March 1781. *Greene Papers*. 7:399.

165 Greene, Nathanael. Letter to Andrew Pickens. Written at North Side of Haw River, N.C. 8th March, 1781, *Greene Papers*. 7:410.

166 Pickens, Andrew. Letter to Nathanael Greene. Written at Camp Shearers, N.C ., 5th March 1781. *Greene Papers*. 7:399.

167 Lee, Henry. Letter to General Nathanael Greene. Written at Alamance County, N.C. 1st March, 1781. *Greene Papers*. 7:379-380. (including Note 4.)
168 Babits, Lawrence E. and Howard, Joshua B. Long, Obstinate and Bloody. *The Battle of Guilford Courthouse* (hereafter Babits and Howard, *Guilford Courthouse*.). The University of North Carolina Press. Chapel Hill. 2009. P. 44. Babits and Howard cite Fries, *Records of the Moravians*. 4:1684, 1746.
169 Preston, William. Letter to Governor Thomas Jefferson. Written at Montgomery County, April 13, 1781. *Virginia State Papers and Other Manuscripts*. 1652-1781 Volume 2. W. M. Palmer, M.D., editor. (hereafter *Virginia State Papers, Volume 2.*) Pp. 34-36.
170 Magill, Charles. Letter to Virginia Governor Thomas Jefferson. Written at Head Quarters near High Rock Ford, March 10th, 1781. In *Calendar of Virginia State Papers and Other Manuscripts. 1652-1781 Volume 1*. W. M. Palmer, M.D., editor P. 567.
171 Graham, *Papers*. P. 346.
172 Robinson, Blackwell P. The Revolutionary War Sketches of William R. Davie (hereafter Robinson, *Davie*.) The North Carolina Department of Cultural Resources, Division of Archives and History. Raleigh. 1976. P. 30.
173 Greene, Nathanael. Letter to Joseph Reed, President of the Pennsylvania Council. March 18th, 1781. Written at "Camp near the Iron Works." *Greene Papers* Page 7: 449.
174 Williams, *Narrative* (in Johnson, *Greene*.) P. 508.
175 Robinson, *Davie*. P. 25
176 Williams, Otho Holland. "*Some Notes & Remarks on His History of the War in South Carolina*" sent to Historian David Ramsay. Forwarded with a letter to Ramsay, written at Camp at Pon Pon, Quarters at Mr. Hayne's. 2nd February, 1782. *Williams Papers*. Part 1/8. (Item #139 is the letter; Item 140 is the enclosure with Williams' comments on Ramsay's text.)
177 *Williams*, Narrative (In Johnson, *Greene*.) P. 499.
178 Williams, Otho Holland. "*Some Notes & Remarks on His History of the War in South Carolina*" sent to Historian David Ramsay. Forwarded with a letter to Ramsay, written at Camp at Pon Pon, Quarters at Mr. Hayne's. 2nd February, 1782. *Williams Papers*. Part 1/8. (Item #139 is the letter; Item 140 is the enclosure with Williams' comments on Ramsay's text.)
179 Lee, *Memoirs*. P. 265.
180 Greene, Nathanael. Letter to George Washington. March 10th, 1781. Written at "Head Quarters, Iron Works, North Carolina *Greene Papers*. 7:422.
181 Williams, Otho Holland. Letter to Nathanael Greene. March 8th, 1781. Written at "Dobb's on Troublesome Creek." *Greene Papers*. 7:413-414.
182 Lee, Henry, Jr. Letter to Nathanael Greene. March 7th, 1781 Written "near Reedy Fork Creek." *Greene Papers*. 7:412.
183 Greene, Nathanael. Letter to Colonel Henry Lee, Jr. March 9th, 1781. Written at "Camp at High Rock Ford." *Greene Papers*. 7:415-416.
184 Notes attached to Greene's March 9th, 1781 letter to Colonel Henry Lee, Jr.. Written at "Camp at High Rock Ford." *Greene Papers*. 7: 415.
185 Magill, Charles. Letter to Virginia Governor Thomas Jefferson. Written at Head Quarters near High Rock Ford, March 10th, 1781. In *Calendar of Virginia State Papers and Other Manuscripts. 1652-1781 Volume 1*. W. M. Palmer, M.D., editor. P. 567.
186 Graham, *Papers*. Pp. 343-344.
187 Williams, Otho. Letter to his brother Elie Williams. Written at High Rock Ford on the Haw River, March 10th, 1781. *Calendar of the Otho Holland Williams Papers in the Manuscript Collections of the Maryland Historical Society*. MS 908. Part 1 of 8. Item #95.
188 Cornwallis, Charles to Lord Germain. Written at Guilford, 17th March, 1781. Stevens, *Campaign in Virginia*. P. 362.
189 Konstam, Angus. *Guilford Courthouse 1781. Lord Cornwallis's Ruinous Victory* Praeger Illustrated Military History Series. Originally published in Oxford: Osprey Publishing Limited, Elms Court, Chapel Way, Botley, Oxford. 2002. Pp. 54 and 58 (inset on map entitled "Initial Deployments at Guilford Courthouse, 15 March, 1781.)

CHAPTER 7

THE BATTLE OF GUILFORD COURTHOUSE

Colonel Otho Williams commanded the Maryland Continental troops that awaited the attack of the British army led by Lord Cornwallis on the crisp, clear morning of March 15th, 1781, at Guilford Courthouse in North Carolina.

General Nathanael Greene, had positioned his forces in three successive lines, stationed several hundred yards apart, in an alignment first employed by Daniel Morgan at the Battle of Cowpens just two months earlier. Here at Guilford Courthouse, Greene had stationed militia from North Carolina in the front line and Virginia militia in the second. These two lines of militia were to fire a few volleys that were intended to slow and weaken the British advance before they hit the third line of Continental troops, whose discipline and training had prepared them to stand firm, and then beat back the British attack.

Otho Williams commanded the left of the third line, which consisted of the First Maryland Regiment under Colonel John Gunby, seconded by Lieutenant Colonel John Eager Howard on the right, and the Second Maryland Regiment under of Lieutenant Colonel Benjamin Ford, seconded by Major Archibald Anderson, on the left. To the right of Williams' command in the third line were Virginia Continental troops led by Brigadier General Benjamin Huger.[1]

Williams' two regiments differed significantly. The First Maryland was one of the best and most experienced units in the Continental army, led by capable officers with combat experience. The second-in-command, John Eager Howard, would be awarded a Silver Medal by Congress for his exceptional battlefield performance at Cowpens, and some of the First Maryland troops who were here at Guilford Courthouse had also served under Howard at Cowpens and during the Race to the Dan.

On the other hand, the Second Maryland was filled with new recruits, and was short of officers. There had been a recent dispute between veteran officers and officers who had recently come south with the new recruits. John Eager Howard described the resulting situation in the Second Maryland:

> *There was a new regiment sent out from Maryland which had been raised by the state, and it was thought that the officers had been more favored than the officers of the old regiments. It joined us a few days before the action and there were such jealousies among the officers that Genl. Greene sent all the new officers*

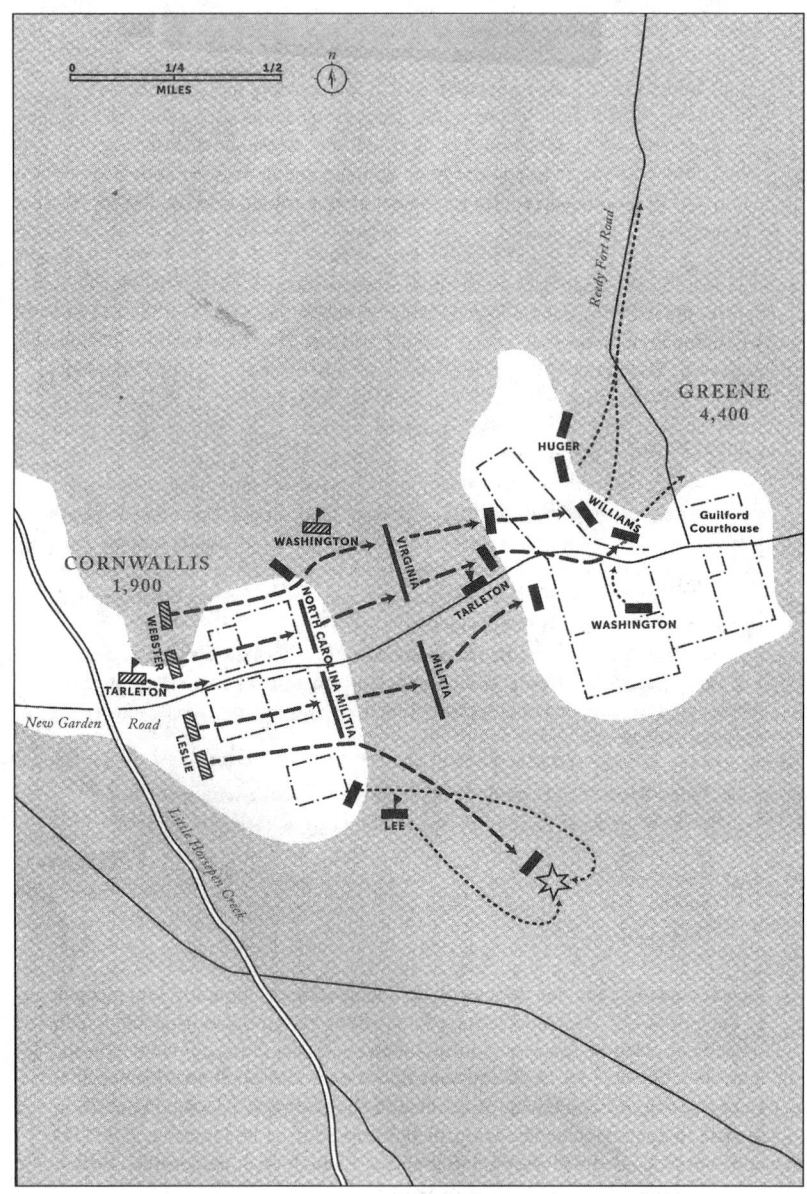

Map 6 - The Battle of Guilford Courthouse

> *home, and made a new arrangement of the two regiments. This was at the time my light infantry joined their regiments. The most of the new men were thrown into the second regiment which was very deficient in officers.*[2]

In addition to the differences in experience and leadership, the physical positions of the First and Second Maryland regiments in the third line were slightly separated, as described by Howard:

> *The 1st regiment under Gunby was formed in a hollow in the wood to the right of the cleared ground about the Courthouse. The Virginia Brigade under Genl. Huger were to our right. The second regiment was at some distance to the left of the first, in the cleared ground with its left flank thrown back so as to form a line almost at right angles with the 1st regt.*[3]

Cornwallis launched his attack shortly after noon,[4] and after pushing back the first line fairly quickly, the British hit stronger resistance from the Virginia militia in the second line, as described by Otho Williams in a letter that he wrote to his brother the day after the battle:

> *The Virginia Brigades of militia commanded by Generals Stevens and Lawson gave the enemy so warm a reception, and continued their opposition with such firmness…during which time the roar of musquetry and cracking of rifles were almost perpetual and as heavy as any I ever heard.*[5]

Howard believed that the fine performance of the Virginia militia was due to the care that General Greene had taken to attract militia officers of good quality into the field, in contrast to the often haphazard efforts of the past, as he described for a historian years later:

> *When Lord Cornwallis was advancing through North Carolina, Genl. Greene wrote to Genl. Stephens, Genl. Lawson, and other officers who he had known in the army and pressed them to come out with their neighbours, for that the militia sent out under your laws were useless. High bounties were given to worthless substitutes who deserted from county to county to get new bounties, and when they were got into the field they had no intention of fighting, Stephens, Lawson, Beverly Randolph, St. George Tucker and other officers of character joined Genl.*

> Greene with their neighbors the yeomanry of the country. You
> have General Greene's account of the brave conduct of these men
> in the action.⁶

As the second line of Virginians finally pulled back, the British pushed forward, even though they had been on their feet for some ten hours and had fought through the woods for several hundred yards. Their advance now brought them to a clearing, and when they looked ahead, they saw a line of Continentals standing in solid formation, on rising ground, several hundred yards in front of them.

Webster's Attack on the Continentals

The heavy fighting and terrain had broken the British line into six separate groups, and each group approached the American third line at separate times and places. The first to arrive was the 33rd Regiment, commanded by the respected Lieutenant Colonel James Webster. Webster attacked the right and center of the American third line, the section manned by Virginia Continentals and Williams' First Maryland Regiment.⁷ True to their training and reputation, these American regulars delivered devastating, well timed volleys and stood their ground. Beaten back by heavy musketry and artillery fire, Webster retreated across the shallow valley that fronted the third line, and took a position on high ground to regroup. During the attack, Webster received a serious wound in the leg that destroyed his kneecap and femur. He would die from this wound about two weeks after the battle.⁸

On the battlefield at this instant, it seemed that the Americans were on the verge of a complete victory, as the tired, thinned British ranks were being held off by Greene's Continentals. Lieutenant Colonel Henry Lee recounted that:

> General Greene was well pleased with the present prospect, and
> flattering himself with a happy conclusion, passed along the line
> exhorting his troops to give the finishing blow.⁹

The Collapse of the Second Maryland

However, Greene's optimism was short-lived. The British Second Guards Battalion had advanced on the far right of the American third line, and was now moving to attack the Second Maryland Regiment. Colonel Otho

Williams started to move from his position with the First Maryland toward the Second, fully expecting that Ford's Second Regiment would stand as firm as Gunby's First Regiment had done just a few minutes earlier. Then "… unaccountably, the second regiment gave way, abandoning to the enemy the two field pieces."[10] Major Archibald Anderson, the Second Maryland's deputy commander, was killed in this fighting, and the loss of his leadership contributed to their poor performance in this battle.[11]

The collapse of the Second Maryland exposed the American left flank to potential disaster. In Greene's report of the battle to the President of Congress, he wrote that this action prompted his decision to withdraw his army from the battlefield:

> *They having broken the 2nd Maryland Regiment, and turned our left flank, and got into the rear of the Virginia Brigade and appeared to be gaining our right, which would have encircled the whole of the Continental Troops, I thought it most adviseable to order a retreat.*[12]

Otho Williams saw the same danger that prompted Greene to order a retreat, and he acted to stem the advancing British tide. The First Maryland might possibly break this attack from the Guards, but from their position, they could not see the British penetration behind their left flank. Deputy Adjutant General John Gibson was sent to inform the First Maryland of the perilous situation, and he made contact with John Eager Howard.

In the meantime, William Washington had also spotted the breach, and moved quickly, charging with his fast-moving cavalry.

Receiving the message from Captain Gibson, Howard passed the word to his commander, John Gunby, and the First Maryland rushed to the point of danger, where they hit the attacking British line hard. Meanwhile, Nathanael Greene, Edward Carrington and Otho Williams tried, without success, to rally the Second Maryland.[13]

Howard described this encounter with the British Guards in detail:

> *The guards after they had defeated Genl. Stephens pushed into the cleared ground and ran at the 2 regiment, which immediately gave way, owing I believe in a great measure to the want of officers & having so many new recruits. The guards pursued them into our rear where they took two pieces of artillery. This transaction was in a great measure concealed from the 1st regiment by the woods and unevenness of the ground.*

> *But my station being on the left of the regt. and next to cleared ground, Capt. Gibson, Deputy Adjutant General, rode to me and informed me that a part of the enemy, inferior in number to us, were pushing through the cleared ground and into our rear, and that if we would face about & charge them, we might take them. We had been for some time engaged with a part of Webster's Brigade, though not hard pressed, and at that moment their fire had slackened. I rode to Gunby and gave him the information. He did not hesitate to order the regiment to face about and we were immediately engaged with the guards. Our men gave them some well directed fires and we then advanced and continued firing.*[14]

Otho Williams wrote that:

> *The first Regiment embraced the opportunity and…they bayoneted and cut to pieces a great number of British Guards, who had taken our field pieces.*[15]

John Eager Howard explained why he had assumed command of the First Maryland Regiment during the encounter:

> *At this time Gunby's horse was shot, and when I met him some time after he informed me that his horse fell upon him, and it was with difficulty he extricated himself. Major Anderson was killed about this time. As we advanced I observed Washington's horse, and as their movements were quicker than ours they first charged and broke the enemy. My men followed very quickly and we passed through the guards, many of whom had been knocked down by the horse without being much hurt. We took some prisoners and the whole were in our power.*[16]

The quick and determined actions of William Washington, John Gunby and John Eager Howard had prevented a disaster for the American side. Howard described his withdrawal of the 1st Maryland from the conflict:

> *…After passing through the guards as before stated, I found myself in the cleared ground, and saw the 71st regt. near the Courthouse and other columns of the enemy appearing in different directions. Washington's horse having gone off, I found it necessary to retire, which I did leisurely, but many of the*

guards who were laying on the ground & who we supposed were wounded, got up and fired at us as we retired[17]

Greene's Withdrawal

Nathanael Greene's decision to withdraw was prudent. While some generals might have taken additional risks for the satisfaction of winning a battle, Greene realized that the larger issue was to keep his army intact. The fact his troops had a safe, protected line of retreat gives testament to his strategic foresight and tactical good sense. He was also aided in the retreat by very able senior officers.

General Benjamin Huger, who had received a slight wound in his right hand during the fighting,[18] commanded the withdrawal of the Virginia Continentals on the right of the third line, and Colonel Otho Williams commanded the withdrawal of the Maryland Continentals on the left.[19] Williams would write that "the artillery horses being shot, we were obliged to leave four six pounders in the field which was almost our only considerable loss. The General ordered the troops to retire, which was executed with such good order and regularity…"[20] Major Charles Magill, who served as an aide to Huger during this battle, stated that "…never were Troops drawn off in better order."[21]

General Greene ordered Colonel John Green (Light Horse Harry Lee called him "one of the bravest of the brave") to move his Virginia regiment of Continentals to form a rear guard across the Reedy Fork Road. Contingents of the British army were sent ahead to pursue the retreating Americans, but were soon exhausted and returned to the main army.[22] Otho Williams wrote to a friend that "the enemy did not presume to press our rear with any spirit they followed only three miles where the regular troops halted and a great many of the militia formed."[23]

Williams wrote home the day after the battle that it was the "longest and severest" action he had ever been involved in,[24] and on the following day, the 17th, he described the retreat to Colonel Carvel Hall back in Maryland, noting that "The general ordered the troops to retire, which was executed with such good order and regularity that the enemy did not presume to press our rear with any spirit. They followed only three miles…"[25]

Condition of the Armies after the Battle

It had been a devastating day for Cornwallis and the British army. They had lost one-fourth of their force in killed and wounded. Among those who would never fight again were gallant soldiers like James Webster, who received a mortal wound during his attack on the third line, and Colonel Duncan Stuart of the 2nd Guards battalion, who fell to a broadsword in the fight on the American left. Cornwallis and his army were veteran professionals, but they felt deeply the loss of such men. Cornwallis was particularly saddened by the loss of James Webster, stating aloud when he heard the news of Webster's death that "I have lost my scabbard." His letter to Webster's father reflects a fighting man's gloom that always accompanies the loss of a brave comrade-in-arms:

> *It gives me great concern to undertake a task which is not only a bitter renewal of my own grief, but must be a violent shock to an affectionate parent...You have for your satisfaction that your son fell nobly in the cause of his country, honoured and lamented by fellow soldiers; that he led a life of honour and virtue, which must secure to him everlasting happiness...*[26]

Cornwallis put the best face he could on the battle in his report to his superiors in England:

> *My Lord, I have the satisfaction to inform Your Lordship, that His Majesty's Troops under my command, obtained a signal Victory on the 15th Inst over the Rebel Army, commanded by General Greene.*[27]

However, Cornwallis' subordinate, Brigadier General Charles O'Hara was much more realistic in his description of the army's desperate situation:

> *...we feel at the moment the sad and fatal effects of our loss on that Day, nearly one half of our best Officers and Soldiers were either killed or wounded, and what remains are so completely worn out by the excessive Fatigues of the campaign, in a march of above a thousand miles, most of them barefoot, naked and for days together living upon Carrion which they had often not time to dress... Tho you will not find it in the Gazette, every part of our Army was beat repeatedly, on the 15th of March, and were obliged to fall back twice.*[28]

When Charles James Fox, a prominent Irish Member of Parliament, reviewed the reports of the battle, and the casualty figures, he quipped that "Another such victory would ruin the British army."[29]

British officer, Charles Stedman, described the state of Cornwallis' army, and his decision to retreat to Cross Creek, North Carolina:

> *When the extent of the British loss was fully ascertained, it became too apparent that Lord Cornwallis was not in a condition either to give immediate pursuit, or to follow the blow the day after the action. Added to its other distresses, the army was almost destitute of provisions. Under such circumstances, although a victory had been gained, a retreat became necessary towards that quarter from whence supplies could be obtained. About seventy of the wounded, not in a condition to travel, were left at the Quakers' Meeting House, under a flag of truce; and on the third day after the action, Lord Cornwallis began to retire, by easy marches, towards Cross Creek.*[30]

Cornwallis' eventual destination was Wilmington, North Carolina, where British shipping could provide a secure supply of provisions and other supplies.

★ ★ ★ ★ ★

Greene Pursues Cornwallis and Seeks Another Battle

In the aftermath of the battle, leaders on the American side sensed that the British Army, though still dangerous, was on the run. Three days after the battle, General Nathanael Greene wrote to his friend Joseph Reed that

> *I have never felt an easy moment since the enemy crossed the Catawba until...the defeat of the 15th, but now I am perfectly easy, being persuaded it is out of the enemies power to do us any great injury.*[31]

Three days later, Greene wrote to his young cavalrymen Henry Lee that he intended to "fight the enemy again."[32]

Otho Williams was an eye-witness to these events and was probably the author of the section of William Gordon's *History of the Rise, Progress, And Establishment, of the Independence of the United States of America* that described the American army's urge to grapple once again with Cornwallis' army:

> So great was the avidity of the Americans to renew the conflict with Cornwallis, that notwithstanding the weather was very wet and the roads deep, they marched almost constantly without any regular supply of provisions. On the morning of the 28th, they arrived at Ramsay's [Ramsey's] mills on Deep river, a strong position which his lordship evacuated a few hours before, by crossing the river on a bridge erected for that purpose. Evident signs of precipitation were found in and about his lordship's environment. Several of the dead were left on the ground unburied. Beef in quarters was found in the slaughter pen on which the hungry continentals set greedily; but that not being sufficient to allay their keen appetites, they eat without a murmur the garbage which was meant for the buzzards.[33]

Williams wrote to his brother on March 27th that he was "exceedingly well and in good spirits," and that Cornwallis had been "…so severely managed that he had to retire towards Cross Creek on the Cape Fear River, leaving seventy odd wounded behind." Williams reported that the Americans were taking prisoners every day as they marched in pursuit of the British Army.[34]

Otho Williams at the Battle of Guilford Courthouse

Otho Williams was very active in the Battle of Guilford Courthouse. He was a close advisor to Nathanael Greene in the preparations for this battle, and as Adjutant General he carried out the assignment to position the troops.[35] He was with the First Maryland when they blunted James Webster's 33rd Regiment's attack on the American third line, he rushed to the position of the Second Maryland when the British Guards attacked there, and he worked hard with Nathanael Greene to rally those troops. He helped inform the First Maryland of their opportunity to strike, and he provided steady leadership as the army withdrew safely from the field of battle. He led the Maryland troops in their orderly retreat from the battlefield.

Nathanael Greene was grateful to Williams for his actions, and, knowing that his wife, Catherine Littlefield Greene, was interested in the Marylander, Greene wrote to her three days after the battle to assure her that Williams had been much engaged in the fight, but was unhurt:

Many fell, but none of your particular friends. Col. Williams is adjutant General of the Army and was very active and greatly exposd.[36]

Despite positive comments from the American commander in the days after the battle, the historical record of Guilford Courthouse includes criticism of Williams written by William Richardson Davie some years after the battle, in similar tone to the criticism that Davie wrote of Williams at Weitzel's Mill. In a sense, Davie's Guilford Courthouse criticism is much more damning than his critique of Weitzel's Mill because his comments about Guilford Courthouse deal with the near-fatal collapse of the Second Maryland Regiment at a crucial point in the fight:

> *I have always understood that the disgrace of the 2d Regiment that day was owen to the mistaken conduct of Colo Ford & Colo Williams - that Ford ordered a charge, that proceeded some distance, and were halted by Colo Williams, and perhaps ordered again to fall back and dress wt the line. The British continued to advance. This manouvre was performed under a heavy fire - when the men were again ordered to advance they all faced about, except a single company on the left which I think was Capt Oldhams.*[37]

Lawrence E. Babits and Joshua B. Howard, in their excellent study of this battle, *Long, Obstinate and Bloody. The Battle of Guilford Courthouse*, construct a credible narrative of what might have happened to cause Davie to make such a comment, namely that Ford ordered the Second Maryland to change front and advance to meet the Guards, that Williams saw that the line was advancing irregularly and recalled it, and that in the confusion the inexperienced and under-officered Maryland troops panicked and fled The authors also suggest that the death of the Second Maryland's second-in-command, Major Archibald Anderson, also contributed to the demise of the Regiment.[38]

When Williams wrote about the battle in a letter to Maryland Colonel Josias Carvel Hall two days later, he noted that:

> *The Maryland troops formed two regiments at present. The Second has but 8 comm'd officers to 6 comp'ys and has a large proportion of State troops. I can give no better reason why that regiment refused to charge when it was ordered.*[39]

In a closing line to Hall, Williams added a guide for Hall's recruiting efforts, "remember our line is exceedingly deficient in number of officers."[40]

However, no other source, first-hand or otherwise, has been found which supports Davie's indictment of the what he deemed "the mistaken conduct" of Williams and Maryland's Benjamin Ford.[41]

Davie's writing on the Battle of Guilford Courthouse did not limit his criticisms to Williams and Ford. Of American commander Nathanael Greene, Davie wrote that "General Greene's letter will give the outline of this action better than any other account, his own mistakes and the behavior of some part of the troops were of course not mentioned." Davie also wrote that the Americans had been out-generaled by his British counterpart on the field of battle: "…while the contest depended upon mere manouvre General Greene evinced his superiority upon every movement; but when they came to action the ascendancy of the British General was apparent - "[42]

Davie also criticized Greene's dispositions at Guilford Courthouse:

> *It was certainly a great mistake to draw up the militia to await the attack of regular troops for several hours, and the position of the front line was actually advantageous to the Enemy, the elevated grounds enabled them to display with order and dispatch, and a common rail fence behind which about half the No. Carolina Militia were posted was a cover too insignificant to inspire any confidence, the rest of the line was as much exposed as any Troops could be in the woods…His 2d line was too remote from the 1st to give it any support, and the position of the continentals forbad any movement that could either succour the 2d line or second their efforts…*"[43]

Davie was an able soldier, and, as head of the commissary department, he occupied a position in Greene's command that would have given him direct access to the discussions at army headquarters. Light Horse Harry Lee wrote that Davie contributed greatly to the success of the southern campaigns by "…his talents, his zeal, his local knowledge, and his influence.'[44] Davie's criticism of Otho Williams must stand as a part of the historical record. However, like his other criticisms of Williams, his remarks about the Battle of Guilford Courthouse were written long after the battle, and do not appear to be corroborated by other contemporary sources.

A Final Word on Otho Williams at Guilford Courthouse

Perhaps the individual whose view should have the most weight in assessing the performance of Otho Williams at the Battle of Guilford Courthouse is Williams' direct superior, the Commanding General, Nathanael Greene, who worked closely with Williams in the preparations for battle and in the actual fighting, sometimes shoulder-to-shoulder. Three days after the battle, when he described the action to his friend Joseph Reed, President of the Pennsylvania Council, Greene mentioned only one of his senior officers:

> *Col Williams who acts as Adjutant General was very active and to this Officer I am greatly indebted for his assistance.*[45]

---

1 Babits and Howard, *Guilford Courthouse*) Pp. 69-72.
2 Howard, John Eager. Letter Answering Questions on Cowpens, Guilford Courthouse, and Hobkirk's Hill. Bayard Papers. MS 109, Box 4. Maryland Historical Society (MdHS). The letter in the MdHS files does not have a date that it is written, or to whom it is written. Babits and Howard have established that this letter was written to John Marshall in 1804 in answer to questions that Marshall had written to Howard about the Battle of Cowpens. Ref: Babits and Howard. P. 161. Footnote 11 to the Preface.
3 Ibid.
4 Babits and Howard, *Guilford Courthouse*. P. 96.
5 Williams, Otho Holland. Letter to Elie Williams, Hagerstown, Maryland Written at Speedwell Furnace, North Carolina. March 16, 1781. Williams Papers. Part 1/8. (Item #97.) (Cited in Babits and Howard, *Guilford Courthouse*. P. 125.)
6 Howard, John Eager. Letter Answering Questions on Cowpens, Guilford Courthouse, and Hobkirk's Hill. Bayard Papers. MS 109, Box 4. Maryland Historical Society.
7 Lee, *Memoirs*. P. 279.
8 Babits and Howard, *Guilford Courthouse*. P. 166 and P. 174.
9 Lee, *Memoirs*. P. 279.
10 Ibid. P. 280.
11 Babits and Howard, *Guilford Courthouse*. P. 150.
12 Greene, Nathanael. Letter to Samuel Huntington, President of the Continental Congress. Written at Camp at the Iron Works, 10 miles from Guilford Courthouse. March 16th, 1781. *Greene Papers*. 7:435.
13 Lee, *Memoirs*. P.281.
14 Howard, John Eager. Letter Answering Questions on Cowpens, Guilford Courthouse, and Hobkirk's Hill. Bayard Papers. MS 109, Box 4. Maryland Historical Society.
15 Letter from Otho Williams to Josiah Carvel Hall. March 17, 1781. Guilford Courthouse National Military Park Collection. Cited in Babits and Howard, *Guilford Courthouse*. P. 158.
16 Howard, John Eager. Letter Answering Questions on Cowpens, Guilford Courthouse, and Hobkirk's Hill. Bayard Papers. MS 109, Box 4. Maryland Historical Society.
17 Ibid.
18 Babits and Howard, *Guilford Courthouse*. P. 166. They cite: "Morton, "Col. William Morton": pension application of Lewis Griffin, 6 Aug. 1833. 378. RWP (Revolutionary War Pension Application Files, Microcopy M803, National Archives, Washington, D.C.)
19 Lee, *Memoirs*. P. 282
20 Letter from Otho Williams to Josiah Carvel Hall. March 17, 1781. Guilford Courthouse National Military Park Collection. Cited in Babits and Howard, *Guilford Courthouse*. P. 165.
21 To Thomas Jefferson from Charles Magill, 16 March 1781," Founders Online, National Archives(http://founders.archives.gov/documents/Jefferson/01-05-02-0211[last update: 2014-10-23]). Source: The Papers of Thomas Jefferson, vol. 5, 25 February 1781–20 May 1781, ed. Julian P. Boyd. Princeton: Princeton University Press, 1952, pp. 162–163.
22 Babits and Howard, *Guilford Courthouse*. Pp. 165 and 167.
23 Letter from Otho Williams to Josiah Carvel Hall. March 17, 1781. Guilford Courthouse National Military Park Collection. Cited in Babits and Howard, *Guilford Courthouse*. P. 170.
24 Williams, Otho. Letter to his brother Elie Williams. Written at Speedwell Furnace, North Carolina. March 16, 1781.

Calendar of the Otho Holland Williams Papers in the Manuscript Collections of the Maryland Historical Society. MS 908. Part 1/8. (Item # 97.)
25 Letter from Otho Williams to Josiah Carvel Hall. March 17, 1781. Guilford Courthouse National Military Park Collection. Cited in Babits and Howard, *Guilford Courthouse*. P. 170.
26 Babits and Howard, *Guilford Courthouse*. P. 174. They cite: Lamb, American War, 360n; Charles Cornwallis to Dr. Webster, 23rd Apr, 1781, in Ross, *Cornwallis Correspondence*, 1:93.
27 Cornwallis, Charles to Lord Germain. Written at Guilford, 17th March, 1781. Ross, Cornwallis Papers. P. 520.
28 Buchanan, Road to *Guilford Courthouse*. P. 381-382.
29 Symonds, *Battlefield Atlas*. P. 93.
30 Stedman, *History*. Pp. 347-348.
31 Greene, Nathanael. Letter to Joseph Reed. Written at Camp near the Iron Works, North Carolina. March 18th, 1781. *Greene Papers*. 7: 450-451.
32 Greene, Nathanael. Letter to Henry Lee, Jr. Written at Headquarters. March 21, 1781. *Greene Papers*. 7:456.
33 Gordon, *History. Vol. IV*. P. 58.
34 Williams, Otho. Letter to his brother Elie Williams. Written at Rocky River, North Carolina. March 27, 1781. *Williams Papers*. Part 1/8. (Item #99.)
35 Regarding the position of the Adjutant General in battle, Charles James in the 1802 Military Dictionary states that "*In a day of battle the adjutant-general sees the infantry drawn up, after which he places himself by the general to receive orders*" Ref: James, Military Dictionary. Pp. ACC/ADJ and ADV/AGE. (pages are not numbered in the text; the progression of the definitions is alphabetical.)
36 Greene, Nathanael. Letter to Catharine Greene. March 18, 1781. Written at the Camp at the Iron Words near Guilford Courthouse. *Greene Papers*. Page 7:446.
37 Robinson, *Davie*. Pp. 31-32.
38 Babits and Howard, *Guilford Courthouse*. Pp. 148-150.
39 Williams, Otho. Letter to Colonel Josias Carvell Hall, 4th Maryland. Written at Camp Speedwell Furnace, North Carolina. 17th March 1781. Guilford Courthouse National Military Park Library Collection, Greensboro, North Carolina.
40 Ibid.
41 The author believes that the events that Davie described in this letter have a distinct similarity to actions at the Battle of Hobkirk's Hill, which are described in a future chapter. It seems conceivable that Davie's memory was imperfect in his assertion on Williams' performance at Guilford Courthouse, which was written long after the War. No other contemporary account has been found that makes the assertion that Williams and Ford were the cause of the poor performance of the Second Maryland at Guilford Courthouse, including writers such as John Eager Howard, who was present at the Battle. As noted previously in the discussion of the skirmish at Weitzel's Mill, Davie made several critical comments about Otho Holland Williams long after the War was over, and there seem to be plausible reasons for his dislike of the Marylander. None the less, Davie was an accomplished soldier, an active and well informed participant in these events, and a credible witness whose observations deserve due consideration.
52 Robinson, *Davie*. P. 32.
43 Ibid. Pp. 32-33
44 Lee, *Memoirs*, P. 578.
45 Greene, Nathanael. Letter to Joseph Reed, President of the Pennsylvania Council. March 18th, 1781. Written at "Camp near the Iron Works." *Greene Papers*. 7:450.

CHAPTER 8

THE BATTLE OF HOBKIRK'S HILL

Greene Returns to South Carolina

When Lord Cornwallis withdrew from the battlefield of Guilford Courthouse and marched toward Wilmington, North Carolina, Nathanael Greene led his army in pursuit. The American general continually looked for opportunities to attack, even though much of his army had melted away after Guilford Courthouse, and his force was, once again, inferior to Cornwallis. Typical of the situation facing Greene was the disposition of the Virginia militia commanded by General Robert Lawson, a unit that had fought very well at Guilford Courthouse. Two weeks after the battle, on April 1st, 1781, Deputy Adjutant General Otho Williams wrote to Lawson that his troops had fulfilled their six weeks of service and were discharged, with General Greene's thanks for their "faithful services and patient perseverance in times uncommonly difficult."[1] In the coming campaign, Greene and Williams would have to rely on their core Continental units from Maryland and Virginia, and hope that reinforcements of militia would come to them when needed to confront the British in direct combat.

As Cornwallis' army headed for the safety of Wilmington, Nathanael Greene realized that it would be difficult to attack the British if they were able to reach that port city, where they would have good defenses, additional troops, and the ability to receive supplies from the sea. Given these realities, Greene pondered his options, writing to George Washington:

> *If the enemy fall down towards Wilmington, they will be in a position where it would be impossible for us to injure them…In this critical and distressing situation, I am determined to carry the war immediately into South Carolina. The enemy will be obliged to follow us or give up their posts in that State.*[2]

Cornwallis and his Army reached Wilmington, North Carolina on April 7th, a little more than three weeks after the Battle of Guilford Courthouse. They were transported down the last leg of the Cape Fear River with the assistance of the Royal Navy.[3]

With Cornwallis now in a strong defensive position and well supplied, Greene swung the American Army away from Wilmington and headed toward South Carolina, intent on recapturing that state. Cornwallis decided to move north into Virginia rather than follow Greene into South Carolina. His explanation sounds as though he considered Nathanael Greene a very troublesome adversary, who used terrain and all available resources very effectively:

> *if we are so unlucky as to suffer a severe blow in South Carolina, the spirit of revolt in that province would become very general, and the numerous rebels in this province be encouraged to be more than ever active and violent. This might enable General Greene to hem me in among the great rivers and by cutting off our subsistence, render our arms useless...*[4]

Greene and Williams knew from hard experience that reliance on militia troops would be difficult, but there was no other way to raise a force that was sufficient to directly challenge the British in South Carolina and Georgia. Some of the difficulties of managing militia troops were in evidence on April 20th, 1781, when Greene and Williams tried valiantly to convince a North Carolina militia contingent to stay with the Army when they thought that their enlistments were expiring:

> *In the afternoon of the twentieth a most unpleasant and disturbing circumstance occurred which seemed for a moment to disturb even the Equanimity of the general himself. Lieutenant Colonel Webb's battalion of militia, which with my own constituted the command of Colonel Read, insisted on their discharge, insisting that their term of service had expired.... finding our entreaties unavailing, one of us went to the general and gave him the unpleasing information, when he, with great condescension, mounted his horse, and accompanied by Col. O. H. Williams, rode into our camp on the aforesaid eminence at a short distance from the regular troops and used all his persuasion and eloquence to detain them but a few days longer, when, as before observed to them, they might be of important service. The general was seconded by Colonel Williams, who in the most persuasive manner reasoned with them and urged their delay, but all to no purpose. Captain R. and the others became more clamorous, and General Greene, mortified and disgusted, directed Colonel Williams to write their discharge...*[5]

In addition to the difficulties of keeping together sufficient troops to pursue their mission, Greene and Williams continued to face enormous challenges in supplying the army, which would consume much of their attention and energy during the coming campaign. Otho Williams was especially involved in the management of arms and ammunition, as the Assistant Inspector of the Army.[6]

In addition to their supply problems, the leaders of the southern army would continue to deal with the frustrations of negotiating with important local military leaders such as Thomas Sumter, who seemed attuned to their own prerogatives and uninclined to work under the orders of Continental leadership. Further, Greene and Williams would never receive the level of support from the various states that they desired, and temporary troops continued to come and go from their camps with maddening regularity.

The pressure on these two men was enormous. Both would write home during this time, as Williams did to his sister, that the campaign was "inconceivably fatiguing," and that he "had seldom taken off his sword, coat or boots to sleep since he began the retreat from the Pee Dee River in January."[7]

Greene, supported by his Deputy Adjutant General Otho Williams, could not count on having superior resources in the fight against the British. If they were going to achieve their objectives, it would have to be by strategy, planning, and masterful use of very limited resources. They would prove to be up to the task.

As Greene moved into South Carolina, he deployed his small force as effectively as he could to achieve multiple objectives in the shortest possible time. While he moved with his main force directly toward Camden, South Carolina, he sent Light Horse Harry Lee and his Legion on ahead to join Francis Marion to attack Fort Watson, located on the Santee River about sixty miles northwest of Charleston, thus beginning an effort to cut the British supply lines that extended inland from Charleston and the coast using the Santee/Wateree rivers as the route. The supply line was protected by several small posts at key points along that route, of which Fort Watson was one of the most important. This effort is known as the "War of Posts."

★ ★ ★ ★ ★

Greene's Army Arrives at Camden, South Carolina

Greene and Williams arrived near Camden, South Carolina with their army on April 19th and 20th.[8] Greene inspected the town's defenses on April 20th and decided that he could not attack successfully until he had more men. He ordered his troops back to a good defensive position on Hobkirk's Hill, a sandy ridge about eighty feet high, located about a mile-and-a-half north of the city.⁹ The "Great Waxhaw Road" ran from Camden northward, up and over the center of the ridge,¹⁰ which runs east-west on either side of the road. There were several springs on the eastern end of the hill, which merged into a creek (referred to as a "rivulet" in some accounts) that ran east from the hill into Little Pine Tree Creek.¹¹

British troops from other parts of South Carolina were trying to reach Camden to reinforce the garrison there, and to help join the fight against Greene and his army. Greene moved his troops to the east of Camden, to reach out to reinforcements from Marion and Lee, who were besieging Fort Watson, and also to intercept any British reinforcements coming from that direction. The ground was swampy east of Camden, so Greene sent his heavy wagons and artillery up the Great Waxhaw Road where they would be safe from the British, while he marched his troops to the east. The supply situation was very difficult east of Camden,¹² and when he learned that Lee and Marion were making good progress at Fort Watson and that British reinforcements were being delayed, Greene ordered his men back to the good defensive position at Hobkirk's Hill. He also directed that the artillery and wagons be brought back to support the Army.¹³

Greene had ordered Thomas Sumter and his South Carolina militia to join him, which would have given him a large enough force to conduct a siege of Camden and take the town by cutting off food supplies. Sumter ignored Greene's orders, which Light Horse Harry Lee said was much to the "… surprise, regret, and dissatisfaction of the American general, and very much to the detriment of his plans and measures."¹⁴ With an inadequate force to blockade Camden, Greene had little choice but to leave his Army sitting atop Hobkirk's Hill, awaiting developments.

★ ★ ★ ★ ★

The Battle of Hobkirk's Hill

General Greene stationed his army atop the hill, with Colonel Otho Williams commanding the Maryland troops to the left of the road and Brigadier General Isaac Huger commanding the Virginia Continentals to its right. Williams' two regiments were the First Maryland, commanded by Colonel John Gunby, on his right, and the Second Maryland, commanded by Lieutenant Colonel Benjamin Ford, on his left. Ford's command held the far left flank of Greene's army. Huger's two regiments were the First Virginia, commanded by Lieutenant Colonel Richard Campbell, and the Second Virginia, commanded by Lieutenant Colonel Samuel Hawes. Hawes'

THE BATTLE OF HOBKIRK'S HILL 219

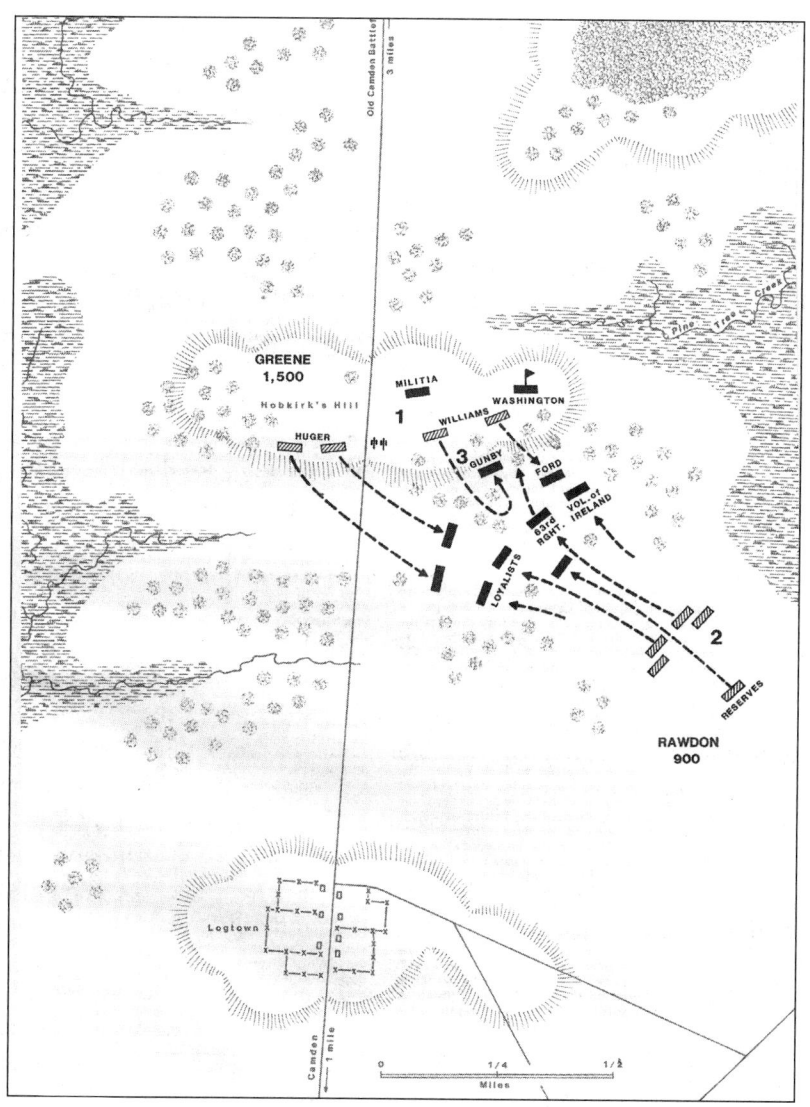

Map 7 - The Battle of Hobkirk's Hill

command formed the far right flank of Greene's army.[15] The American lines faced south down the Great Waxhaw Road, which was the expected route of advance for any British attack. Pickets were stationed ahead of their lines to provide early warning of any approaching enemy. (A map of the Hobkirk's Hill area and battle is included on page 219.)

Fort Watson surrendered to Marion and Lee on April 23rd, and they sent a number of prisoners from the fort to Greene at Camden. These prisoners arrived at Greene's lines on Hobkirk's Hill the next day, April 24th. Some of these prisoners were former American soldiers who had gone over to the British, but Greene was desperate for more troops, and he therefore accepted their avowals that they had only signed up with the British because they hoped they would receive better treatment. One of these turncoats, a drummer in the Maryland Brigade named Jones, deserted again that very day, went to the British lines, and gave a largely accurate description of the American position to the British commander at Camden, Lord Rawdon.[16] The deserter Jones also gave Rawdon the invaluable information that that Greene's army had not been reinforced by Sumter, adding that the Americans were short on provisions and had sent their cannon away from the front lines.[17]

Rawdon was an impressive leader, who one observer called "...a man of uncommon address."[18] He commanded a small force of less than 1,000 men at Camden, and had thought that he would act on the defensive and wait for reinforcements.[19] However, the Maryland drummer's report convinced him that if he moved quickly, he might be able to attack Greene successfully, which Rawdon hoped to do before the Americans could be reinforced by Francis Marion, Henry Lee, and Thomas Sumter, who he had heard were "coming to Greene."[20] Rawdon decided to try to surprise the larger American force of some 1,500 men[21] by approaching their lines under the cover of the woods instead of advancing in the open straight up the Great Waxhaw Road, as the Americans apparently expected.

The Americans held a good position on Hobkirk's Hill, and they had stationed competent pickets in front of their lines to protect them from any surprise. However, many soldiers had relaxed their guard on the morning of April 25th, when an order was issued that 'The troops are to be furnished with two days provisions and a gill of spirits per man as soon as the stores arrive," a message that was undoubtedly encouraging to troops who were used to living on meager rations. The officers and men were not expecting an attack. Many were cooking their food and washing clothes in the rivulet. Greene's second-in-command, General Isaac Huger, was washing his feet in the rivulet with several other officers, while a number of soldiers were washing their kettles nearby. Nathanael Greene was at breakfast.[22]

At about 10 a.m. firing was heard from the pickets who were stationed in front of the army, and who were the first to meet Rawdon's attack. Colonel Williams was able to ride the two- or three-hundred yards from the front line to headquarters, undoubtedly to confer with Greene, and then back to the lines before the fighting became more widespread.[23] Militia officer Guilford Dudley was marching his command up the back side of the hill with artillery when they met Williams, who ordered them to "March to the right and support Colonel Campbell," there being no time for more elaborate instructions.[24]

The firing from the pickets was totally unexpected; it alarmed the men behind the American lines and spurred them to action. The pickets, commanded by Captain Benson of Maryland and Captain Morgan of Virginia, did a professional job of slowing the British advance, and they were soon supported by the intrepid Robert Kirkwood and his veterans from Delaware.[25] Kirkwood and the pickets were able to slow Rawdon's advance, but their small force was slowly pushed back.

Meanwhile, the men from the Maryland and Virginia regiments who had been at the stream immediately grabbed their weapons and rushed up the hill to join their comrades in formation. Some were barefoot; most did not have on their coats.[26]

The American lines were formed in a hurry. Some early writers maintained that the Army fell into an orderly formation very quickly. For example, Light Horse Harry Lee wrote that "…the American army, notwithstanding its short notice, was quickly ranged for action."[27] Similarly, Nathanael Greene's battle report would state that "The line was formed in an instant."[28] However, subsequent events seem to support views like those of Lieutenant-Colonel John Eager Howard, who wrote years later that the response to Rawdon's surprise attack was not quite so crisp and perfect:

> *The officers made every exertion to have their men paraded, but before many who were washing could join their regiments the line was attacked…the line was not well formed…*[29]

It seems possible that the sudden appearance of Rawdon and his assault column shocked the Continental troops at Hobkirk's Hill, and threw them into an unaccustomed state of confusion as they prepared to meet the oncoming British troops. In previous battles when these Continental troops had been so effective, there had been ample time to form their lines and make careful preparations for the ordeal ahead. At Hobkirk's Hill, everything was done in a rush and under the threat of an imminent attack, which must have been unsettling for both officers and men.

Since Rawdon had chosen to swing through the woods on his right, his initial attack hit the American left, which was occupied by the Maryland Continentals under the overall command of Colonel Otho Williams. Rawdon would be charging straight into the teeth of some of the American army's best fighting units, who were led by an experienced commander in Williams. Also, unbeknownst to Rawdon and in contradiction to what he had been told by the deserter, American artillery had been brought back to the front lines, and was "well posted and doing great execution."[30]

The British troops were deployed in a long column so that they could move quickly and present a narrow front that would avoid detection by the Americans for as long as possible. Greene saw their formation as an opportunity, and thought that his men should be able to overlap Rawdon's narrow column and take a large toll on the British troops by firing on them from both flanks. Greene quickly issued orders that would execute this movement, which would result in a "double envelopment," with Rawdon's men caught between troops on both flanks. This was the type of maneuver that had led to the impressive American victory at Cowpens, just three months earlier.

To execute this plan, Greene sent orders to his far left Regiment under Maryland's Lieutenant Colonel Ford and his far right regiment under Virginia's Lieutenant Colonel Richard Campbell to swing around the British flanks and start the encirclement. Greene's center regiments under Maryland's John Gunby and Virginia's Samuel Hawes were ordered to advance down the hill and "charge them in front" while their comrades on either side worked their way around the British flanks. Greene also ordered William Washington and his cavalry to skirt the British left flank and attack them from the rear.[31] Greene led the Virginia troops in person,[32] while Williams commanded the Maryland troops on the left, probably an indication of Greene's trust in the Marylander's military judgment.

Greene sensed that he was about to win a decisive victory, which would be a great step forward in his campaign to re-take the South. The past four months of retreat, loss, tension, and despair had made the American General hungry for a win. He was convinced that he was about to smash Rawdon.

As the American flanking units under Benjamin Ford on the left and Richard Campbell on the right started their movements, Gunby's First Maryland and Hawes' Second Virginia moved straight ahead down the hill, with orders not to fire but to engage the enemy with the bayonet when the lines finally met. There was some disorder on the right of Gunby's line, and some troops fired their weapons, in spite of orders to attack with the bayonet. About this time, a British bullet claimed the life of the respected Captain William Beatty, who commanded one of the companies on Williams' and Gunby's right. Greene, Williams and Lieutenant Colonel John Eager Howard would all mention Beatty's death as a factor in the performance of the First Maryland in this battle.

The result of this confusion was that the two Maryland companies on the right of Gunby's line lagged behind the four companies on his left, which were led smartly ahead by Howard, Gunby's second-in-command. Sensing growing disarray, Gunby ordered his companies on the right to halt and regroup, and ordered Howard to bring his advancing companies back to reform into one consolidated line with the companies on the right. The combination of these confusing orders, the loss of the respected leader Beatty and the steady advance of a determined British battle line was too much for the Maryland troops. They broke and lost formation.

Suddenly, and without warning, Greene's hopes for victory were smashed by the astonishing collapse of the most reliable troops in his command, the First Maryland Regiment. Colonel Otho Williams, Colonel John Gunby and Lieutenant Colonel John Eager Howard all tried vigorously to rally the first Maryland,[33] but the tide of battle had turned, and it was too late to reconstruct a solid battle front. On the American left, Benjamin Ford, commander of the Second Maryland, received a very serious wound, which undoubtedly affected the morale of his troops and the effectiveness of communications with Commanding General Greene.

It was a confusing situation, which Otho Williams was still struggling to explain to his brother two days after the battle:

> *The first Maryland regiment particularly, was ordered to charge bayonets, without firing, but for some cause not yet clearly ascertained, the regiment received orders to retire and then broke.... The unfavorable consequences were that the army lost a glorious opportunity of gaining a complete victory, taking the town, and biasing the beam of Fortune greatly in favor of our cause...*[34]

As the American lines began to fall back, Nathanael Greene rushed to the front and plunged into the effort to turn the tide, as Williams, Gunby and

Howard had done earlier. North Carolina militia officer Guilford Dudley wrote that he had seen "…the general himself, with his cool intrepidity risking his invaluable person in the thickest of the battle," and that Greene had "…personally exposed himself during the conflict, especially on the left…"[35] William Richardson Davie summarized Greene's battlefield heroics on this day:

> *Nothing was more conspicuous this day than the personal bravery of Genl Greene who behaved more like a Capt of Grenadiers than a Major General; but these were exertions to retrieve the fortune of the day.*[36]

Despite the best efforts of the senior leaders, the retreat of the First Maryland started a chain of events that led to the withdrawal of the entire American army.

William Washington and his cavalry had been able to move into the rear of the British attacking force, and they were able to take a number of prisoners. Greene praised these efforts in his battle report, although other commentators have criticized Washington for being slow to support the disintegrating American line, instead spending his time making prisoners of wounded soldiers and non-combatants such as wagoners and camp followers.[37]

Greene's army retreated in good order north up the Great Waxhaw Road and established a defensive position at Sander's Creek. They were able to carry off all their artillery and much of their baggage, plus six British officers as prisoners. There was occasional fighting along the road to hold off Rawdon's pursuit, but about 4 o'clock, William Washington attacked the British lead units with a combined force of cavalry and infantry. Rawdon ended his pursuit and withdrew back to Camden.[38]

★ ★ ★ ★ ★

Controversies Regarding the Battle of Hobkirk's Hill

The sound of the guns had barely faded before the men in the southern army began to try to understand what had happened to cause the highly reliable First Maryland Regiment to perform so poorly at the Battle of Hobkirk's Hill, and the performance of these veteran troops has been a topic of study for historians ever since. Controversy, confusion, and complexity still seem to cloud our understanding of the Battle of Hobkirk's Hill. William Richardson Davie, a Continental Officer from North Carolina who headed Nathanael Greene's commissary operations, embroiled Otho Holland Williams in the controversy, as he had done in comments on the skirmish at Weitzel's Mill and the Battle of Guilford Courthouse. In his criticism of Williams at Hobkirk's Hill, Davie seems to have taken particular offense at some of the writing about the battle that appeared in William Gordon's *The History of the Rise, Progress, And Establishment, of the Independence of the United States Of America*, to which Williams was known to have contributed.

Twenty-three years after the Battle, John Eager Howard, a friend of Otho Williams and a close companion during much of the 1780/1781 campaign, provided some thoughtful, balanced insights on the First Maryland's collapse at Hobkirk's Hill. Howard had been second-in-command of the unit during the Battle, and was therefore a direct participant in the controversial events. He provided input and analysis to several Revolutionary War historians over the years, and his observations stand out for their sober, careful, thoughtful tone and for the absence of overt efforts to enhance his own reputation. Howard's detailed explanation included discussion of the items such as the troops forming slowly because of cooking and washing, and the death of William Beatty, but in the end Howard concluded of the First Maryland:

> *"The truth is they behaved bad."*[39]

In 1819, long years after he had participated in the battle, Samuel Mathis called on distant memories to try to explain the First Maryland's collapse:

> *This was the critical moment. Altho' our left was giving way, yet Gen. Huger on our right was gaining ground and was beginning to advance upon the enemy and Col. Gunby's regiment of brave soldiers, veterans of the Maryland Line, had all got to their arms, were well formed and in good order, but too impatient waiting the word of command. Some of them had begun to fire in violation of orders, and seeing the British infantry coming up the hill in front of them, Col. Gunby suffered them to come within a few paces and then ordered his men to charge without firing. Those near him, hearing the word, first rushed forward, whereby the regiment was moving forward in the form of a bow. Col. Gunby ordered a 'halt' until the wings should become straight: this turned the fate of the day...*[40]

When Otho Williams wrote about the Battle of Hobkirk's Hill just two days after it occurred, he noted that the fighting was at long range, and was therefore less intense than other battles, because there wasn't any hand-to-hand fighting or bayonet charges:

> *The action was at no time very warm, but it was durable, and our troops by the gallant exertions of our officers, were rallied frequently, but always fought at long shot. A convincing testimony that this was generally the case, is that none or very few of our men were wounded with buck shot or bayonet... The cavalry, the light infantry, and the guards, acquired all the honor, and the infantry of the battalions all the disgrace that fell upon our shoulders. The cavalry, led on by Washington, behaved in a manner truly heroic...*[41]

There were many other attempts to explain the events of April 25th, 1781. Light Horse Harry Lee attributed the loss to "...the deranging effects of unlimited confidence," emphasizing that Greene should have kept Washington's cavalry in reserve to support any unit like the First Maryland that faltered.[42] William Richardson Davie felt that "The battle was lost for want of troops to form the second line or proper reserve, a single half battalion to have replaced the two companies in Gunby's regiment which fell back would have restored the fortune of the day."[43] There are many other opinions in the written record.

From the moment that the battle ended, Nathanael Greene was absolutely convinced that there was one cause, and one cause alone of the debacle at Hobkirk's Hill, and that was the actions of the commander of the first Maryland, Colonel John Gunby. Greene reached that conclusion immediately, and he never deviated from it. His letter report to the President of Congress two days after the battle contained unusual public criticism of a brother officer:

> *The Enemy were staggered in all quarters, and upon the left were retiring while our Troops continued to advance, when unfortunately two Companies of the right of the First Maryland Regiment got a little disordered, and unhappily Colo Gunby gave an order for the rest of the regiment then advancing to take a new position in the rear, where the two companies were rallying. This impressed the whole Regiment with an Idea of a retreat, and communicated itself to the 2d Regiment which immediately followed the first on their retiring.*[44]

Greene was still fuming at Gunby three months after the battle, in a letter to Joseph Reed:

> *The troops were not to blame in the Camden affair; Gunby was the sole cause of the defeat; and I found him much more blameable afterwards, than I represented him in my public letters.*[45]

Nathanael Greene was furious. An opening victory in the campaign to free South Carolina had been in his grasp, only to be snatched away by the inexplicable performance of the normally reliable First Maryland Regiment. This same Regiment had performed brilliantly at Guilford Courthouse just a month before, and under the same leaders, Colonel John Gunby and his second-in-command, John Eager Howard. In the General's mind, their poor performance demanded an explanation.

Gunby requested a court martial, and Greene had calmed down enough by four days after the battle to write that an official inquiry would decide whether the loss was "...owing to an order of Col Gunby's, or the misconduct of the Maryland Troops."[46] This was the closest that Greene would ever come to a balanced view on the subject.

Gunby's trial was held on May 2nd. The court concluded that:

> *It appears, from the above report, that Colonel Gunby's spirit and activity were unexceptionable. But his order for the regiment to retire, which broke the line, was extremely improper and unmilitary, and, in all probability, the only cause why we did not obtain a complete victory.*[47]

Otho Williams apparently avoided public involvement in the controversy regarding Gunby. He was in a ticklish position. He was the direct subordinate and friend of the Commanding General Nathanael Greene, who was very clear in his mind that Gunby alone had lost the day. On the other hand, Gunby was a brother officer from Maryland and Williams' direct subordinate during the controversial actions. The record of Williams' activities regarding the trial, including his personal correspondence, do not directly condemn Gunby or shed further light on the situation.

A. A. Gunby, a descendent of the Colonel who had been the focus of Greene's fury after Hobkirk's Hill, wrote the treatise "Colonel John Gunby of the American Line," which was published in Cincinnati in 1902. This well written report presents a lawyerly case that John Gunby, a fine combat officer, was unfairly slighted by history as the scapegoat of Hobkirk's Hill. It presents a compelling case that Greene's fury and the quick court martial of Gunby may well have rendered judgments that were unfair to this good soldier.

One of Nathanael Greene's most recent biographers criticized the General for his reactions to Hobkirk's Hill and his visceral attack on Gunby:

> *This was Greene at his worst: petulant, filled with self-pity, and desperately trying to protect his reputation from those confounded critics who were ever so willing to find fault with him. He chose Gunby as a scapegoat when, in fact, his own decisions to counterattack on Rawdon's flanks and send Washington's cavalry into the fray may have tipped the battle in Rawdon's favor.*[48]

Otho Holland Williams rendered his own personal verdict about the Battle of Hobkirk's Hill in a letter to his sister written a few days after the battle. He noted that the army had lost many killed and wounded in the fight, and they had lost the best possible chance to take the town of Camden and its stores. Williams felt sure that they would have succeeded "if the troops had behaved as they should have."[49]

The American Army had suffered a disappointing loss at Hobkirk's Hill, but these were tough, resilient men who had recovered from loss in the past. Their well-managed retreat from the battlefield was solid testament that they retained their fighting spirit and discipline. In spite of General Greene's disappointment and dismay, he described his army in positive terms when he wrote to the President of Congress that: "Our Army is in good spirits, and this little repulse will make no alteration in our general plan of operation."[50]

★ ★ ★ ★ ★

William Richardson Davie's Critique of Greene, Williams and Gunby

William Richardson Davie once again turned his pen on Otho Williams regarding the Battle of Hobkirk's Hill:

> *Mr. Gordon I observe has taken this account of the action before Camden on the 25th of Ap.81 from Colo Williams's M.S.S. in which William's dislike of Gunby is apparent - Was this mistake of Gunby the reason why the 2(nd) Maryland regiment behaved so ill? - Or could Gunby's conduct influence the behavior of the Virginia line, who were repeatedly led up to action by Genl Greene in person, and could not be induced to stand the fire of*

the enemy; the presence of the General seconded by the exertions of Huger Hawes & Campbell.[51]

Davie introduces new information that Hawes' Regiment of Virginians would not charge the British, in spite of the personal intervention of Nathanael Greene. Davie also implied that Gordon's view had been distorted largely by the dislike that Otho Holland Williams had for Gunby. Williams was a significant contributor to Gordon's history, however, Gordon had many other possible sources for his conclusions, including the court martial of Gunby, which had found that the Colonel was responsible for the poor performance of the First Maryland and that Gunby's order for that unit to retire was probably the direct cause of the defeat. Gunby's trial was presided over by General Isaac Huger, and included Colonel Charles Harrison and Colonel William Washington as members.[52] The court's findings were endorsed by Nathanael Greene, and published in his General Orders. If Davie was correct that the criticism of Gunby was unfair, he could have also censured the members of the Court as soundly has he chose to condemn Otho Williams. As noted elsewhere in this text, Davie also wrote critically of Williams' performance at Weitzel's Mill and Guilford Courthouse, and seemed to be alert to opportunities to point out the Marylander's shortcomings.

However, there may be a kernel of truth in Davie's assertion that Otho Williams was not a particular friend of John Gunby, but the existing evidence is slight, and virtually none exists that supports Davie's contention that Williams had a "dislike" for Gunby . Williams had a close friendship with Samuel Smith, a Baltimore businessman who was very familiar with Maryland politics and the interactions between the state's senior military officers.[53] Smith was inclined to give Williams advice on how to advance his military standing in the state, such as his advice in April, 1779 to "…push the settlement of the matter of rank between [Col. John Hoskins] Stone and [Col. John] Gunby; the decision will go against Stone, and Williams will then have no one to dispute the regiment with him after the war is over."[54] Smith's correspondence may imply that Gunby and Williams had divergent interests relative to rank and seniority in the Maryland military's pecking order, but by the time of the Battle of Hobkirk's Hill, such issues had been resolved, as Williams was clearly senior to Gunby.

Finally, the narrative about Hobkirk's Hill in *Gordon's History of the Rise, Progress and Establishment of the United States of America* is consistent with other writing on the subject, including the record of Gunby's court martial, pension records, and the observations of other contemporary writers. The record does not appear to support Davie's assertion that our understanding of the Battle of Hobkirk's Hill is distorted by Williams' "dislike" of Gunby.

Morale in the Maryland Line after Hobkirk's Hill

In his pension statement written in 1832, Guilford Dudley described Greene's army as "mortified troops, whose spirits were yet rather depressed by their late repulse before Camden."[55] It would seem natural that soldiers like the men in the First Maryland, who had performed so gallantly at the Battles of Camden, Cowpens and Guilford Courthouse would be dismayed by their actions at Hobkirk's Hill.

Morale in the Maryland command would also have undoubtedly been affected by the loss of respected soldiers in this battle. Captain William Beatty's loss was felt so deeply that Nathanael Greene mentioned it in a letter to the President of Congress:

> *Enclosed is the returned of the killed and Wounded. Among the former is Captain Baty (William Beatty) of the Maryland Line, a most excellent officer and an ornament to his profession.*[56]

Otho Williams mentioned to his sister, Mrs. Mercy Stull, that he deeply lamented Beatty's death.[57] The respect shown for Beatty by both the army commander and the Adjutant General seems to emphasize this officer was so widely admired that his death could well have unsettled his company and contributed to the unfortunate maneuvers that caused the First Maryland regiment to break formation at the Battle of Hobkirk's Hill.

Another loss that was deeply felt was that of Lieutenant Colonel Benjamin Ford, who had been badly wounded during the battle. Williams would later report to his brother Elie the death of his "worthy little friend."[58]

The loss of respected fellow officers and the disgrace of his unit's poor performance weighed heavily on Otho Williams, as he shared with his brother in a letter written two days after the battle:

> *Many of our officers are mortally mortified at our late inglorious retreat. I say mortally, because I cannot doubt that some of us must fall, in endeavoring the next opportunity, to re-establish our reputation. Dear Reputation, what trouble do you not occasion, what danger do you not expose us to! Who but for it, would patiently persevere in prosecuting a war, with the mere remnant of a fugitive army, in a country made desolate*

by repeated ravages, and rendered sterile by streams of blood. Who but for reputation would sustain the varied evils that daily attend the life of a soldier, and expose him to jeopardy every hour. Liberty, thou basis of reputation, suffer me not to forget the cause of my country, nor to murmur at my fate."[59]

The natural bravery and military competence of the Maryland Line would certainly be important factors in their future performance on the battlefield, but Williams seems to have felt that in future combat they would be willing to hazard unusual risks to overcome the memory of their poor performance at Hobkirk's Hill.

An Emotional Defense of Greene and the Southern Army

Otho Holland Williams would occasionally wield his pen in public statements that defended his own actions or those of his friends. On May 15th, 1781, a spirited defense of Nathanael Greene and the southern army appeared in the *Maryland Journal and Baltimore Advertiser* which has all the hallmarks of having been written by Williams (the editors of the Papers of General Nathanael Greene state that the author is "undoubtedly Otho Williams.") These sentiments are those of a front-line soldier who was outraged by the criticisms of the arm-chair strategists who sat comfortably at home while the Army endured danger and privation to fight for the country's freedom. This essay provides an important look into the inner sentiments of Otho Williams as a proud and determined warrior:

> *When I say that our Commander has behaved himself as heretofore, I only barely do him justice. Look back into our Proceedings, with so Little Means, where have you read so much having been done? Let this Man be unfortunate, or let him be successful, in either Case he will be a great Man. When we get more Troops, we will win Battles; and when we have better Means, we will recover lost Countries. If the Southern States should be overrun, blame no one in this Quarter. We have done our Duty; would to God I could say the same thing of these States from whom we have been so long expecting Succour. Tell me, you who know something of public Affairs, what Policy is it, that has prevented you from sending us black Troops, if you could not get white ones; what Policy is it, that has kept*

> *from us, as I am told, about 300 new Levies, for near three Months, which might have given us two Victories? As soon as 20 or 30 of your Levies had got together, why have they not been forwarded, under proper Officers? Is it the Officers who do not exert themselves on such Occasions, or is it the Government that fall asleep over their Businesses? Whatever be the Cause, I know who will experience its Effects. We are not many. We have been tried by great Sufferings, and ye all know, whether we have shrunk from our Duty. But the Sufferings we must feel, arise from the Supineness of some of our Countrymen.*[60]

Greene Considers Going to Virginia

An interesting sidelight to the story of the Battle of Hobkirk's Hill involves Greene's morale and attitude in the immediate aftermath of the battle. He was apparently despondent at the defeat, disgusted with Sumter's lack of support and cooperation, deeply disappointed in the support he was receiving from the various state governments and their militia, and furious at Colonel Gunby. Greene expressed these feelings in a letter to his friend Joseph Reed, President of the Pennsylvania Council, a week-and-a-half after the battle.:

> *The prospects here are so unpromising, and the difficulties so great, that I am sick of the service, and wish my self out of the Department. When I made this last Movement I expected 2000 Virginia Militia to operate with us, and 1000 men with Sumter, but both have failed me; and I am in the greatest distress. The tardiness of the people puts it out of my power to attempt anything great...*[61]

No surviving remarks of Otho Holland Williams express feelings as dark and despondent as those above written by Greene in his private correspondence. Yet the Army's Adjutant General was almost certainly aware of the Commanding General's feelings, based on their joint responsibilities and frequent interaction.

Greene contemplated the possibility of going north to Virginia to join the fight there in his May 9th letter to Light Horse Harry Lee, where he indicated that "...much is to be done in Virginia..." and that "...more advantage will result from (Greene's) going than staying, for he can serve them more effectively there than here..."[62]

In later years, John Eager Howard remembered clearly that Greene had considered leaving South Carolina and heading north to take command of the troops in Virginia, where he might do more good for the Revolutionary cause. Howard's friend William Washington had told him that Greene was preparing for the trip north:

> *I can say positively that Washington's horse had orders to be in readiness to attend General Greene to Virginia. The reason given by the General for his determination to retreat was that Sumter would not act with him and supply him with provisions as he had promised and that he could be of more service to his Country in Virginia...*[63]

Since Greene ultimately remained in South Carolina, he clearly worked through his despair, and resolved to continue the fight in the southern theater. It seems highly likely that Otho Williams would have been involved in these discussions, both as Greene's friend and close associate, and as one of his key staff officers and commanders.

Even while he was dealing with his own inner personal feelings of despair, Greene worked diligently to keep a positive spin on news that was disseminated about the Battle of Hobkirk's Hill. Perhaps some of this was his own pride and defensiveness, but he also realized that positive news was also vital to maintaining the strongest possible support from the various state governments and the people in the countryside. The Commanding General of the southern army was quick to try to squelch reports that the American army had suffered a significant defeat, as indicated in his very precise instructions to Francis Marion:

> *Capt Conniers has just arrivd in Camp, and says that reports are below that we were routed and totally dispersed.*
> *You will take measures to have the account contradicted and the public properly informed. By mistake we got a slight repulse. The injury is not great. The Enemy Sufferd much more than we did. What has happened will make no alteration in our plan of operations and therefore I wish you to pursue the same plan as you had in contemplation before.*[64]

Rawdon Evacuates Camden

Once he was able to look past the disappointment of Hobkirk's Hill, Nathanael Greene realized that he still had the opportunity to dislodge Lord

Rawdon from Camden, and to move forward with his aggressive plans for regaining control of South Carolina. He ordered Francis Marion, "Light Horse Harry" Lee, and Thomas Sumter to block any British troops that tried to reinforce Camden, so that the Americans could maintain their numerical superiority in the area. Sumter seemed reluctant to have his movements controlled by Greene, as usual, but Marion and Lee were always cooperative, and, in accordance with Greene's wishes, they maneuvered back and forth across the Carolina countryside trying to keep Watson from reinforcing Rawdon. In spite of the best efforts of Marion and Lee, Colonel Watson and his command of about 500 men plus two pieces of artillery reached Camden on May 7th.[65] The addition of Watson's troops and artillery gave the aggressive Rawdon enough strength to once again seek battle with Greene.[66]

Rawdon moved north in search of Greene's army, and found him at a new position at Sawney's Creek (which Greene called "Sandy Creek",) in what Guilford Dudley called "...the strongest position I ever saw in South Carolina or perhaps anywhere else." Greene's army was posted on the summit of a "...stupendous hill faced with rock, having a difficult pass of steep ascent to climb up, his artillery posted in the road, on the eminence..." General Greene and Adjutant General Otho Williams had personally directed the positioning of the American troops in battle array on these formidable heights.

"A handsome firing took place" between Rawdon's advanced troops and Greene's screening force of pickets and the cavalry of William Washington. When Greene learned that Rawdon might find a path to the rear of his hilltop position, he fell back three or four miles to another strong position on a still, deep creek.

Rawdon was impressed with Greene's dispositions, and realized that direct action against the main American army would be disastrous. The British commander decided to withdraw all the way to Charleston, since he found that Greene was:

> *...everywhere so strong, that I could not hope to force it without suffering such a Loss, as must have crippled my Force for any future Enterprise...(and) I could not hope that Victory would give us any Advantage.*[67]

Rawdon evacuated Camden and set off for Charleston on May 10th. He tried to alert the British garrison at Ninety-Six of his decision, but the countryside was so effectively patrolled by the American army and partisans that none of Rawdon's communications got through.⁶⁸ Lee noted that when Rawdon left Camden, he:

> ...burned the jail, the mills, and some private houses, and destroyed all the stores which he could not take with him. He carried off four or five hundred negroes, and all the most obnoxious loyalists accompanied him.⁶⁹

Rawdon's withdrawal from Camden demonstrated that Greene's campaign to regain the South was succeeding, even in the face of his army's disappointing defeat at Hobkirk's Hill. While the British had clearly prevailed on the battlefield on April 25th, 1781, subsequent events would show that Green's aggressive strategy had put the British on the defensive, and had started to force their slow, steady withdrawal from the interior of South Carolina.⁷⁰

These events affirmed the statement that Greene had made in a letter to the Chevalier de La Luzerne: "We fight get beat rise and fight again."⁷¹ Greene usually did not prevail on the field of battle, but that he usually achieved his strategic objectives in spite of tactical setbacks.

As soon as he learned that Rawdon and his troops had withdrawn from Camden, Greene set his army in motion to pursue, and he also began to look for opportunities to capture additional British outposts. He thought that Rawdon might try to reinforce the important post of Fort Motte at the juncture of the Congaree and Wateree Rivers, so he ordered Marion and Lee to take the fort before Rawdon could reach it. The Americans got to the fort first, and with Mrs. Motte's daring aid, used fire arrows to set her roof on fire. Her house was the center of the improvised fort. Marion and Lee then forced the fort to surrender with the fire and artillery.⁷²

After the victory at Fort Motte, Greene continued to put pressure on British outposts. He ordered Lee to Fort Granby, upriver on the Congaree toward Ninety-Six, and he sent Marion to Georgetown, near the mouth of the Great Pee Dee River. Lee induced Fort Granby to surrender on the day he arrived, May 15th, by permitting the greedy garrison commander to leave unharmed with much of his loot and captured slaves. The Georgetown garrison evacuated by sea and sailed for Charleston on May 23rd.⁷³

Greene was enjoying outstanding success in his campaign to dislodge the British from their various fortifications, which Otho Williams summarized in a letter to his brother on June 12th, pointing out that the British had evacuated or lost Camden, Fort Watson, Fort Motte, Fort Granby, Nelson's Ferry, Georgetown, and Fort Dreadnought (part of the defenses at Augusta,

Georgia) in the past few weeks. After these successes, the only remaining British garrisons in South Carolina were Charleston and Ninety-Six.[74] Greene had been confronted by myriad difficulties, but in spite of all these manifold challenges, his campaign to retake the South was enjoying astonishing success.

The Southern Army Commander wanted to keep the strongest possible pressure on the British, and to continue pushing them out of the countryside and into their coastal enclaves at Charleston and Savannah. He ordered Lee to proceed to Augusta, Georgia to help the local forces under Andrew Pickens and Elijah Clarke attack that important post, while Greene and Williams marched with the main army toward the Loyalist garrison at Ninety-Six.

---

1   Williams, Otho Holland. Letter to General Robert Lawson. Written at Camp at Ramsey's Mill, North Carolina. April 1st, 1781. *Greene Papers*. 8:19.
2   Greene, Nathanael. Letter to George Washington. Written at Head-quarters at Colonel Ramsay's on Deep River. March 29, 1781. *Greene Papers*. 7:481.
3   Tarleton, *History*. P. 289.
4   Cornwallis, Charles. Letter to Lord George Germain. Dated Wilmington. April 23rd, 1781. Tarleton, *History*. P. 335.
5   Dudley, Guilford. 1832 deposition submitted with his Pension Statement. In Dann ed., *Accounts*. P. 218.
6   Von Steuben, Baron. Letter to Nathanael Greene. Written at Chesterfield Courthouse, Virginia. April 2nd, 1781. Letter contents, plus note 7. Greene Papers. 8:30-31; Von Steuben, Baron. Letter to Nathanael Greene. Written at May's Mill on the West Side of the Pee Dee on Camden Road, North Carolina, 15th April, 1781. Letter plus note 4. *Greene Papers*. 8:99.
7   Williams, Otho. Letter to Mrs. Mercy Stull. May 4, 1781. *Williams Papers*. Part 1/ 8. (Item # 102.)
8   Seymour, *Journal*. P. 380.
9   The author used the information from John Robertson's "The Global Gazetteer of the American Revolution," to determine that Hobkirk's Hill is 6.7 miles south of the site of the disastrous defeat of the American Army at the Battle of Camden, which occurred nine months earlier, on August 16th, 1780. Ref: http://gaz.jrshelby.com/
10 Dudley, Guilford. Pension Statement. 1832. In Dann ed., *Accounts*. P. 219.
11 Kirkland, Thomas J. and Kennedy, Robert M. *Historic Camden. Part One. Colonial and Revolutionary*. (hereafter Kirkland and Kennedy, *Historic Camden*.) The State Company. Columbia, South Carolina. 1905. P 226; Dudley, Guilford. Pension Statement. 1832, Dann, ed., *Accounts*. P. 219; Lee, *Memoirs*. P. 336.
12 Howard, John Eager. Letter Answering Questions on Cowpens, Guilford Courthouse, and Hobkirk's Hill. Bayard Papers. MS 109, Box 4. Maryland Historical Society.
13 Lee, *Memoirs*. Pp. 334-335.
14 Ibid. P. 333.
15 The description of the army's positions is taken from the map on page 1174 of Commager and Morris.
16 Lee, *Memoirs*. P. 335.
17 Kirkland and Kennedy, *Historic Camden*. P. 228.
18 Mathis, Samuel. Letter to W. R. Davie. Written at Camden. June 26, 1819. Commager and Morris. P. 1177.
19 Symonds, *Battlefield Atlas*. P. 94.
20 *Greene Papers*. 8:157. (Note 1 to letter from Nathanael Greene to Samuel Huntington, President of Congress. Written at Camp Sanders's Creek, South Carolina. April 17th, 1781.)
21 Symonds, *Battlefield Atlas*. P. 94.
22 Gordon, *History. Volume IV*. Pp. 82-83; Moultrie, William. *Memoirs of the American Revolution, Volume 2*. P. 276.
23 Gordon, *History. Volume IV*. P. 83.
24 Dudley, Guilford. 1832 deposition submitted with his Pension Statement. In Dann, ed., *Accounts*. P. 219.

25 Greene, Nathanael. Letter to Samuel Huntington, President of the Continental Congress. Written at Camp, Sanders' Creek, South Carolina. April 27, 1781. *Greene Papers*. 8:155.
26 Kirkland and Kennedy, *Historic Camden*. P. 231.
27 Lee, *Memoirs*. P 336.
28 Greene, Nathanael. Letter to Samuel Huntington, President of the Continental Congress. Written at Camp, Sanders' Creek, South Carolina. April 27, 1781. *Greene Papers*. 8:155.
29 Howard, John Eager. March 22, 1782 letter to John Gunby. Bayard Papers. MS 109. Maryland Historical Society.
30 Gordon, *History. Volume IV*. P. 83.
31 Greene, Nathanael. Letter to Samuel Huntington, President of the Continental Congress. Written at Camp, Sanders' Creek, South Carolina. April 27, 1781. *Greene Papers*. 8:156.
32 Gordon, *History. Volume IV*. P. 83.
33 Lee, *Memoirs*. P. 338.
34 Williams, Otho Holland. Letter to Elie Williams. Written at Camp before Camden. April 27, 1781. From Tiffany, *Sketch*. P. 19.
35 Dudley, Guilford. 1832 deposition submitted with his Pension Statement. In Dann, ed., *Accounts*. P. 220.
36 Robinson, *Davie*. P. 33.
37 Greene, Nathanael. Letter to Samuel Huntington, President of the Continental Congress. Written at Camp, Sanders' Creek, South Carolina. April 27, 1781. *Greene Papers*. 8:157 and Note 4 on P. 159.
38 Gordon, *History. Volume IV*. P. 84.
39 Howard, John Eager. Letter Answering Questions on Cowpens, Guilford Courthouse, and Hobkirk's Hill. Bayard Papers. MS 109, Box 4. Maryland Historical Society.
40 Mathis, Samuel. Letter to William Richardson Davie. Written at Camden. June 26, 1819. Commager and Morris. P. 1177.
41 Williams, Otho Holland. Letter to Elie Williams. Written at Camp before Camden. April 27, 1781. From Tiffany, *Sketch*. P. 20; though Williams called the action "durable," an individual who lived in Camden and kept a diary recorded on April 25th that "Between 11 and 12 o'clock heard a very heavy fire of cannon and musketry lasting fifteen minutes...." The same diarist wrote the next day that "Understand ye firing we heard was an engagement above Camden. Ref: Kirkland and Kennedy, *Historic Camden*. P. 252.
42 Lee, *Memoirs*. P. 340.
43 Robinson, *Davie*. P. 44.
44 Greene, Nathanael. Letter to Samuel Huntington, President of the Continental Congress. Written at Camp, Sanders' Creek, South Carolina. April 27, 1781. *Greene Papers*. 8:156.
45 Pancake, *This Destructive War*. Pp. 195-198. Pancake cites: "Greene to Reed, July 6, 1781, Reed, Reed, 2: p. 362."
46 Greene, Nathanael. Letter to Colonel Henry Lee, Jr. Written at Camp, Rugeley's Mill, South Carolina. 29 April, 1781. *Greene Papers*. 8:172.
47 General Orders of Nathanael Greene. Written at Camp near Rugeleys, South Carolina. Wednesday, 2nd May 1781. *Greene Papers*. 8:187.
48 Golway, Terry. *Washington's General. Nathanael Greene and the Triumph of the American Revolution*. New York. 2005.. P. 269.
49 Williams, Otho Holland. Letter to Mrs. Mercy Stull. May 4, 1781. Calendar of the Otho Holland Williams Papers in the Manuscript Collections of the Maryland Historical Society. MS 908. Part 1 of 8. Item # 102.
50 Greene, Nathanael. Letter to Samuel Huntington, President of the Continental Congress. Written at Camp, Sanders' Creek, South Carolina. April 27, 1781. *Greene Papers*. P. 8:157.
51 Robinson, *Davie*. P. 33.
52 General Orders. At Camp near Rugeleys, South Carolina. 2nd May, 1781. Footnote 1. *Greene Papers*. 8:187, footnote 1.
53 Samuel Smith had served as a Continental Officer early in the war, and had been commended for his outstanding performance during Battle of Long Island and the campaign around Philadelphia in 1777/78, but he had resigned his commission after that and returned to his business activities in Baltimore. He would later serve as the commander of the Baltimore defenses in the War of 1812, which included the defense of Fort McHenry during the time in which Francis Scott Key wrote the Star Spangled Banner. In addition to friendly social banter and advice on Williams' military career, Smith's correspondence with Williams also discusses their joint investments, principally in shipping. Smith apparently guided some investment funds for Williams. Their investments in shipping were high-risk, high-reward. The correspondence sometimes mentions losses, sometimes sizeable gains.
54 Smith, Samuel. Letter to Otho Holland Williams. Written at Baltimore Town, April 15, 1779. *Williams Papers*. Part 1/8. (Item #30).
55 Dudley, Guilford. 1832 deposition submitted with his Pension Statement. In Dann, ed., *Accounts*. P. 222.
56 Greene, Nathanael. Letter to Samuel Huntington, President of the Continental Congress. Written at Camp Sander Creek, South Carolina. April 27th, 1781. *Greene Papers* 8:157.

57 Williams, Otho. Letter to Mrs. Mercy Stull. Written May 4th, 1781. *Williams Papers*. Part 1/8. (Item # 102.)
58 Williams, Otho. Letter to Elie Williams. Written at Bush River, South Carolina. June 23rd, 1781. *Williams Papers*. Part 1/8. (Item # 107.)
59 Williams, Otho Holland. Letter to Elie Williams. Written at Camp before Camden. April 27, 1781. From Tiffany, *Sketch*. P. 20.
60 Footnote #2 is appended to a letter from Dr. James McHenry to Nathanael Greene. Written at Baltimore, May 23, 1781. *Greene Papers*. 8:303.
61 Greene, Nathanael. Letter to Joseph Reed, President of the Pennsylvania Council. Written at Camp near Camden on the West side of the Wateree. May 4th, 1781. *Greene Papers*. 8:201.
62 Greene, Nathanael. Letter to Colonel Henry Lee, Jr. Written at Colonel's Creek, South Carolina. May 9, 1781. *Greene Papers*. 8:228.
63 A transcript of this letter was provided to the author by historian Sam Fore. It is from Lee Family materials called the Rocky Mount Collection at the DuPont Library at Stratford Hall. From context, Professor Babits and Sam Fore believe it to have been written by John Eager Howard to Judge William Johnson after the publication of Johnson's Life of Greene in 1822.
64 Greene, Nathanael. Letter to General Francis Marion. Written at Camp Rughlys, South Carolina. April 27, 1781. *Greene Papers*. 8:160.
65 Greene, Nathanael. Letter to Colonel Henry Lee, Jr. Written at Colonel's Creek, South Carolina. May 9, 1781. *Greene Papers*. 8:229, Note 3.
66 Dudley, Guilford. 1832 deposition submitted with his Pension Statement. In Dann ed., *Accounts*. Pp. 222-223.
67 Pancake, *This Destructive War*. P. 200.
68 Lee, *Memoirs*. P. 344.
69 Ibid. Pp. 344-345.
70 Symonds, *Battlefield Atlas*. P. 95.
71 Greene, Nathanael. Letter to the Chevalier de La Luzerne. Written at Camp near Camden, South Carolina. April 28th, 1781. *Greene Papers*. 8:168.
72 Lee, *Memoirs*, pp. 249-352.
73 Pancake, *This Destructive War*. P. 200-202.
74 Williams, Otho Holland. Letter to Elie Williams. Written at Camp before Ninety Six, South Carolina. June 12, 1781. *Williams Papers*. Part 1/8. (Item # 106.)

CHAPTER 9

THE SIEGE AT NINETY-SIX[1]

Nathanael Greene's and Otho Williams' next objective was the well-fortified settlement named Ninety-Six,[2] which was situated on good, defensible ground some one-hundred-and-eighty miles northwest of Charleston. The British had chosen to fortify this spot because it gave them a strong presence in the deep interior of South Carolina, where they hoped that a permanent fortification would encourage their allies and threaten their enemies. A member of the British force described the post as:

> ...*a village or country town - contains about twelve dwelling houses, a court house and a jail...Ninety Six is situated on an eminence, the land cleared for a mile around it, in a flourishing part of the country, supplied with very good water, enjoys a free, open air, and is esteemed a healthy place.*[3]

The garrison at Ninety-Six was ably led by Lieutenant-Colonel John Harris Cruger of New York, whose approximately 550 men included battalions of Loyalist troops from New York and New Jersey, and militia from South Carolina. Cruger had taken command of the post in August, 1780, and had worked diligently to strengthen its defenses.[4] These included a stockade around the town, strengthened by bastions and blockhouses. There was a "stockade fort" to the west of town, a fortified jail within the town's walls, and an earthen fortress built in the form of a star (called the "Star Redoubt") to the north.[5] The main sources of water were a spring and "rivulet" to the west of the town, which were protected by the stockade fort and the fortified jail.[6] All the various defensive positions were linked together by a network of trenches,[7] which enabled the British defenders to move troops quickly to any threatened point.

All of Greene's force, which included about 1,000 men and three brass six-pound cannon, had arrived at Ninety-Six by the evening of May 22nd.[8] The Commander of the Southern Army and his Chief Engineer, Thaddeus Kosciusko, reconnoitered the British position and decided that it was too strong to be taken by a frontal assault. Greene wrote to Harry Lee that Ninety-Six was much better fortified and manned than he had expected.[9]

Since a direct attack was too risky, the Americans decided to lay siege to the works, in which they would surround the garrison, cut it off from supplies and support, and thereby force it to surrender. Much of siege warfare consisted of digging a series of parallel trenches, where the attacking force inched closer and closer to the enemy fortifications until they would finally be in a position where artillery and small arms fire could force the defenders to surrender. Although knowledge of how to conduct a siege was an important part of military education in Europe, very few American officers had any appreciation for the complexities of this type of warfare, and neither Greene nor his Deputy Commander Otho Williams had ever received such training. Greene therefore relied on his Chief Engineer Thaddeus Kosciusko, an officer with European schooling and experience, to plan and direct the siege.

Kosciuszko decided that the main target should be the Star Redoubt, and he directed the Americans to begin digging a trench near the redoubt on the very first night of May 22nd. The alert Cruger sensed the danger immediately, and ordered a small party out to attack this first American outpost the next day. The British drove the Americans off, took their entrenching tools, and destroyed the works that they had begun to build.[10] In this first day of fighting at Ninety-Six, the tone had been set. Cruger and his men were going to be tough adversaries.

Chastened by this early setback, Kosciusko began his next trenches and fortifications much farther back from the British positions. The American artillery began regular bombardments from their three six-pound cannon,[11] and the siege settled into a daily routine of digging, cannonading, and exchanging small arms fire. It was a gritty and dangerous type of warfare, with the Americans trying to dig their way closer to victory, and the British trying every tactic they could think of to delay what appeared to be their inevitable surrender. The only hope that Cruger and his men had was that a relief column from Charleston could reach Ninety-Six and drive the Americans away before the garrison was forced to surrender.

During the daylight hours, the Americans exchanged artillery and small arms fire with the British, and prepared for the dangerous night work in the trenches, when the digging began under the cover of darkness, and the British inevitably sent small parties out to surprise and attack the Americans. Much of the hard work of digging was performed by slaves, who were protected by heavily armed soldiers.

By June 3rd, Greene felt that he was in a dominant position, and he sent Otho Williams to the British lines under a flag of truce to deliver this ultimatum to Cruger:[12]

> *The very distant situation of the British Army commanded by Lord Cornwallis - Lord Rawdons retreat - The reduction of all the British posts upon Wateree, Congaree and Santee Rivers; and*

> *your present circumstances (which are not more truly known to yourself than to your adversary) Leave you no hope but in the generosity of the American Army. The Honourable Major Gl Greene has therefore commanded me to demand an immediate Surrender of your Garrison. A moral certainty of success, without which the previous measure wo'd not have been taken, induces the General to expect a compliance with this Summons, which I am authorized to assure you, most Seriously will not be repeated. You will therefore consider yourself answerable for the consequences of a vain resistance or destruction of Stores.*
>   *I have the Honor to be Sir*
>   *Your most Obededt Hble Servant*
> *O.H. Williams.*[13]

Cruger firmly rejected the demand to surrender:

> *I am honor'd with your Letter of this Day, intimating Major General Greene's immediate Demand of the surrender of His Majesty's garrison at Ninety-Six, a Compliance with which my Duty to my Sovereign renders inadmissible at present.*[14]

On Monday, June 4th, the Americans tried to use fire arrows to set the British soldiers' quarters aflame. Cruger doused the flames and then tore the shingles off the roofs to prevent any further attacks of that kind.[15]

Colonel Otho Williams was able to participate in a humanitarian gesture during the siege of Ninety-Six when he received a request from Lieutenant-Colonel Cruger to permit a sick officer to pass through the American lines on his way to Charleston. Cruger had emphasized that the officer's "...unhappy situation will justify, on every principle of humanity, the application." Williams granted the request, and permitted an attendant, a British soldier, and two horses to take the young officer in a litter through the American lines.[16]

Greene and Williams did their best to stretch their meager resources in their effort to conduct a successful siege at Ninety-Six, but they also had to keep an eye out for possible British reinforcements coming from Charleston. They learned on June 6th that a sizeable number of British transports had arrived at Charleston, and Greene expressed his dismay in a letter to the Marquis de Lafayette on June 7th:

> *The…fleet with …reinforcements arrived on the 2d of this instant at Charles Town. It is said they amount to upwards of 2,000 men. It is reported also that they are advancing this way. If so I expect they will raise the siege. This will be mortifying after the incredible fatigue we have gone through in carrying on our approaches, and the losses we have sustained in the Siege…*[17]

Light Horse Harry Lee and his Legion arrived at Ninety-Six to reinforce Greene on Friday, June 8th, and Andrew Pickens and his South Carolina militia arrived soon afterwards.[18] Lee and Pickens had been helping with the attack on Augusta, Georgia, some sixty miles due south of Ninety-Six. When the British force at Augusta had surrendered on June 5th, it freed Lee and Pickens to move quickly to Ninety-Six to help Greene.

With his characteristic self-confidence and bravado, Lee decided that Kosciusko's strategy for the siege was incorrect, and that the Americans should be concentrating on Ninety-Six's water supply in the rivulet and spring west of the town instead of on the Star Redoubt.[19] The bold young Legion commander prevailed with his Commanding General, and Greene directed Lee to build approaches that would threaten the water supplies. Lee promptly set about constructing works that threatened Cruger's defenses on the western side of the stockade.

Never one to hide his light under a bushel, Lee openly criticized Kosciusko in his *Memoirs* for ignoring Ninety-Six's water supply,[20] even though Greene's Chief Engineer later wrote that he and Greene had felt that the British could easily have found water by digging wells inside the stockade.

By now, the siege at Ninety-Six had settled into a grueling, relentless, dangerous series of small military operations that were being conducted in the increasingly hot Carolina summer. Light Horse Harry Lee captured the sense of fear, tension, fatigue and danger in his *Memoirs*:

> *The besiegers advancing closer and closer, with caution and safety, both on the right and left, Lieutenant-Colonel Cruger foresaw his inevitable destruction, unless relieved by the approach of Lord Rawdon. To give time for the desired event, he determined, by nocturnal sallies,*[21*] *to attempt to carry our trenches; and to*

---

*A sally is a sudden assault or raid. Defensive fortifications typically had "sally ports," or gates which were designed to allow troops to get through quickly for a raid, or "sally."

> *destroy with the spade whatever he might gain by the bayonet. These encounters were fierce and frequent; directed sometimes upon one quarter and sometimes upon another...*[22]

Lee further noted that the frequent attacks by the British became "... extremely harassing to the American army, whose repose during the night was incessantly disturbed and whose labor in the day was incessantly pressed."[23] Otho Williams wrote home in the midst of the siege that he was experiencing "great fatigue and danger."[24]

Nathanael Greene gave a full description of the difficulties in his letter to the President of Congress on June 9th, 1781:

> *We have been prosecuting the Seige at this place with all possible diligence with our little force, but for want of more assistance the approaches have gone on exceeding slow, and our poor Fellows are worne out with fatigue, being constantly on duty every other Day and sometimes every Day. The Works are strong and extensive. The position difficult to approach and the Ground extremely hard. The Garrison numerous and formidable when compared to our little force. They have sallied more or less every Night; but have been constantly driven in.*[25]

Greene peppered Thomas Sumter and Francis Marion with instructions to do all they could to hold back Rawdon and his reinforcing column, and he also dispatched Andrew Pickens and his South Carolina militia to help delay Rawdon's advance.[26] Meanwhile, Greene, Williams, and Lee worked as hard as they could to try to defeat Cruger before Rawdon arrived.[27]

On June 12th, Light Horse Harry Lee sent out a small detachment during a dark, violent, rainless storm to try to set fire to Cruger's stockade Fort. Lee's description of this encounter gives the flavor of the hard fighting between small groups of men during the siege:

> *...a sergeant with nine privates of the Legion infantry, furnished with combustible matter, was directed to approach the stockade in the most concealed direction, under cover of the storm, while the batteries in every quarter opened upon the enemy, and demonstrations of striking the star redoubt were made, with the expectation of diverting his attention from the intrepid party, which, with alacrity, undertook the hazardous enterprise. The sergeant conducted his gallant band in the*

> best manner; concealing it whenever the ground permitted, and when exposed to view crawling along upon the belly. At length he reached the ditch with three others; the whole close behind. Here unluckily he was discovered, while in the act of applying his fire. Himself and five were killed; the remaining four escaped unhurt, although many muskets were discharged at them running through the field before they got beyond the nearest rise of ground which could cover them from danger.[28]

That evening, a daring rider foiled the American sentries and was able to deliver a dispatch to Cruger from Lord Rawdon, announcing that he was en route with 2,000 men to raise the siege. This raised morale inside the garrison, and, once the Americans learned what had happened, it gave them a renewed sense of urgency to force a surrender before British reinforcements arrived.

On June 14th, the Americans completed a log structure called a "Maham Tower," which had been devised by a Lieutenant-Colonel Ezekiel Maham of Francis Marion's command during the attack on Fort Watson. A Maham Tower was constructed from overlapping logs and built to a height of some thirty feet above the ground to provide riflemen with a vantage point to fire down on enemy troops within their fortifications. The Tower at Ninety-Six was constructed near the Star Redoubt, and enabled Greene's riflemen to send the British infantrymen and artillerymen scurrying for cover.[29]

The same day, Greene learned that Rawdon had passed through Orangeburg, a little over one hundred miles away. He sent an urgent message to William Washington to take his cavalry and Lee's Legion cavalry to join Sumter and do everything possible to slow Rawdon's advance.[30] A combination of the small size of the American Army, the militia not turning out to join the fight, the ineptitude or indifference of some American leaders, and Rawdon's astute management of his march all combined to let Rawdon march toward Ninety-Six virtually unimpeded. Greene would have to force the siege to a completion very quickly, or give up the effort and retreat.

On the 17th, Lee's artillery forced the British to evacuate the stockade fort that protected the rivulet and spring, making their main source of water unavailable. In the intense, humid summer heat, Cruger's men dug a well inside the Star Redoubt, but did not strike water.[31] The situation inside the British lines was about to become desperate for lack of water.

While Cruger and his men were suffering greatly inside the garrison at Ninety-Six, things were coming quickly to a head for Greene. As Lee later described it, Greene would either have to launch an all-out assault, march out to meet Rawdon (who outmanned him significantly,) or retreat. Normally, Greene could have been expected to follow the most prudent strategy and retire to fight another day, but, Lee asserts, the American Army "with one voice, entreated to be led against the fort." Lee also alluded to the troops' desire to make amends for the bad performance of one regiment at Guilford Court House (the Second Maryland Regiment) and another at Hobkirk's Hill (the First Maryland Regiment.)[32] After the Battle of Hobkirk's Hill, Otho Williams had predicted that these earlier disgraces would motivate certain Maryland officers to dare greatly to wash away the shame of these prior failures.[33]

Greene was persuaded by the remonstrances of his troops, and he issued orders for the assaults to be launched at noon on June 18th. The assault on the left was to be commanded by Lieutenant Colonel Richard Campbell of Virginia, and carried out by a detachment from the Virginia and Maryland brigades. The assault on the right was to be commanded by Light Horse Harry Lee and carried out by Lee's Legion Infantry and Robert Kirkwood's Delaware Regiment. These were desperate attacks, and each assault party was led by a small group of men called a "forlorn hope," meaning that they were not expected to survive the battle. Lieutenants Duval of Maryland and Seldon of Virginia led the forlorn hope on the left; Captain Rudolph of the Legion led the forlorn hope on the right.

On the final signal at noon, the entire American line began to fire - the artillery from their emplacements, riflemen from the Maham Tower, and infantrymen from every available American position. The assaulting troops rushed into the trenches carrying iron hooks to pull down sandbags from atop the enemy's emplacements and "fascines" (bound bundles of sticks) to fill up enemy ditches. Lee asserts that the assault force was "...manifesting delight in the expectation of carrying by their courage the great prize in view."[34]

Cruger and his men launched desperate counter-attacks through their sally ports, and fought tooth and nail to keep the Americans at bay. Lieutenants Duval and Seldon were badly wounded,[35] which sapped the energy from the attack on the left. The aggressive counter-attacks by the British resulted in desperate hand-to-hand fighting, which left some thirty Americans dead, and the survivors scrambling to get back to the safety of their lines as best they could.[36] Greene decided to end the assault, even though Lee maintained that his men had gained a position on the right that would have supported a successful attack on the town. Greene withdrew his troops from the assault lines and prepared to retreat from Ninety-Six. He offered Cruger a truce to collect and bury the dead, but the British commander rejected the offer because he felt that acceptance would have been acknowledgment of defeat. Lee reported that "…gloom and silence pervaded the American camp - every one disappointed - every one mortified."[37]

Greene and Cruger exchanged several notes over the next day as they bartered over prisoner exchanges, and Greene issued a proclamation that did its best to cast a positive light on events:

> *The General takes pleasure to acknowledge the high opinion he has of the gallantry of the troops engaged in the attack of the Enemys Redoubts. The judicious and alert behavior of the Light Infantry of the Legion, and those commanded by Captain Kirkwood, directed by Lieut. Colonel Lee met with deserved Success, - And there is great reason to believe that this attack on the Star Battery, directed by Lieutenant Colonel Campbell, wou'd have been equally fortunate if the brave Lieutenants Duvall and Selldon, who most valiantly led on the advanc'd Parties, had not been unluckily wounded. Their conduct merits the highest Encomiums and must insure them perpetual Honor… The General presents his thanks, most cordially, to both Officers and Soldiers: and hopes to give them an early opportunity of reaping the fruits of their superior spirit by an attack, in the open Field, upon the Troops now led by Lord Rawdon. The Army will be prepared to change Camp tomorrow by Sun rise.*[38]

The night air was filled with the mournful sounds of the groans of the American wounded that had been left in the trenches around Ninety-Six, and it seemed a point of honor for the Americans to be able to bury their honored dead. Therefore, on the morning of June 19th, Otho Williams sent a note to Lieutenant-Colonel Cruger:

> *Major General Greene proposes that parties may be mutually admitted to bury the Dead of both armies that fell Yesterday between the Lines and within the Trenches. The Genl relies upon the promises of Lt. Colo. Cruger for Humanity & attention to such wounded American soldiers as may have fallen into his hands.*[39]

Cruger replied that he would give every possible consideration to the American wounded that he had captured, and agreed to forward to the Americans all of the bodies in his custody of those who had been killed in the prior days fighting.[40]

During the siege of Ninety-Six, Otho Williams served in three distinct capacities - as Commander of the Maryland Brigade; as second-in-command to Greene (Brigadier General Isaac Huger was not present at the Siege of Ninety-Six;) and as Greene's Adjutant General. In this latter capacity, he had continued to demonstrate a sense of precision and organization that characterized his administrative work. Williams' broad scope of responsibilities and his precise manner of handling his duties are illustrated in the "Return of Killed, Wounded and Missing at the Siege of Ninety Six in So. Carolina" dated June 20th, 1781:

	Killed	Wounded	Missing
Headquarters and Staff	-	1	-
Virginia Brigade	41	36	16
Maryland Brigade	13	26	3
Light Infantry	1	9	1
Legion Infantry	2	2	-
Virginia Militia	1	2	-
Total	58	76	20

Greene Retreats from Ninety-Six

Early on the morning of June 20th, 1781, Nathanael Greene led his Army away from Ninety-Six, a tacit acknowledgement that he had failed in his twenty-eight day attempt to take the fortress and town by siege. Lord Rawdon was reported to be only twenty-five miles away,[41] and Greene did not have the strength to meet him in the open field, even though he had so confidently told his soldiers in the General Orders of the 18th that he was ready to do so. Greene knew that he had to save his Army, which was the soul of the Revolution in the Carolina's and Georgia. He took great pains to communicate to the general populace through trusted figures like Andrew Pickens that he was not abandoning the Whigs in the region, but would stay in the field and rise to fight again.

Lord Rawdon arrived at Ninety-Six on June 21st, completing his grueling two-week march in time to save Ninety-Six from capitulation. His troops had suffered mightily in the brutal summer heat during their march to save Cruger's command. They marched in this heat for over two weeks wearing heavy woolen uniforms, first in the rush to reinforce the garrison at Ninety-Six, and then in pursuit of Greene. They were completely spent. It was reported that over fifty of them died of heat exhaustion.[42]

Greene marched his Army toward Charlotte, protecting his retreat with cavalry commanded by Lee and Washington. He also dismantled the mills that he passed, as a way to deprive any pursuing British forces of food.[43]

After he had given his men a brief rest and assessed the situation at Ninety-Six with Cruger, Lord Rawdon set out after Greene, but quickly discovered that the fast pace of the American foot soldiers, the summer heat and the excellence of the American cavalry gave him little hope of overtaking Greene's Army. His Lordship therefore gave up the pursuit on June 26th and began to retire toward Ninety-Six, where he ordered that the post be abandoned and that his entire force retreat to Charleston. Hearing this, Greene turned back from the road to Charlotte and looked for an opportunity to attack the British column. Rawdon stopped at Orangeburg, and took a defensive position there, while Cruger gathered various Loyalist families from the Ninety-Six area, razed the defensive works that he had defended so gallantly, and marched toward Charleston by a separate route.

Greene's main army and his cavalry under Lee and Washington tried to shadow Rawdon and Cruger, and to find a favorable opportunity to offer battle. These maneuverings in late June and early July, 1781 were summarized by Otho Holland Williams in a letter to Major Pendleton, an aide-de-camp to Greene:

> *After you left us at Ninety-Six we were obliged to retrograde as far as the cross-roads above Winnsborough. Lord Rawdon's return over Saluda induced the general to halt the army, and wait for intelligence respecting his further manoeuvres, and hearing a few days after that his lordship was on his march to Fort Granby, our army was ordered to march toward that place by way of Winnsborough. Before we could arrive at Congaree, Lord Rawdon retired to Orangeburgh, and, as he had left a considerable part of his army at Ninety-Six, General Greene detached the cavalry and light infantry to join General Marion, and endeavor to intercept Colonel Stewart, who was on his*

THE SIEGE AT NINETY-SIX

march from Charleston, with the third regiment &c., consisting of three hundred, convoying bread, stores, &c., of which Lord Rawdon's troops were in great want. Stewart, however, joined his lordship at Organgeburgh; and General Greene, from the information he had received, was encouraged to expect success from an attack upon the British army at that post…General Greene reconnoitered the position of the enemy, and found it materially different from what it had been represented…. These considerations induced the general rather to offer than to give battle. The enemy declined the opportunity, and put up with the insult. General Greene, therefore, ordered our troops to retire in the afternoon to Colonel Middleton's plantation…[44]

Light Horse Harry Lee described the army's desperate state at Orangeburg:

We had experienced in the course of the campaign want of food, and had sometimes seriously suffered from the scantiness of our supplies, rendered more pinching by their quality; but never did we suffer so severely as during the few days' halt here… Of meat we had literally none; for the few meager cattle brought to camp as beef would not afford more than one or two ounces per man…[45]

On July 13th, Greene sent Francis Marion, Thomas Sumter and the Legion cavalry to attack the small forts (Greene called them "nothing but churches occupied") at Moncks Corner and Dorchester, in hopes of drawing Rawdon out of Orangeburg to defend them.[46] When Rawdon stood fast, Greene decided to lead his tired troops toward a place where they could enjoy a much-needed rest.

The Army Rests at the High Hills of the Santee

Greene established his camp on James's Old Field at Midway Plantation in an area called the High Hills of the Santee.[47] Otho Williams noted that they had reached this site by "slow, easy marches," and had left various detachments behind to intercept British convoys and generally harass Rawdon, Cruger, and Alexander Stewart, who was bringing supplies from Charleston.[48] Williams and Greene also continually tried to devise ways to pester the formidable British force that was stationed in Charleston.

Greene had picked a delightful spot where his exhausted troops could enjoy the relative luxuries of some well-deserved rest and ample supplies of decent food. The campaign had been exhausting, especially in the intense heat and humidity of a Carolina summer, and the troops were greatly in need of this rest. Otho Williams talked openly about his own exhaustion in a letter to his sister in Maryland, where he noted that "campaigning has been inconceivably fatiguing."[49]

Light Horse Harry Lee described the pleasures of this American camp at the High Hills of the Santee, where Williams and the troops were finally able to enjoy some rest and relief from the daily tensions of army operations in the field:

> *The troops were placed in good quarters, and the heat of July rendered tolerable by the high ground, the fine air, and good water of the selected camp. Disease began to abate, our wounded to recover, and the army to rise in bodily strength...*
> *The soldiers of Greene's army may truly call these hills benignant. Twice our general there resorted, with his sick, his wounded, and worn-down troops; and twice we were restored to health and strength, by its elevated dry situation, its pure air, its fine water, and the friendly hospitality of its inhabitants.*[50]

For the next six weeks, Greene's Continental infantry would enjoy their rest, while Lee's Legion, Washington's cavalry, Marion's partisans and Sumter's militia tried to keep the British off balance.

In spite of the need for the men to rest and regain their strength, Greene and Otho Williams did not relax their firm system of military discipline. On July 17th, Greene announced that Williams would issue directives for troop discipline in his capacity as Assistant Inspector General, and that all orders that he issued as Deputy Adjutant General were to be "respected and obeyed." Williams' duties as Deputy Inspector General included conducting inspections of "every thing relative to organization, recruiting, discharges, administration, accountability of money and property, instruction, police, and discipline of the several corps of the army." In his capacity as Deputy Adjutant General, he directed the Army's administrative paperwork and supervised daily camp details, including guards and work parties.[51]

Soldiers who strayed from strict military performance were tried by courts martial, and, if found guilty, they were severely punished. Greene's General Orders for Sunday, August 5th noted that Sergeant John Radley was found guilty of "Expressing himself in a Disaffected manner in the presence of the Soldiers," speaking "Disrespectful" of Lieutenant Colonel John Eager Howard (his commanding officer) and "frequently saying in presence of the Soldiers, he would never endeavor to injure the Enemy." That same date it was also recorded that Joden Roziers of the North Carolina Line was convicted of "... desertion, joining the Tories & bearing Arms against the United States" and "Passing thro' Camp with a Fictitious Name." When both of these soldiers were convicted and sentenced to death, Nathanael Greene approved their sentences.[52] Greene issued the Death Warrant for Sergeant Radley on August 6th, which ordered Sergeant Levi Smith to have Radley "shot to death." Smith signed the warrant, certifying that the execution had been carried out between 6 and 7 p.m. that date.[53] Roziers' Death Warrant was issued on August 10th, in which Sergeant Robert McCorkle was ordered to have Roziers "hang'd by the Neck till he be Dead" between 5 and 6 p.m.. Sergeant McCorkle signed an accompanying document, certifying that Roziers had been executed as directed. This same date, McCorkle also certified that Private John Barrott and Private James Pallet had also been hung, both for deserting and bearing arms against the United States.[54]

The General Orders of August 5th also reported the results of other courts martial. One convicted deserter was sentenced to fifty lashes; another to fifty lashes plus an extension of his time in the service; a third, who had repeatedly deserted and had forged his colonel's name, was sentenced to 100 lashes and an extension of service. A fourth deserter, John Sullivan of the North Carolina line, was found guilty but "in consideration of his being detained by his Master from joining agreeable to his Furlough," the court recommended only that his term of service be extended. Finally, a soldier who was convicted of deserting, stealing three blankets, a pair of shoes, and a knapsack, and of losing his musket, was sentenced to 100 lashes and to "make Restitution for those things stolen."[55]

★ ★ ★ ★ ★

Personal Glimpses of Otho Holland Williams

On June 23rd, Williams wrote to his brother Elie that the Southern army had conducted the siege of Ninety-Six from May 22nd until they were forced to give up the task on June 20th under the threat of an attack by Lord Rawdon's reinforcements. Williams also reported the death of his "worthy little friend" Benjamin Ford, who had died of wounds received at the Battle of Hobkirk's Hill. As he would do wistfully in so many of his letters home, he expressed the hope to be able to return to Maryland for a visit "in the fall," although he would not wish to leave the field "at any improper time, for fear of disappointing" his General, Nathanael Greene.[56]

On June 24th, just after he had raised the siege at Ninety-Six, Nathanael Greene mentioned to Light Horse Harry Lee that "Col. Williams' servant was one of the deserters who went to the enemy day before yesterday. He was detected in plundering, and made his escape for fear of punishment."[57] It was undoubtedly a matter of grave concern that an individual who had been so close to the Adjutant General had gone over to the enemy.

On July 5th, Otho Williams undertook the delicate task of explaining to his Commanding General that his servant (Dominique) had returned, and that Williams had pardoned him because he was so "...circumstancial and consistant in his reports, and he has been so expeditious in his return..." Williams begged Greene's indulgence in this decision.[58]

On July 6th, 1781, Adjutant General Williams wrote to General Greene with an indictment of Major Henry Hardman, who as "Field Officer of the Day" on July 4th

> ...not only neglected but positively refused to visit Capt. Anderson's guard, or to furnish him with the parole and the countersign, though ordered to do so. The rude ungentlemanly behavior of Major Hardman was observable on other occasions that Day, and the manner in which he declared his intentional disobedience obliges me to report him. When orders are received with contempt and rejected with insolence, examples are requisite to reestablish Subordination - the basis of Discipline.[59]

Hardman had come in to the Army as a Captain on July 18th, 1776,[60] and he had been chosen to command one of the two Maryland Battalions that were established under Williams' command after the Battle of Camden.[61] In early February, 1781, Greene had given Major Hardman command of the contingent that had remained South of the Dan River to protect the crossings while Williams and his Screening Force crossed, a post of honor. Hardman would serve with distinction on a future battlefield.

There is no further record of disciplinary action on Hardman in the Greene or the Williams papers, and Henry Hardman became one of the Original Members of the Society of the Cincinnati after the War,[62] indicating that any damage to Hardman's reputation from Williams' accusations was temporary, at best.[63] The story, however, illustrates the prickly perfectionism of Otho

Holland Williams, and his willingness to face controversy head on when he felt that it was justified.

There was also a softer side to Williams. Nathanael Greene's wife, Catharine, was apparently quite fond of him, and passed pleasant personal messages to him through her letters to her husband on a number of occasions. This excerpt from a letter that Greene sent to Mrs. Greene from the High Hills of the Santee on July 18, is a sample:

> *I delivered your letter to Col Williams without reading it, and did not notice its not being sealed till afterwards. The Col was polite enough to shew it me notwithstanding; and I think it very pretty. The stile and sentiments were very cleaver...*[64]

Wives of Williams' other friends also seemed to be concerned about the Colonel, and to want to involve themselves with match-making for this very eligible bachelor. Nathaniel Ramsay, a Baltimorean and one of the heroes of the Battle of Monmouth in 1778, wrote Williams a friendly letter dated August 4th, 1781, and after exchanging some interesting news, added that "...Mrs. Ramsay sends greetings, and wishes to know whether you received a Letter which She dispatched to you last Winter from a fair hand on long island."[65]

Otho Holland Williams had entered the American Army at the very outset of the War in 1775, and he had served in highly responsible posts that required assiduous attention to detail and monumental amounts of work for the past several years. In retrospect, it is easy to discern that he had contracted a serious illness (probably tuberculosis) while he was a prisoner-of-war in New York from December, 1776 through February, 1778. His once robust health was in a steady decline. During his service in the South, Williams experienced grueling heat and the malarial low country of the South during the summer, and he had his share of bone-chilling cold and driving rain in the winter. His tough work schedule, the demands of senior leadership responsibilities, and his active participation on the front lines of all of Greene's campaigns must certainly have accelerated his illness.

Greene Advances from the High Hills of the Santee

From mid-July to mid-August, 1781, while Greene and his army were comfortably settled in their Camp in the High Hills of the Santee, he was very active in sending out small units to harass the British forces as best he could. But he also constantly sought ways to force a decisive battle with the main British forces, and to use any legitimate means possible to push them out of as much territory as possible. Control over territory meant control of the sentiments of the local population, and Greene wanted that control. When there was a strong military presence in a region, there was a greater likelihood that people would provide provisions for the troops, sign up for militia duty, supply valuable intelligence and generally support that army.

The editors of the Papers of Nathanael Greene emphasize that his strategy must also be understood in the context of a principle of international diplomacy called *ut possedetis*, which means that contending armies retain the land that they hold at the end of hostilities. Greene feared that the British would try to negotiate on the basis of this principle in any peace discussions, and he wanted Great Britain to have as small a foothold as possible in the South when peace negotiations began.[66]

In mid-August, Greene learned of an opportunity to attack a large enemy force at Thompson's Farm, about a half-mile from Fort Motte on the Congaree River. He led his Continentals down from the High Hills of the Santee on August 23rd. However, the crossings of the Wateree and Congaree Rivers required them to make a long, circuitous march, which gave the British time to move away.[67] Greene led his troops to Motte's Plantation and learned that the British had marched forty miles away to Eutaw Springs, where they were planning to establish a permanent post. He decided to attack Eutaw Springs, and moved in that direction "by slow and easy marches," both to disguise his eventual objective, and to give Francis Marion and his partisan band time to catch up with him. Marion arrived at Greene's camp just a few miles from Eutaw Springs on September 7th, and Greene prepared to attack at the first opportunity.[68]

Greene was able to approach the British camp at Eutaw Springs undetected, a fact that shows clearly how the residents of the South Carolina countryside were now very averse to helping the British army. The British were losing the battle for the hearts and minds of the populace.[69] Another factor that gave the British difficulty in obtaining good intelligence was the work of American partisan bands and Greene's cavalry to harass British communications. American cavalry and light troops in the South continued to far out-perform their mounted peers on the British side. Light Horse Harry Lee felt that the speed, mobility, and endurance of his troops were far superior to their British counterparts, and he attributed this advantage largely to his troops having better mounts and generally superior horsemanship. Whatever the reasons, the British were almost operating blind when they ventured outside of Charleston.

1   A major source of information on the siege of Ninety-Six is: Greene, Jerome A. *Historic Resource Study and Historic Structure Report. Ninety-Six: A Historical Narrative.* (hereafter Greene, Jerome. *Ninety-Six.*) Published by the National Park Service (Denver Service Center; Branch of Historic Preservation; Southeast/Southwest Team. National Park Service. United States Department of the Interior.) Denver Colorado. 1979. Reprinted 1998, 2004, 2005.
2   The most likely origin of the name "Ninety-Six" is that the site is approximately ninety-six miles from Keowee, the Cherokee village closest to South Carolina settlements. Ref: Greene, Jerome, *Ninety-Six.* P. 4.
3   Ibid. P. 84. Greene cites "Diary of Anthony Allaire, pp. 19-20, and notes that this was initially published in Lyman C. Draper, *King's Mountain and Its Heroes* (Cincinnati: Peter G. Thompson, 1881.)
4   Ibid. Pp. 86; 99-102; 113.
5   Ibid. P. 113.
6   Lossing, *Field-Book.* P. 485.
7   Greene, Jerome, *Ninety-Six.* P. 113.
8   Ibid. Pp. 120-121.
9   Greene, Nathanael. Letter to Colonel Henry Lee, Jr. Written at Ninety Six, South Carolina. May 22nd, 1781. *Greene Papers.* 8:291.
10 Lossing, *Field-Book.* P. 485.
11 Greene, Jerome, *Ninety-Six.* Pp. 128-129.
12 Ibid. P. 136.
13 Williams, Otho Holland. Letter to Lieutenant-Colonel Cruger. June 3, 1781. Cited in Greene, Jerome, *Ninety-Six.* Pp. 136-137. Greene cites "Greene Papers, Clements Library." *Greene Papers.* 8:339.
14 Greene, Jerome, *Ninety-Six.* P. 137. Greene notes that this message is reproduced in William Johnson's *Life and Correspondence of Nathanael Greene, II.* P. 144. It is also summarized in the *Greene Papers.* 8:340.
15 Ibid. P. 138.
16 Ibid. P. 139
17 Greene, Nathanael. Letter to the Marquis de Lafayette. June 7, 1781. Cited in Greene, Jerome, *Ninety-Six.* P. 153. Greene cites Greene Papers, Library of Congress, VI.
18 Lossing, *Field-Book.* P. 485.
19 Greene, Jerome, *Ninety-Six:.* Pp. 141-142. Greene cites Alexander Garden's *Anecdotes of the Revolutionary War in America* (Charleston: A.E. Miller, 1822), p. 65.
20 Lee, *Memoirs.* P 371.
21 See Footnote.
22 Lee, *Memoirs.* P. 372.
23 Ibid. P. 372.
24 Williams, Otho Holland. Letter to Elie Williams. Written at Camp before Ninety Six, South Carolina. June 12, 1781. *Williams Papers.* Part 1/8. (Item #106.)
25 Greene, Nathanael. Letter to the President of Congress. Written at Camp before Ninety-Six, South Carolina. June 9, 1781. *Greene Papers.* 8:363-364.
26 Lossing, *Field Book.* P. 486.
27 Lee, *Memoirs.* P. 373.
28 Ibid. P. 373-374.
29 Greene, Nathanael. Letter to the President of Congress. June 9, 1781. Cited in Greene, Jerome, *Ninety-Six.* Pp. 148-149. Greene cites Kosciuszko, by Haiman. Page 114.
30 Greene, Nathanael. Letter to the Colonel William Washington. Written at Camp before Ninety-Six, South Carolina. 14 June, 1781. *Greene Papers.* 8:389. Cited in Greene, Jerome, *Ninety-Six:.* P. 157.
31 Greene, Nathanael. Letter to the Colonel William Washington. Written at Camp before Ninety-Six, South Carolina. 14 June, 1781. *Greene Papers.* 8:389. Cited in Greene, Jerome, *Ninety-Six:.* P. 157.
32 Lee, *Memoirs.* P. 375.
33 Williams, Otho Holland. Letter to Elie Williams. Written at Camp before Camden. April 27, 1781. From Tiffany, *Sketch.* P. 20.
34 Lee, *Memoirs.* P. 376.
35 The mettle of the American officers and men that fought in the Southern Army is highlighted by the story of the amputation of Lieutenant Selden's right arm after the assault at Ninety-Six, as related by Alexander Garden in his *Anecdotes of the Revolutionary War In America*, p. 408. "While his right arm was raised with the intention of drawing down a sand-bag…, a ball entered his wrist, shattered the bone of the limb nearly to the shoulder. For so severe a wound, the only remedy was amputation. It is well known, that on such occasions, the operating Surgeon requires the assistance of several

persons to hold the patient's limb, and to support him. To this regulation Seldon would not submit. It was his right arm he was about to lose. He sustained it with his left during the operation, his eyes fixed steadily on it; nor uttered a word, till, the saw reached the marrow, when in composed tone and manner, he said, 'I pray you, Doctor, be quick." This impressive display of Seldon's grit happened long before the discovery of chloroform.

36 Greene, Jerome, *Ninety-Six*. Pp. 161-163. Jerome Greene cites numerous sources from which he constructed this summary of the fighting at Ninety-Six on June 18th, 1781.

37 Lee, *Memoirs*. Pp. 378.

38 Greene, Nathanael. General Orders. Issued at Camp before 96, South Carolina. Monday, 18th June, 1781. *Greene Papers*. 8:408-409.

39 Williams, Otho Holland. Note to Lieutenant-Colonel Cruger. June 19th, 1781. Cited in Greene, Jerome, *Ninety-Six*. P. 166. Jerome Greene cites "Williams to Cruger, June 19th, 1781. Greene Papers, Clements."

40 Ibid. P. 166. Jerome Greene cites "Williams to Cruger, June 19, 1781. *Greene Papers*, Clements."

41 Ibid P. 168.

42 Pancake, *This Destructive War*. P. 214. Pancake cites: "Thayer, Greene, p. 362; Tarleton, Campaigns, p. 323; Balfour to Clinton, July 20, 1781, BHP ." (BHP is "Sir Guy Carleton Papers, more familiarly known as British Headquarters Papers, Colonial Williamsburg.")

43 Greene, Nathanael. Letter to Thomas McKean, President of Congress. Written at Head Quarters on the High Hills of Santee, South Carolina. July 17th, 1781. *Greene Papers*. P. 9:28.

44 Williams, Otho Holland. Letter to Major Pendelton, Aide-de-Camp to General Greene. Written at the High Hills of the Santee. July 16, 1781. In Lee, *Memoirs*. Pp. 385-386.

45 Lee, *Memoirs*. P. 386.

46 Greene, Nathanael. Letter to Thomas McKean, President of the Continental Congress. Written at Head Quarters on the High Hills of the Santee, South Carolina. July 17th 1781. *Greene Papers*. 9:29.

47 Greene's General Orders. Written at Camp at Waring's Plantation, South Carolina. Monday, July 16, 1781. Footnote 1. *Greene Papers*. 9:18.

48 Williams, Otho Holland. Letter to Major Pendelton, Aide-de-Camp to General Greene. Written at the High Hills of the Santee. July 16, 1781. From Lee, *Memoirs*. Pp. 385-386.

49 Williams, Otho Holland. Letter to Mrs. Mercy Stull. May 4th, 1781. *Williams Papers* Part 1/8. (Item #102.)

50 Lee, *Memoirs*. Pp. 393; 448.

51 General Orders of Nathanael Greene. 17 July, 1781. (Including Note 1.) *Greene Papers*. 9:22.

52 General Greene's Orders. High Hills of the Santee, S.C., Sunday, 5 August, 1781. *Greene Papers*. 9:131.

53 Death Warrant for Sergeant John Radley. Issued at the High Hills of the Santee, South Carolina. 6th August, 1781. *Greene Papers*. 9:134.

54 Warrants for the Execution of Private John Bartrott, Private Joden Roziers and James Pallet. From the High Hills of the Santee, South Carolina. 10th August, 1781. *Greene Papers*. 9:158.

55 General Orders of Nathanael Greene. High Hills of the Santee, South Carolina. Sunday, 5th August, 1781. *Greene Papers*. 9:131.

56 Williams, Otho Holland. Letter to Elie Williams. Written at Bush River, South Carolina. June 23rd, 1781. *Williams Papers*. Part 1/8. (Item # 107.)

57 Greene, Nathanael. Letter to Colonel Henry Lee, Jr. Written at Broad River, South Carolina. June 24th, 1781. *Greene Papers*. 8:452.

58 Williams, Otho Holland. Letter to Nathanael Greene. Written at Rice Creek, South Carolina. July 5th, 1781. *Greene Papers*. 8:500.

59 Williams, Otho Holland. Letter to Nathanael Greene. Written at Camp Crane Creek, South Carolina. July 6th, 1781. *Williams Papers*. Part 1/8. (Item # 108.)

60 *Muster Rolls and Other Records of Service of Maryland Troops in the American Revolution*. Maryland Archives Online. Volume 18. P. 48.

61 Williams, Otho. *Brigade and Regimental Orders*. O. H. Williams, Comm. September 13, 1780. February 10, 1781. Maryland Historical Society Manuscript Collection. MS 768. Entry for September 13, 1780.

62 Steuart, *Maryland Line*. P. 168.

63 In 1785, Williams would write to a friend that he was sorry to hear of the misfortunes of Hardman, "…with whom he used to be intimate…." but Hardman has been guilty of a thousand ",,,improprieties and rudenesses." (Letter from Otho Holland Williams to Dr. Philip Thomas. Written at Baltimore, February 10, 1785. *Williams Papers*. Part 2/8. (Item #299.)

64 Greene, Nathanael. Letter to Catharine Greene. Written at Camp, High Hills, Santee, South Carolina. July 18th, 1781. *Greene Papers*. 9:35

65 Ramsay, Nathaniel. Letter to Otho Holland Williams. Written at Baltimore, Maryland. August 4th, 1781. *Williams Papers*. Part 1/8. (Item # 109.)

66 *Greene Papers*. 9: xi.

67 Williams, Otho Holland. Letter to Elie Williams. Written at Fort Motte, on Congaree River, South Carolina. September 4, 1781. *Williams Papers*. Part 1/8. (Item # 114.)
68 Greene, Nathanael. Letter to Thomas McKean. Written at Head Quarters, Martins Tavern, near Ferguson Swamp, South Carolina. September 11th, 1781. *Greene Papers*. 9:328.
69 Symonds, *Battlefield Atlas*. P. 97

CHAPTER 10

THE BATTLE OF EUTAW SPRINGS[1]

Nathanael Greene's army reached Burdell's Tavern, just seven miles from the British encampment at Eutaw Springs, on the afternoon of September 7th, 1781, and spent a restful night.[2] At 4 a.m. on the next morning, his army marched toward the British. Greene's units were arrayed according to the plan worked out by Otho Williams with the regimental commanders. The South Carolina State troops and Lee's Legion, commanded by Colonel William Henderson, led the way, and were followed by the North and South Carolina militia, commanded by Francis Marion. The third line was made up of the Continentals (with Williams in command of the Maryland troops,) under the command of General Jethro Sumner, and the rear units were Robert Kirkwood's Delaware Regiment and William Washington's cavalry. The artillery was interspersed between the columns. These dispositions were made for the march so that the troops could move quickly to their assigned positions when they reached the battlefield.[3]

The British commander at Eutaw Springs, Lieutenant Colonel Alexander Stewart, was initially unaware that Greene was in the vicinity, and he had sent a "rooting party" of about 100 men forward to gather sweet potatoes that morning. Two deserters from the North Carolina troops informed Stewart that Greene was nearby, and the British commander took the precaution of sending Captain Coffin and his cavalry forward to reconnoiter, and to recall the rooting party, if necessary. Coffin found Greene's advanced American troops, mistook them for an isolated body of militia, and charged. The British cavalry were easily repulsed, as Coffin found that he was attacking a formidable force. Coffin's command turned about and galloped back toward Eutaw Springs, leaving their dead and wounded on the ground. The rooting party heard the commotion and headed for the fighting. The entire party was captured by the Americans.[4]

Stewart was concerned that his troops would be vulnerable to the American superiority in cavalry if he retreated, so he decided to stand and fight. Rather than advance his entire corps and expose his flanks to the American cavalry, he held his main line steady at his Eutaw Springs camp and sent a screening force ahead to confront and slow the American advance.[5]

Greene wanted his troops to be fully ready for the coming fight, so he halted his columns, distributed a ration of rum, and formed his men in line of battle. The Americans then resumed their eastward advance in full battle formation, with the following alignment in the front line - South Carolina militia on the right, commanded by Francis Marion; North Carolina militia in the center, commanded by Colonel Malmady; South Carolina militia on the left, commanded by Andrew Pickens; the right flank protected by Light Horse Harry Lee with his Legion; the left flank was covered by Colonel William Henderson with South Carolina State troops.[6]

The second line was composed entirely of Continental troops. General Jethro Sumner commanded three battalions totaling 350 North Carolina troops on the right; Colonel Richard Campbell commanded two Virginia Battalions with 350 men in the center; and Colonel Otho Williams commanded two Maryland battalions with 250 men on the left. The woods on both sides of the road, while not thick, required the troops to advance slowly in order to preserve their alignment.[7]

Two three-pound cannon were assigned to the front line, and two six-pound cannon advanced with the second line. Colonel Washington and Captain Robert Kirkwood brought up the rear, where they served as a general reserve.[8] Altogether, Greene commanded approximately 2,400 men, who would face Stewart's 2,000.[9]

The good defensive position occupied by the British is illustrated in the map on page 260.

The Charleston road roughly bisected the British camp, and their line of battle, which was positioned a few hundred paces west of the camp. Stewart formed his line with Irish Buffs to the right of the Charleston Road; Tories in the center under Lieutenant-Colonel Cruger (who had performed so effectively during the siege of Ninety-Six); and British regulars of the sixty-third and sixty-fourth regiments to the left of the road. Major John Majoribanks commanded the British grenadiers and light infantry, stationed on the far right of the British position, beyond the Charleston road. This was on the edge of a ravine that dropped sharply to a branch of the Santee River.[10] A brick mansion and garden were situated to the right and slightly to the rear of the British camp. The British artillery was posted in the main road.[11]

The advanced British unit engaged the American front line about two or three miles from the British camp.[12] When British artillery raked the American lines, Otho Williams brought up Gaines' artillery at a "full gallop," and their fire soon had a good effect, permitting the advance to continue.[13]

Greene's front ranks pushed the British back until they reached Stewart's prepared lines, which extended from the Eutaw Creek on their right across the road to the left of their line, which was "in the air," or unprotected by any natural obstacle. The British defenses for the left consisted of Coffin's cavalry

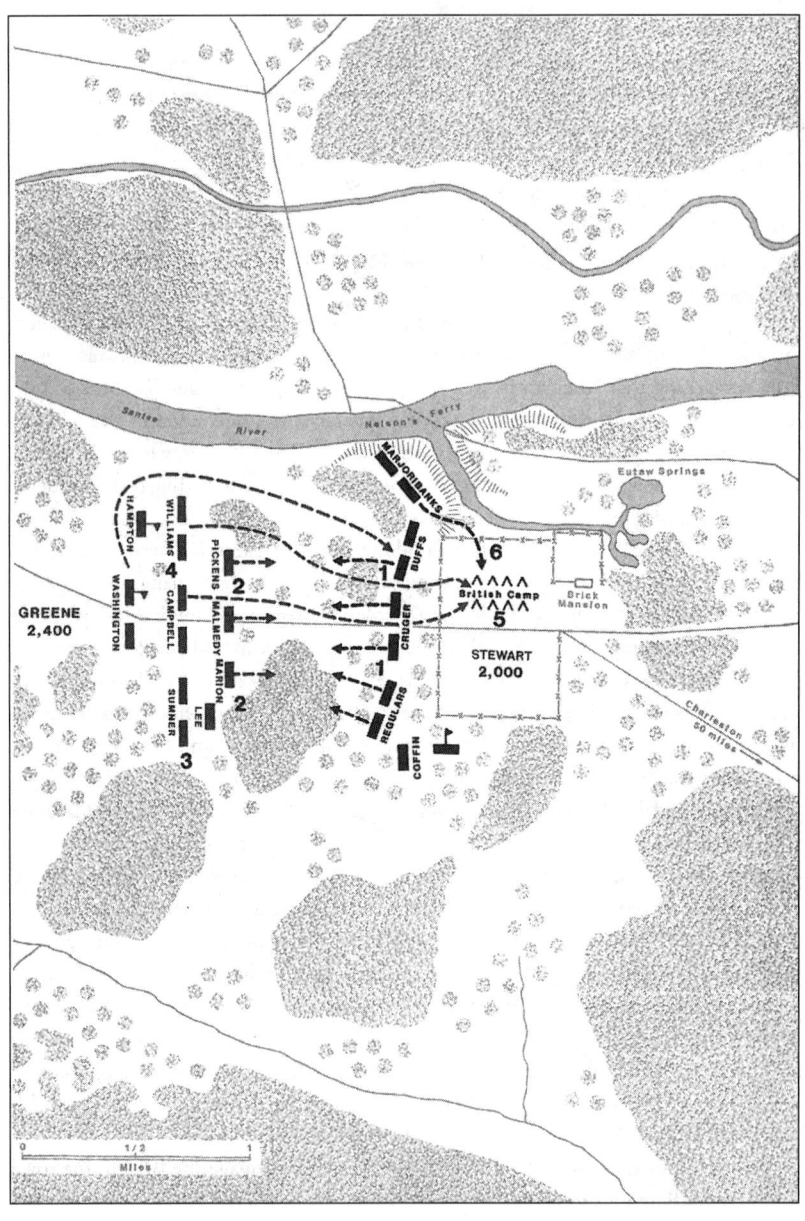

Map 8 - The Battle of Eutaw Springs

and a detachment of infantry in woods a convenient distance from the front line.[14]

A stand-up fight of musketry and artillery ensued between Greene's front line and the British defenders, described by Williams as "steady and desperate" and "bloody and obstinate in the extreme," resulting in carnage that was "equal and severe." Governor Rutledge of South Carolina, who was a few miles from the action, reported later that the militia were engaged long enough to fire seventeen rounds. They endured heavy artillery fire in addition to the enemy's musketry.[15]

These militia troops performed extremely well, which Nathanael Greene, a frequent critic of militia, took pleasure in describing:

> *General Marion, Colo Malmady and General Pickens conducted the Troops with great gallantry and good conduct, and the Militia fought with a degree of spirit and firmness that reflects the highest honor upon this class of Soldiers.*[16]

Otho Williams seconded this admiration for these men of the front:

> *Nor had the militia been wanting in gallantry and perseverance. It was with equal astonishment, that both the second line and the enemy, contemplated these men, steadily, and without faltering, advance with shouts and exhortations into the hottest of the enemy's fire, unaffected by the continual fall of their comrades around them.*[17]

Williams noted that "…it was impossible that this could endure long, for these men were, all this time, receiving the fire of double their number."[18]

Greene ordered General Sumner to advance to support his front line. Sumner commanded inexperienced troops, but they, too, performed so well that they drew the praise of their Commanding General:

> *These were all new Levies, and had been under discipline but little more than a month, notwithstanding which they fought with a degree of obstinacy that would do honor to the best of veterans; and I could hardly tell which to admire most the gallantry of their Officers or the bravery of the Troops.*[19]

Both armies reinforced their front lines, and the firing continued unabated. Sumner's North Carolina Continentals finally started to give way, and the left of the British line, sensing opportunity, leaped to the attack so aggressively that they lost their formation. With a fine tactical eye, Greene ordered Otho Williams forward.[20] Williams and his men moved straight ahead into intense artillery and musket fire.[21]

Otho Williams noted in a later narrative that the Maryland troops were "...emulous to wipe away the recollections of Hobkirk's Hill," and that they "...advanced with a spirit expressive of the impatience with which they had hitherto been passive spectators of the action."[22]

When the second line approached the British within forty yards, the Virginians under Campbell fired a destructive volley, and then the entire line "...with trailed arms, and an animated pace, advanced to the charge."[23]

The right and center of the British line were able to keep their order, but the left became disordered and started to retreat. Williams noted the "good conduct of Col Lee" at this point, when the Legion infantry "wheeled and poured in upon them a destructive enfilading fire," throwing the British left wing into "irretrievable disorder." Greene would write three days after the fight that Lee turned the British left flank with "...great address, gallantry, and good conduct," and was charging them from the rear at the same time the Virginia and Maryland troops were charging them in front.[24] Colonel William Henderson, who Greene called "a most valuable officer," was wounded on the American left, and his command in that sector passed to Lieutenant Colonel Wade Hampton.[25]

While their left was collapsing, the British center and right remained in formation, awaiting attack with "unshaken constancy." They were hit by the charge of the American second line, and began to be forced back by retreating soldiers from their own troops, when the Marylanders delivered a volley that broke the entire British formation.[26]

Williams recalled that "shouts of victory resounded through the American line," and the American efforts were now concentrated on keeping the British troops from retreating to the brick house. This was tough fighting and there were many American casualties, including the fine leader of the Virginia Continentals, Richard Campbell (whom Williams called "the gallant Campbell.") Campbell clung to life, supported in his saddle by his son, but the wound in his chest would prove mortal.[27]

Williams' interjects in his narrative that at this moment a well-timed charge by the cavalry of Lee's Legion might well have been decisive, as cavalry was

---

*Lee's location and actions at various times on the battlefield of Eutaw Springs are subjects of controversy. In this text, we give precedence to the the observations of our subject, Otho Williams.

the "means for rendering disorder irretrievable."²⁸* However, the charge was not made, which Williams surmised might have been because Lee himself was with his Legion infantry or because Coffin's British cavalry had more men than Lee's cavalry at the point of attack, and the officers that Lee had left in command decided not to charge. Concerning the lost opportunity for a decisive cavalry charge, Williams rued that the "…position was highly favorable to such a movement. Why this was not done, has never been explained."²⁹

The British line had a strong anchor on its far right. The troops of Major John Majoribanks held a good position in the thickets along Eutaw Creek, and the right of the main British line remained largely intact. The British left was pushed back while the right held firm, resulting in the two armies performing what Williams called a "half wheel, which brought them into the open ground in front of the house."³⁰

Greene quickly realized that Majoribanks had to be dislodged, or he would pose a dire threat to the left of Williams' line as it advanced. The American General ordered the reserve of William Washington and Robert Kirkwood to attack Majoribanks.

Washington leapt to the task, and galloped promptly toward the woods, leaving Kirkwood's supporting infantry well to the rear. Unfortunately, Washington "…attempted a charge, but it was impossible for cavalry to penetrate the thicket." He tried to find a path around the British left and into their rear, but this movement brought his line into the sights of Marjoribanks' troops, and "…a deadly and well directed fire, delivered at that instant, wounded or brought to the ground many of his men and horses, and every officer except two."³¹ Washington himself was wounded and captured.

Otho Williams' ability to construct a compelling narrative is well illustrated in his powerful description of the fury, chaos, and destruction on the Eutaw Springs battlefield at this moment:

> *On the left, Washington's Cavalry, routed and flying, horses plunging as they died, or coursing the field without their riders, while the enemy with poised bayonet, issued from the thicket, upon the wounded or unhorsed rider. In the fore-ground, Hampton covering and collecting the scattered Cavalry, while Kirkwood, with his bayonets, rushed furiously to revenge their fall, and a road strewed with the bodies of men and horses, and the fragments of dismounted Artillery. Beyond these, viewed over the whole American line advancing rapidly, and in order: And*

> *on the right, Henderson borne off in the arms of his soldiers, and Campbell sustained in his saddle by a brave son, who had sought glory at his father's side.*[32]

The British center and left were retreating steadily, which spread fear and panic behind their lines. Commissaries destroyed their stores. Civilian loyalists and American Army deserters grabbed any transportation they could find, and jammed the road to Charleston in their desperate attempts to get away safely. The British set fire to their supplies that had been stored along the road, and felled trees to impede any American advance.[33]

Otho Williams recorded that the victorious American troops reached the main British camp, where they were bedazzled by food, drink, and comparative riches before them. Hot, hungry, thirsty, tired, and poorly clad, some of the men could not resist the temptation of such treasures, and they lost their formation as they fell out to partake of the veritable feast before their eyes. Many "…fastened upon the liquors and refreshments they afforded, and became utterly unmanageable."[34*] The attack lost its momentum, and "the American line got into irretrievable confusion." The few American officers who pursued the fleeing British beyond the camp found themselves unsupported and in a precarious situation.[35]

Meantime, the remaining British forces north of the Charleston road had slowly put together defensible positions in the thicket, in the large three-story brick mansion, and in the garden that surrounded the house. The American units which had avoided the temptations of the British camp began to focus on the brick house; one of these units was the Legion infantry, who chased some fugitives from the far American right into the brick house, where the door was slammed shut to keep them out, and some of the fleeing British troops were also locked out. These were soon captured, and used as shields for the American troops to protect them from the fire coming from the house.[36]

The British defenders poured a heavy fire into the American troops, and Greene's efforts were now focused on taking the brick house and the thicket. The Americans moved four six-pounder artillery pieces into position to attack the house, two of the Americans' own and two that had been abandoned by

---

*Some authors question whether or not American troops were distracted by looting the riches of the British camp. As with other matters of historical controversy, when there is no direct, contemporary evidence to the contrary, we give precedence to the writings of Otho Holland Williams, who was present on the field.

the British, but "in the ardour to discharge a pressing duty" the artillery was pushed too close to the brick house, where the artillerymen were very soon all killed or wounded.[37] "Never were pieces better served," said Greene, but "most of the Men and Officers were either killed or Wounded."[38] Majoribanks' men then rushed from the garden beside the brick house and captured the cannons. Otho Williams felt that the loss of these four cannons prompted Greene' decision to retire from the battlefield, as small arms fire would never be able to take the brick house.[39]

British forces on the left and center began to push back against the Americans when they sensed the loss of momentum in the American attack. Majoribanks on the British right and Coffin on their left saw the disorder among the American troops, and simultaneously moved against the American line. Perceiving this threat, Greene ordered Captain Pendleton of his staff to order the Legion cavalry to attack Coffin, but Lee was not with the cavalry and his subordinate, Major Eggleston, made the attack unsuccessfully.[40] Coffin, as soon as he had beaten off Eggleston, charged the rear of the Americans who were strewn among the tents. Learning of this attack, and apparently unhappy that Lee was not with his cavalry, Greene also realized that his troops were not prevailing in any part of the battlefield. He ordered a retreat.[41]

Greene sent Wade Hampton's cavalry up the Charleston road to cover the retreat, and Hampton repulsed a sharp attack by the British cavalry under Coffin, but when the Americans pursued their retreating prey in Coffin's command too far, they received a devastating volley from Majoribanks' men in the woods near the road. Hampton pulled his surviving men back to a defensible position along the road. After Majoribanks had captured the American artillery that had been firing at the brick house, and pulled it back within the British lines, he was reinforced by parties from the brick house, and he charged the Americans who were dispersed among the tents, driving them out.[42] About this time, Maryland Lieutenant Colonel John Eager Howard was beginning an attack near the head of the ravine, but the attack faltered when Howard was seriously wounded.[43]

Slowly, most of the American troops extricated themselves from the British camp, and joined the units that had been attacking the brick house in a slow, steady retreat to the west. They were able to form a line under the cover of the woods, and the British troops, who had received quite a battering, did not venture beyond the area in which they were covered by the protecting fire from the house.[44]

Greene took care to bring off all his dead and wounded that he could reach, although he was forced to leave behind any that were within range of the deadly British muskets in the brick house. The American Army retreated to Burdell's, seven miles away, the closest point where there was enough water to slake the mighty thirsts that had built up on this long, hot, and horribly bloody day. According to Williams:

> *Not a spring or rivulet was near, but that in possession of the enemy; and the water in our canteens had been exhausted early in the battle. The day was extremely sultry, and the cry for water was universal. Much as Greene wished to avail himself of the evident advantage he had gained, by sitting down close to Stewart, he was forced to forego this desire, and to retire several miles to the spot which afforded an adequate supply of water.*[45]

Once again, the British Army held the field at the end of the day's fighting, and could therefore claim the fortunes of the day. However, Stewart retreated toward Charleston the next evening, and he left unmistakable signs of distress in his wake - 60 wounded men were left behind to be cared for by Greene, and 60 of his unburied dead were left on the field.[46] The British also broke apart 1,000 muskets and threw them into the spring, and destroyed substantial amounts of stores.[47] These are not the acts of men who have won a battlefield victory.

The fighting at Eutaw Springs had been unusually brutal and bloody, even in comparison to the savage combat of the previous battles of the southern campaign. Nathanael Greene called the encounter at Eutaw Springs "by far the most obstinate and bloody I ever saw."[48] Stewart counted 84 killed, 351 wounded, and 257 missing, not including the rooting party that had been captured early on the morning of the 8th. This loss amounted to more than 40% of his army. Greene reported 139 killed, 375 wounded, and 8 missing. The American loss was about 25% of Greene's command, although the heavy loss in officers included 16 killed and 43 wounded.[49] Marylander John Eager Howard reported that:

> *Nearly one-half my men were killed or wounded, and I had seven officers out of twelve disabled - four killed and three severely wounded.*[50]

Another measure of the bloody toll this day was the rate of casualties for the six officers who commanded Continental Regiments at Eutaw Springs. Of these six, three were wounded (John Eager Howard, William Washington, and William Henderson), and one (Richard Campbell) was killed. The only commanders of Continental Regiments who were unhurt were Light Horse Harry Lee and Otho Holland Williams.[51] A 58% casualty rate among Howard's officers, and 67% among Continental regimental commanders give grim testimony to the severity of the combat at Eutaw Springs, and to the front-line leadership style of the American officers in Greene's army.

As for the Maryland troops under the command of Colonel Williams, they were worn down to a mere shadow of their former strength by months of arduous marching and heavy fighting. Greene recognized the impact of this battle on these troops, who he respected so deeply:

> *Many brave fellows have fallen and a great number of Officers are wounded among the number is Lt Col Howard. The Maryland line made a charge that exceeded any thing I ever saw. But alas their ranks are thin and the officers few.*[52]

When he had had time to reflect on the events of the day, Greene singled out the Maryland troops for special praise in a letter to General William Smallwood, who was back in Maryland on recruiting duty:

> *Nothing could exceed the gallantry of the Maryland line. Col Williams, Howard and all the Officers exhibited acts of uncommon bravery, and the free use your line and some other Corps made of the bayonet gave us the victory.*[53]

★ ★ ★ ★ ★

The Aftermath of Eutaw Springs

The war was not yet officially over and there were many days of sparring and small unit actions still ahead, but the bloody fight at Eutaw Springs was the last major engagement between American and British soldiers in the Carolinas.

It had been a fierce battle, and both sides claimed victory. The British held the field, but they evacuated it quickly, and returned toward the safe confines of the city of Charleston. At first, Greene pursued the British on the road toward Charleston, but Stewart showed no signs of slowing his retreat, so Greene's "… wounded and prisoners requiring attention, he resolved to retire again to the High Hills of the Santee."[54] The battered American army would once again return to an area where it could rest and regain its strength in a pleasant environment.

Greene's report to Congress singled out his Adjutant General for particular praise:

> *I cannot help acknowledging my obligations to Colonel Williams for his great activity on this and many other occasions in forming the army, and for his uncommon intrepidity in leading on the Maryland troops to the charge, which exceeded any thing I ever saw.*[55]

Congress was generous in its praise of the officers and men who fought at Eutaw Springs. It passed a resolution that two pieces of field Ordnance be presented to Nathanael Greene by the Commander-in-Chief, with a motto engraved "from the United States in Congress Assembled to Major Genl. Greene, in honour of the Victory obtained under his Command near the Eutaw Springs in So Carolina on the 8th September A. D. 1781." It also resolved that "a British standard be presented to Major General Greene, as an honorable testimony of his merit, and a golden medal emblematical of the battle and victory aforesaid."[56]

Otho Holland Williams was also singled out for praise by Congress as well, when they awarded him a sword for "... his great military skill and uncommon exertions on this occasion."[57]

---

1 While multiple references have been consulted in this description of the Battle of Eutaw Springs, the narrative presented here relies primarily on the writing of Otho Holland Williams (with additions by Colonels Hampton, Polk, Howard, and Watt) on the battle, which was published in *Documentary History of the American Revolution Consisting of Letters and Papers Relating to the Contest for Liberty, Chiefly in South Carolina in 1781 and 1782* by R. W. Gibbes, M.D., published in Columbia, South Carolina in 1853. Pp. 144-158. As noted in Chapter 1, this reference is cited herein as Williams, *Battle of Eutaw*, in Gibbes
2 Brooks, N.C. The Battle Ground of America. No. VI – *Battle of Eutaw Springs, From Original and unpublished MSS.* (hereafter Brooks, *Battle of Eutaw Springs*, in Graham's Magazine.) *Graham's American Monthly Magazine of Literature and Art.* George R. Graham, Editor. Volume XXVII. Philadelphia. George R. Graham & Co. 1845. P. 253.
3 Williams, *Battle of Eutaw*, in Gibbes. Pp. 144-145.
4 Williams, *Battle of Eutaw, in Gibbes*, P. 145; Greene Nathanael. Letter to Thomas McKean, President of the Continental Congress. (Report of the Battle of Eutaw Springs.) Written at Martin's Tavern, South Carolina, September 11th, 1781. *Greene Papers*. P. 9:329.
5 Stewart, Alexander. Report of the *Battle of Eutaw Springs*. Dated Eutaw, September 9, 1781. Excerpt included in Lee, *Memoirs*. P. 604.
6 Williams, *Battle of Eutaw*, in Gibbes. P. 146.
7 Ibid, P. 146.
8 Ibid. P. 146; Brooks, *Battle of Eutaw Springs*, in Graham's Magazine, P. 254.
9 Symonds, *Battlefield Atlas*. P. 97
10 Lee, *Memoirs*. Pp. 467-468.
11 Williams, *Battle of Eutaw*, In Gibbes. Pp. 147-148.
12 Greene, Nathanael. Letter to Thomas McKean, President of the Continental Congress. (Report of the *Battle of Eutaw Springs*.) Written at Martin's Tavern, South Carolina, September 11th, 1781. *Greene Papers*. 9:329.
13 Brooks,, *Battle of Eutaw Springs*, in Graham's Magazine. P. 254.
14 Williams, *Battle of Eutaw*, in Gibbes. P. 147.
15 Ibid. P. 148.
16 Greene Nathanael. Letter to Thomas McKean, President of the Continental Congress. (Report of the *Battle of Eutaw Springs*.) Written at Martin's Tavern, South Carolina, September 11, 1781. *Greene Papers*. 9:329.

17 Williams, *Battle of Eutaw*, in Gibbes. P. 148.
18 Ibid. P. 148.
19 Greene Nathanael. Letter to Thomas McKean, President of the Continental Congress. (Report of the Battle of Eutaw Springs.) Written at Martin's Tavern, South Carolina, September 11th, 1781. *Greene Papers*. 9:329.
20 Williams, *Battle of Eutaw*, in Gibbes. P. 149.
21 Greene Nathanael. Letter to Thomas McKean, President of the Continental Congress. (Report of the Battle of Eutaw Springs.) Written at Martin's Tavern, South Carolina, September 11, 1781. *Greene Papers*. 9:331.
22 Williams, *Battle of Eutaw*, in Gibbes. P. 150.
23 Ibid. P. 150.
24 In spite of Nathanael Greene's praise for Lee in his report to Congress on the Battle of Eutaw Springs, criticism of the Legion commander was lodged from several sources and his performance at this battle remains a topic of historical analysis and discussion. For example, the Greene Papers state in Note 11 on 9:335-336 that an 1826 article in the Charleston Gazette published an accusation by Samuel Hammond that Lee had been distracted from the main fight by arguing with some officers about who should take command in place of the fallen Richard Campbell. Lee would leave the army in early 1782, before the end of the war, and return to Virginia. The reasons for his departure seem complex, but most researchers seem to have concluded that an important part of his decision was based on criticisms that he had received regarding the Battle of Eutaw Springs, and on his feeling that Greene had not appropriately praised his actions in reports of that battle. The author believes that a definitive conclusion on Lee's location on the field at various critical times and his specific actions at Eutaw Springs await future substantive research. Given the many years since the battle and the fact that currently available primary documentation has been studied for many years without producing irrefutable answers, a final, definitive explanation may be unattainable.
25 Greene Nathanael. Letter to Thomas McKean, President of the Continental Congress. (Report of the Battle of Eutaw Springs.) Written at Martin's Tavern, South Carolina, September 11, 1781. *Greene Papers*. 9:331.
26 Williams, *Battle of Eutaw*, in Gibbes Pp. 150-151.
27 Ibid. Pp. 150-153.
28 See footnote.
29 Williams, *Battle of Eutaw*, in Gibbes. P. 151.
30 Ibid. Pp. 151-152.
31 Ibid. P. 152.
32 Ibid. Pp. 152-153.
33 Ibid. P. 153.
34 See Footnote.
35 Williams, Battle of Eutaw, in Gibbes. Pp. 153-154.
36 Ibid. P. 154.
37 Ibid. P. 155.
38 Greene Nathanael. Letter to Thomas McKean, President of the Continental Congress. (Report of the Battle of Eutaw Springs.) Written at Martin's Tavern, South Carolina, September 11, 1781. *Greene Papers*. 9:331.
39 Williams, Otho Holland. Draft of a letter to Major Edward Giles. Written at the High Hills of the Santee, South Carolina. September 23, 1781. *Williams Papers*. Part 1/8. (item # 116.)
40 The criticism of Light Horse Harry Lee at this battle, mentioned previously, included a commentary in the Gibbes "*Battle of Eutaw*" by Captain Nathanael Pendleton of Greene's staff that Light Horse Harry Lee "rode about the field, giving orders and directions, in a manner the General did not approve of. Gen. Greene was, apparently, disappointed when I informed him Col. Lee was not with his Cavalry, and that I had delivered the order to Major Eggleston." The Gibbes article is dated 1858, and indicates that Otho Williams is the author, with additions by Cols. W. Hampton, Polk, Howard and Watt. It is not known if Otho Williams was the source of the information on the observations of Captain Nathanael Pendleton, but such criticisms of Lee have not been found in the Williams Papers or other sources that he would have authored.
41 Williams, *Battle of Eutaw*, in Gibbes. Pp. 154-155.
42 Ibid. P. 156.
43 Brooks, *Battle of Eutaw Springs*, in Graham's Magazine. P. 256.
44 Williams, *Battle of Eutaw*, in Gibbes.. Pp. 156.
45 Lee, *Memoirs*. P. 474.
46 Williams, Otho Holland. Draft of a letter to Major Edward Giles. Written at the High Hills of the Santee, South Carolina. September 23, 1781. *Williams Papers*. Part 1/8. (item # 116.)
47 Williams, *Battle of Eutaw*, in Gibbes. P. 156.
48 Greene, Nathanael. Letter to William Smallwood. Written at the High Hills of the Santee, S.C. September 18, 1781. *Greene Papers*. 9:369.
49 Greene. Nathanael. Letter to Thomas McKean, President of the Continental Congress. (Report of the Battle of Eutaw Springs.) Written at Head Quarters, Martins Tavern, near Fergusons Swamp, South Carolina. September 11th, 1781.

(Notes 22 and 24.) *Greene Papers*. 9:338.
50   Scharf *Maryland*. P. 427.
51   Lee, *Memoirs*. P. 472.
52   Greene, Nathanael. Letter to William Smallwood. Written at the High Hills of the Santee, S.C. September 18, 1781. *Greene Papers*. 9:370.
53   Greene, Nathanael. Letter to William Smallwood. Written at the High Hills of the Santee, S.C. September 18, 1781. *Greene Papers*. 9:369-370.
54   Williams, *Battle of Eutaw*, in Gibbes. P. 157.
55   Greene Nathanael. Letter to Thomas McKean, President of the Continental Congress. (Report of the Battle of Eutaw Springs.) Written at Martin's Tavern, South Carolina, September 11, 1781.   *Greene Papers*. 9:333.
56   Journals of the Continental Congress. Volume XXI. 1781. July 23--December 31. Monday, October 29, 1781. Pp. 1084-1085. From the Library of Congress web site.
57   Journals of the Continental Congress. Volume XXI. 1781. July 23--December 31. Monday, October 29, 1781. P. 1085. From the Library of Congress web site.

CHAPTER 11

WILLIAMS' FINAL DAYS WITH GREENE'S ARMY

Recovery After Eutaw Springs

The Battle of Eutaw Springs had been a brutal four-hour slugfest, fought in the bright sun, sweltering heat, and dripping humidity of a late summer day. Casualties in both armies were heavy, and the troops were exhausted, but that did not stop Nathanael Greene from looking for every possible way to hit the British again.

The morning after the battle, General Greene sent Francis Marion with his South Carolina militia and "Light Horse Harry" Lee with his Legion to patrol the area between Eutaw Springs and Charleston. Their mission was to slow Stewart's retreat and to cut off any British reinforcements that were being sent from Charleston. Greene followed with his army, marching as far as Ferguson's Swamp on the road to Charleston, where he wrote on September 11th that he was looking for an opportunity to fall on his retreating foe and "put a finishing stroke on our successes." Greene's high hopes were foiled, however, when Marion and Lee's small forces were not able to prevent Major MacArthur from reinforcing Stewart. Facing a strong British force, Greene decided to call a halt to the pursuit, rest for a few days, and then proceed to the army's old position at the High Hills of the Santee.[1] The British advantage in manpower grew larger when Stewart and MacArthur were further reinforced by General Paston Gould[2]* near Monck's Corner.[3]

Greene moved ahead to the High Hills, leaving Otho Williams behind in command of the army to deal with the complex logistics of crossing the Santee River and then following Greene to camp.[4] The army reached the High Hills on September 16th,[5] eight days after the battle. Nathanael Greene turned immediately to writing Governor Thomas Nelson of Virginia,[6] Colonels Isaac Shelby and John Sevier (two of the leaders of the frontier riflemen who had helped win the Battle of King's Mountain in October, 1780. He wrote to South Carolina militia General Thomas Sumter to report a victory at Eutaw Springs and to ask for reinforcements. His letters to Shelby, Sevier and Sumter expressed concern that the arrival of a French fleet off of the Chesapeake Bay would result in Cornwallis leaving Virginia and marching through North Carolina to reach Charleston.[7] He asked Shelby and Sevier to bring "as large

---

*Gould was the senior British officer in Charleston, having relieved Stewart on September 12th, 1781.

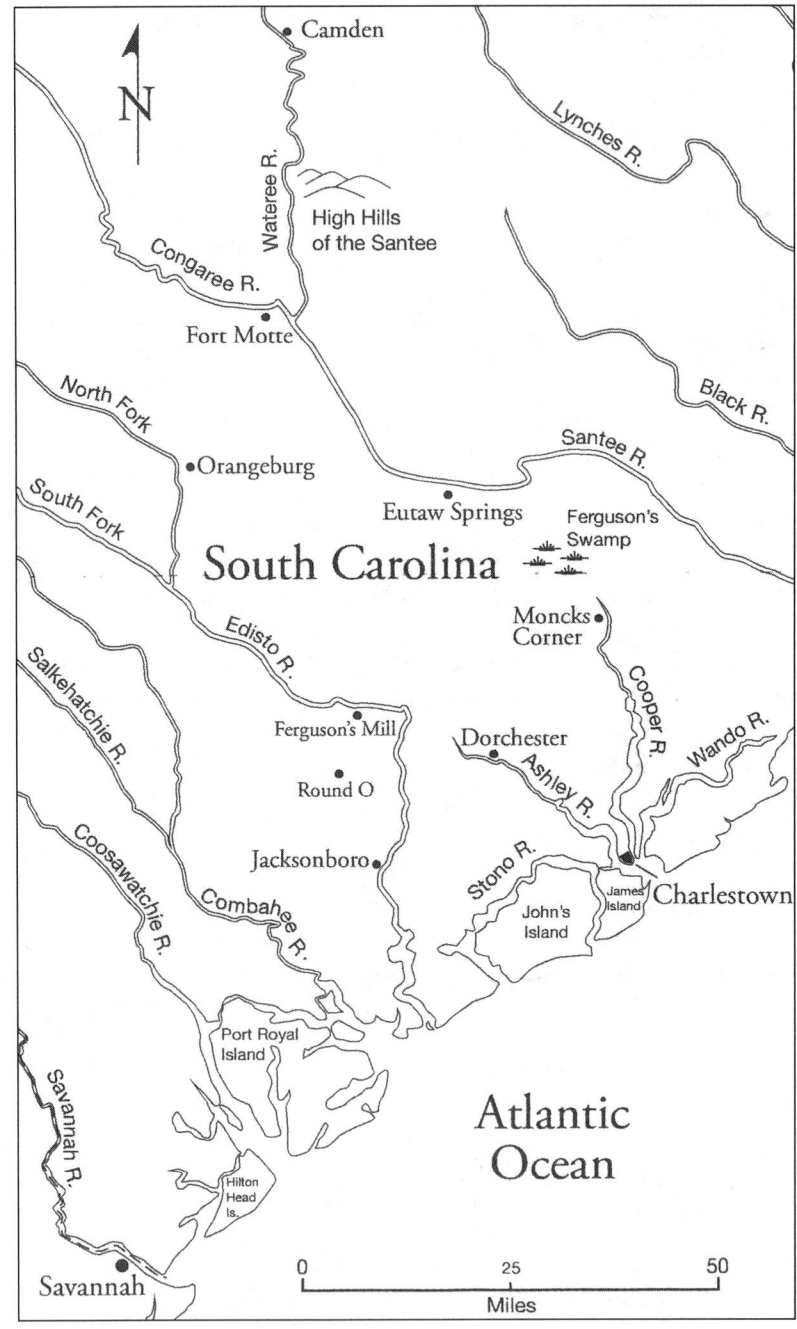

Map 9 - Forces in the Charleston area after Eutaw Springs

a body of riflemen as they can" to Charlotte, North Carolina, keeping Greene informed of their expected arrival.[8]

Greene must have met some difficulties on his trip, since Williams wrote to him on September 16th from St. Mark's Church that he was "...sorry for the accidents and mistakes..." that had deprived Greene of:

> *"...the pleasure of spending a few days agreeably on your route to the high Hills, particularly as by hastening your movements they have occasioned you to take cold; but I hope all will soon come right and that your health will be perfectly restored."*[9]

Williams expressed his belief that Cornwallis would be leaving Virginia to re-enter North Carolina, and was aware of Greene's efforts to obtain reinforcements from riflemen from the "upper Country." He reported his plans to have the troops and wagons under his command cross the Santee River on their route to the High Hills, and he also described for Greene the grim situation of the men who had been wounded at Eutaw Springs:

> *The condition of the Wounded was deplorable. We found them without necessaryes, some of them scarcely attended, and others wholly neglected; many had their wounds animated with fly blows,*[10*] *and all together they exhibited one of the most humiliating and distressing scenes I ever beheld... I interested myself as much as possible for their relief but had not means to alleviate their misery.*[11]

The distressing condition of the many wounded men was one heavy burden, but sickness was also raging through the American army at an alarming rate. "Light Horse Harry" Lee attributed the rampant disease to exhaustion from the campaign; the rigors of the battlefield; the hot, sultry days; and the heavy dew at night.[12] All these factors undoubtedly contributed to the Army's distress, but Lee and his contemporaries did not know that the swarms of lowland insects caused the widespread suffering from malaria and yellow fever. The medicine of that era was helpless against these scourges. Writing two weeks after the battle, Williams described the army's situation and the benefits of taking the army to the High Hills of the Santee:

---

*Fly blows are fly eggs deposited in animal flesh.

> *This expedition was made in the season of the year which is most sickly in this country In August and September agues and fevers particularly the bilious are almost universal complaints to avoid which was the general's principal inducement to return to this position which is almost the only one in this state where those annual diseases do not prevail over every constitution.*[13]

The General Orders of September 16th directed the troops to "Wash & Clean their Arms" by 4 p.m., and then begin the March to the High Hills where they will be given "…time to refresh after their Glorious Expedition in which they behaved with such Extraordinary fortitude & bravery."[14]

Although the troops had undoubtedly looked forward to a time of rest and revitalization at their camp in the High Hills, there was no relaxation of military discipline. The General Orders of the next day, September 17th, reflected the kind of precision that always characterized the administration of Otho Holland Williams: brigade field returns were due by noon the following day.[15] The army settled into the routine of camp life, as the troops tried to rest, heal and regain their fighting edge after the rigors of the last campaign.

About two-and-a-half weeks later (on October 4th or 5th[16]), Greene left Williams in charge of the army at the High Hills and rode the approximately 130 miles to Charlotte, North Carolina, explaining his purpose to George Washington on October 7th that:

> *I came to this place to try to get out a body of militia to drive the Enemy all into Charles Town but how far I shall succeed is uncertain and how far the army will be able to second the attempt is uncertain as they are getting sickly.*[17]

Otho Williams wrote to Greene on October 10th, reporting on the shortage of physicians and surgeons, some of whom were "sick and unfit for duty." The three surgeons who were well enough to work were treating as many wounded officers as possible, but "Several of our Soldiers are Dead and others dying yit (sic.) the number of sick does not decrease." The fever had become so prevalent that "Battalions can scarce form Companies," and he hoped that "this dreadful Season will soon be over." To add to Williams' woes, the army had "…not a Cartridge nor an ounce of powder in Store," and was unable to fill Francis Marion's request for ammunition. Williams avowed that he would send ammunition to Marion when an expected shipment arrived.[18] "We are in a truly calamitous situation," opined Williams, "tho' I hope the Enemy, weakened by similar causes will not be able to disturb us. If they shou'd; I fear our mountain Friends will not arrive (in) time enough to give us the necessary assistance." Finally, Williams expected "every Hour" to hear "most agreeable intelligence" from Greene,[19] a hint that Greene and Williams were expecting important news from Yorktown, Virginia, where a combined French and American army under George Washington had their old adversary Cornwallis under siege at Yorktown, Virginia.[20]

On October 11th, Greene wrote from Charlotte to Colonels Isaac Shelby and John Sevier to inform them that Lord Cornwallis was besieged at Yorktown, Virginia by an army of twenty-thousand men commanded by George Washington, and that the British commander would almost certainly surrender soon, removing the danger that he would be invading North and South Carolina. Greene was hoping that Washington would bring his troops to the South, but he still requested that Shelby and Sevier join him in the effort to keep the British penned up in Charleston and prevent them from gathering supplies from the countryside. He admonished them that "We wait only your arrival to begin operations." Sevier eventually joined Greene's army with "a large body of rifle Men" on October 24th and Shelby arrived a few days later.[21] They served under the command of Francis Marion.[22]

Greene had returned from Charlotte to the army's camp at the High Hills of the Santee, by October 15th, when he wrote to Governor Rutledge of South Carolina that he desired to have Andrew Pickens and his two regiments of South Carolina militia concentrate on operations in the frontier regions.[23] Before the end of October, Pickens attacked the Cherokee town of Chota and several nearby villages in his effort to "protect the frontier."[24]

When the Commanding General returned from his trip to Charlotte, he and Otho Williams were almost immediately faced with significant morale problems in the army.

Daily life in the southern army was filled with many difficulties, and some of the long-suffering troops had reached the end of their tethers. There was a hint of mutiny in the air. The tiny contingent that remained of the Maryland Continental regiments submitted petitions to Greene requesting opportunities to go home. They complained of their need for clothing, and recounted their long and honorable service. They gathered into small groups where they talked seriously of these issues and of their low pay. Discontent spread to other army units, until a tipsy South Carolina soldier named Timothy Griffin openly implored the men to defy their officers. Greene ordered him seized, court martialed, and executed by a firing squad with the entire army looking on.[25] The execution was carried out on October 21st, 1781,[26] and it seemed to quiet the situation for the time being.[27]

However, executions did not eliminate the many difficulties that the army faced. Greene described the destitute condition of his army to Colonel Thomas Pickering, Quartermaster General of the Continental Army:

> *We have had a most distressing campaign. The resources of this Country are so small, and our supplies have been so scanty that we have suffered numberless inconveniences … We are in great distress this moment for want of Tents, those we have are almost all worn out, & the number we have had in the best State has not afforded us more than one (tent) to ten Men, and many of those of an indifferent kind… Among other things we are suffered greatly for want of Canteens and are now in want of axes. Nothing has been more distressing to us than the want of Artificers.*[28*] *The few that came from the Northward, their time of service soon expired after their arrival, and we were left with few except such as we could draft from the line. In this Country, where there are so few manufacturing towns and artizans generally so scarce & hard to be got, treble the number of artificers are necessary that are to the Northward, where things at the last moment may be procured with so much ease and dispatch.*[29]

Greene knew that it would take time for the regular infantry to regain its fighting trim, and his command was down to a "… whole collective strength that don't exceed One thousand men fit for duty."[30] Even in these straightened circumstances, the restless Commander wanted to harass the British any way he could. He sent his fast-moving light troops, under Marion and Lee, to do whatever damage they could to the enemy. He described this approach to the President of Congress in a letter written on October 25th:

> *Our force here is too small and sickly to attempt any thing further until reinforcements arrive, unless it is in the partisan way, in which I hope we shall be able to effect something cleaver, as a considerable number of riflemen have come down from the mountain to join us, & are gone down to General Marion.*[31]

---

*Artificers included various skilled trades, including "armourers, smiths, carpenters, harness makers, and wheel wrights.

In the last week of October,[32] Greene and his men learned that George Washington and the main American Army had won a landmark victory at Yorktown, Virginia, where Lord Cornwallis had been forced to surrender his entire command.

General Greene wanted the French fleet and the bulk of Washington's Army to come south after the victory at Yorktown[33] to help him drive the remaining British out of their only remaining strongholds in the South - - Wilmington, North Carolina; Charleston, South Carolina; and Savannah, Georgia. However, Washington wrote on October 31st that:

> *Every Argument & Persuasive had been used with the French Admiral to induce him to aid the Combined Army, in an operation against Charlestown, but the advanced Season, The Orders of His Court, and his own Engagements to be punctual to a certain Time fixed on for his ulterior operations, all forbid his Compliance, & I am obliged to submit. Nothing therefore remains, but to give you a respectable Reinforcement; & to return myself to the Northward with the Remainder of the Troops.*

Washington added that the reinforcements would be commanded by Major General Arthur St. Clair and would consist of Continental troops from Pennsylvania, Maryland, and Virginia, plus their cavalry.[34] St. Clair's command included the brigades of Brigadier Generals Mordecai Gist of Maryland and Anthony Wayne of Pennsylvania.[35] Washington gave St. Clair discretionary orders, but made clear that, if practicable, he wanted him to capture Wilmington, the last remaining British stronghold in North Carolina:

> *You will march them by the most convenient rout, and in the most expeditious manner (without fatiguing the Troops) towards Wilmington in North Carolina; or other Posts in that State of which you will endeavour to dispossess the enemy if their situation from the intelligence you shall receive as you advance shall, in your judgment, render it practicable and advisable. If it does not you will continue your March to the Southern Army, and put yourself under the command of Majr Genl. Greene.*[36]

St. Clair began his march south to reinforce Greene on November 5th.[37] British General Alexander Leslie took command in Charleston on November

8th, and immediately ordered the evacuation of Wilmington, as he was concerned that the garrison would be cut off by St. Clair's advance. The British troops left Wilmington by sea on November 14th and sailed to Charleston.[38] This freed St. Clair to take the much more favorable inland route to join Greene.[39]

When he learned from George Washington that the French fleet would not be available and that he would be receiving only a small reinforcement, Greene was momentarily discouraged. However, he quickly recovered, and looked for an opportunity to move against the British with his smaller-than-hoped-for force, as soon as the weather was cool enough to support sustained operations.[40]

On November 18th, as the weather grew cooler, Greene led his army out of the encampment at the High Hills of the Santee and marched toward the British. On the 27th, he left Otho Williams in charge of the main army and personally led a detachment of 200 cavalry and 200 infantry toward Dorchester.[41] By this phase of the war, it was clear that Greene had complete confidence in Colonel Otho Williams' ability to command the army in his absence.

On November 29th, Greene drew the British cavalry out of Dorchester and initiated a brief, intense fight, making such an aggressive demonstration that the British garrison, consisting of about 150 cavalry, 500 infantry, and 200 Tories evacuated the post and retreated to the Quarter-House on Charleston Neck. This retreat, precipitated by Greene's astute management of his small force, gave control of all the rice between the Ashley and Edisto Rivers to the American army.[42] A British force at Goose Creek also retreated, leaving Greene in "quiet possession of the country."[43]

On December 2nd Greene informed Williams of his successful operations:

> *I wrote you yesterday from Vandomeres plantation of our little skirmish before Dorchester. The enemy evacuated it the same Night and burnt their works, Stores and forage and retired to the Quarter House. They appear to have been much alarmed and have disgraced themselves not a little by their precipitate retreat.*[44]

In this letter, Greene also instructed Williams to take the Army to Round O,[45]* sending their engineer (Colonel Thaddeus Kosciuszko) to find a good camp. Greene then informed Williams of his plans to station his troops so that they could most effectively keep the British confined to the area around Charleston. In the process, Greene paid his Adjutant General a compliment for his known skill at leading the flying army:

> *I propose General Sumter to occupy the Post at Orangeburg and Four Holes Bridge, General Marion St Thomases & St Stephen's parish and if Col Lee is but well enough to command the horse with a detachment of infantry for the cover of the Country between Ashley and the Edisto. I think this plan would answer until we are strong enough to move to Dorchester with all our force. There is great quantities of forage in this quarter. But without Col Lee is well enough to take command of the flying Army I shall be at a loss how to cover it unless the Adjutant General will take the command.*[46]

The authors of The Papers of Nathanael Greene summarize Greene's plan as follows:

> *Protection of the area northeast of Charleston became the responsibility of Francis Marion's militia brigade, augmented by the mounted South Carolina State Troops of Peter Horry and Hezekiah Maham. Greene and his army defended the area west and south of the South Carolina capital, while John Barnwell's militia brigade shielded the southernmost part of the state. The militia forces of Thomas Sumter and his successor William Henderson, protected central South Carolina, and Andrew Pickens defended the west against incursion by Indian tribes.*[47]

Williams wrote to Greene on the same day to report that they had marched 13 miles the day before to reach a camp at Buck's Creek, and that he was making arrangements to obtain enough corn meal to feed the troops. This included an agreement with Thomas Sumter to deliver some meal, to send out a party to collect more corn, and to operate a mill near Nelson's Ferry. Williams wrote a

---

*The name Round O was given by settlers to a friendly Native American warrior whose name was difficult to pronounce and who had an O painted on his chest."

note on a letter from Sumter: "I applied in person.... The more consequence you impute to some men the more they will exert themselves to serve you." Sumter's biographer considered Williams contemptuous in making such a statement.[48] There was considerable and lasting friction between Sumter and the officers like Otho Williams who were loyal to Nathanael Greene.

Greene provided more detail on his strategic intentions to Governor Rutledge on December 3rd, 1781:

> *The Army for the present will take post at the Round O. Sumter at Orangeburg and the Four Holes, General Marion in St. Stevens and St Thomas Parish and I propose to form a flying Army of the Cavalry and a detachment of Infantry for the security of the Country between Ashley and Edisto. This will be our disposition until we are stronger and the enemies future plan more fully explained.*[49]

Greene had acted on the offensive since the Battle of Guilford Courthouse on March 15th, 1781, a strategy that had led to battles at Hobkirk's Hill, Ninety-Six, and Eutaw Springs. He was now posting his forces in strategic locations that were essentially defensive, all with an eye to protecting the countryside from British incursions and keeping them bottled up as close to Charleston as possible. Greene would continue to look for ways to keep pressure on the British troops in Charleston and eventually force the evacuation of that city, but he would never have the number of troops or the supporting naval forces that were needed to make such a strategy successful.

Greene's ability to maneuver the British out of Dorchester was characteristic of the small, contained actions that would be fought for the rest of the war. Williams congratulated Greene for achieving his objective "without risking a general action," and hoping that he could hold his gains until General St. Clair arrived.[50] Two days later, Williams wrote that the army had struggled to march twelve miles "with a great number of Pioneers & the best guides in the Country," and that he would encamp at Ferguson's Mills until Colonel Kosciuszko returned from his mission to identify a proper campground near Round O.[51] The General Orders for December 7th were written at "Camp at Colo Sanders, Round O, South Carolina," and they established the stern military discipline that was characteristic of the camps of Greene and Williams:

> *The Camp Guards are to be disposed in such a manner as to prevent the Soldiers from Going out of camp without leave.*

> *Whoever is found guilty of Trespassing against Genl Orders by Stealing or plundering shall suffer the severest penalty.*[52]

The Orders for the next day were characteristic of the daily activities in a camp run by these leaders- "Brigades will exercise every afternoon by battalion. Guards are to be relieved daily at 8 a.m."[53]

Nathanael Greene's correspondence began to be dated from "Head Quarters Round O., S.C." on December 9th,[54] indicating that he had rejoined the main army after his excursion to Dorchester. Greene, Williams, and their main fighting force were now encamped some 40 miles northwest of Charleston, with the British army "all closely pent up on Charles Town Neck."[55] From that strategic spot, the Americans could command the land route between the British outposts at Charleston and Savannah. Greene described the advantages of his position to Governor Nathan Brownson of Georgia on December 10th:

> *...the Enemy have retired to Charles Town that is to the Quarter House in the Neck and have only one out post at Stono at the crossing place on to Johns Island. We have now full command of all the Country.*[56]

The daily General Orders during the army's encampment at Round O. provide glimpses of what life was like for Otho Williams and the troops with whom he served. There were many routine days, such as December 15th, 1781:

> *As there is great plenty of Deer and wild Fowl in this neighborhood, the Depy Adjutant General is authorized to grant permits to huntsmen to kill Game for the use of the Officers, for which a small allowance of loose ammunition will be made.*[57]

On December 18th, 1781, the orders stipulated that "The quartermaster will obtain oyster shells for use by the commissary; troops will receive and immediately cook provisions for tomorrow,"[58] There were also stern and bitter days, such as Tuesday, December 11th, when the orders announced that General Greene had approved sentences of 100 lashes on the bare backs of four soldiers convicted of leaving camp without permission and "Plundering the Inhabitants." The sentences were ordered to be carried out that afternoon. On that same day, Greene approved a death sentence for Maryland soldier William Poland for desertion and joining the enemy, although Greene later pardoned him.[59]

Occasionally the routine of camp life was interrupted for a less military message, as with the General Orders for Christmas Day 1781, wherein Greene "wishes the Army a Merry Christmas; and that it may be so, he directs that the usual proportion of Sprits be issued to the officers and Men."[60]

There were occasional short respites such as Christmas Day for Nathanael Greene and Otho Williams, but they never stopped searching for any possible way to increase the size of their command so that they could confront the British successfully on the battlefield. The Commanding General appealed directly to state governments, Continental officers, and militia commanders for more troops, and the former Quaker also tried to convince the governments of South Carolina and Georgia to recruit slaves for the American Army. He made clear his preference to grant freedom to those who would serve honorably. Greene sent his observations to South Carolina Governor John Rutledge on December 9th, 1781:

> *The natural strength of this country in point of numbers, appears to me to consist much more in the blacks, than the whites Could they be incorporated, and employed for it's defence, it would afford you double security. That they would make good Soldiers I have not the least doubt and I am persuaded the State has it not in its power to give sufficient reinforcements without incorporating them, either to secure the country, if the Enemy mean to act upon an offensive plan, or furnish a force to dispossess them of Charlestown, should it be defensive.*[61]

Greene added that he would like to see a corps of pioneers[62*] and a corps of artificers formed, plus a force of four regiments, two as part of the continental army and two as state troops, who should "…have their freedom, and be cloathed, and treated in all respects as other soldiers; without which, they will be unfit for the duty expected from them."[63] Greene repeated the recommendation on January 21st, 1782.[64][65]

The initiative to accept slaves into the army was supported by John Laurens, an impressive and widely admired young soldier, and also by the Army's Adjutant General, Otho Holland Williams.[66][67] There was an intense debate over the proposal, but Greene had to report to George Washington on March 9th that "I persuaded the Legislature to raise black Regiments but could not prevail; not because they objected to the expence (for they

---

*Pioneers repaired roads and worked on fortifications.

give a most enormous bounty for white men, and pay in Slaves) but from apprehension of the consequences."[68]

Although the legislatures would not support providing the black troops that he had hoped for, Greene continued to try to attract soldiers from any available source, and to deploy his small force wisely with the goal of keeping the British bottled up in Charleston. His army was given a temporary boost when General Arthur St. Clair and his command reached Greene's camp on January 4th, 1782.[69]

With Greene's forces deployed in an arc around Charleston, the state of South Carolina held an election and decided to convene the General Assembly at Jacksonboro, approximately thirty-six miles from Charleston, on January 18th, 1782. The General Assembly should have been a tempting target for a British or Tory raiding party, but British strength, morale and influence had sunk so low that they were unable to disturb this meeting of the legislature, even though it was being held so close to their last remaining bastion in the state.[70]

After St. Clair's force arrived from Yorktown, Greene sent General Anthony Wayne and his Pennsylvanians to Georgia to try to take control of that state. Wayne's orders included an admonition to:

> *Try by every means in your power to soften the malignity and deadly resentments subsisting between the Whigs and tories, and put a stop as much as possible to that cruel custom of putting people to death after they have surrendered themselves prisoners.*[71]

Greene added that "The practice of plundering you will endeavor to Check as much as possible." Not only did Greene want to achieve these goals and also put pressure on the British garrison at Savannah, he probably wanted to separate Wayne and St. Clair, who apparently had a long-standing dislike for each other, which had resurfaced in an intense disagreement on their march from Yorktown to join Greene's army.[72]

Williams Leaves the Southern Army and Returns to the North

One inevitable result of dwindling numbers of soldiers was that the army now had too many senior officers for the smaller number of troops. With so few Marylanders still in the Southern army, and with the arrival of Brigadier General Mordecai Gist, the Maryland Line in Greene's army was "top heavy."

This permitted Otho Williams to contemplate an honorable way to leave the rigors of the War in the South, and return to his beloved Maryland home for some well-deserved rest.

---

1 Greene, Nathanael. Letter to Thomas McKean, President of the Continental Congress. Written at Head Quarters, Martins Tavern, near Fergusons Swamp, So Carolina, September 11th, 1781. *Greene Papers.* 9:332.
2 See Footnote.
3 Greene, Nathanael. Letter to Thomas McKean, President of the Continental Congress. Written at Head Quarters, Martins Tavern, near Fergusons Swamp, So Carolina, September 11th, 1781. Note 21. *Greene Papers.* 9:338.
4 Williams, Otho Holland. Letter to Nathanael Greene. Written at Camp at St. Mark's Church, 20 Miles from James' Old Field, S.C. 16th September 1781. *Greene Papers.* 9:353.
5 *Greene Papers* 9:xlvi.
6 Thomas Nelson had been elected Governor of Virginia on June 12th, succeeding Thomas Jefferson, whose term had legally ended on June 2nd. The short delay in electing the new governor occurred because the members of the Virginia legislature had been scattered by a British raid on Charlottesville on June 3rd. (Ref: Note 1 to Letter from Nathanael Greene to Thomas Jefferson. Written at Camp near the Cross Roads between Broad River and the Catawba, South Carolina. June 27th, 1781. *Greene Papers.* 8:465.)
7 Greene's concern that Cornwallis would leave Yorktown, Virginia and march to Charleston, South Carolina was not realized. George Washington led a combined French and American army that besieged Cornwallis in Yorktown and accepted the surrender of his army on October 19, 1781.
8 Greene, Nathanael. Letters to Thomas Nelson of Virginia, Colonels Isaac Shelby and John Sevier, and General Thomas Sumter. Written at the High Hills of the Santee. September 16, 1781. *Greene Papers.* 9: 350-352.
9 Williams, Otho Holland. Letter to Nathanael Greene. Written at Camp at St Marks Church 20 Miles from James' Old Field, S.C. 16th September, 1781. *Greene Papers.* 9:353.
10 See Footnote.
11 Williams, Otho Holland. Letter to Nathanael Greene. Written at Camp at St. Marks Church 20 miles from Jame's Old Field, S.C. 16th September, 1781. *Greene Papers* 9:350-352.
12 Lee, *Memoirs.* Pp. 475-477.
13 Williams, Otho Holland. Letter to Major Edward Giles. Written at the High Hills of the Santee. September 23rd, 1781. *Williams Papers.* Part 1/8. (Item #116.) This letter is also reproduced in the article *The Battle Grounds of America. No. VI. Battle of Eutaw Springs. From Original and Unpublished MSS.* By N. C. Brooks. Graham's American Monthly Magazine, Volume XXVII. Philadelphia. George R. Graham & Co. 1845. Pp. 256-258.
14 General Orders issued at Camp At Scott's Lake, S.C. 16 September, 1781. *Greene Papers.* 9:350.
15 General Orders, Camp High Hills Santee, S.C. 17 September, 1781. *The Papers of Nathanael Greene.* 9:355.
16 Greene wrote to George Washington from the High Hills of the Santee on October 4th and the next letter he wrote was from approximately 130 miles to the northwest at Charlotte, North Carolina on October 7th. *Greene Papers.* 9: 426 and 428
17 Greene, Nathanael. Letter to George Washington. Written at Charlotte, N.C. October 7, 1781. *Greene Papers* 9:430.
18 One of Greene's objectives on his trip to Charlotte was to obtain a supply of ammunition. Note 4 to letter from Colonel Otho H. Williams to Nathanael Greene. Written at the High Hills of the Santee. 10 October, 1781. *Greene Papers.* 9:441.
19 Williams, Colonel Otho H. Letter to Nathanael Greene. Written at High Hills of the Santee, S.C. 10 October, 1781. *Greene Papers.* 9:440-441.
20 Lord Cornwallis' army would surrender to Washington just nine days later, on October 19th, 1781.
21 Greene, Nathanael. Letter to Colonels Isaac Shelby and John Sevier. Written at Charlotte, N.C. October 11, 1781. Including notes. *Greene Papers.* 9:442-443.
22 Marion, Francis. Letter to Nathanael Greene. Written at Peyres Plantation East of Santee, S.C. 18th November, 1781. *Greene Papers.* 9:589.
23 Greene, Nathanael. Letter to Governor John Rutledge of South Carolina. Written at Head Quarters. The High Hills of the Santee. October the 15th, 1781. *Greene Papers.* 9:447.
24 Note 1 to Letter from Governor John Rutledge of South Carolina to Nathanael Greene. Written at the High Hills of Santee, South Carolina. 15th October, 1781. *Greene Papers* 9:446.
25 Gordon, History. Volume IV. Pp. 172-173.
26 Death Warrant for Private Timothy Griffin, Camp, High Hills of the Santee, S.C. 21 October, 1781. *Greene Papers.* 9:459.
27 Pancake, *This Destructive War.* P. 236.

28 See Footnote.
29 Greene, Nathanael. Letter to Colonel Timothy Pickering. Written at Head Quarters. The High Hills of the Santee, S.C. October 21st, 1781. *Greene Papers.* 9: 461.
30 Greene. Nathanael. Letter to Governor Thomas Nelson of Virginia. Written at Head Quarters, High Hills of the Santee, South Carolina. October 24th, 1781. *Greene Papers.* 9:473.
31 Greene, Nathanael. Letter to Thomas McKean, President of the Continental Congress. Written at Head Quarters High Hills Santee, S.C., October 25th, 1781. *Greene Papers.* 9:483.
32 Greene's first mention of the surrender of Cornwallis is in letters to Colonel Peter Horry and General Francis Marion written on October 30th, 1781. Greene Papers. 9:496. He penned his congratulations to George Washington on November 2nd, 1781. *Greene Papers.* 9:519.
33 Pancake, This Destructive War. Pp. 236-237.
34 Washington, George. Letter to General Nathanael Greene. Written at Head Quarters near York, Va. 31st Oct 1781. *Greene Papers.* 9:504-505.
35 Lee, *Memoirs.* P. 518.
36 Washington, George. Letter to Arthur St. Clair. Written at Head Quarters near York, Virginia. October 29, 1781. *Washington Papers.*
37 Washington, George. Letter to Nathanael Greene. Written at Mount Vernon. November 16th, 1781. The Papers of George Washington.
38 Martin, Alexander. Acting Governor of North Carolina. Letter to Nathanael Greene. Written at Salem. November 28, 1781. *Greene Papers.* 9:634-635.
39 Greene's aide Captain Nathanael Pendleton wrote to Greene from Guilford, North Carolina on November 27th that if St. Clair marched by the "lower Road" on the coastal plain that his march would be "exceedingly impeded" by having to collect provisions in a "disaffected Country." On the other hand, provisions "are or will be ready at every post" on the upper route." Ref: *Greene Papers.* 9:632-633.
40 Lee, *Memoirs.* P. 521.
41 Gordon, *History.* Volume IV. P . 176.
42 Ibid. P. 176.
43 Morris, Lewis, Jr. Letter to his father, 10 December 1781. In Note 2 to letter from Nathanael Greene to Colonel Otho H. Williams. Written at Mr. Warrings Plantation 7 Miles from Dorchester, S.C. December 2nd 1781. *Greene Papers.* 9:650.
44 Greene, Nathanael. Letter to Colonel Otho H. Williams. Written at Mr. Warrings plantation 7 Miles from Dorchester, S.C, December 2nd, 1781. *Greene Papers.* 9:649.
45 See Footnote.
46 Greene, Nathanael, Letter to Colonel Otho H. Williams. Written at Mr. Warrings plantation 7 Miles from Dorchester, S.C., December 2nd, 1781. *Greene Papers.* 9:649:650.
47 *Greene Papers.* Introduction to Volume 10. 10:xi-xii.
48 Williams, Otho H. Letter to Nathanael Greene. Written at Camp Buck Creek, S.C. 2nd December, 1781. With notes. *Greene Papers.* 9:655.
49 Greene, Nathanael. Letter to South Carolina Governor John Rutledge. Written at Head Quarters near Dorchester, S.C. December 3rd 1781. *Greene Papers.* 10:4.
50 Williams, Otho H. Letter to Nathanael Greene. Written at Riedelsperger's, S.C. 4th December, 1781. *Greene Papers.* 10:7.
51 Williams, Colonel Otho H. Letter to Nathanael Greene. Written at Fergusons Mills, S.C. 6th December, 1781. *Greene Papers.* 10:10-11.
52 General Greene's Orders. Written at Colo Sanders, Round O, S.C. 7th December, 1781. *Greene Papers.* 10:11.
53 General Greene's Orders. Written at Camp at Colo Sanders's, S.C. 8 December , 1781. *Greene Papers.* 10:15.
54 Greene, Nathanael. Letter to Colonel Stephen Drayton. Written at Head Quarters Round O., S.C. December 9th, 1781. *Greene Papers.* 10:16.
55 Greene, Nathanael. Letter to General John Twiggs. Written at Head Quarters near Parkers Ferry, S.C. December 7th, 1781. *Greene Papers.* 10:13.
56 Greene, Nathanael. Letter to Governor Nathan Brownson of Georgia. Written at Head Quarters at the Round O., S.C. December 10th, 1781. *Greene Papers.* 10: 25.
57 General Greene's Orders. Written at Head Quarters Round O., S.C. Saturday, December 15th, 1781. *Greene Papers.* 10:57.
58 General Greene's Orders. Written at Round O., S.C. Tuesday, 18 December, 1781. *Greene Papers.* 10:72.
59 General Green's Orders. Written at Camp at Colo Sanders's. Tuesday, 11 December, 1781. Note 1. *Greene Papers.* 10:34.
60 General Greene's Orders. Written at Round O. S.C. Tuesday, 25 December, 1781. *Greene Papers.* 10:102.
61 Greene, Nathanael. Letter to Governor John Rutledge of South Carolina. Written at Headquarters at the Round O,

S.C. December 9, 1781. *Greene Papers*. 10:22.
62　See Footnote.
63　Greene, Nathanael, Letter to Governor John Rutledge of South Carolina. Written at Headquarters at the Round O, S.C. December 9, 1781. *Green Papers*. 10:22.
64　Greene's position on enlisting African-Americans in the army aroused the suspicion among some South Carolina landowners that the plan was designed to open the door to emancipation. Aedanus Burke, a participant in the debate in the South Carolina House of representatives is quoted: "The northern people I have observed regard the condition in which we hold our slaves in a light different from us. I am much deceived indeed, if they do not secretly wish for a general Emancipation, if the present struggle was over." The legislature eventually approved a law for recruiting slaves from confiscated estates as "waggoners, Pioneers, Artificers and servants for the officers," but never discussed again their service as soldiers. Ref: Greene, Nathanael. Letter to Governor John Rutledge of South Carolina. Written at Head Quarters, Skirving's S.C. January 21, 1781. *Greene Papers*. 10:228-230. Note 4. While both Otho Williams and Nathanael Greene expressed support for enlisting black soldiers to fight against the British, it did not mean that they were abolitionists. In fact, both men owned slaves after the war.
65　Greene, Nathanael. Letter to Governor John Rutledge of South Carolina. Written at Head Quarters, Skirving's S.C. January 21, 1781. *Greene Papers*. 10:228-230.
66　This letter, written to Edward Giles in June, 1781, shows that Williams supported the recruitment of African-Americans for service in the Continental Army. There is further evidence in his article in the *Maryland Journal and Baltimore Advertiser* of May 15, 1781, which is cited in *Greene Papers* 8:303.
67　Giles, Edward. Letter to Otho Holland Williams. Written at Mt. Felix, Harford County, Maryland on June 1, 1781. *Williams Papers*. (Part 1/8. (Item # 105.)
68　Greene, Nathanael. Letter to George Washington. Written at Headquarters Ponpon, S.C. March 9th, 1782. *Greene Papers*. 10:472.
69　Note 1 to letter from Nathanael Greene to Governor John Rutledge of South Carolina. Written at Head Quarters. Round O. S.C. January 4th, 1782. *Greene Papers*. 10:51.
70　Ibid. 10:51-52.
71　Greene, Nathanael. Letter to General Anthony Wayne. Written at Head Quarters Round O., S.C. January 9th, 1781. (Including notes.) *Greene Papers*. 10:175-176.
72　Greene, Nathanael. Letter to General Anthony Wayne. Written at Head Quarters Round O., S.C. January 9th, 1781. (Including notes.) Greene Papers. *10:175-176*.

CHAPTER 12

RETURN TO THE NORTH

A few weeks after General Mordecai Gist arrived with his Maryland troops at the Southern army's camp on January 4th 1781, Colonel Otho Williams was relieved of his duties with the Southern army and was permitted to return home. General Nathanael Greene announced in his General Orders of February 1st, 1782, that Colonel Josiah Harmar was relieving Williams as Deputy Adjutant General, and he thanked his friend Williams "not only for his particular services in the Adjt Genls Department, but in the general operations of the Campaign."[1]

Greene arose early on February 9th, 1781 and wrote to a friend, Jeremiah Wadsworth, that Williams would be delivering the letter that he was writing. Williams was anxious to head for home, and Greene confided in Wadsworth that "Had I time I would write to you more correctly, and in a fairer hand; but the Colonel is in a hurry to be gone; and I have got up a little earlier than common to finish this and some other letters before breakfast."[2]

Otho Williams set out on his journey north with the high honor of carrying dispatches from Nathanael Greene to the Continental Congress. Greene wrote to Williams on February 9th with specific instructions for his journey, including stops at Camden, Charlotte, Salisbury and Richmond to monitor the distribution of clothing, the procurement of wagons, the movement of prisoners and the repair of weapons.[3] During his journey, Williams wrote periodically to Greene to report on his activities.[4] He occasionally included personal notes, such as his regret that he had not been able to meet with Greene's wife as she traveled south to rejoin the General, accompanied by his aide, Major Ichabod Burnet. Williams asked Greene to tell Catherine that he was "infinitely Obliged by the introduction that she left for me at St. George Tucker's. With all her affable severity I'm persuaded that her opinion of me is not unfavorable. I flatter myself that it is not unfriendly."[5]

Greene also instructed Williams that he was to emphasize to the government of Maryland that the needs of the southern army were urgent, and to support General William Smallwood in sending troops to reinforce it.[6]

One of the documents that Williams carried north was a letter from Greene to Congress recommending that Williams be promoted to Brigadier General. This letter, dated February 10th, was Greene's second to Congress on the subject of Williams' promotion. The first had been written on October 30th, and had contained a solid justification for granting the Marylander a Brigadier General's commission, noting that "few Officers merit more, or will be more studious to discover such honor as Congress may think proper to bestow."⁷

Greene had written on the same date to George Washington on the subject of Williams' promotion, requesting that the Commander-in-Chief support what Greene presented as a well-justified reward for Williams' valuable service, describing him as:

> ...an officer, whose zeal and long service, give him a just claim to public attention, and to your friendship. I am under many and singular obligations to him, for his uncommon exertions, to promote the operations in this department, and shall think myself happy, if my recommendation will add to his estimation, in your opinion, and contribute in the least to procure him, that promotion which his standing, and justice, authorize him to claim.⁸

Congress had referred Greene's recommendation to the Secretary of War on November 29th.⁹ On December 4th, George Washington endorsed Williams' promotion in his letter to Congress, subject to Congress agreeing that it was proper to fill the vacancy at that time:

> If it is necessary to add any thing to the recommendation of General Greene, I can assure Congress, that Colo. Williams, as an Officer of merit, has ever stood high in my estimation, and that it is my opinion, that his long services, military abilities and good conduct justly entitle him to the promotion mentioned, provided Congress should think proper, at this time, to fill the vacancy ¹⁰

Washington also notified Greene that he had forwarded his recommendation for Williams' promotion to Congress, noting that "...if thought proper at this time, there is no doubt of Colo. Williams being promoted."¹¹ This opinion was reinforced by Captain William Pierce, Jr., one of Greene's aides who had been honored to carry his commander's dispatches from the Battle of Eutaw Springs to Congress. Pierce reported on October 24th from Philadelphia that "Colo Williams stands high on the List of fame, and I hope will be noticed for his singular merit, as I have heard several Members of Congress speak of him in very affectionate terms."¹²

Although Generals Washington and Greene had endorsed him and there appeared to be favorable sentiment in Congress, the question of the promotion was deferred. Congress referred the matter to a five-man Committee of Congress that was working with Washington on plans to fill the ranks of the Army for the coming year.[13]

By the time that Williams was starting his trip home to Maryland early in February, 1782, it had been over three months since Greene's initial correspondence to the Commander-in-Chief and Congress regarding his promotion, and Greene's February 10th letter sought to reinvigorate action on the matter. In addition to the new letter from Greene, Colonel Williams planned to go to Philadelphia, where it was hoped that his presence would give additional weight to that recommendation. Williams wrote to his brother that Nathanael Greene was his friend, and had promised him "every indulgence, consistent with the good of the service."[14] Greene's February 10th letter is a fine testament to the service of the Maryland Colonel:

> *This will be handed to your Excellency by Colo. Williams who is on his return to the Northward. I am obliged to refer him to Congress to learn their determination respecting his promotion recommended to General Washington and by him addressed to Congress. I have only to observe that I believe his right of promotion is unquestionable, his merit known and confessed, and that the hope of promotion is the soul of an Army.*[15]

There were clear reasons why Williams' promotion did not pass immediately. Congress thought that the war would soon be over, and they wanted to limit the size and cost of the army, which argued against commissioning new brigadiers. Also, many states had a "favorite son" who they thought was at least as deserving of promotion as the Colonel from Maryland. This resulted in several votes of the full Congress in which Williams' promotion was considered along with others, and did not pass.[16]

By April 27th, Williams had reached Philadelphia, where he was openly fretting about his prospects. Maryland Congressional Delegate John Hanson wrote to his friend Philip Thomas that:

> *Colo. Williams is now here Anxious about his promotion which I think there is little Doubt of. His own merit as an Officer and the strong recommendation he has from General Green, must prevail.*[17]

Williams' promotion finally passed on day, May 9th, 1782, when James Madison moved that the Marylander be promoted to Brigadier General.

Madison had opposed Williams on all previous ballots, but he now emphasized that General Greene had "...recommended Colonel Otho Williams, as an officer whose distinguished talents and services give him a just pretension to such appointment..." and that the appointment was also supported by the Commander in Chief.[18]

The newly minted Brigadier General Williams probably breathed a sigh of relief. It had been seven months since Greene had submitted his initial letter of recommendation, and the new Brigadier had learned some lessons about parliamentary procedures along the way. It had taken some time, but Williams would soon receive a letter from his mentor, Nathanael Greene addressed to "My Dear General."[19] It must have been a very gratifying experience to have been so honored.

★ ★ ★ ★ ★

Home to Maryland

Williams soon left Philadelphia for Maryland to attend to his military duties and personal affairs. He traveled first to Baltimore, which he found "dull and gloomy" because the merchants were suffering from a loss of business caused by the war. Then he proceeded to Annapolis, where society was more brilliant, more like Philadelphia.[20]

When he reached Annapolis, a very happy Otho Williams wrote to Nathanael Greene to thank him for supporting his promotion,[21] and the next day, he wrote a similar letter of thanks to Commander-in-Chief Washington. He also informed Washington that he planned to remain in Maryland until Greene called him back to the South, and that he intended to help obtain support for the southern army from the Maryland legislature.[22]

Washington answered graciously on July 9th that Williams' promotion had been to "...your Merit more than any Interest of mine."[23]

Williams carefully preserved his Brigadier General's Commission, signed by John Hanson, President of Congress and Benjamin Lincoln, Secretary of war, "to take rank from May 9th, 1782."[24] Today, it is a part of the Otho Holland Williams Papers at the Maryland Historical Society.

Williams was also pleased that he sensed favorable public support for the Southern army and its Commander Nathanael Greene. He proudly informed his Commanding Officer that:

> To say what all sorts of people in all places think and how they speak of the Southern Army and its commander (as far as I

> *have comprehended opinions) would be to express the greatest applause that men can deserve...*[25]

While Williams and his friends and were pleased by his promotion, there were a number of ambitious Colonels who protested because they considered themselves senior to him and therefore more deserving of promotion to Brigadier. The basis for their objection was that, while Williams was the most senior Marylander available for the promotion to command Maryland troops, they were senior to him when viewed from the perspective of the entire Army, not just Maryland's officers.

General Nathanael Greene was drawn into the controversy, responding to a disgruntled Colonel Charles Cotesworth Pinckney of South Carolina that: "... I have very great respect for Col Williams but I should never have recommended him for promotion to the prejudice of one officer much more 18 or 20."[26]

Greene stood by his friend Williams, and assured officers such as Pinckney who claimed offense that he had acted with propriety. He also did what he could to assuage his friend Williams' concerns:

> *I wrote you some time past in answer to your letter of the first of June. In that letter I congratulated you upon your promotion from which I felt a singular happiness; but observed at the same time, that the manner was more honorable to you than satisfactory to the Colonels of the Army. ... The love of rank is so strong a principle in the breast of a soldier that he who has a right to promotion will never admit another over his head willingly upon a principle of merit. You are not to expect therefore that every body will subscribe to the justice of your promotion. You must content your self with having obtained it; and that no man is without his enemies but a fool...*[27]

Greene ended this show of support for his friend Williams with some personal notes that showed, once again, the interest that Mrs. Greene took in the newly-minted Brigadier, noting that "Mrs. Greene says you must get married, that you owe it to society, and that your own happiness depends on it." Greene closed this letter by referring to himself as Williams' "affectionate friend."[28]

Personal Matters and Health

Williams requested that Greene allow him to remain in Maryland to assist General William Smallwood with recruiting, and also informed his Commander of his intention to make a "short visit" to his home in the western part of the state.[29] The subject of Williams' health was being mentioned frequently during these first months back in Maryland, and it would become an increasingly frequent topic in his correspondence for the remainder of his life. Writing to General William Smallwood from Hagerstown, Maryland on July 20th, Williams mentioned that he had not fully recovered from an illness he had experienced in Baltimore.[30] Two days later, he wrote to Nathanael Greene that he was suffering from rheumatism, and was going to Bath, Virginia "to get rid of it."[31] Mrs. Nathanael Greene sent word by her husband from South Carolina that rheumatism was a curse on Williams because of the "tyranny he has shown to some of the fair ladies."[32]

By October 15th, a correspondent in Philadelphia commented that he was glad that Williams' health was better.[33] Williams was only thirty-three years old when he was promoted to Brigadier General, and yet this young man was beset by persistent concerns with his health. Clearly, his war service had sapped much of the strength of his once-vigorous body.

During his time in the army, Williams had often dreamed of being home in Maryland, living the rural lifestyle that he had enjoyed in his youth. Now that he was home, he began to pursue that long-cherished dream. He purchased 412 acres in "Monacacy Manor" from the State of Maryland on September 10th, 1782,[34] and began to work on arrangements to operate his farms. His brother Elie wrote from Hagerstown to Otho in Frederick that slaves were for sale near Frederick.[35]

Williams was trapped in the odious culture of his time and place, in which many of his fellow citizens condoned slavery. His conscience was active enough to point out that his father had never owned slaves, and that he personally believed in a gradual movement toward full emancipation. Although he felt that slavery was "a mortal sin entailed on us by our forefathers," he convinced himself that he was justified in buying slaves more than he was in selling, because he felt that he could assure good treatment under his ownership. His internal contradictions were revealed in his criticism of some who, "from purest humanity," had freed their slaves and given liberty to a number of "ignorant ill disposed barbarians," who have injured society more than they have helped it.[36]

It is unpleasant to contemplate the horrid fact that many of our forefathers who fought for independence from Great Britain owned slaves, and lived in a society with strong prejudices.

★ ★ ★ ★ ★

Support for Veterans

Williams felt a sense of obligation to his comrades-in-arms, and played an active role in presenting their case to the authorities. George Washington had commended him for his intention to work with the Maryland legislature on behalf of "the Sick and Wounded Soldiery of your Line,"[37] and Williams stood ready to use his pen and his influence in support of that cause.

On June 2nd, 1782, he wrote to the General Assembly of Maryland on behalf of the entire soldiery of Maryland, and paid particular attention to the plight of the men who had been disabled in the service. Congress had established a corps of invalids at the national level, but Williams told his state's legislature that there were many problems with that approach, among them that members had to be away from their home state to serve in that corps, and that they were required to serve under officers who did not know them, and who were therefore not as concerned with their ease and comfort as their own Maryland officers would be. Williams noted that a number of men had chosen begging over serving in the Continental Army's Invalid Corps, and some were becoming a nuisance to society. Williams requested that the State form its own Invalid Corps and suggested that it could serve as a defense force and a training school for new recruits.[38]

The legislature responded. On Saturday, June 8th, the General Assembly noted that a memorial had been submitted by Generals Smallwood and Williams, Colonel Gunby and others recommending the establishment of an invalid corps. The memorial was referred to the Maryland Delegates at the Continental Congress, who were requested to seek the legislature's instructions.[39]

Though he was dealing with a variety of ailments, Williams wrote an elegant statement supporting the troops of the Maryland Line to the Governor of Maryland on July 7th, 1782. Williams noted that the Maryland regiments were:

> ...the only troops who have constantly kept the field under every difficulty, since the spring of 1780, without a shilling of pay real or nominal, with out a supply of clothing at any time equal to their necessities; and without any other subsistence

> than what, with the assistance of the rest of the army, they have occasionally collected by force of arms, in a country once entirely in subjugation, and in a very great degree attached to the enemy. No distresses, no dangers have ever shaken the firmness of their spirits, nor induced them to swerve from their duty. They have a long time patiently suffered the neglect of their country, not without murmuring, it is true, but without mutiny or disaffection to a cause which they are endeavoring to maintain with their blood...[40]

The subsequent actions of the Maryland Government are testimony to Williams' influence. Just nine days after he sent this letter to the Governor, the Maryland Council gave urgent directions to raise funds to support the Maryland troops who were serving with Greene.[41]

On the same date, the Council of Maryland noted that "We have also undertaken to pay £32.10.0 for 50 Hats purchased for the Invalids, to enable them to march to Frederick Town, to act as a Guard over the Prisoners there."[42] Later in the year, on November 2nd, the Council directed their Commanding Officer at Annapolis to order a specific list of 40 Invalids "to march without Delay to Frederick Town, to guard the British Prisoners, where they may render essential Service."[43]

Maryland had encountered as many difficulties as any other state in providing pay, supplies and support to their troops in the field during the Revolution. The record of the Maryland troops during the War was one of distinction, and their state government at least made an honest, if not always effective, effort to acknowledge their service. As the war was slowly coming to its conclusion, Nathanael Greene wrote to the Governor of Maryland that he was very pleased "to hear of the generous measures which this State is pursuing for rewarding that band of veterans who have been the greatest support of our southern operations."[44]

The Journals of the Maryland Senate, General Assembly, and Governor's Council have many entries that show a government struggling, in a time when resources were strained, to show proper support for the men in the field. They disbursed funds, purchased clothing, and made some provisions for the sick and wounded. They grappled often with the difficult problem of compensating the officers and soldiers for the loss in the value of their pay due to rampant inflation. Finally, the state set aside land west of Fort Cumberland to be laid out in lots, and in 1788, each officer was granted four lots of fifty acres each, and each soldier received one fifty acre lot.[45]

Many Maryland officers deserve credit for their efforts to bring the plight of their troops to the attention of the governor and legislature. Otho Williams remained a staunch advocate for Maryland's veterans for the rest of his life.

Army Matters

While Williams tended to his personal affairs and to the recruiting service in Maryland, he also made sure that George Washington and Nathanael Greene knew that he would like to have an active command with the army. However, he found that there were no openings for Brigadiers because the size of the northern and southern armies was small and the pace of military operations was slow.

When he first arrived home, Williams had offered his services to Washington, and had been told that "… the present inactive State of Affairs does not render your presence here necessary…" although the Commander-in-Chief emphasized that he would be pleased to have Williams with him if circumstances changed, and if a transfer could be done "with propriety."[46] Greene wrote a friendly letter to Williams on November 12th, 1782, and included the news that he would be happy to have him back in the field, but that he had "…no command for even the officers now with him." Greene also reported that most of the Maryland and Pennsylvania troops would be going home soon, with each group leaving behind only one regiment to continue to serve with the southern army.[47]

Williams visited army headquarters in Newburgh, New York in November, 1782,[48] and he stopped off in Philadelphia on his way home in December, where he talked with Secretary of War Benjamin Lincoln about a "legion plan for cavalry."[49] Williams followed up his discussions with Lincoln by writing to George Washington that he would be "glad to be appointed" to lead that unit.[50] The Commander-in-Chief replied thoughtfully that "…in case any arrangement should take place, by which a command suitable to your rank can be conferred on you without injury to the feelings of other Gentlemen, it will be extremely satisfactory to me."[51]

To keep all his options open, Williams also continued to correspond with Nathanael Greene about a possible return to active service with the Southern army. The British had evacuated Charleston on December 14th, 1782, and Greene was living comfortably in Governor Rutledge's "very elegant" house in Charleston when he wrote to Williams on January 8th, 1783. Greene noted that the imminent departure of Brigadier General Mordecai Gist and the illness of Brigadier General Anthony Wayne might require that Williams be ordered to rejoin the Southern army.[52] However, by the time he received this letter, Williams was well along in his plan to retire from the army and assume a significant position in the civilian world.

★ ★ ★ ★ ★

Retirement from the Army

When Greene was writing his letter of January 8th, 1783 from Charleston, he did not know that Williams had skillfully negotiated a lucrative position with the government of his home state. Two days before Greene wrote that letter, Williams was appointed by the State of Maryland to the post of Naval Officer of the Port of Baltimore, with responsibilities that involved the collection of customs duties for goods passing through the port. Some people in Maryland had opposed his receiving such a "highly esteemed" appointment, and tried to block him by insisting that he could not hold that post while he was still on active duty in the Army. The Governor's Council cleared the way for Williams to accept the post when it determined that a retired officer on half pay could hold the Office of Naval Officer of the Port.[53] All Williams had to do now was to resign from the Army.

Having tried for over a year find a suitable post with the army, Williams petitioned the War Office on January 15th, 1783 to allow him to retire and accept the Naval Officer position. He injected a sense of urgency by emphasizing that there were ships that wanted to leave Baltimore harbor, but they could not do so until the new Naval Officer of the Port arrived.[54] Assistant Secretary of War William Jackson wrote to the President of Congress the same day, recommending that Williams should be allowed to retire from the Army, with the understanding that Congress would allow him to retire with "...the emoluments allowed to supernumerary officers."[55] Congress approved the recommendation the next day,[56] and Jackson forwarded a copy of their resolution to Williams on January 20th, 1783.[57] By then, Williams had hurried on to Baltimore to assume the duties of Collector of the Port, accepting the commission in a letter to Governor Paca on January 20th, the same day that Jackson sent him Congress's resolution.[58]

Williams confided in his friend Dr. Philip Thomas of Frederick, Maryland that he had arranged his half-pay status with Congress during a visit to Philadelphia before his appointment to the Naval Officer position by Maryland. He had deftly balanced his appointment to a state position with his military responsibilities, and had come to a solution that was very much in his favor. He would have a prestigious and financially rewarding position on the payroll of the state of Maryland, and he would receive the half-pay of a retired Brigadier General of the Continental Army.[59]

Nathanael Greene would soon write to congratulate his friend on his "easy competency" as Naval Officer of Baltimore.[60]

Naval Officer of the Port of Baltimore

Williams' first days in his new position were a little overwhelming, as he found the office in considerable disarray. The Deputy Naval Officer treated him with disrespect, and turned documents over to him only very reluctantly. Furthermore, Williams was beset by many applicants for positions on his staff.

Nonetheless, Williams dove headlong into the challenge, and his penchant for administrative work helped him to bring a sense of order to the office fairly quickly. He was also determined to build a capable office staff, starting with the appointment of a capable assistant.[61] [62]

By the Spring of 1783, Williams was enmeshed in all aspects of the office, and he called upon Samuel Chase, a local attorney who had signed of the Declaration of Independence and would become a future Associate Justice of the United States Supreme Court, to help him clarify the laws relating to customs duties, and to seek amendments where appropriate. Always a stickler for precision, Williams wanted clear guidelines for a process that had apparently been handled fairly loosely in the past.

Otho Williams identified many difficulties with the existing laws for Chase, including the fact that many procedures had not been officially published but were known only to the officers executing them. Ship captains claimed that other ports only required them to pay duties on goods that they put ashore, while Baltimore was charging fees for all the goods on board. The law specified the percentage that was to be charged, but was not clear about what the percentage applied to. Williams had made it a practice not to charge duties on goods that had been produced in the United States, but sought official approval for that approach. Williams also sought Chase's support for retaining the power of the Collector's office if the General Assembly chose to create an additional office for collection of import duties.[63]

In this first year in office, Williams learned that cash flow was an important consideration in the execution of his responsibilities. Ship captains and others could delay their payments for several months, but the State could call for funds whenever it was deemed appropriate. There is a sense of panic in his private correspondence in the early spring of 1783 when he learned that he was short of the funds required to pay his obligations to the State.

He had to call upon old friends like "Light Horse Harry" Lee for loans that would let him pay what he owed, noting that he had "…only ten days to pay the balance…," and that he wished to do everything possible to avoid the "…mortification of not paying."[64] Lee responded with a firm show of support, assuring his friend that he would do whatever was necessary so that Williams would not have to suffer the embarrassment of being in arrears to the state.[65]

Formation of the Society of the Cincinnati

On May 10th, 1783, Major General Henry Knox called together all the General Officers who remained with the army on the Hudson River, plus one officer from each regiment to discuss the establishment of a hereditary organization to be called the Society of the Cincinnati,[66] which was to be comprised of the officers of the Continental Army and their descendants. These officers had endured common hardships and common dangers for many years. They had lost comrades to sickness and combat; shed their own blood; and endured the rigors together of life in camp, on the march, and in battle in what had often seemed an unending and unwinnable struggle. The statement of organizational purpose embodied these sentiments:

> …as the mutual friendships which have been formed under the pressure of common danger, and, in many instances, cemented by the blood of the parties, the officers of the American Army do, hereby, in the most solemn manner, associate, constitute and combine themselves into one Society of Friends, to endure as long as they shall endure, or any of their eldest male posterity…[67]

It was logical that these soldiers would want to maintain bonds of friendship in civilian life, but the establishment of the organization set off alarm bells for some civilian leaders who felt they had just been freed from the British aristocracy, and they didn't want to be ruled by another that would be home grown in America. Although this controversy was a topic of lively debate during the formative years of the Society, soldiers like Otho Holland Williams supported the organization and participated in its activities.

In November, 1783, six months after General Knox's meeting in New York, Maryland's senior officer, Major General William Smallwood published a notice in the Maryland Gazette that called on all "officers of the Maryland Line, upon the present and half-pay establishments" to meet in Annapolis on November 20th, where "several matters very interesting to the line will be communicated." Otho Williams was elected to be the acting Chairman of the meeting, when the two Maryland officers who were senior to him, Major General William Smallwood and Brigadier General Mordecai Gist were unable to attend. The meeting established the Society in Maryland, and elected Smallwood to be President, Gist to be Vice President, and Brigadier General Otho Williams to be Secretary. They also named Smallwood, Williams, Governor William Paca, and Colonel Nathan Ramsay as delegates to the national society meeting,[68] which was to be held in Philadelphia on the first Monday in May, 1784.[69]

End of the War

Ever since Cornwallis' surrender at Yorktown in October 1781, it had been clear that the British government no longer had the stomach to keep on fighting. Negotiations dragged on, and the American Army had to keep an eye on the British troops who remained in the states, but the final result seemed inevitable.

The British had evacuated Charleston in December, 1782, and by the summer of 1783, there was no longer any need for Maryland troops in the south. In late July of that year, Brigadier General Mordecai Gist and the last 500 men of the Maryland Line from the Southern Army landed at Annapolis. From there, they marched to Baltimore, where they arrived on July 27th.[70]

These fine troops came home with the praises of their thankful Commanding General ringing in their ears. Before they left for home, Greene had written Maryland Governor Paca that he would be "...wanting in gratitude not to acknowledge the singular merit and the importance of their services. They have spilt their blood freely in the service of their country, and have faced every danger and difficulty without a murmur or complaint."

Greene then gave special notice to his former Adjutant General:

> *I beg leave to recommend Colonel Williams, who has been at the head of your Line, to the particular notice of your State, as an officer of great merit and good conduct.*"[71]

Greene himself then began his own journey north, arriving in Annapolis on September 25th. He moved on to Baltimore, where he noted in his diary that "Here I had the pleasure of meeting two of my old officers, General Williams and Colonel Howard. The pleasure of meeting is easier felt than described."[72]

George Washington's Farewell

The Continental Congress was meeting in Annapolis at the end of 1783, providing this small state the singular honor of hosting the session where the Commander-in-Chief, George Washington, resigned his commission just before Christmas that year. This event is one of the most important moments in the history of the United States of America, for the victorious warrior relinquished all his power to the representatives of the people, and returned to private life. If an intensely ambitious man like Napoleon Bonapante or Charles Lee or Benedict Arnold had commanded the American armies, our new republic could conceivably have been nipped in the bud, and instead may have become a military dictatorship.

Brigadier General Otho Holland Williams was an active participant in the events leading up to the resignation ceremony. He had the honor to present an address to Washington on behalf of the inhabitants of Baltimore when the Commander-in-Chief arrived in the city,[73] and then he followed the great man to Annapolis, where he was present for many of the dinners, dances and celebrations that marked the events

General Washington returned his commission to Congress at the Maryland State House in Annapolis on December 23rd, 1783, and then rode to Mount Vernon to enjoy his first Christmas at home in nine years.[74] Like their Commander-in-Chief, Otho Williams and his comrades looked forward to the joys of life in a nation without war.

Williams had taken up arms over eight-and-a-half years earlier, as a twenty-six year old Lieutenant in a Maryland Rifle Company. He had served with distinction in many capacities, earned the respect of men like George Washington and Nathanael Greene, and won promotion to Brigadier General at age thirty-three. His future in the peacetime world would be built on the foundation of an outstanding military reputation and a well-cultivated network of influential friends.

1 General Greene's Orders. 1 February, 1782. *Greene's Papers*. 10:291.
2 Greene, Nathanael. Letter to Jeremiah Wadsworth. Written at Head Quarters Pon Pon, S.C. February 9th, 1782. *Greene's Papers*. 10:339.
3 Greene, Nathanael. Letter to Colonel Otho H. Williams. Written at Camp, Pon Pon, South Carolina, February 9th, 1782. *Greene Papers*. 10:341-342.
4 Williams, Otho Holland. Letter to Nathanael Greene. Written at Salisbury, N.C. 23rd February, 1782. *Greene Papers*. 10:403-404.
5 Williams, Otho Holland. Letter to Nathanael Greene. Written at Richmond, Va. 12 March, 1782. *Greene Papers*. 10:493.
6 Greene, Nathanael. Letter to Otho Holland Williams. Written at Camp Pon Pon, S.C. February 9, 1781. *Greene Papers*. 10:341.
7 Greene, Nathanael. Letter to Thomas McKean, President of Congress. Written at High Hills of the Santee. 30 October, 1781. *Greene Papers*. 9:496.
8 Greene, Nathanael. Letter to George Washington. Written at the High Hills of the Santee, South Carolina. October 30, 1781. *Greene Papers*. 9:497-498. (Also in the Washington Papers.)
9 Hanson, John. Letter to Philip Thomas. January 29, 1782. Footnote 3. Library of Congress. *Letters of Delegates to Congress: Volume 18. March 1, 1781 - August 31, 1781.* Page 315. Library of Congress web site.
10 Washington, George. Letter to the Continental Congress. December 4, 1781. *Washington Papers*.
11 Washington, George. Letter to Nathanael Greene. December 15, 1781. *Washington Papers*.
12 Pierce, William, Jr. Letter to Nathanael Greene. Written at Philadelphia. October 24th, 1781. *Greene Papers*. 9:475.
13 Hanson, John. Letter to Philip Thomas. January 29, 1782. Footnote 3. Library of Congress. *Letters of Delegates to Congress: Volume 18. March 1, 1781 - August 31, 1781.* John Hanson to Philip Thomas. Page 315. Library of Congress web site.
14 Williams, Otho Holland. Letter to Elie Williams. Written at High Hills of Santee. November 10, 1781. *Williams Papers*. Part 1/8. (Item # 142.)
15 Greene, Nathanael. Letter to His Excellency John Hanson, Esq., President of Congress. Written at Head Quarters, Ponpon, South Carolina. February 10, 1782. U.S. Continental Congress Papers, Manuscript Division, Library of Congress. Microfilm 22,339, Reel No. 175. Item No. 155, II, Folio 417. Photocopy in the possession of the author was obtained from the Library of Congress. This letter is mentioned in Note 2 for the May 8, 1782 entry in the Journals of the Continental Congress.
16 Journals of the Continental Congress. Volume 22. P. 143. Friday, March 22, 1782.
17 Hanson, John. Letter to Philip Thomas. Written at Philadelphia. April 27, 1782. Letters of Delegates to Congress: Volume 18. March 1, 1781 - August 31, 1781. Pp. 474-475.
18 Journals of the Continental Congress. Vol. 22. P. 251-52. Thursday, May 9th, 1782.
19 Greene, Nathanael. Letter to Otho Holland Williams. September 17th 1782. Written at Head Quarters Ashley River. *Greene Papers*. 11:669.
20 Williams, Otho Holland. Letter to Nathanael Greene. Written at Annapolis, Maryland. June 1, 1782. *Williams Papers*. Part 1/8. (Item 152.)
21 Ibid.
22 Williams, Otho Holland. Letter to George Washington. Written at Annapolis, Maryland. June 2, 1782. *Williams Papers*. Part 1/8. (Iitem 153.)
23 "From George Washington to Otho Holland Williams, 10 July 1782," Founders Online, National Archives (http://founders.archives.gov/documents/Washington/99-01-02-08898 [last update: 2015-03-20]). Source: this is an Early Access document from The Papers of George Washington. IT IS NOT AN AUTHORITATIVE FINAL. *Williams Papers*. Part 1/8. (Item 157.)
24 Brigadier General's Commission of Otho Holland Williams. *Williams Papers*. Part 1/8. (Item 151.)
25 Williams, Otho Holland. Letter to Nathanael Greene. 1st June 1782. Written at Annapolis. *Greene Papers*. 11:279.
26 Greene, Nathanael. Letter to Charles C. Pinckney. June 27, 2782. Written at "Head Quarters (near Bacon's Bridge, S.C.) *Greene Papers* 11:376.
27 Greene, Nathanael. Letter to Otho Holland Williams. September 17th 1782. Written at "Head Quarters Ashley River. *Greene Papers*. 11:669.
28 Ibid. 669;671.
29 Williams, Otho Holland. Letter to Nathanael Greene. Written at Annapolis, Maryland. June 1, 1782. *Williams Papers*. Part 1/8. (Item#152.)
30 Williams, Otho Holland. Letter to William Smallwood. Written at Hagerstown, Maryland. July 20, 1782. *Williams Papers*. Part 1/8. Item # 158.

31 Williams, Otho Holland. Letter to Nathanael Greene. Written at Hagerstown, Maryland. July 22, 1782. *Williams Papers*. Part 1/8. (Item #159.)
32 Greene, Nathanael. Letter to Otho Holland Williams. Written at Ashley River, North Carolina. November 12, 1782. *Williams Papers*. Part 1/8. (Item #167.)
33 Pettit, Charles (Assistant Quartermaster General). Letter to Otho Holland Williams. Written at Philadelphia. October 15, 1782. *Williams Papers*. Part 1/8. (Item #165.)
34 Williams, Otho. To the State of Maryland. September 10, 1782. *Williams Papers*. Part 1/8. (Item # 163); Monocacy Manor" was confiscated from its Loyalist owners by the State of Maryland and set aside to be sold for certificates that were granted to Maryland' Continental troops. (See Archives of Maryland; Kilty's Land-Holder's Assistant, and Land-Office Guide, Volume 73, page 336.) Williams paid principal and interest to the State on these properties. He was granted full possession of lots #31 and #32 in April 1787. See *Williams Papers*. Part 3/8. Transfers of Land from State to Otho Holland Williams, #385 and #386 and Williams' letter to Dr, Philip Thomas, March 29, 1788, #398.
35 Williams, Elie. Letter to Otho Holland Williams. Written at Hagerstown, Maryland. October 26, 1782. *Williams Papers*. Part 1/8. (Item #166.)
36 Williams, Otho Holland. Letter to William Lewis. Written at Baltimore, June 15, 1786. *Williams Papers*. Part 3/8. (Item #352.)
37 "From George Washington to Otho Holland Williams, 10 July 1782," Founders Online, National Archives (http://founders.archives.gov/documents/Washington/99-01-02-08898 [last update: 2015-03-20]). Source: this is an Early Access document from The Papers of George Washington. IT IS NOT AN AUTHORITATIVE FINAL VERSION.
38 Williams, Otho Holland. Address to the General Assembly of Maryland. June 3, 1782. *Williams Papers*. Part 1/8. (Item 154.)
39 Votes and Proceedings of the General Assembly of Maryland. MSA SC M 3196, Page 1438. Saturday, June 8, 1782.
40 Williams, Otho Holland. Letter to Maryland Governor Thomas Sim Lee. July 7, 1782. *Williams Papers*. Part 1/8. (Item 156.) This letter is reproduced in Scharf, *Maryland*. Pp. 486-487.
41 Journal and Correspondence of the Council of Maryland, 1781-1784. Volume 48, Page 215. July 16 Liber No. 78, page 359. Archives of Maryland Online.
42 Ibid.
43 Journal and Correspondence of the Council of Maryland, 1781-1784. Volume 48, P. 296. November 2. , Liber No. 78. P. 359. Archives of Maryland Online.
44 Greene, Nathanael. Letter to Governor Paca of Maryland. Written at Annapolis, September 27, 1783. Reproduced in full in Scharf, *Maryland*. Pp. 493-494.
45 Scharf, *Maryland*. P. 507.
46 "From George Washington to Otho Holland Williams, 10 July 1782," Founders Online, National Archives (http://founders.archives.gov/documents/Washington/99-01-02-08898 [last update: 2015-03-20]). Source: this is an Early Access document from The Papers of George Washington. IT IS NOT AN AUTHORITATIVE FINAL VERSION. Also in *Williams Papers*. Part 1 of 8. (Item #157.)
47 Greene, Nathanael. Letter to Otho Holland Williams. Written at Ashley River, South Carolina. November 12, 1782. *Williams Papers*. Part 1/8. (Item #167.)
48 Williams' letter to Baron Von Steuben of November 28, 1781, was written at "Camp Newbergh, N.Y." *Williams Papers*. Part 1/8. (Item #168.)
49 Williams, Otho Holland. Letter to George Washington. Written at Philadelphia, January 1, 1783. *Williams Papers*. Part 2/8. (Item #173.)
50 Williams, Otho Holland. Letter to George Washington. Written at Philadelphia, January 1, 1783. *Williams Papers*. 2/8. (Item #174.)
51 Washington, George. Letter to Otho Holland Williams. January 12, 1783. *Washington Papers*.
52 Greene, Nathanael. Letter to Otho Holland Williams. Written at Charleston, South Carolina. January 8, 1783. *Williams Papers*. Part 2/8. (Item #179.)
53 Journal and Correspondence of the Council of Maryland, 1781-1784. Volume 48, Page 338; Williams' Commission as Naval Officer, 4th District, Baltimore County is preserved in the *Williams Papers*. Part 2/8. (Item # 176.)
54 Williams, Otho Holland. Letter to Assistant Secretary of War William Jackson. Written at Philadelphia, January 15, 1783. *Williams Papers*. Part 2/8. (Item #184.)
55 Jackson, William (Major.) Letter to the President of Congress (Elias Boudinot.) Written at Philadelphia, January 15, 1783. *Williams Papers*. Part 2/8. (Item #183.)
56 Journals of the Continental Congress, Library of Congress edition, January 16, 1783. vol. XXIV, January 1 - August 29, 1783. p. 47. Cited in the *Williams Papers*. Part 2/8. (Item # 185.)
57 Jackson, William. War Office. Letter to Otho Holland Williams. Written at Philadelphia, January 20, 1783. *Williams Papers*. Part 2 /8. (Item #187.)
58 William, Otho Holland. Letter to Governor William Paca. Written at Baltimore, January 20, 1783. *Williams Papers*. Part 2/8. (Item #188.)

59 On May 15, 1783, Williams attended a meeting of the Maryland officers who were on half-pay. He wrote and signed their "Resolution of Acceptance," in which they accepted a lump sum payment of five years' pay in lieu of half-pay for life. (Minutes of Meeting of Half-Pay Officers. Annapolis. May 15, 1783. *Williams Papers*. Part 2/8. (Item # 206.)

60 Greene, Nathanael. Letter to Otho Holland Williams. Written at Charleston, South Carolina, July 2,, 1783. *Williams Papers*. Part 2/8. (Item #214.)

61 Williams, Otho Holland. Letter to Dr. Philip Thomas. Written at Baltimore, February 3, 1783. *Williams Papers*. Part 2/8. (Item # 191.)

62 Williams selected Robert Denny, formerly a Lieutenant in the 5th Maryland Regiment, as his Assistant. Denny worked as Williams' Assistant in the Collector's Office for several years, and Williams later recommended him to Secretary of the Treasury Alexander Hamilton for the position of Collector of Annapolis. (Williams letter to Alexander Hamilton, written at Ceresville, Frederick County, July 6, 1793. *Williams Papers*. Part5/8. (Item #805.)

63 Williams, Otho Holland. Letter to Samuel Chase. Written at Baltimore, May 21, 1783. *Williams Papers*. Part 2/8. (Item #208.)

64 Williams, Otho Holland. Letter to Col. Henry Lee, Jr. Written at Baltimore, April 10, 1784. *Williams Papers*. Part 2/8. (Item #245.)

65 Lee, Henry, Jr. Letter to Otho Holland Williams. Written at Stratford, Virginia, April 17, 1784. *Williams Papers* Part 2/8. (Item #247.)

66 Scharf, *Maryland*. P. 501.

67 Society of the Cincinnati. *Register of the Society of the Cincinnati of Maryland. Brought Down to February 22, 1897*. (hereafter Society of the Cincinnati, *Register*.) Published by Order of the Society. Press of A. Horn & Company. Baltimore. 1897. P. 3.

68 State Society of the Cincinnati, Annapolis, November 21, 22, 1783. *Williams Papers*. Part 2/8. (Item #228.) This story is also described in Scharf, Maryland. Pp. 501-502.

69 Washington, George. Letter to Henry Knox. Written at Mount Vernon. February 20, 1784. *Washington Papers*.

70 Scharf, *Maryland*. P. 492.

71 Greene, Nathanael. Letter to Governor Paca of Maryland. June or July, 1783. Cited in Scharf, *Maryland*. P. 492.

72 Greene, Nathanael. Diary entries for September, October, 1783. Cited in Scharf *Maryland*. P. 493.

73 Williams, Otho Holland. Address to General Washington. December 18, 1783. *Williams Papers*. Part 2/8. (Item #231.)

74 Scharf, *Maryland* 499-501.

CHAPTER 13

AFTER THE WAR.

Building a Civilian Life

Most soldiers spend a considerable part of their leisure moments thinking about home, and Otho Holland Williams was certainly no exception. His private correspondence during the war contains many touching references to the home of his youth and the joys of family life. Osmond Tiffany, an early chronicler of Williams' life, quoted a particularly touching letter to his brother:

> *My disposition is wholly domestic; my feelings flow with excess of tenderness whenever I indulge the thoughts of home. There I will be as soon as I can quit the field with honor...*[1]

Williams went on to say that when he arrived home:

> *Then will I take you and my fond sisters in my arms, and live with you in peace.*[2]

As George Washington traveled home to Mount Vernon after he resigned his commission in Annapolis, Otho Holland Williams could feel confident about his own prospects for a successful civilian career. He had obtained a lucrative position as Naval Officer of the Port of Baltimore (sometimes referred to as the "Collector" of the port), and he was also receiving half-pay as a retired Brigadier General of the Continental Army. He had gained the means to begin to accumulate land and establish farms in the western part of his home state, and he was looking for further opportunities to expand his holdings.

Williams also took a keen interest in horses and racing, and he had a sharp eye for well-bred animals. He would boast one day that he owned "the finest stud in America,"[3] and he would even offer its services to George Washington,[4] who also loved owning, riding, and breeding horses.

When he returned from the army, Otho Williams had proven his effectiveness as a senior military officer, and he had a strong network of influential friends to advance his civilian career. His duties at the Port of Baltimore gave him an important role in the business affairs of a city that would grow rapidly after the war. Reflective of the dynamism of the time, Williams was Collector of the Port when the first ship with goods from China arrived in Baltimore on August 9th, 1785. John O'Donnell, the owner of the vessel that brought these goods, named a section of Baltimore "Canton" in honor of this event.[5] Today, Canton is a waterfront community, popular with tourists and residents for its restaurants and ambience.

Williams played a prominent role in the affairs of Baltimore during these post-war years along with other veterans of the Continental Army, including Samuel Smith, and John Eager Howard. Williams and Howard were particularly close. They traveled together, dined together, and loaned each other money.[6] Friendships with men like Howard and Smith were important to Otho Williams, much as former military men have always valued their relationships with fellow veterans. Williams, Howard, and Smith were all prominent former army officers who had shared common hardships during the war, and it was natural for them to carry their relationships into their commercial activities - Smith as a prominent merchant, Howard as a large Baltimore City landholder and real estate developer, and Williams in a prominent government role associated with the business of the city. With all that, Williams was not an easy person to get to know. While he appeared to be very pleasant in most situations, he was apparently capable of expressing his opinions very directly for individuals that he found reason not to hold in high regard. Light Horse Harry Lee described these aspects of Williams' personality in his Memoirs:

> *His countenance was expressive, and the faithful index of his warm and honest heart. Pleasing in his address, he never failed to render himself acceptable, in whatever circle he moved, notwithstanding a sternness of character, which was sometimes manifested with too much asperity. He was cordial to his friends, but cold to all whose correctness in moral principle became questionable in his mind.*[7]

★ ★ ★ ★ ★

The Society of the Cincinnati

Having presided at the organizational meeting of the Maryland State Society of the Cincinnati at Annapolis on November 21st, 1783, Williams had also been chosen to attend the first meeting of the national society, in Philadelphia from May 4th-18th, 1784.[8] Williams traveled to the meeting with John Eager Howard.[9]

The national meeting elected him to a prestigious group that included Governor John Dickinson of Pennsylvania; Colonel Henry Lee of Virginia; Colonel W. S. Smith of New York; and General Henry Knox of Massachusetts to serve on a committee to review certain changes to the Society's charter,[10] which were part of the effort to make its elite and hereditary nature less objectionable to powerful critics such as Thomas Jefferson and John Adams, who worried that it would become the basis for a new aristocracy. The Society changed some provisions to make it more acceptable to the general public, and Williams participated actively as long as he lived.

This initial national meeting also elected Williams to serve as Assistant Secretary of the national Society, under the Secretary Henry Knox, a position that he held until 1787.

Williams participated actively in Society affairs, and was elected by the Maryland Society in 1784, 1787, and 1792 to attend the national meetings.[11] In 1792, he succeeded William Smallwood as President of the Society of the Cincinnati of Maryland, a post in which he served for the rest of his life. He valued the opportunity to maintain his bonds of friendship and comradery with his fellow veterans.

★ ★ ★ ★ ★

Williams' Social Life

Williams' correspondence has many references to his love life. He enjoyed female companionship, having a number of romantic attachments during and after the war. He could tell one of his correspondents that "Philadelphia is full of fine women,"[12] and he would write to his old mentor, Nathanael Greene that he had delayed writing until he could tell him certainly about the "outcome of a love affair." The affair ended badly, Williams reporting that he was suffering extreme misery because of the "perfidy" a young woman had shown him in dissolving the relationship.[13]

Williams spent a few happy-go-lucky days after the war with his friend John Eager Howard, writing on one occasion that he and Howard had yesterday "returned from an elegant party of pleasure."[14] Williams' health was never robust after the war, and his correspondence tells of many depressing days when he was suffering from one ailment or another. He noted on one occasion that he had stayed indoors and lived on tea and barley broth until a pleasant day, when his friend Howard had taken him on a ride in Howard's coach. At the end of the ride, Howard and Williams had joined "...a more beautiful and more agreeable party of ladies...," which also seemed to help revive Williams' spirits.[15] Williams' papers contain several letters from the enthusiastically amorous Thaddeus Kosciusko, who invariably provided his effusive observations on the women that he had encountered and sought similar information from Williams.

Many women seemed to feel solicitous about his well being as though they were caring for a beloved younger brother. For example, Mrs. Nathanael Greene dictated many personal notes to Williams which were included in her husband's letters to his friend.

★ ★ ★ ★ ★

Marriage and Family

Williams finally found an enduring relationship with Mary Smith, the second daughter of William Smith, a prominent member of the Baltimore business community. They were married in the First Presbyterian Church of Baltimore on October 18th, 1785,[16] and Williams soon wrote to his friend William Jackson that he was as happy as he had ever hoped he might be, and that "my Girl is all I thought her and all I wish her."[17] Home and family were important to Williams, and he now looked forward to the prospect of a happy family life.

When Williams had to go to Annapolis and leave Mary at home during the early months of their marriage, she wrote to him that "I am sure you will be proud when I say you are the first gentleman that I ever honord with a letter."[18] Soon, Williams and his friends began to call his wife "Polly."

On July 25th, 1786, Williams wrote excitedly to his good friend Dr. Philip Thomas that Polly had delivered their first child, a "fine, full-formed, healthy looking" boy named Robert. The first-time father wrote that fatherhood "opens a thousand new avenues to the Heart."[19]

While his own family was starting to grow, Williams endured the deaths of two of his sisters during these years. These were heavy losses for a former orphan who loved his family so dearly. On April 4th, 1787, he wrote that, while he was prosperous, he felt deeply the loss of his sister, Mercy (Mrs. John) Stull, and a year and a half later, on January 6th, 1789, he received the sad news that another sister (Priscilla) had died. The sisters were buried beside each other in a cemetery that overlooked the Potomac River near their childhood home.[20]

While Williams mourned the loss of his sisters, he had the joy of seeing his family grow steadily. Polly would have four more sons: William Elie, Edward Greene, Henry Lee and Otho Holland.[21] William Elie's middle name was for Otho's brother; Edward Greene's middle name was for his former Commander; Henry Lee was named for his wartime friend; and his fifth and youngest son was his own namesake. Williams was a loving father who placed importance on the education of his sons, and, rather than being aloof and distant, enjoyed playing with them.²²

His pride in his family and his deep attachment to his army friends are illustrated in his letter to Henry Lee announcing the naming of his third son:

> *Henry Lee Williams was born on the 23d day of December, in the first hour of the morning. I name my son with the approbation of his mother, not after the governor of Virginia, but after the man whose merit hath exalted him to that high office. I call him Henry Lee, to perpetuate in my family the remembrance of that friendship which originated at a time when the test of merit could not be mistaken; when the exertions for liberty were most necessary, and when the arms of freemen were most effectual. At an early period of our acquaintance you inspired me with esteem, and I have often been happy in occasions to believe that disposition reciprocal. One of those occasions 1 shall ever remember. The retreat of the southern army to Dan River, though now forgotten, was, in my estimation, one of the most masterly and fortunate manoeuvres of our beloved Greene. The ardour, activity, and enterprise with which you conducted the legion, then attached to the light infantry, which covered the retreat, and which I had the honour to command; the readiness with which you aided all my endeavours, and the soldierly sympathy which, in the most critical exigencies, you felt and expressed for me, as the responsible officer, left on my mind indelible impressions of gratitude and affection.*²³

Williamsport

A primary path to wealth in the early years of the Republic was investment in land, as described by George Washington in a letter to his stepson John Parke Custis from the dreary camp at Valley Forge in the winter of 1777/78:

> *…Land is the most Permanent Estate we can hold, & most likely to increase in its value.*²⁴

Like many of his generation, Otho Williams followed that path with investments in land in western Maryland, the home of his youth.

During the war, Williams had often thought longingly of the specific plot of land where he had grown up, where the Conococheague Creek flows into the Potomac River. Accordingly, he petitioned the Maryland legislature to permit him to establish a community there, and the enabling legislation was passed on January 20th, 1786:

> *That Thomas Hart, Thomas Brooke, Moses Rawlings, Richard Pindell and Alexander Clagett, or any three or more of them, be and are hereby appointed commissioners to survey a quantity of land, not exceeding one hundred and fifty acres, being part of a tract of land called Ross's Purchase, and another called Leeds, contiguous to the mouth of Conococheague creek, in Washington county, and the same, when surveyed, to lay out into lots, streets, lanes and alleys, (the main streets running east and west, or nearly so, not to be less than eighty feet wide, and the streets crossing the said main streets not to be less than sixty-six feet wide) to be erected into a town, and to be called and known by the name of Williams's Port.*[25]

With a new town named for him, the future must have seemed very promising. If Williamsport could grow and prosper, it would be a financial boon for Otho Williams. He would always be able to find time in his busy schedule to deal with the affairs of the town that he had founded.

★ ★ ★ ★ ★

Appointment as Collector of Baltimore by the Federal Government

When the Articles of Confederation were found inadequate to govern the new nation and a new Constitution was written to provide a stronger national government, Williams held decidedly pro-Federal-government sentiments, and he supported the ratification of the United States Constitution, submitting a letter to the Editor of the Maryland Journal and Baltimore Advertiser that proclaimed that the choice was either anarchy or peace, prosperity and tranquility.[26]

He also foresaw that his state position as Naval Officer of the Port of Baltimore would be replaced by a Federal Government position, and he moved quickly to be sure that he remained in his lucrative post. From January through April, 1789, he wrote to influential friends such as Henry Lee and Robert Morris to solicit their help in gaining the appointment,[27] and these friends helped him to contact others such as Lee's relative, Richard Henry Lee.[28]

Having mustered all the support that he could, Williams wrote directly to President Washington to apply for the Federal Post of Collector of the Port of Baltimore on April 18th, 1789, almost two weeks before Washington was even inaugurated President.[29]

Williams traveled to New York to influence the decision, and, while he was there, he wrote to the President's aide, David Humphreys, on May 12th, 1789 to present further arguments in support of his case.[30] He was back in Baltimore by June 7th, where he wrote of his interesting trip to New York, which had included a two-hour personal discussion with President Washington. He maintained that Washington was "anxious for repose and speaks to his private friends of his home and a quiet life in very moving terms."[31]

President Washington faced the enormous task of building an entire national government, one step at a time. The position of Collector of Baltimore was foremost in the mind of Otho Holland Williams, but it was a small matter in the grand scheme. Williams' request ground slowly through the halting machinery of a new government, slowed down even further when the President became seriously ill, and had to have what Williams' father-in-law William Smith called a large boil on his thigh lanced. Congressman Smith was valuable eyes and ears for Williams at the seat of government, and he provided advice on how best to win the appointment, including a recommendation that Williams write a flattering letter to Senator Richard Henry Lee and that he reach out to Maryland Senator Charles Carroll of Carrollton.[32]

The coveted appointment finally arrived in Baltimore on August 8th, and Williams responded with a note to Washington the next day, reporting that he had received the Commission and a copy of the legislation regarding the collection of duties.[33] His initial review of the new Federal Government's customs regulations convinced him that he would have a lighter workload than formerly, and he intended to enjoy more leisure.[34] However, by February, 1790, he was complaining of the amount of work and low pay.[35]

Williams had also added to his personal workload by accepting a commission as a Judge of the Criminal Court of Baltimore County in June, 1788.[36] The records of the State Council of Maryland from 1788 through 1792 reveal that Williams was commissioned as an Associate Justice on the Baltimore County Court of Oyer and Terminer[37] ten times, often serving with Samuel Chase, who was later an Associate Justice on the U.S. Supreme

Court. The purpose of these courts was to try criminal cases when the regular courts were not in session. The governing legislation stated that:

> *the great hazard and danger of keeping prisoners until they are brought to trial at the stated and fixed times of holding courts, as established by law, it is thought reasonable, for the more effectually expediting of justice, that the governor be invested with power to issue commissioners of oyer and terminer and gaol delivery*[38]

John Eager Howard was Governor of Maryland from 1788 through 1791, and chaired the Governor's Council which appointed Williams to this court during his governorship.[39] Williams and Howard maintained their friendship after the war, including when Howard was governor. Otho Williams and his wife hosted Governor and Mrs. Howard for dinner July 1st, 1789.[40]

While Williams may have accepted these judgeships in expectation that his work at the Port would lessen, he may have underestimated the impact on his life of his new direct superior, a dynamo Secretary of the Treasury named Alexander Hamilton. Hamilton was brilliant, and he loved immersing himself in an enormous amount of detail. He corresponded regularly with Williams about the business of the Port of Baltimore, and he delved deeply into its affairs. Hamilton was a stern task master. He wanted things done right, and he wanted them done quickly. He was an ardent and energetic advocate for the federal government, and he wanted his Port Collectors to be aggressive and effective in collecting federal revenue.

To make things even more challenging, Williams was dealing with an energetic superior at a time when everything was new – the government structure, the associated legislation, the operating procedures, and the people in the organization. Hamilton drove very hard to provide clear directions to Treasury officials like Williams, and he wanted strict obedience to the rules. He dug into virtually everything associated with the collection of customs duties, and no detail was too insignificant to escape the Secretary's attention. For example, Williams and Hamilton corresponded on the fact that Philadelphia and Baltimore had been measuring the alcoholic content of distilled spirits differently, because they were using different measuring instruments. The Secretary of the Treasury sent a thermometer and hydrometer to Williams that were to be used in measuring the strength (proof) of distilled spirits.[41]

While Williams' long-established routines were upset by the need to keep an aggressive new superior happy, the job of Collector of the Port was still an important one, and it gave Williams significant stature in the community. Duties for one two-month period during his tenure amounted to $110,000.[42] Annual imports were $3,500,000 in his last year in office, comprised of wine, molasses, sugar, salt, and European dry goods. Exports were $2,500,000 that year, comprised of grain, lumber, naval stores and re-exported imports.[43] Williams ran a busy office in a thriving port city.

In addition to collecting customs duties, Secretary Hamilton directed Williams to manage the work of fortifying the port.[44] In this capacity, he appointed him to be the Chief Artillery Officer of the Port and directed him to work with the Secretary of War to put Baltimore in a "state of defence."[45] Baltimore's defenses at that time included an earthen and timber fort known as Fort Whetstone, which would be renamed Fort McHenry in 1798, the site of the 1814 battle during which the Star Spangled Banner was written by Francis Scott Key.[46]

★ ★ ★ ★ ★

Williamsport Considered as a Candidate for the National Capital

Otho Holland Williams had high hopes that Williamsport might become the capital of the United States. He did his best to analyze all available information on the Federal Government's intentions for a national capital, and he characteristically sought to apply whatever influence he could to help drive the decision he wanted.

On August 23rd, 1789, his father-in-law, Congressmen William Smith, gave him a list of the cities that had received mention in Congress as possible sites of the future capital, including Trenton, New Jersey; Lancaster, York, Harrisburg, and Wright's Ferry, Pennsylvania; Fort Cumberland, Conococheague, Havre de Grace, Baltimore and Annapolis, Maryland; and Georgetown, Virginia.[47] While Williams was undoubtedly pleased that Conococheague was mentioned, he also must have realized from the length of the list that the competition was going to be formidable.

While Williams was trying to give Williamsport the best possible chance of becoming the national capital, there were alarming signs that his health continued to decline. When he attended church on Sunday, December 20th, 1789, he coughed and burst a small blood vessel, which caused a significant flow of blood. A doctor was sent for while Williams was "blubbering through my mouth and nose great quantities of warm, fresh blood from the lungs." He went home, where two doctors attended him, draining blood from his arm, or bleeding him.[48]

While he was struggling with his health, the process of selecting a national capital moved slowly forward. Seven months after he had burst a blood vessel in church, Congressman Smith gave him the best available information on the requirements that Congress was establishing for the location of the capitol. Congress had given President George Washington the power to make the selection.[49] Williams was at Sweet Springs, Virginia when he received this information, and made his plans to put Williamsport forward in the best possible light.

On October 20th, 1790, Williams wrote to his friend Dr. Philip Thomas that he understood that President Washington was conducting his tour of locations along the Potomac River, and he urged Thomas to get word to his brother Elie Williams, so that he could be present when the President visited Williamsport.[50]

The people of Washington County were very excited after the President's visit, and hoped that their little town would win the coveted honor. A local newspaper carried an optimistic announcement:

> *The Residence Law of Congress, and the late visit of our illustrious President, encourage the Citizens of Washington County to hope that the Seat of the Federal Government will be located therein* [signed] *An Inhabitant. October 26, 1790.*[51]

A few days after this newspaper announcement, Otho tried to further strengthen the case by writing directly to President Washington to describe the benefits of selecting Williamsport. He noted that he would be willing to give the government whatever land it would need for public buildings, although there was an acre that he wished to retain because his parents and some dear friends were buried there. He noted that the streets and alleys of Williamsport had been laid out much wider than was normal for the time, and that there was plenty of land in the vicinity, so that the town could accommodate significant growth. Finally, Williams revealed that he had been working to raise funds to build the federal district, and enclosed for the President a printed layout.[52]

But, sadly for Williams, the President decided on a spot some seventy-five miles downstream, which is now Washington, D.C. William Smith broke the news to Otho Williams on January 24th, 1791, and then wrote again a few days later to say that he was glad that his son-in-law was taking it like a "philosopher and a Christian."[53]

Interest in the Governorship of Maryland

On March 22nd, 1792, Otho Williams wrote to President Washington with an unusual proposal, one that he had considered for quite some time before approaching the President. The term of Governor George Plater of Maryland was about to expire, and while several men had expressed interest in the office, none had yet gained a clear advantage. Williams and a group of respected advisers felt that his reputation for competence and integrity might help him to win the election, even though he had never previously solicited the support of a political party or faction.

Williams implied to the President that if he became Governor, he would be a friend to the Federal Government, but then he unveiled his dilemma. The position of Governor paid significantly less than his current post as Collector of the Port of Baltimore, and he could not sustain such difference in income for an extended period. He suggested that Washington appoint his father-in-law, William Smith, to replace Williams as Collector of the Port, with the understanding that Williams would be reappointed when his service as Governor was completed. Recognizing the questionable nature of this proposal, Williams told the President that "My hesitation arose from the delicate nature of the subject which I have not mentioned, and will not mention, even to Mr. Smith, without your approbation."[54]

Day after day went by with no response from the President, and Williams grew more and more worried about Washington's interpretation of his proposal. He finally wrote to the President about four weeks later, sounding like a wayward schoolboy who was sorry for offending a stern and highly respected teacher:

> *If my letter of the 22nd ultimo. has been the cause of the least displeasure to you it will prove a source of lasting regret to me. A regret which I shall feel the more sensibly as this object of my proposal was, in my own estimation, too inconsequential to have induced the smallest risque of your disapprobation.*
>
> *Your silence, my Dear Sir, and my own reflections induce the apprehension that some impropriety may have appeared to you of which I was unconscious.*
>
> *If my apprehension is not founded in error, I wish, not that you would give yourself the trouble, or me the pain, of showing me my fault; but that you would have the goodness to cancel the letter, and obliterate from your memory every trace of an incident which whatever it may be, while it is remembered*

by you will not fail to inflict on me the severest regret and mortification.
With the most reverential respect and Esteem, and allow me to add, with the sincerest affection.[55]

Washington's reply of April 26th offers a gentlemanly and conciliatory tone as he ends the discussion on a positive note:

Your letter of the 18th. Instt. came duly to hand, as did the one to which it alludes. To the latter I could make no reply for reasons which will (perhaps have) occurred to you. Sensible however, if you had not assured me of it, that you meant not to give me pain by the proposition therein contained, I can assure you that I feel none, and that, with the same esteem and regard I always professed to have for you, I remain, Dear Sir: "Your most obedient and affectionate G. Washington[56]

Simply stated, there weren't going to be any under-the-table deals in George Washington's administration, if he could help it.

Washington's statement that he still maintained high regard for Williams would be confirmed a short month later, when he offered the chastened Marylander a high military appointment.

★ ★ ★ ★ ★

George Washington's Offer of an Army Appointment

On November 4th, 1791, General Arthur St. Clair had been badly defeated by a combined force of Native Americans of the Miami, Shawnee and Delaware tribes at the Battle of the Wabash, near present-day Fort Recovery, Ohio. One of the casualties at this disaster was the gallant Robert Kirkwood, who had served so ably as the commander of the Continental troops from Delaware in the Revolutionary War in the South. President Washington forced St. Clair to resign, which left several openings in an Army that was being reorganized to counter the Whiskey Rebellion and deal with the Native Americans on the frontier.

The President compiled a document called "Opinion of the General Officers" to try to summarize the strengths and weaknesses of the various candidates for senior army appointments. His observations were brutally frank, as he, Knox and Hamilton grappled with the difficult task of finding qualified officers who would accept commissions. The Commander-in-

Chief's appraisal of Otho Holland Williams gives clear insight into how he perceived the Marylander:

> Brigadier General Williams. Is a sensible man, but not without vanity. No doubt, I believe, is entertained of his firmness: and it is thought he does not want activity; but it is not easy, where there is nothing conspicuous in a character, to pronounce decidedly upon a Military man who has always acted under the immediate orders of a superior Officer; unless he had been seen frequently in Action. The discipline, interior oeconomy and police of his Corps is the best evidence one can have of his talents in this line and of this, in the case of Genl. Williams I can say nothing; as he was appointed a Brigadier after he left the Northern to join the Southern army. But a material objection to him is delicate health (if there has been no change in his Constitution), for he has gone to the Sweet Springs two or three years successively in such bad health as to afford little hope of his ever returning from them.[57]

Washington's unfamiliarity with the details of Otho Williams' service in the South was apparently a factor that weighed upon the Marylander's chances for an appointment. Williams' friend, mentor and commander, Nathanael Greene had died in 1786. Had he been alive when Washington was selecting officers for the nation's army, Greene would probably have been able to refresh Washington's memory of his friend's distinguished service.

There was another consideration regarding Otho Williams as a candidate for a senior position in the army. The President would have preferred to name Light Horse Harry Lee to the command,[58] but both Washington's Memorandum on General Officers" and Thomas Jefferson's notes the Cabinet meeting on March 9, 1792 make reference to a key consideration regarding Lee, Jefferson noting:

> Lee. a better head & more resource than any of them. but no economy, & being a junior officer, we shd lose benefit of good seniors who wd not serve under him.[59]

In spite of Washington's reservations about Williams' capabilities and his reluctance to serve under Lee,[60] Otho Williams received a letter from Secretary of the Treasury Alexander Hamilton dated March 28th, 1782, that he was being considered to replace St. Clair, even though his health was a serious concern.⁶¹ Williams answered Hamilton on April 5th that he was very gratified for being mentioned, and that, while his health was better, there didn't seem to be much about the command to "excite ambition or any other passion."⁶²

On May 3rd, 1792, Secretary of War Henry Knox wrote to Williams to inform him that Daniel Morgan had been offered a Brigadier Generalship and the position of second-in-command of the Army, but that he anticipated that Morgan would decline. Knox wanted to know if Williams would consider the position, and was convinced that the President would be very pleased if Williams were appointed.⁶³ The surviving copy of this letter in the Maryland Historical Society's manuscript collection contains a revealing note in Williams' handwriting, indicating that he was not pleased with the offer of a position that was probably subordinate to Henry Lee, who he had outranked during the Revolution.⁶⁴ Williams' reaction proved the validity of President Washington's concern that officers who had been senior to Lee during the Revolution would balk at serving under him.

Williams answered Knox in a private letter on May 6th that he was honored by the suggestion, but since his health was poor and he had responsibilities to his family and to a number of orphans, he asked to be permitted to decline.⁶⁵ At this point, Williams did not mention his irritation at the prospect of being superseded by Henry Lee.

On the same date that Williams was writing this private letter to Knox, the Secretary was drafting the official notification that Williams had been appointed a Brigadier General by the President with the consent of the Senate.⁶⁶ Knox wrote again the next day asking for Williams' decision, noting that "I wish to God you could find it convenient to accept."⁶⁷ Presidential aide Tobias Lear wrote on May 13th, asking Williams to inform the President at Mt. Vernon whether or not he accepted the position.⁶⁸ While Lear was writing to Williams, Williams wrote two letters to Knox – a public letter officially declining the appointment citing his health and private concerns, and a private letter that also revealed that his "ambition was not tempted" by the offer to be second-in-command.⁶⁹

Williams also wrote to President Washington on the 13th, noting that he had just received the official appointment at 10 o'clock that night, and was responding immediately. He informed the President that he declined the appointment, citing "his physician's advice, the wishes of his friends, and other reasons of private inconvenience."⁷⁰

Otho Williams was one of the few men that President Washington had considered for top positions in the nation's army. He had been nominated by the President and confirmed by the Senate for the rank of Brigadier General. Circumstances required that he decline the appointment, but the offer was a fitting ending to his fine record of military service.

A Defense of Nathanael Greene's Widow

When Nathanael Greene died unexpectedly at age forty-three, he had left a significant unresolved issue for his estate. Toward the very end of the war, when he was desperate for any possible means to feed and clothe his little army, Green had reportedly offered his personal guarantee on some financial transactions that would provide the needed supplies for his troops. Several years after Greene's death, his widow appealed to Congress to help discharge this debt, and a firestorm of opposition appeared in the House of Representatives, led by none other than Congressman Thomas Sumter of South Carolina. Greene had sometimes been frustrated in his efforts to coordinate movements with Sumter during the war, and Sumter's hard feelings must have lasted long after Greene's death.

Sumter's remarks infuriated Greene's friends, including Alexander Hamilton, Henry Lee, Edward Carrington and Otho Holland Williams. These four men tried to use their influence to support Mrs. Greene's cause, and to coordinate a series of public statements in defense of a man that they all greatly admired.

Lee started this effort in February, when he noted Sumter's "undeserved reflections" on Greene's name, and asked Williams to provide Lee with any facts he had from his close official association with Greene.[71] Williams responded that many of his official papers had been lost when they were being returned to him from historian William Gordon, but that he would do his best to assemble his recollections.[72] Williams sent his comments to Lee on March 19th,[73] which were quite disparaging of Sumter, as Lee returned them in a letter dated March 26th with "some of the asperities softened."[74] Williams sent the work to Hamilton, noting that while he felt that General Sumter's speech had been "shameful," he hesitated to publish his remarks,

---

*Sweet Springs is now in West Virginia, about twenty-five miles south of The Greenbrier Resort in White Sulfur Springs, West Virginia.

and asked that Hamilton review them, and, if he thought appropriate, to have them published, perhaps in a Philadelphia paper.[75*]

Williams' efforts to publish his support for Greene were overtaken by events, as the House passed the resolution supporting Greene's estate by a vote of 29-26 on April 4th, 1792.[76] President Washington informed Congress three weeks later that he had signed legislation entitled "An act to indemnify the estate of the late Major General Nathaniel Greene for a certain bond entered into by him, during the late war."[77]

After all the commotion had died down, Hamilton wrote to Williams on June 9th that he had withheld publication of Williams' statement because it had appeared to him that the measure was going to pass anyway, and that it did not seem wise to start a "new game."[78] For the time being, Thomas Sumter's unkind reflections on the memory of Nathanael Greene had faded into obscurity.

★ ★ ★ ★ ★

The Curtain Closes

Williams' health continued to deteriorate, and he sought the best available remedies. At that time, considerable faith was placed in the freshness of country air and the healing waters of warm springs. His letter to Secretary of the Treasury Alexander Hamilton in October, 1792 describes a hopeful stay in the country when he had found some relief from his illness, but then expresses the agony as the symptoms of his illness return:

> *My stay in the Country was attended with so many indications of returning health that I thought the time well spent; and was returning home full of confidence that business would again be a pleasure to me when a very unexpected and violent attack on my breast banished all my sanguine expectations, and reduced me almost to the last extremity. An Hemorrhage from the lungs, which continued several days, attended by the most alarming symptoms, made it requisite, in the opinion of my Physicians, to make among other applications repeated and liberal use of the launcet which, in addition to the loss of blood from the lungs and a fever, which attended me for about two weeks, weakened me extremely. I have happily recovered much apparent health and strength, but my lungs remain very sore and irritable: and*

> *my Physicians recommend a Voyage to some of the West India Islands for the Winter as the best means of restoring my health perfectly.*[79]

Williams accordingly requested the permission of the President to leave the country.[80] On November 1st, Hamilton forwarded the President's approval of the trip, and, ever business-like added that "It is not doubted that due care will previously be taken to secure the proper management of the public business in your absence."[81]

Williams left soon afterwards for Barbados in hopes of regaining his vigor. He was back in the United States by March 28th, when he began a two-week stay in Charleston. While there he either visited or received a visit from Dr. David Ramsay, General Isaac Huger, Colonel William Washington, and General Charles Cotesworth Pinckney (who had been so unhappy with Williams' promotion to Brigadier in 1782).[82] He had returned to Baltimore by May 18th, when he received a letter from a friend welcoming him home.[83] Alexander Hamilton wrote a personal note from Philadelphia dated June 21st, 1793, in which he stated that "I learnt with real pleasure, your return from the West Indies in improved health. Be assured, that I interest myself, with friendship, in your welfare."[84]

Otho and Polly's oldest son Robert had become desperately ill and had died while Williams was away on this trip. After he returned to Baltimore, he wrote to his friend Dr. Philip Thomas that he and Polly were in deep mourning for the loss of their oldest child.[85]

Williams had less and less stamina, and he slowly began to reduce his workload to a level that he could bear. He resigned from his Baltimore County judgeships in 1792.[86]

Williams had built the office of the Collector of the Port of Baltimore into an efficient operation, with a highly capable staff. This enabled the office to continue to function effectively, even while the Collector himself was becoming steadily weaker. In late June, 1792, he reported to Secretary of the Treasury Alexander Hamilton that he had to leave Baltimore because of his health,[87] and from that point, a number of his business letters were written from Ceresville, Maryland, near Frederick, over fifty miles from his office in Baltimore. He corresponded regularly with his principal assistant, Daniel Delozier, who consistently displayed professional competence, a conscientious attitude, and complete loyalty to Williams. When President Washington appointed Delozier to be Surveyor of the Port of Baltimore in 1793 (a position subordinate to Williams, but a promotion from Assistant

Collector,) he noted that Delozier appeared to have been doing a great part of the business of that department because of the illness of General Williams.[88]

A little over a year later, in the last days of the summer of 1793, it was clear to Williams and to all who came in contact with him that he did not have long to live. He wrote to his old friend Philip Thomas on August 11th, 1793 that he had enjoyed a recent visit to Williamsport, but that "God only knows in how short a time I must leave that and objects infinitely more dear."[89] Near year's end, he told Thomas that he only went outside when the weather was good, and played soldier with his sons when it was not.[90]

The new year of 1794 brought no relief. On January 3rd, he told Dr. Thomas that he was very tired, and that he had only a few moments when he felt good, which was only from a "reconcilement of pain."[91] His correspondence discussed many remedies that he tried, including the practice of blistering and the use of a variety of natural medications, including Indian turnip, Ruspine's styptic, and different teas, including rattle weed root, yarrow, and Ellicompain. He once proudly reported to Dr. Thomas that he had been able to go to sleep without using laudanum,[92] and he also wrote that he smoked two cigars a day, which he considered "of use."[93] All of the medicine of the day was ineffective against the advance of his disease, probably tuberculosis, which he had almost certainly contacted when he was a prisoner-of-war in New York from late 1776 to early 1778.

Sensing that the end was near, Williams prepared his Last Will and Testament on June 5th, 1794.[94]

Williams had often traveled in the heat of the summer to seek the comfort of the baths in western Virginia. It is a 250 mile trip from Ceresville, Maryland to Sweet Springs, Virginia, and it was an arduous trek in 1794.[75] Williams' old Army friend Edward Carrington had once written with advice for the trip: "...all the fords are good, save two, and they are passable...;" "...you will get plenty of oats and hay, but you must depend upon your own baggage for both lodging and food..." Carrington warned Williams to be sure not to set out when the water was high.[96] This demanding trip would put heavy stress on Williams' steadily weakening body.

The path from Ceresville to Sweet Springs was well traveled, and Williams had made the trip many times. He had described the route in a letter to his friend Dr. Philip Thomas several years earlier: the first stop was at Horatio Gates' home, Traveler's Rest near Shepherdstown, Virginia (about 40 miles from Ceresville); then to Daniel Morgan's home, Saratoga, near Boyce, Virginia (about 28 miles from Gates' home); and then 100 miles to Staunton,

Virginia, making various stops along the way. The visits with Gates and Morgan, two of his friends from the war years, had likely been a source of pleasure for Williams.[97]

But his old friends who only saw him occasionally also sensed his deep decline and imminent death. Morgan wrote him a quick note after they had crossed paths in Winchester, Virginia a year earlier, and had told Williams that he hoped he would recover, and that he should "…fight hard before he dies."[98]

Otho Holland Williams never made it to Sweet Springs in the summer of 1794. He reached Woodstock, Virginia and could go no farther. He died there on July 15th, 1794, at the age of forty-five.

His body was returned to Williamsport, where he was buried on the high ground of the Riverside Cemetery, overlooking the confluence of Conococheague Creek and the Potomac River, the land that he had dreamed about so often while he was far away from home, fighting for our independence, during the Revolutionary War.[99]

---

1 Tiffany, *Sketch*. Pp. 26-27
2 Ibid.
3 Williams, Otho Holland. Letter to Dr. Philip Thomas. Written at Baltimore, February 12th, 1790. *Williams Papers*. Part 4/8. (Item #549.)
4 Williams, Otho Holland. Letter to George Washington. Written at Baltimore, March 17th, 1790. *Williams Papers*. Part 4/8. (Item #565.)
5 O'Connell, John. Letter to Otho Holland Williams. Written at Baltimore, June 30th, 1786. The information on Chinese imports and the naming of Canton is in an "Editor's Note" at the bottom of this letter. *Williams Papers*. Part 3/8. (Item #355.)
6 Williams, Otho Holland. Letter to Uriah Forrest. Written at Baltimore. April 28, 1784. *Williams Papers*. Part 2/8. (Item # 252.); Williams, Otho Holland. Letter to Dr. Philp Thomas. Written at Baltimore. March 19th, 1785. *Williams Papers*. Part 2/8. (Item #303.); Howard, John Eager. Letter to Otho Holland Williams. Written at Baltimore. April 23rd, 1785. *Williams Papers*. Part 2/8. (Item #314.)
7 Lee, *Memoirs*. P. 593.
8 Society of the Cincinnati, Register. Pp. 29-32; Williams, Otho Holland. Letter to Uriah Forest. Written at Baltimore, April 28th, 1784. *Williams Papers*. Part 2/8. (Item # 252;) George Washington to Gilbert Simpson, 13 February 1784," Founders Online, National Archives "From (http://founders.archives.gov/documents/Washington/04-01-02-0084, ver. 2014-05-09). Source: *The Papers of George Washington, Confederation Series, vol. 1, 1 January 1784–17 July 1784*, ed. W. W. Abbot. Charlottesville: University Press of Virginia, 1992, pp. 117–118
9 Williams, Otho Holland. Letter to Uriah Forrest. Written at Baltimore. April 28th, 1784. *Williams Papers*. Part 2/8. (Item # 252.)
10 Society of the Cincinnati, *Register*. P. 19.
11 Ibid. Pp. 40, 43, and 45.
12 Williams, Otho Holland. Letter to Dr. Philip Thomas. Written at Philadelphia. May 11th, 1784. *Williams Papers*. Part 2/8. (Item # 256.)
13 Williams, Otho Holland. Letter to Nathanael Greene. Written at Baltimore, January 14th, 1784. *Williams Papers*. Part 2/8. (Item #236.)
14 Williams, Otho Holland. Letter to Dr. Philip Thomas. March 25th, 1784. *Williams Papers*. Part 2/8. (Item #243.)
15 Williams, Otho Holland. Letter to Dr. Philip Thomas. Written at Baltimore, April 27th, 1784. *Williams Papers*. Part 2/8. (Item # 250.)
16 "Maryland, Marriages, 1666-1970," index, *Family Search* (https://familysearch.org/pal:/MM9.1.1/F4JQ-6YG : accessed 19 Jul 2014), Otho Holland Williams and Mary Smith, 18 Oct 1785; citing First Presbyterian Church, Baltimore, Baltimore, Maryland, reference ; FHL microfilm 13699.
17 Williams, Otho Holland. Letter to William Jackson. Written at Baltimore, November 20th, 1785. *Williams Papers*.

Part 2/8. (Item # 335.)
18 Williams, Mary Smith (Mrs. O.H.) Letter to Otho Holland Williams. Sunday, January 1st, 1786. *Williams Papers*. Part 2/8. (Item #339.)
19 Williams, Otho Holland. Letter to Dr. Philip Thomas. Written at Baltimore, July 25th, 1786. *Williams Papers*. Part 3/8. (Item # 360.)
20 Williams, Otho Holland. Letter to Dr. Philip Thomas. Written at Baltimore, April 4th, 1787. Williams Papers. Part 3/8. (Item #378;) Pindell, Richard. Letter to Otho Holland Williams. January 6th, 1789. *Williams Papers* Part 3/ 8. (Item #429.); Smith, Edward. *Historic Resource Study. Williamsport, Maryland. Chesapeake and Ohio Canal National Historical Park*. National Park Service. July 25, 1979. P. 7.
21 Last Will and Testament of Otho Holland Williams. Written at Baltimore, June 5th, 1794. *Williams Papers*. Part 5/8. (Item #969.)
22 Last Will and Testament of Otho Holland Williams. Written at Baltimore, June 5th, 1794. Williams Papers. Part 5/8. (Item #969.); Williams, Otho Holland. Letter to Dr. Philip Thomas. Written at Baltimore, December 14th, 1793. *Williams Papers*. Part 5/8. (Item #848.)
23 Lee, Henry, IV. *The Campaign of 1781 in the Carolinas: With Remarks, Historical and Critical on Johnson's Life of Greene*. (Philadelphia. Published by E. Littell, 1824.) Pp. 125-126.
24 "From George Washington to John Parke Custis, 1 February 1778," Founders Online, National Archives (http://founders.archives.gov/documents/Washington/03-13-02-0355 [last update: 2014-12-01]). Source: *The Papers of George Washington, Revolutionary War Series, vol. 13, 26 December 1777–28 February 1778*, ed. Edward G. Lengel. Charlottesville: University of Virginia Press, 2003, pp. 435–437.
25 Laws of Maryland 1785-1791. Volume 204, Page 153. Archives of Maryland Online.
26 "Otho Holland Williams, A Marylander. To the Editor of the Maryland Journal and Baltimore Advertiser." March 20th, 1788. *Williams Papers*. Part 3/8. (Item #397.)
27 Williams, Otho Holland. Letter to Henry Lee, Jr. Written at Baltimore January 3rd, 1789; Williams Papers. Part 3/8. (Item #427;) Williams, Otho Holland. Letter to Robert Morris. January 3rd, 1789. Written at Baltimore. *Williams Papers*. Part 3/8. (Item #428.)
28 Lee, Henry, Jr. (Light Horse Harry.) Letter to Otho Holland Williams. February 17th, 1789. *Williams Papers*. Part 3/8. (Item #439.)
29 "To George Washington from Otho Holland Williams, 18 April 1789," Founders Online, National Archives (http://founders.archives.gov/documents/Washington/05-02-02-0068 [last update: 2015-03-20]). Source: *The Papers of George Washington, Presidential Series, vol. 2, 1 April 1789– 15 June 1789*, ed. Dorothy Twohig. Charlottesville: University Press of Virginia, 1987, pp. 71–72; This letter is also included in the Williams Papers. Part 3/8. (Item #460.) This Historical Society's Calendar lists the date as April 16th instead of April 18th.)
30 Williams, Otho Holland. Letter to Col. David Humphreys. Written at New York, May 12th, 1789. *Williams Papers*. Part 3/8. (Item #464.)
31 Williams, Otho Holland. Letter to Dr. Philip Thomas. Written at Baltimore, June 7th, 1789. *Williams Papers*. Part 3/8. (Item #465.)
32 Smith, William. Letter to Otho Holland Williams. Written at New York. June 21st, 1789. *Williams Papers*. Part 3/8. (Item #470.)
33 Williams, Otho Holland. Letter to George Washington. Written at Baltimore, August 9th, 1789. *Williams Papers*. Part 3/8. (Item #507.)
34 Williams, Otho Holland. Letter to Dr. Philip Thomas. Written at Baltimore, August 5th, 1789. *Williams Papers*. Part 3/8. (Item #505.)
35 Williams, Otho Holland. Letter to General Benjamin Lincoln, Collector of the Port of Boston, Mass. Written at Baltimore, February 21st, 1790. *Williams Papers*. Part 4/8. (Item #554.)
36 Journal and Correspondence of the Council of Maryland, 1784-1789. Volume 71. Page 268.
37 *Blackstone's Commentaries on the Laws of England* state that Courts of Oyer, Terminer and General Gaol delivery were commissioned by the monarch, and the judges were to inquire, hear and determine all treasons, felonies, and misdemeanors. (Ref: *An Abridgment of Blackstone's Commentaries on the Laws of England*, by Sir John E. Eardley-Wilmot – Bart. London. Longman, Greene, Brown and Longmans. 1853. P. 270.) Maryland passed a law on May 27th, 1788 that authorized Baltimore County to " to issue a commission of oyer and terminer and gaol delivery for the trial of any felony, or other crime, offence or misdemeanor, at any time heretofore committed, or hereafter to be committed…" These provisions were enacted "For the more effectual punishment of criminals," since it was represented that "the commission of burglary, robbery, horse-stealing, and other crimes hath greatly increased in this state." (Ref: *Laws of Maryland, 1785-1791. Volume 204. Laws of Maryland made and passed at a Session of Assembly, Begun and held at the city of ANNAPOLIS, on Monday the fifth of November, in the year of our Lord one thousand seven hundred and eighty-seven. Annapolis*. Printed by Frederick Green, printer to the state. P. 300.)
38 Laws of Maryland 1785-1791, Volume 204. Page 250.
39 Journal and Correspondence of the Council of Maryland, Volume 71 (November 27, 1784 - February 23, 1789), page

268 and Volume 72 (February 23, 1789 to November 11, 1793,) pages 45, 50/51, 70, 89, 96, 163-165, 182/183, 245, and 246/247.
40   Williams, Otho Holland. Letter to Doctor Philip Thomas. Written at Baltimore. July 1st, 1789. *Williams Papers*. Part 3/8. (Item # 473.)
41   Delozier, Daniel. Letter to Otho Holland Williams. Written at Baltimore. January 11th, 1781. *Williams Papers*. Part 4/8. (Item #624.)
42   Delozier, Daniel (Deputy Collector.) Letter to Otho Holland Williams.   Written at Baltimore, June 29th, 1791. *Williams Papers*. Part 4/8. (Item #660.)
43   "Estimate of imports, exports & c. Baltimore" 1793. *Williams Papers*. Part 5/8. (Item #862.)
44   Hamilton, Alexander. Letter to Otho Holland Williams. Written at the Treasury Department, April 3rd, 1794. *Williams Papers*. Part 5/8. (Item #939.)
45   Williams, Otho Holland. Letter to Louis Henry Bouteiller. Written at Baltimore, April 4th, 1794. *Williams Papers*. Part 5/8. (Item #942.)
46   On March 20th, 1794, Congress authorized the building of coastal fortifications at sixteen designated sites, including Baltimore. The post at Baltimore was then an earthen and timber fortification known as Fort Whetstone. It was re-named Fort McHenry in 1798. Ref: Kauffmann, J.E. and Kaufmann, H.W. Fortress America: *The Forts That Defended America, 1600 to the Present*. DeCapo Press. 2004. Pp. 142-144.
47   Smith, William. Letter to Otho Holland Williams. Written at New York, August 23rd, 1789. *Williams Papers*. Part 3/8. (Item #512.)
48   Williams, Otho Holland. Letter to Dr. Philip Thomas. Written at Baltimore, December 23rd, 1789. *Williams Papers*. Part 3/8. (Item #536.)
49   Smith, William. Letter to Otho Holland Williams. Written at New York, July 15th, 1790. *Williams Papers*. Part 4/8. (Item #595.)
50   Williams, Otho Holland. Letter to Dr. Philip Thomas. Written at Baltimore, October 20th, 1790. *Williams Papers*. Part 4/8. (Item #608.)
51   The Maryland Press, 1777-1790 by Joseph Towne Wheeler. The Archives of Maryland Online, Volume 438, Page 206.
52   Williams, Otho Holland. Letter to George Washington. Written at Hagerstown, November 1st, 1790. *Williams Papers*. Part 4/8. (Item #609.)
53   Smith, William. Letter to Otho Holland Williams. Written at Philadelphia. January 24th, 1791. *Williams Papers*. Part 4/8. (Item #627.); Smith, William. Letter to Otho Holland Williams. Written at Philadelphia, February 3rd, 1791. *Williams Papers*. Part 4/8. (Item #633.)
54   To George Washington from Otho Holland Williams, 22 March 1792," Founders Online, National Archives (http://founders.archives.gov/documents/Washington/05-10-02-0087, ver. 2014-05-09). Source: T*he Papers of George Washington*, Presidential Series, vol. 10, *1 March 1792–15 August 1792*, ed. Robert F. Haggard and Mark A. Mastromarino. Charlottesville: University of Virginia Press, 2002, pp. 146–148.
55   To George Washington from Otho Holland Williams, 18 April 1792," Founders Online, National Archives (http://founders.archives.gov/documents/Washington/05-10-02-0175, ver. 2014-05-09). Source: *The Papers of George Washington*, Presidential Series, vol. 10, 1 March 1792–15 August 1792, ed. Robert F. Haggard and Mark A. Mastromarino. Charlottesville: University of Virginia Press, 2002, pp. 289–290.
56   From George Washington to Otho Holland Williams, 26 April 1792," Founders Online, National Archives (http://founders.archives.gov/documents/Washington/05-10-02-0198, ver. 2014-05-09). Source: *The Papers of George Washington*, Presidential Series, vol. 10, 1 March 1792–15 August 1792, ed. Robert F. Haggard and Mark A. Mastromarino. Charlottesville: University of Virginia Press, 2002, pp. 321–322.
57   Memorandum on General Officers, 9 March 1792," Founders Online, National Archives (http://founders.archives.gov/documents/Washington/05-10-02-0040, ver. 2014-05-09). Source: *The Papers of George Washington*, Presidential Series, vol. 10, 1 March 1792–15 August 1792, ed. Robert F. Haggard and Mark A. Mastromarino. Charlottesville: University of Virginia Press, 2002, pp. 74–79.
58   Washington would write Lee regarding this decision that "I have no hesitation in declaring to you that the biass of my inclination was strongly in your favor…" Ref: "From George Washington to Henry Lee, 30 June 1792," Founders Online, National Archives (http://founders.archives.gov/documents/Washington/05-10-02-0339 [last update: 2014-12-01]). Source: *The Papers of George Washington, Presidential Series, vol. 10, 1 March 1792–15 August 1792*, ed. Robert F. Haggard and Mark A. Mastromarino. Charlottesville: University of Virginia Press, 2002, pp. 506–509.
59   "Thomas Jefferson's Memorandum of a Meeting of the Heads of the Executive Departments, 9 March 1792," Founders Online, National Archives (http://founders.archives.gov/documents/Washington/05-10-02-0039 [last update: 2014-12-01]). Source: *The Papers of George Washington*, Presidential Series, vol. 10, *1 March 1792–15 August 1792*, ed. Robert F. Haggard and Mark A. Mastromarino. Charlottesville: University of Virginia Press, 2002, pp. 69–73.
60   Williams' reluctance to serve under Light Horse Harry Lee would prove moot, as Washington eventually decided to give the command to "Mad" Anthony Wayne, a decision which deeply disappointed Lee. Ref: Washington, George.

Letter to Henry Lee. Written at Philadelphia, June 30, 1792. *Washington Papers*. In that letter, Washington had told Lee that "I have no hesitation in declaring to you that the biass of my inclination was strongly in your favor."
61 Hamilton, Alexander. Letter to Otho Holland Williams. Written at Philadelphia, March 28th, 1792. *Williams Papers*. Part 4/8. (Item #696.)
62 Williams, Otho Holland. Letter to Alexander Hamilton. Written at Baltimore, April 5th, 1792. *Williams Papers*. Part 4/8. (Item #697.)
63 Knox, Henry. Letter to Otho Holland Williams. Written at Philadelphia, May 3rd, 1792. *Williams Papers*. Part 4/8. (Item #708.)
64 Note written by Williams on the letter from Henry Knox to Otho Holland Williams, written at Philadelphia, May 3rd, 1792. *Williams Papers*. Part 4/8. (Item #708.)
65 Williams, Otho Holland. Letter to Henry Knox. Written at Baltimore, May 6th, 1792. *Williams Papers*. Part 4/8. (Item #709.)
66 Knox, Henry. Letter to Otho Holland Williams. Written at the War Department, May 8th, 1792. *Williams Papers*. Part 4/8. (Item #710.)
67 Knox, Henry. Letter to Otho Holland Williams. Written at Philadelphia, May 9th, 1792. *Williams Papers*. Part 4/8. (Item #711.)
68 Lear, Tobias. Letter to Otho Holland Williams. May 13th, 1792. *Williams Papers*. Part 4/8. (Item #712.)
69 Williams, Otho Holland. Letter to Henry Knox, Secretary of War. Written at Baltimore, May 13th, 1792. *Williams Papers*. Part 4/8. (Item #713.); Williams, Otho Holland. Letter to Henry Knox. Written at Baltimore, May 13th, 1792. *Williams Papers*. Part 4/8. (Item #714.)
70 Williams, Otho Holland. Letter to President of the United States George Washington. Written at Baltimore, May 13th, 1792. *Williams Papers*. Part 4/8. (Item #715.)
71 Lee, Henry (Light Horse Harry.) Letter to Otho Holland Williams. February, 1792. *Williams Papers*. Part 4/8. (Item #682.)
72 Williams, Otho Holland. Letter to Governor Henry Lee (Light Horse Harry.) Written at Baltimore, March 15th, 1792. *Williams Papers*. Part 4/8. (Item #688.)
73 Williams, Otho Holland. Letter to Governor Henry Lee (Light Horse Harry.) Written at Baltimore, March 19th, 1792. *Williams Papers*. Part 4/8. (Item #689.)
74 Lee, Henry (Light Horse Harry.) Letter to Otho Holland Williams. Written at Richmond, Virginia. March 26th, 1792. *Williams Papers*. Part 4/8. (Item #694.)
75 Williams, Otho Holland. Letter to Alexander Hamilton. Written at Baltimore, April 5th, 1792. Part 4/8. (Item #697.)
76 Journal of the House of Representatives of the United States, 1789-1793. Wednesday, April 4th, 1792. The Library of Congress Web Site.
77 Journal of the House of Representatives of the United States, 1789-1793. Friday, April 27th, 1792. The Library of Congress Web Site.
78 Hamilton, Alexander. Letter to Otho Holland Williams. Written at the Philadelphia, June 9th, 1792. *Williams Papers*. Part 4/8. (Item #722.)
79 "To Alexander Hamilton from Otho H. Williams, 29 October 1792," Founders Online, National Archives (http://founders.archives.gov/documents/Hamilton/01-12-02-0441, ver. 2014-05-09). Source: *The Papers of Alexander Hamilton, vol. 12, July 1792–October 1792*, ed. Harold C. Syrett. New York: Columbia University Press, 1967, p. 629.
80 Ibid.
81 "From Alexander Hamilton to Otho H. Williams, 1 November 1792," Founders Online, National Archives (http://founders.archives.gov/documents/Hamilton/01-13-02-0004, ver. 2014-05-09). Source: The Papers of Alexander Hamilton, vol. 13, November 1792–February 1793, ed. Harold C. Syrett. New York: Columbia University Press, 1967, p. 2.
82 Memorandum of visits received and made in Charleston, S.C. March 28th-April 13th, 1793. *Williams Papers*. Part 5/8. (Item #782.)
83 Irwine, M. H. Letter to Otho Holland Williams. Written at Baltimore, May 15th, 1793. *Williams Papers*. Part 5/8. (Item #784.)
84 "From Alexander Hamilton to Otho H. Williams, 21 June 1793," Founders Online, National Archives (http://founders.archives.gov/documents/Hamilton/01-15-02-0013, ver. 2014-05-09). Source: *The Papers of Alexander Hamilton*, vol. 15, *June 1793–January 1794*, ed. Harold C. Syrett. New York: Columbia University Press, 1969, pp. 13–14.
85 Williams, Otho Holland. Letter to Dr. Philip Thomas. Written at Baltimore, May 16th, 1793. *Williams Papers*. Part 5/8. (Item #786.)
86 Williams, Otho Holland. Letter to Governor Thomas Sim Lee and the Council. Written at Baltimore, May 1st, 1792. *Williams Papers*. Part 4/8. (Item #706;) Williams, Otho Holland. Letter to Governor Thomas Sim Lee and Council. Written at Baltimore, November 1st, 1792. *Williams Papers*. Part 4/8. (Item #753.)
87 Williams, Otho Holland. Letter to Alexander Hamilton. Written at Ceresville, Frederick County, Maryland, June

28th, 1792. *Williams Papers*. Part 4/8. (Item #732.)
88 Washington, George. Letter to Charles Carroll. Written at Philadelphia, August 25th, 1793. The Papers of George Washington at the Library of Congress.
89 Williams, Otho Holland. Letter to Dr. Philip Thomas. Written at Elizabeth Town (near Hagerstown), August 11th, 1793. *Williams Papers*. Part 5/8. (Item#816.)
90 Williams, Otho Holland. Letter to Dr. Philip Thomas. Written at Baltimore, December 14th, 1793. *Williams Papers*. Part 5/8. (Item#848.)
91 Williams, Otho Holland. Letter to Dr. Philip Thomas. Written at Baltimore, January 3, 1794. *Williams Papers*. Part 5/8. (Item #863.)
92 Williams, Otho Holland. Letter to Dr. Philip Thomas. Written at Elizabeth (now Hagerstown) on October 9th, 1792. *Williams Papers*. Part 4/8. (Item #748.)
93 Williams, Otho Holland. Letter to Dr. Philip Thomas. Written at Baltimore, December 14th, 1793. *Williams Papers*. Part 5/8. (Item# 848.)
94 Last Will and Testament of Otho Holland Williams. Written at Baltimore, June 5th, 1794. *Williams Papers*. Part 5/8. (Item #969.)
95 Sweet Springs is now in West Virginia, about twenty-five miles south of The Greenbrier Resort in White Sulfur Springs, West Virginia.
96 Carrington, Edward. Letter to Otho Holland Williams. Written at Staunton, Virginia, July 20th, 1790. *Williams Papers*. Part 4/8. (Item #596.)
97 Williams, Otho Holland. Letter to Dr. Philip Thomas. Written at General Daniel Morgan's home Saratoga, June 26th, 1790. *Williams Papers*. Part 4/8. (Item #592.)
98 Morgan, Daniel. Letter to Otho Holland Williams. September 10th, 1793. *Williams Paper*s. Part 5/8. (Item #821.)
99 Tiffany, *Sketch*. Pp. 30-31.

BIBLIOGRAPHY

Collections of Manuscripts and Papers

Bayard Papers. Maryland Historical Society. MS 109.

Calendar of the Otho Holland Williams Papers in the Manuscript Collections of the Maryland Historical Society. MS 908.

Papers of General Daniel Morgan. Theodorus Bailey Myers Collection Series V. The New York Public Library. Manuscripts and Archives Division. New York, New York.

Proceedings of a General Court Martial, Held at Brunswick, in the state of New Jersey, by order of His Excellency Gen. Washington…for the trial of Major General Lee. July 4th, 1778. Major General Lord Stirling, president. New York. Privately Printed. J.M. Bradstreet & Sons, Printers. 1864.

Smallwood, William. *Proceedings of several General Courts-Martial held by the order of Brigadier General Smallwood on the trials of Colonel J. Carvil Hall and Capt. Edward Norwood.* Annapolis. Printed by Frederick Green. MDCC,LXXIX (1779). Maryland Historical Society Manuscript Rare UB 856 .H17.

The Papers of General Nathanael Greene. Showman, Richard K.; Conrad, Dennis M.; and Roger N. Parks, et. al., Eds. *The Papers of General Nathanael Greene*. University of North Carolina Press, Chapel Hill Detailed entries for specific volumes are listed separately in the Bibliography under Books. The following volumes are referenced:

Volume	Editor	Published
v. 7. 26 December 1780-29 March 1781	Showman	1994
v. 8. 30 March-10 July 1781	Conrad	1995
v. 9. 11 July 1781-2 December 1781	Conrad	1997
v. 10. 3 December 1781-6 April 1782	Conrad	1998
v. 11.7 April-30 September 1782	Conrad	2000

The Papers of George Washington at the Library of Congress and at Founders Online, National Archives.

Williams, Otho. *Brigade and Regimental Orders, O.H. Williams Commd* Maryland Historical Society Manuscript Collections. MS 768. (Covers the period from September 13, 1780 through February 9, 1781, when Williams was in command of the combined regiments of Maryland and Delaware troops.)

Books

Allen, Ethan. *A Narrative of Col. Ethan Allen's Captivity, Written by Himself and Now Published for the Information of the Curious in All Nations* Published by Thomas & Thomas, from the Press of Charter and Hale. Walpole, New Hampshire. 1807.

Babits, Lawrence E. *A Devil of a Whipping. The Battle of Cowpens.* The University of North Carolina Press. Chapel Hill and London. 1998.

Babits, Lawrence E. and Howard, Joshua B. *Long, Obstinate and Bloody. The Battle of Guilford Courthouse.* The University of North Carolina Press Chapel Hill. 2009.

Bright Jeffrey G and Dunaway, Stewart E. *Like A Bear with his Stern in a Corner. The NC Campaign during the American Revolution.* Self Published. LaVergne, Tennessee. 2010.

Balch, Thomas, ed. *Papers Relating Chiefly to the Maryland Line during the Revolution.* Printed for the Seventy-Six Society. T.K. and P.G. Collins, Printers. Philadelphia. 1857.

Boyle, Esmeralda and Pinkney, Frederick. *Biographical Sketches of Distinguished Marylanders.* Kelly, Piet and Company. Baltimore. 1877.

Buchanan, John. *The Road to Guilford Court House.* John Wiley & Sons, Inc. New York et. al. 1997.

Burrows, Edwin G. *Forgotten Patriots: The Untold Story of American Prisoners During the Revolutionary War.* Basic Books. New York. 2008.

Cashin, Edward J. *The King's Ranger - Thomas Brown and the American Revolution On The Southern Frontier.* University of Georgia. Athens. 1999.

Cecere, Michael. *They Are Indeed a Very Useful Corps.* Heritage Books. Westminster, Maryland. 2006.

Clarke, John. *Military Institutions of Vegetius in Five Books, Translated from the Original Latin. With a Preface and Notes.* By Lieutenant John

Clarke,Printed for the Author and Sold by W. Griffin in Catharine Street. London. 1767.

Codman, John 2nd. *Arnold's Expedition to Quebec.* Second Edition. The Macmillan Company. New York. 1902.

Commager, Henry Steele and Morris, Richard B., Eds. *The Spirit of Seventy Six. The Story of the American Revolution as told by Participants.* Harper & Row Publishers. New York, Evanston and London. 1967.

Conrad, Dennis, M., Editor; Parks, Roger N, Senior Associate Editor; King, Martha J., Assistant Editor; Showman, Richard K, Editor Emeritus. *The Papers of General Nathanael Greene. Volume VIII. 30 March – 10 July, 1781.* The University of North Carolina Press. Chapel Hill and London. Published for the Rhode Island Historical Society. 1995.

Conrad, Dennis, M., Editor.; Parks, Roger N. Senior Associate Editor, and King, Martha J. Assistant Editor. *The Papers of General Nathanael Greene. Volume IX. 11 July 1781 - 2 December 1781.* The University of North Carolina Press. Chapel Hill and London. Published for the Rhode Island Historical Society. 1997.

Conrad, Dennis, Editor; Parks, Roger N., Senior Associate Editor; King, Martha J. *The Papers of General Nathanael Greene. Volume X. 3 December 1781 – 6 April 1782.* The University of North Carolina Press. Published for the Rhode Island Historical Society. Chapel Hill and London. 1998.

Dandridge, Danske. *American Prisoners of the Revolution.* The Michie Company, Printers. Charlottesville, Virginia. 1911.

Dann, John C., Ed. *The Revolution Remembered. Eyewitness Accounts of the War for Independence.* The University of Chicago Press. Chicago and London. 1980.

Desjardin, Thomas A. *Through A Howling Wilderness.* St. Martin's Press. New York. 2006.

Ewald, Johann. *Diary of the American War: A Hessian Journal.* Translated and edited by Joseph P. Tustin. Yale University Press, New Haven and London, 1979

Fischer, David Hackett. *Washington's Crossing*. Oxford University Press. Oxford, New York et. al. 2004.

Garden, Alexander. *Anecdotes of the Revolutionary War in America, with Sketches of Character*. Printed for the author by A.E. Miller. Charleston, South Carolina. 1822.

Gibbes, Robert W., M.D. *Documentary History of the American Revolution, Consisting of Letters and Papers Relating to the Contest for Liberty, Chiefly in South Carolina, in 1781 and 1782*. Published by Banner Steam Power Press. Columbia, South Carolina. 1853.

Golway, Terry. *Washington's General. Nathanael Greene and the Triumph of the American Revolution*. Henry Holt and Company. New York. 2005.

Gordon, William, D.D. *The History of the Rise, Progress, And Establishment, of the Independence of the United States Of America: Including An Account Of The Late War and of the Thirteen Colonies, From Their Origin To That Period. In Four Volumes. (Volume 3.)* Printed for the Author; and sold By Charles Dilly, in the Poultry; and James Buckland, in Pater-Noster Row. London. 1788.

Gordon, William, D.D. *The History of the Rise, Progress, And Establishment, of the Independence of the United States Of America: Including An Account Of The Late War and of the Thirteen Colonies, From Their Origin To That Period. In Four Volumes. (Volume 4.)* Printed for the Author; and sold By Charles Dilly, in the Poultry; and James Buckland, in Pater-Noster Row. London. 1788.

Graham, William Alexander. *General Joseph Graham and his Papers on North Carolina Revolutionary History*. Published for the Author by Edwards & Broughton. Raleigh. 1904.

Graydon, Alexander. *Memoirs of a life, chiefly passed in Pennsylvania: within the last sixty years*. Printed For William Blackwood and T. Cadell, Strand, London. Edinburgh. 1822. (This is a reprint of the original document which was printed in Harrisburg, Pennsylvania by John Wyeth in 1811.)

Greene, George Washington. *The Life of Nathanael Greene, Major-General of the Army of the Revolution in Three Volumes. Volume 3* Hurd and Houghton. Cambridge University Press. New York. 1871.

Greene, Jerome A. *Historic Resource Study and Historic Structure Report Ninety-Six: A Historical Narrative*. Denver Service Center; Branch of Historic Preservation; Southeast/Southwest Team. National Park Service. United States Department of the Interior. Denver Colorado. 1979. Reprinted 1998, 2004, 2005.

Gunby, A.A. *Colonel John Gunby of the Maryland Line. Being Some Account of His Contribution to American Liberty*. The Robert Blake Company. Cincinnati. 1902

Hawks, F. L., Ed. *Official And Other Papers Of The Late Major-General Alexander Hamilton: Compiled Chiefly From The Originals In The Possession Of Mrs Hamilton. Vol. I*. Wiley & Putnam. New York and London. 1842.

Heitman, Francis B. *Historical Register of the Officers of the Continental Army During the War of the Revolution, April, 1775 to December, 1783 New, Revised and Enlarged Edition*. The Rare Book Shop Publishing Company, Inc. Washington, D.C. 1914.

Higginbotham, Don. *Daniel Morgan, Revolutionary Rifleman*. University of North Carolina Press. Chapel Hill. 1961.

Holmes, Richard. *Redcoat. The British Soldier in the Age of Horse and Musket* Harper Collins Publishers. London. 2001.

Jacob, John J. Biographical *Sketch of the Life of the late Captain Michael Cresap*. Cincinnati, Ohio, 1866.(Reprinted from the Cumberland Edition of 1826, with Notes and Appendix for William Dodge, by Jno. F. Ulhorm, Steam Job Printer, 38 West 3d St.)

James, Charles. *A New and Enlarged Military Dictionary*. Printed for T. Egerton, at the Military Library, near Whitehall. London. 1802.

Johnson, William. *Sketches of the Life and Correspondence of Nathanael Greene, Major General of the Armies of the United States in the War of the Revolution. Vol. I*. Published for the Author by A.E. Miller. Charleston, South Carolina. 1822.

Kapp, Friedrich. *The Life of John Kalb, Major General in the Revolutionary Army*. Henry Holt and Company. New York. 1884.

Kauffmann, J.E. and Kaufmann, H.W. *Fortress America: The Forts That Defended America, 1600 to the Present.* Da Capo Press. 2004.

Kirkland, Thomas J. and Kennedy, Robert M. *Historic Camden. Part One Colonial and Revolutionary.* The State Company. Columbia, South Carolina. 1905.

Kirkwood, Robert. *The Journal and Order Book of Captain Robert Kirkwood of the Delaware Regiment of the Continental Line.* (Edited by Reverend Joseph Brown Turner.) The Historical Society of Delaware. Wilmington, 1910.

Konstam, Angus. *Guilford Courthouse, 1781. Lord Cornwallis's Ruinous Victory.* Praeger Illustrated Military History Series. Originally published in Oxford: Osprey Publishing Limited, Elms Court, Chapel Way, Botley, Oxford. 2002.

Lee, Henry. *The Revolutionary War Memoirs of General Henry Lee.* Edited by Robert E. Lee with an Introduction by Charles Royster. DaCapo Press New York. 1998.

Lee, Henry, IV. *The Campaign of 1781 in the Carolinas; with Remarks Historical and Critical on Johnson's Life of Greene.* Published by E. Littell William Brown, Printer. Philadelphia. 1824.

Leckie, Robert. *George Washington's War. The Saga of the American Revolution.* Harper Collins Publishers. New York. 1992. Harper Perennial edition published 1993. New York.

Lossing, Benson J. *Pictorial Field-Book of the Revolution.* Harper Brothers. New York. 1850.

Lossing, Benson J. *Pictorial Field-Book of the Revolution, Volume 2.* New York Harper & Brothers Publishers. 1852.

Lowell, Edward J. *The Hessians and the other German Auxiliaries of Great Britain in the Revolutionary War.* Harper & Brothers, Franklin Square. New York. 1884.

McCullough, David. 1776. Simon & Shuster. New York. 2005.

Morrill, Dan. *Southern Campaigns of the American Revolution.* The Nautical and Aviation Publishing Company of America. Charleston. 1993.

Moultrie, William. *Memoirs of the American Revolution, So Far as it Related to the States of North and South Carolina, and Georgia. Volume 2.* Printed by David Longworth for the Author. New York. 1802.

Myers, T. Bailey, Ed. *Cowpens Papers. Being Correspondence of General Morgan and the Prominent Actors. From the Collection of Theodorus Bailey Myers. Contributed to the Centennial Celebration. May 11, 1881* The Charleston News and Courier. Charleston. 1881.

Onderdonk, Henry, Jr. *Revolutionary Incidents Of Suffolk And Kings Counties; With An Account Of The Battle Of Long Island, And The British Prisons And Prison Ships At New York. New York.* Leavitt & Company, 191 Broadway, New York.1849.

Palmer, Wm. P, M.D., ed. *Calendar of the Virginia State Papers and Other Manuscripts. Volume I.* R.F. Walker, Superintendent of Public Printing Richmond. 1875.

Palmer, Wm. P., M.D., ed. *Calendar of the Virginia State Papers and Other Manuscripts, Volume II.* James E. Goode, Printer. Richmond. 1881.

Pancake, John S. *This Destructive War. The British Campaign in the Carolinas, 1780-1782.* The University of Alabama Press. Tuscaloosa and London. 2003.

Pearson, Michael. *Those Damned Rebels. The American Revolution As Seen Through British Eyes.* First Da Capo Press Edition. 2000.

Piecuch, Jim. *The Blood Be Upon Your Head: Tarleton and the Myth of Buford's Massacre.* Lugoff, South Carolina. The Southern Campaigns of the American Revolution Press. 2010

Piecuch, Jim. *The Battle of Camden. A Documentary History.* The History Press. Charleston and London. 2006.

Piecuch, Jim and Beakes, John. *Cool Deliberate Courage. John Eager Howard in the American Revolution.* The Nautical and Aviation Publishing Company of America. Charleston. 2009.

Piecuch, Jim and Beakes, John. *Light Horse Harry Lee in the War for Independence.* The Nautical and Aviation Publishing Company of America. Charleston. 2013.

Ramsay, David. *The History of the Revolution of South Carolina, from a British Province to an Independent State.* Trenton: Printed by Isaac Collins. 1785

Ross, Charles, Esq., Ed. *Correspondence of Charles, First Marquis Cornwallis In Three Volumes. Vol. I.* Second Edition. John Murray, Albemarle Street. London. 1859.

Robinson, Blackwell P. *The Revolutionary War Sketches of William R. Davie.* The North Carolina Department of Cultural Resources, Division of Archives and History. Raleigh. 1976.

Saffell, W.T.R. *Records of the Revolutionary War Containing the Military and Financial Correspondence of Distinguished Officers.* Third Edition. Charles C. Saffell. Baltimore. 1894.

Scharf, J. Thomas. *History of Maryland from the Earliest Period to the Present Day. Vol. II.* Published by John B. Piet. Baltimore. 1879.

Scharf, J. Thomas. *The Chronicles of Baltimore; Being a Complete History of Baltimore Town and Baltimore City from the Earliest Period to the Present Time.* Turnbull Brothers. Baltimore. 1874.

Showman, Richard K., General Editor; Conrad, Dennis, M., Editor; Parks, Roger N, Senior Associate Editor; and Stevens, Elizabeth C. Associate Editor. *The Papers of Nathanael Greene. Volume VII. 26 December 1780 - 29 March 1781.* The University of North Carolina Press. Chapel Hill and London. Published for the Rhode Island Historical Society. 1994.

Smith, Edward. *Historic Resource Study. Williamsport, Maryland. Chesapeake and Ohio Canal National Historical Park.* National Park Service. July 25, 1979.

Smith, Justin H. *Arnold's March from Cambridge to Quebec. A Critical Study.* G.P. Putnam's and sons. New York and London. 1903.

Society of the Cincinnati. *Register of the Society of the Cincinnati of Maryland Brought Down to February 22, 1897.* Published by Order of the Society. Press of A. Horn & Company. Baltimore. 1897.

Stedman, Charles. *History of the Origins, Progress and Termination of the American War, Vol. II.* Printed for the Author and Sold by J. Murray,

Fleet-Street J. Debrett, Piccad1lly ; And J. Kerby, Corner Of Wigmore Street, Cavendish Square. London.1794.

Steuart, Rieman. *A History of the Maryland Line in the Revolutionary War. 1775-1783.* The Society of the Cincinnati. Towson, Maryland. 1969.

Stevens, Benjamin Franklin, ed. *The Campaign in Virginia 1781. An Exact Reprint of Six Rare Pamphlets on the Clinton-Cornwallis Controversy Volume I.* London. 1888.

Symonds, Craig L. (Cartography by William J. Clipson.) *A Battlefield Atlas of the American Revolution.* The Nautical & Aviation Publishing Company of America. Baltimore. 1986.

Tarleton, Banastre. *A History of the Campaigns of 1780 and 1781 in the Southern Provinces of North America.* Printed For Colles, Exshaw, White, H. Whitestone, Burton, Byrne, Moore, Jones, And Dornin. Dublin. 1787.

Tiffany, Osmond. *A Sketch of the Life and Services of Otho Holland Williams.* Read before the Maryland Historical Society on Thursday Evening, March 6, 1851 Baltimore. Printed by John Murphy & Co. No. 178 Market Street. 1851.

Treacy, M.F. *Prelude to Yorktown.* The University of North Carolina Press. Chapel Hill. 1963.

Tyler, Moses Coit. *The Literary History of the American Revolution. Volume II.* 1776-1783. G.P. Putnam's Sons. New York and London. 1897.

Ward, Christopher. (Edited by John Richard Alden.) *The War of the Revolution.* Skyhorse Publishing. 2011.

Waring, Alice Noble. *The Fighting Elder. Andrew Pickens (1739-1817)* University of South Carolina Press. Columbia. 1962.

Weir, John F. (Director of the Yale School of Fine Arts.) *John Trumbull, A Brief Sketch of his Life to Which is Added a Catalogue of His Work. Prepared for the Committee on the Bi-Centennial Celebration of the Founding of Yale College.* Charles Scribner's Sons. New York. 1901.

Wharton, Francis, ed. *The Revolutionary Diplomatic Correspondence of the United States. Volume I. Printed In Conformity with Act of Congress if August 13, 1888.* Government Printing Office. Washington. 1899.

Williamsport Chamber of Commerce. *Williamsport and Vicinity Reminiscences. Early Part of the 18th Century to the Early Part of 1933, Inclusive.* Stouffer Print Company. 1933.

Wilson, Roger B.; Robinson; Donald; Morris James; and Glenn, David. *The River and the Ridge. 300 Years of Local History.* Gateway Press Baltimore. 2003.

Wright, Robert K., Jr. *The Continental Army.* Center Of Military History United States Army, Washington, D. C., 1986.

Zucker, Adolf Eduard. *General De Kalb, Lafayette's Mentor.* (Volume 53 in the University of North Carolina studies in the Germanic Languages and literatures.) University of North Carolina Press. Chapel Hill. 1966.

Commemorative Publications

Fort Washington. *November 16, 1776. A Memorial from the Empire State Society of the Sons of the American Revolution to the Honorable Mayor and Municipal Assembly of the City of New York, praying for the erection of a suitable monument to mark the site of Fort Washington.* By the Empire State Society of the Sons of the American Revolution. New York. 1898.

Magazine Articles

A Journal of the Southern Expedition, 1780-1783. By William Seymour, Sergeant-Major of the Delaware Regiment. Pennsylvania Magazine of History and Biography, Volume VII. Philadelphia. Publication Fund of the Historical Society of Pennsylvania. No. 1300 Locust Street. 1883. ("A Journal of the Southern Expedition by William Seymour," is on pages 286-298.)

Battle of Eutaw Springs. By N.C. Brooks. *Graham's American Monthly Magazine of Literature and Art, Volume XXVII.* George R. Graham, Editor and Proprietor. 98 Chestnut Street, Philadelphia. 1845. (The article on the Battle of Eutaw Springs is on pages 253-258.)

Muster Roll of Captain Thomas Price's Company of Rifle-Men in the Service of the United Colonies. Maryland Historical Magazine. Vol. XXII. September, 1927.

Prelude to Guilford Courthouse. By Robert Dunkerly. In Southern Campaigns of the Revolutionary War. Volume 3, Number 3. March 2006. (Pages 34-43.)

Southern Campaign. 1780. Gates at Camden. By John Austin Stevens. The Magazine of American History, with Notes and Queries. Volume V. (Pages 241 - 281.) A.S. Barnes and Company. New York and Chicago. 1880.

The Battle Grounds of America. No. VI. Battle of Eutaw Springs. From Original and Unpublished MSS. By N. C. Brooks. Graham's American Monthly Magazine of Literature and Art. George R. Graham, Editor. Volume XXVII. Philadelphia. George R. Graham & Co. 1845.

The Battle of Ramseur's Mill. By William A. Graham. In "The North Carolina Booklet. Great Events in North Carolina History, Vol. 4, No.2." (June 1904). E. M. Uzzell and Company, Printers and Binders. Raleigh: North Carolina. Society Daughters of the Revolution, 1904. 1st ed

The Capture of Colonel Moses Rawlings. By Dale J. Schmitt. Maryland Historical Magazine. Vol. 71, No. 2. Summer, 1976.

The Horrors of Civil War: The Tilghman Family in the American Revolution. Maryland Historical Magazine, Volume 101, No. 1. (Spring 2008.) P. 39.

The Old Martyr's Prison. By Edward Hagaman Hall. Presented to The Board of Aldermen of the City of New York by The American Scenic and Historic Preservation Society Reprinted from "The City Record" of October 23, 1902. New York.

On Line Collections

Archives of Maryland Online. http://aomol.msa.maryland.gov/html/index.html

National Archives. Founders Online. Correspondence and Other Writings of Six Major Shapers of the United States: George Washington, Benjamin Franklin, John Adams (and family), Thomas Jefferson, Alexander Hamilton, and James Madison. http://founders.archives.gov/

Sherman, William Thomas. *Calendar and Record of the Revolutionary War in the South: 1780-1781.* Ninth Edition. 2014.

The Writings of George Washington from the Original Manuscript Sources, 1745-1799. John C. Fitzpatrick, Editor. Library of Congress Web Site/ American Memory/ Presidents / Washington, George. http://memory.loc.gov/ammem/gwhtml/gwhome.html

Sources Cited By Others

Bass. Robert D. *The Green Dragoon*: *The Lives of Banastre Tarleton and Mary Robinson*. New York: Henry Holt and Company, 1957. (M.F. Treacy notes: "Contains interesting documentary material. Most of the book concernsTarleton's later career.")

Haiman, Miecislaus. *Kosciuiszko in the American Revolution*. New York: Polish Institute of Arts and Sciences in America, 1943. Reprint; Boston: Gregg Press. 1972.

Mackenzie, Roderick. *Strictures on Lt. Col. Tarleton's "History of the Campaigns of 1780 and 1781, in the Southern Province of North America."* London: Printed for the Author, 1787.

Wickwire, Franklin and Mary. Cornwallis: *The American Adventure* Houghton Mifflin Co., Boston, 1970. (cited by William Thomas Sherman, Calendar and Record of the Revolutionary War in the South: 1780-1781. Fourth Edition.)

Web Sites

Archives of Maryland Online. **http://aomol.net/html/index.html**

Family Search Onlne. "Maryland, Marriages, 1666-1970," index, *Family Search* https://familysearch.org/pal:/MM9.1.1/F4JQ-6YG: accessed 19 Jul 2014

Southern Campaigns Revolutionary War Pension Statements & Rosters. http://revwarapps.org/

The Library of Congress Web Site. http://www.loc.gov/index.html

Published Papers

Bolton, Reginald Pelham. *The Defence and Reduction of Mount Washington. An Account of the Identification of the Site of Fort Washington, New York City, and the Erection and Dedication of a Monument Thereon Nov. 16, 1901* by the Empire State Society of the Sons of the American Revolution. New York. 1902.

Hentz, Tucker. *Unit History of the Maryland and Virginia Rifle Regiment (1776 1781)*: Insights from the Service Record of Capt. Adamson Tannehill Richmond, Virginia Historical Society. Call number E259. H52 2007. http://www.vahistorical.org/research/tann.pdf.

Government Documents

Biographical Directory of the United States Congress, 1774-2005 Superintendent of Documents, U.S. Government Printing Office. Washington, D.C. Library of Congress Control Number 2004114224.

Journal and Correspondence of the Council of Maryland, Volume 12 (July 7 – December 31, 1776,) Volume 71 (November 27, 1784 – February 23, 1789), and Volume 72 (February 23, 1789 to November 11, 1793 Archives of Maryland online.

Journals of the Continental Congress. Library of Congress Web Site.

Laws of Maryland, 1785-1791. Volume 204. *Laws of Maryland made and passed at a Session of Assembly, Begun and held at the city of ANNAPOLIS, on Monday the fifth of November, in the year of our Lord one thousand seven hundred and eighty-seven. Annapolis.* Printed by Frederick Green, Printer to the State. P. 300.

Letters of Delegates to Congress. Library of Congress web site.

Muster Rolls and Other Records of Service of Maryland Troops in the American Revolution. Archives of Maryland Online. Volume 18.

Proceedings of the Convention of Maryland, 1774-1776. Maryland Archives Online. Volume 78.

The Maryland Press. By Joseph Towne Wheeler. Printed by the Waverly Press. 1938. Archives of Maryland online. Volume 438.

INDEX

Adams, John, 37, 306
Adlum, John, 36, 37
Anderson, Maj. Archibald, 201, 205, 211
Annapolis, Maryland, 13
Armand, Col. Charles, 114, 116, 117, 124
Armstrong, John, 103, 105, 107, 111, 130, 156
Arnold, Gen. Benedict, 63-64, 103, 138, 300
  court martial of, 63-64
Ashley River, 278, 279, 280
Baltimore, Maryland, 1, 2, 13, 37, 54, 58, 229, 231, 290, 292, 296, 297, 299, 300, 304, 305, 307, 309, 310, 311, 312, 314, 320
Bannister River, 168
Beatty, Capt. William, 223, 225, 230
Beatty's Ford, 79
Boston, Massachusetts, 5-6, 8, 10, 12-13, 20-24, 49, 55, 138
  Boston, Seige of, 18-24, 138
  map, 18
Boyd's Ferry, 78
Broad River, 76
Brooke, Thomas, 309
Brown, Thomas "Burntfoot", 87, 88
Buford, Col Abraham, 74, 84, 85, 88, 152, 172
Bunker Hill, Battle of, 12
Burgoyne, Gen. John, 48, 88, 138
Butler, Gen. John, 117
Camden, South Carolina, 3, 5, 8, 76, 102, 108, 112-13, 115-118, 123-130, 132-133, 137, 140-143, 150-151, 169, 189, 217-218, 220, 224, 227-228, 230, 234-236, 252, 287

  Battle of, 3, 5, 8, 102, 117-124
  retreat, 125-127
  criticism of Gates' conduct, 129
  map (Smiths Mill and Deep River?), 109
Campbell, Maj. David, 178
Campbell, Col Richard, 8-9, 218, 222, 229, 245, 259, 262, 264, 266
Campbell, Col. William, 181-182, 190-191, 193, 221
Cape Fear River, 76, 78, 210, 215
Carrington, Lt. Col. Edward, 151, 167, 205, 318, 321
Carroll, Charles, 310
Caswell, Gen Richard, 73, 107, 111-112, 117
Catawba River, 79, 154, 159-160
Charleston, 9, 10, 26, 67, 73, 83, 86, 103, 106, 111, 113, 115, 116, 125, 139, 217, 234, 235, 236, 239, 240, 241, 248, 249, 255, 259, 264, 265, 266, 267, 271, 275, 277, 278, 279, 280, 281, 283, 295, 296, 299, 320,
Charlotte, North Carolina, 83-84, 108, 112, 121, 126-128, 137-141, 149, 153, 159, 189, 248, 271, 274-275, 287
Chase, Samuel, 297, 310
Cheraw, South Carolina, 76, 89, 153-157, 159-160, 167
Clagett, Moses, 309
Clapp's Mill, Skirmish at 174-180
Clarke, Col. Elijah, 87-88, 236
Clinton, Gen. Sir Henry, 51-52
Coffin, Maj. John, 258-259, 263, 265
Concord, Battle of, 12
Congaree River, 76, 235, 240, 248, 254

INDEX

Continental Army, 1, 6, 8, 12-13, 21, 23, 28-29, 46, 49-50, 57-58, 67, 83, 94-98, 102-104, 112-113, 119, 121-123, 125, 132-133, 157, 178, 183, 187, 191-193, 201, 205, 215, 217, 221, 225, 250, 259, 266, 267, 275-277, 282, 287, 293, 297-298, 300, 304-305, 315
- administration of discipline, 62
- combat readiness, 64
- organization of, 23
- petition of the Maryland officers, 57
- reorganization of rifle troops, 27

Cooper's Ferry, 51

Cornwallis, Gen. Charles, Earl, 33, 113, 116-118, 121-122, 125, 127 129, 132, 137-140, 149, 153, 158-161, 163, 165-171, 173-174, 177, 179-181, 183, 185-186, 189 194, 201, 203, 208-210, 215, 240, 271, 273, 275, 277, 299
- at Battle of Fort Washington, 33
- reinforces Charleston, 116
- at Battle of Camden, 118, 121, 122, 125
- moves into North Carolina to Charlotte, 128
- retreats to South Carolina, 139-140 in pursuit of Greene (Race to the Dan), 163-167
- at Battle of Guilford Courthouse, 201-206

Cowan's Ford, 79

Cowpens, Battle of, 157-161, 177, 201, 222, 230

"Race to the Dan", 162-168

Cresap, Capt. Michael, 4, 15-17, 22, 58

Cresap, Thomas, 15

Cruger, Lt. Col. John Harris, 121, 239-249, 259

Dan River, 8, 78, 151, 161, 163, 165-171, 173, 252, 308

Davidson, Gen. William, 93, 137, 159

Davie, Col. William R., 6, 55, 88, 137, 186, 188-190, 211-212, 224-226, 228-230

Deep River, 76, 107, 108-109, 111, 194

Delaware River, 51, 80

Demont, Lt. William, 32-33, 37

deserters, 9, 21, 52,63, 89, 94, 135, 220, 222, 251-252, 258, 264, 281
- desertion as court martial offense, 63
- effect of British and American armies, 89-90
- executions for desertion, 89-90, 251

Edisto River, 278- 280

Elk River, 72

Eutaw Springs, Battle of, 3, 5, 8-11, 254-268, 271, 273, 280, 288
- aftermath, 267-268
- map (British defensive positions), 260

Fell, John, experience in The Provost, 47

Ferguson, Maj. Patrick, 128, 137, 139, 157

Ferguson's Mill, 280

Finley, Sgt. James, 21

Ford, Lt. Col. Benjamin, 50, 120, 122, 201, 205, 211-212, 218, 222-223, 230, 251

Fort Cumberland, 294, 312

Fort Dreadnought, 236

Fort Duquesne, 138

Fort Granby, 235-236, 248

Fort Lee, 26, 30, 32, 35, 38

Fort McHenry, 37, 312

Fort Motte, 235-236, 254

Fort Ninety-Six, 78, 84, 86, 235-236, 239-242, 244-248, 251-252, 259, 280
- Siege of, 239-247

Fort Recovery, 315

Fort Ticonderoga, 24

Fort Tryon, 33

342   INDEX

Fort Washington, 4, 8, 26, 30-33, 35, 38, 44, 48-49, 52, 65, 143, 149
  Battle of, 30-38
  map, 34
Fort Watson, 217-218, 220, 236, 244
Fort Whetstone, 312
Fox, Charles James, 209
Frederick, Maryland, 14, 16-17, 49, 296
Fredericksburg, Virginia, 74
Gates, Gen. Horatio, 48, 103-108, 110-118, 121-122, 124-126, 129-133, 136-143, 149-150, 152, 156, 321
  role in Williams' release as prisoner, 48
  appointed to command Southern Army, 103-107
  at Battle of Camden, 117-121
  criticism of conduct after Camden, 129
Georgetown, South Carolina, 83, 156
Germain, Lord George, 169
Giles, Maj. Edward, 130, 131, 157
Gist, Gen. Mordecai, 61, 67, 117, 122, 124, 277, 283, 287, 295, 299
Goose Creek, 278
Gordon, William, 4- 6, 160, 188, 209, 225, 228-229, 318
Graydon, Alexander, 45, 48
Greene, Gen. Nathanael, 2, 4-10, 31-32, 35, 37-38, 59, 81, 89-90, 94, 102, 132, 142-143, 149-156, 158, 160-174, 177-180, 183-194, 201, 203-205, 207-210, 212-213, 215-218, 220-222, 224-236, 239-254, 258-259, 261-262, 264-268, 271, 273-275, 277-283, 287-292, 294-297, 299-300, 306-308, 316, 318-319
  role in Fort Washington, 31-32, 143
  takes command of Southern Army, 142-143, 149

  strategy for the South, 150-151
  Race to the Dan, 166-167
  at Battle of Guilford Courthouse, 201-206
  at Battle of Hobkirk's Hill, 218-214
  at Seige of Ninety-Six, 239-247
  at Battle of Eutaw Springs, 258-267
Greene, George Washington, 2, 4, 102
Guilford Courthouse, Battle of, 5, 6, 8, 161, 163, 193, 201, 210-213, 215, 225, 227, 229-230, 280
  map, 214
Gunby, Col. John, 120, 124, 201, 203, 205, 206, 218, 222, 223, 224, 225, 226, 227, 228, 229, 230, 232, 293
Hall, Col. Josias, 113, 127, 211, 212
Hamilton, Alexander, 1, 3-4, 129, 131-132, 142, 311-312, 315-316, 318-320
Hampton, Col. Wade, 262-263, 265
Hancock, John, 30
Hanson, John, 49, 289-290
Hardman, Maj. Henry, 134, 166
Harlem Heights, 30
Harlem River, 30-31, 33, 35
Harrison, Col. Charles, 229
Hart, Thomas, 309
Haw River, 76, 165, 182, 185
Hawes, Col. Samuel, 218, 222-223, 229
Henderson, Col. William, 258-259, 262, 264, 266, 279
Hessians, 26-27, 31, 35-38, 44, 51, 80, 95-97
High Hills of the Santee, 249-250, 253-254, 267, 271, 273, 275, 278
Hillsborough, North Carolina, 84, 107, 121, 127-128, 133-134, 137-142, 160, 168, 170-172, 179
Hobkirk's Hill, Battle of, 6, 8, 217-220, 225, 229-231, 234-235, 280

Howard, John Eager, 1, 4, 82-83, 113, 124-127, 133, 135, 139, 151, 155, 157, 161, 171-173, 182-183, 191-192, 201, 203, 205-206, 221, 223-225, 227, 233, 251, 265-267, 300, 305-306, 311
Howe, Gen. Sir William, 26, 33, 51
Hudson River, 26, 30-33, 38, 298
Huger, Gen. Benjamin, 86, 201, 207
Huger, Gen. Isaac, 159-161, 163, 218, 220, 229
Hyco River, 172
Irwin's Ferry, 78
Jefferson, Thomas, 1, 3, 73, 81, 152, 167, 187, 193, 306, 316
Johnson, Gov. Thomas, 20-21, 49
Johnson, William, 4
Kalb, Gen. Baron Johann de, 54-55, 58, 67, 72-75, 81, 83, 103-104, 106-108, 112, 116-117, 122, 124, 127-128, 134, 156
  at Battle of Camden, 117-124
  death, 127-128
Kingsbridge, New York, 31, 37
Kirkwood, Capt. Robert, 108, 110, 122, 124, 135, 139, 175-177, 221, 245-246, 258-259, 263, 315
Knox, Gen. Henry, 23, 298, 305-306, 315, 317
Knyphausen, Gen. Wilhelm von, 33, 35-37
Kosciuszko, Col. Tadeusz, 240, 279
Lafayette, Marquis de, 53, 271, 241
Lawson, Gen. Robert, 203
Lee, Gen. Charles, 51, 106, 130, 132, 300
  court martial of, 53, 54
Lee, Lt. Col. Henry, 1, 204, 207, 209, 212, 217-218, 220-221, 226, 232, 234-236, 239, 242-246, 248-250, 252, 254, 258-259, 262-263, 265, 271, 273, 276, 279, 298, 305, 307-310, 316-318

Leslie, Gen. Alexander, 277
Lexington, Massachusetts, 12
Lincoln, Gen. Benjamin, 103, 106, 290, 295
Loring, Joshua, British Commissary of Prisoners, 45
Mackenzie, Capt. Frederick, 33, 37
Madison, James, 1, 289-290
Magaw, Col. Robert, 32-33, 37-38, 45, 65
Maham, Col. Hezekiah, 279
Maham, Lt. Col. Ezekiel, 244
Manhattan Island, 30, 31, 32
Marion, Gen. Francis, 86, 93-94, 110, 126, 156, 217-218, 220, 233-235, 243-244, 248-250, 254, 258-259, 261, 271, 274-276, 279-280
Majoribanks, Maj. John, 259, 263, 265
May's Mill, 110
McCurtin, Pvt. Daniel, 20-22
McHenry, Dr. James, 37, 47, 53, 157
Mercer, Gen. Hugh, 35
militia, 8, 74, 87, 93-96, 102, 106-107, 111-113, 115, 117-121, 123-125, 133, 137, 150, 153, 160, 171-177, 179-184, 186-192, 201, 203, 207, 212, 215-216, 218, 224, 232, 239, 242-244, 250, 254, 258-259, 261, 271, 274-275, 279, 282
Monmouth, Battle of, 51-53, 65, 130, 253
Monroe, James, 1
Morgan, Col. William, 179
Morgan, Gen. Daniel, 4, 14-17, 19, 29-30, 55, 58, 93, 103, 106, 123, 130, 138-141, 153-155, 157-162, 177, 201, 317, 321
Morristown, New Jersey, 59, 61, 66, 72, 154
Nash, Gov. Abner, 111
Nelson, Gov. Thomas, 271

INDEX

Nelson's Ferry, 236, 279
Neuse River, 76
New York City, 4, 8, 22-28, 30-32, 35, 44-45, 49, 51-54, 65-67, 93, 103, 131, 138-139, 170, 239, 253, 298, 305, 310, 321
  campaign 24-27
Newburgh, New York, 295

O'Hara, Gen. Charles, 79, 160, 167, 208
Oldham, Capt. Edward, 175-177, 211
Pee Dee River, 76, 107, 110, 154, 217, 235
Petersburg, Virginia, 72-73, 76
Philadelphia, Pennsylvania, 26, 28-29, 51, 63, 67, 72-73, 103, 105, 143, 149, 288-290, 292, 295-296, 299, 305-306, 311, 318, 320
Phillips, Gen. William, 66
Pickens, Gen. Andrew, 86-87, 93, 171-172, 174-175, 179, 186, 236, 242-243, 247, 259, 261, 275, 279
Pickering, Col. Thomas, 276
Pinckney, Col. Charles C., 291, 320
Pindell, Dr. Richard, 309
Potomac River, 2, 80, 307, 309, 313, 322
Price, Capt. Thomas, 4, 15-17, 19, 21, 23
prisoners, 3-5, 44-49, 51-52, 59, 61, 65-66, 85-90, 116, 120, 122, 130, 158, 172, 175, 180, 206, 210, 220, 224, 246, 253, 267, 283, 311, 321
  exchanges of, 45-48, 65-66, 138, 246
Putnam, Gen. Israel, 31-32, 35
Pyle, Dr. John, 172-173
Radley, Sgt. John, 250-251
Rall, Col. Johann, 35-36, 39
Ramsay, David, 4-5, 162, 164, 190, 320
Ramsay, Lt. Col. Nathaniel, 51, 65, 172, 253, 299

Ramsey's Mill, 172, 210
Rawdon, Lt. Col. Francis, Lord, 81, 113, 116-117, 128, 220-222, 224, 228, 234-235, 240, 242-249, 251
Rawlings, Lt. Col. Moses, 22, 25, 27, 30, 32-33, 35, 36-38, 58, 309
Reuber, John, 35
Roanoke River, 76, 78, 151, 161
Ross, George, 1, 2, 25, 230
Rugeley's Mill, 113
Rutledge, Gov. John, 73, 261, 275, 280, 282, 295
Saluda River, 76, 248
Santee River, 76, 78, 116, 217, 240, 259, 271, 273
Savannah, Georgia, 83, 277
Scammel, Col. Alexander, 59-61, 67, 123, 136
Schmidt, Gen. Martin Conrad, 35
Senf, Col. John Christian, 117
Sevier, Col. John, 271
Seymour, Sgt. William, 110
Shelby, Col. Isaac, 271
Sherill's Ford, 159
Singleton, Capt. Anthony, 117
slaves, 235, 240-241, 282-283, 292, 293
  attitudes toward slavery, 292
  proposals to recruit slaves, 240-241, 282-283
Smallwood, Gen. William, 23, 54, 57, 97, 117, 120, 122, 124, 127, 152, 267, 287, 292-93, 298-299, 306
Smith, Lt. Col. Samuel, 53, 305
Smith, Mary, 307
Smith, Sgt. Levi, 251
Smith, William, 307, 310, 312-314
Smiths Mill, 108-109
Society of the Cincinnati, 252, 298, 305-306
Spuyten Duyvil Creek, 30-31
Stanton River, 168

INDEX

Stedman, Charles, 126, 170, 209
Stephens, Gen. Adam, 203, 205
Stephenson, Col. Hugh, 25, 29
Steuben, Gen. Baron Friedrich von, 50, 53, 57-59, 67, 72, 102, 134, 137, 156-157
Stevens, Gen. Edward, 93, 113-114, 117-118, 151, 179, 203
Stevenson, Col. Hugh, 27, 29, 37
Stewart, Lt. Col. Alexander, 248-249, 258-259, 266-267, 271
Stone, Col. John Hawkins, 229
Stuart, Col. Duncan, 208
Stull, Col. John, 28
Stull, Mercy nee Williams, 1, 230, 307
Sullivan, John, 251
Sumner, Gen. Jethro, 9, 258, 259, 261
Sumter, Gen. Thomas, 93, 115-116, 121, 132, 217-218, 220, 232-234, 243-244, 249-250, 271, 279-280, 318-319
Tarleton, Lt. Col. Banastre, 74, 84-85, 90, 128, 157, 166, 168, 172-173, 176, 180- 182
  "Tarleton's Quarter," 85
  "The Provost" prison in New York, 44, 46
Thomas, Dr. Philip, 68, 289, 296, 307, 313, 320-321
Tilghman, James, 16-17
Tillman, Tench, 53
Trading Ford, 79
Valley Forge, Pennsylvania, 50, 102, 157, 308
Washington, Gen. George, 1, 3, 5, 19, 21, 23-27, 29, 31-32, 35, 37-38, 44, 50-51, 53-59, 62- 67, 72, 74, 80, 94-95, 98, 102-106, 115, 123-124, 131-132, 134, 136, 138-139, 142-143, 149-151, 174, 185, 188, 192, 274-275, 277-278, 282, 288-290, 293, 295, 300, 304, 308
  appointed to command Continental Army, 12
  as President, 6, 310, 313-317, 319 320
Wateree River, 76, 217, 235, 240, 254
Watson, Lt. Col. John, 234
Waxhaws, 74, 84, 85
Wayne, Gen. Anthony, 53, 277, 283, 296
Webster, Lt. Col. James, 176, 180-184, 204, 206, 208, 210
Weitzel's Mill, Skirmish at, 6, 182, 185 190, 193, 211, 225
White Plains, New York, 30
Wilkinson, James, 48
Williams, Elie, 1, 25, 47, 54, 74, 141, 153, 157, 168, 193, 230, 251, 292, 307, 313
Williams, Joseph, 1-2
Williams, Otho Holland, 1-11, 13, 15-17, 19-28, 30, 32-33, 35-38, 44-67, 72, 74, 81, 83-84, 88-90, 94, 97-99, 102-103, 108, 110-114, 116-120, 122-124, 126-127, 129-137, 139-143, 149-169, 171-186, 188-193, 201, 203-207, 209-213, 215- 218, 221-236, 239-241, 243, 245-253, 258-268, 271, 273-275, 278-284, 287-300, 304-322
  early family life, 1
  civilian life before the war, 2
  personality, 6
  physical appearance, 2, 16, 17
  as Lt. in a rifle company, 12-15
  promotion to Capt., 23
  at siege of Boston, 19-24
  offer of promotion to Col. by Maryland, 28
  transfer to New York, 25
  at Battle for Fort Washington, 36
  wounded, 37
  as prisoner-of-war, 3, 44

tended by Dr. McHenry, 47
released on parole, 47
illness, 48, 68
promotion to Col., 3, 49
as member of Gen. Lee's court martial board, 53-54
as sub-inspector under Von Steuben, 58
as acting Adjutant General, 3, 59- 62
transfer to the Southern Theater, 72
at battle of Eutaw Springs, 3, 8-11, 258-267
promotion to Brig. Gen., 3, 289
establishment of Williamsport, 309

Williams, Prudence Holland, 1

Williamsport, 2, 308-309, 312-313, 320, 322

Wilmington, North Carolina, 83, 169, 209, 215, 277

Woodford, Gen. William, 98

Wright's Ferry, 312

Yadkin River, 79, 127, 160, 163